Medusa's Gaze

Medusa's Gaze

*Casuistry and Conscience
in the Renaissance*

Lowell Gallagher

Stanford University Press
Stanford, California   1991

Stanford University Press
Stanford, California
© 1991 by the Board of Trustees of the
Leland Stanford Junior University
Printed in the United States of America

CIP data appear at the end of the book

Published with the assistance of a special grant from the
Stanford University Faculty Publication Fund to help support
nonfaculty work originating at Stanford

Frontispiece: The "Siena Sieve" Portrait, attributed to Zuccari.
Reprinted by permission of Scala/Art Resource.

for the memory of my father

Acknowledgments

"For saying so, there's gold," says Viola, in gratitude for the gift of good words she receives in Illyria. In the course of writing this book I have more than once wished, like Viola, that I could surmount the poverty of words to thank the people whose advice and support I have been lucky to receive. I hope these words will convey something of the spirit of gratitude in which I write them.

A grant from the M. M. Lewis Foundation enabled the initial research on what began as a dissertation project at Stanford University. I am deeply indebted to the teachers and colleagues who were insightful and challenging readers of the manuscript at various stages: John B. Bender, J. Martin Evans, René Girard, and Ronald A. Rebholz. Many thanks as well to Harry Berger, Jr., John Freccero, and Stephen Orgel, whose views on literary problems helped clarify my approach to casuistry. Without the encouragement and influence years ago of Bonniejean Christensen, Richard Hampsten, and Esther Lesér, this book would not have been written: to these early teachers I owe a special debt. In addition, I have benefited from the wisdom and unfailing generosity of Bruce Harvey and Kate McDowell, who have been indispensable in more ways than I can express, both as fellow scholars and as friends. Finally, I wish to thank my mother, for teaching me endurance and the love of books.

L. G.

Contents

Medusa's Gaze

But if ye saw that which no eyes can see,
The inward beauty of her liuely spright,
Garnisht with heauenly guifts of high degree,
Much more then would ye wonder at that sight,
And stand astonisht lyke to those which red
Medusaes mazeful hed.
                    —Spenser, *Epithalamion*

Casuistry in the Elizabethan Church-State; or, The Ambiguities of Ideological Colonization

Among the follies that Alexander Pope assigned to the lunar sphere in *The Rape of the Lock*, after the cages for gnats and the dried butterflies, we find "tomes of casuistry." He made the phrase rhyme with "chains to yoke a flea"—an aptly deflated image for the kind of snare that casuistry had come to represent in the world that Pope knew. In the culture of mid-eighteenth-century England, casuistry—the science of resolving problems of moral choice, known as "cases of conscience"—had lost the reputation it had acquired in the sixteenth and seventeenth centuries as the principal agent of scandal, moral decay, and political subversion—as an "endlesse and living veine of powder & salt-peeter," to borrow the words of one Protestant commentator.[1] Why this change, this descent into the banal, should have occurred has something to do, in part, with the exertion of political and social lines of force that determine what we might call the half-life value of what a culture constitutes as its privileged discourses, a phenomenon that Michel Foucault's work—notably *The Archaeology of Knowledge*—illumined.[2]

In some ways casuistry indeed had the trappings of a residual text in eighteenth-century English culture, particularly insofar as the social and political context in which it had gained notoriety two centuries earlier was no longer a dominant force. The "Catholic problem," especially, had been virtually neutralized, if not entirely resolved; in any case, the existence of a dissident religious population no longer carried the implication of an imminent restructuring of the political identity of the commonwealth, as it did in the days when the word "papist" evoked the image of a network of secret traitors quietly working to bring about a Spanish takeover. Casuistry, the discourse associated with this explosive image, acquired its political charge principally through the cases of conscience of dissident populations, like the English Catholic community's. The cases articulated the efforts of these populations to survive as the ideological Other within an enclosed, ostensibly homogeneous community: to reconcile conflicts between political and religious affiliation, between public and private codes of conduct, between competing legal systems and jurisdictions. Implicitly, casuistry became the discourse of indiscernible— and thus potentially uncontainable—dissent. And it became a figure of ambiguity: ostensibly the vehicle through which the voice of conscience performed its stabilizing, normative function, it was also the perceived harbinger of the disintegration of communally recognized signs of what belonged inside and what outside the structure of cultural norms.

The muting and dispersal in Pope's England of the social and political tensions that had helped define and promote the use of casuistry some two hundred years earlier no doubt contributed to the eventual retreat of casuistry from the arena of public discourse. But such conditions do not tell the whole story. We need to consider as well that casuistical analysis, notorious for its complicated heuristics in the realm of moral theology, for its hair-splitting interpretations of the circumstantial evidence of a case, and for its vision of the world, and of the human mind, as a labyrinthine text, implicitly challenged the adequacy of the rather different construction of reality drawn from the perspective of the so-called "enlightenment," of which Pope, of course, was a privileged and self-proclaimed exponent. In other words, it had become necessary to view casuistry—once the central, if controversial, instrument for drawing order out of a chaotic landscape of conflicting moral, political, and social hierarchies—as the residue of a hopelessly antiquated epistemology and interpretive practice. Such a view, we might say, recalls that of the Renaissance humanists with respect to the arabesques in language and in logic of the medieval scholastics and in stone of the architects of the Gothic cathedrals. In both cases we can read the viewers' absorption in the rhetoric of an acute dislocation between past and present: we can read the determination of the present to escape the authority of the past, to exercise control over the mythological—and, in the case of the mythos of casuistry, the destabilizing—narrative of its own origins.

It is no wonder, then, that "tomes of casuistry" should end up on the moon in Pope's mock-epic. Their fate testifies to his culture's desire to expunge, as though creating a taboo, both the ethos of social and political instability and the Byzantine morality associated with casuistry; their fate testifies as well to the perceived banality of such a taboo, to the reasoned appraisal of casuistry—and of the conditions that fostered it—as an obsolete phenomenon, one that had no place in the current cult of rationalism. Naming casuistry the stuff of lunacy effectively announced the death of a discourse and, through that death, the sealing off of a potentially destabilizing vision of the social and political mechanisms behind the idea of rational human commerce.

What Pope's line does not suggest is where one should look to discover how and in what altered forms casuistry, or the discourse of conscience, survived. In 1971 George Starr contributed a groundbreaking study on the subject, *Defoe and Casuistry*, which charted the secularization of casuistical heuristics in popular literature of the seventeenth and eighteenth centuries and which described how such texts constituted narrative models for Defoe's novelistic practice. Apart from Starr's work, the relationship between casuistry and literary discourse seems to have remained in the lunar orbit in which Pope fixed it. That it has remained so may have to do with the tedium—which few would dispute, I think—of reading the case manuals; or with the assumption—an arguable one—that the kinds of interpretive practices and narrative structures that casuistical discourse elicits are to be found mainly in the manuals themselves. Such an assumption, which considers the manuals as isolated texts, with their characteristics and significance transmitted to them, as though intravenously, through the rarefied channels of a self-propagating intellectual history, is not an assumption that Starr made; nor is it one that governs this study.

The premise I follow in this study is that the exploration of the connections between casuistical discourse and the narrative practices that produced the literary genre we call the novel, though provocatively begun in Starr's work, has not been exhausted—and not merely because the earlier study deliberately confined itself to the works of a single author. The "divine science" of casuistry, as Starr's work suggested, was a central instrument in the social construction of reality, a mediating channel between producers and consumers of the normative text of social order: it taught one how to read the book of the world with a nuanced eye but always under the gaze of received truths; it promoted a taste for empirical investigation in the context of an anticipated telos. What I, unlike Starr, want to emphasize is that casuistry determined, as much as it was determined by, a hermeneutical context fraught with political and social antagonisms and haunted by the suspicion that this condition was itself fueled by an ongoing process of often imperceptible shifts in the relations of power that held together the culture's sense of what was true and what was real.

As the early chapters of this study demonstrate, casuistry had more in common with Pandora's box than with Athena's olive branch. Even in its salad days it was more than a heuristic device meant to draw order and certainty out of chaos and doubt or to quell scandal. Its relation to scandal and doubt, which I see as the nascent loci of a culture's discourse of self-critical inquiry, was intrinsically ambiguous. It reduced anxieties in its capacity as an instrument of pastoral care or social control only to raise others as the vehicle of an epistemology of opacity and contingency and of an interpretive practice that militated against the authority of final answers—against, for example, the capacity of an authorial voice to delimit the range of meanings or perceived intentions in texts designated as the representations of the truth of conscience. What was dangerous about casuistry, ultimately, is that its inescapable involvement in political and ideological conflicts—which by the sixteenth century had percolated into quotidian antagonisms—problematized the culture's received truths, making their immanent character susceptible to interpretation as an arbitrary construct, a house of cards built on insoluble contradictions and upheld, moreover, by a massive suspension of disbelief. Reading the culture's social texts, as well as its written texts, from the casuistical perspective was potentially, then, a hubristic act—yet the potential was rarely realized. This dichotomy, too, turns out to have been part of the vertiginous interpretive practice that casuistry fostered: a practice that promoted ways of exploiting silence and equivocation in order to indicate, allusively, the mechanisms of suppression at work within the culture that permitted the culture's norms to maintain their self-evident aspect.

The first part of this study tells the story I have just described through the lens of one of the central antagonisms of English political history, an episode that illustrates the ambiguous character of casuistry at the height of its popularity and announces the kind of narrative procedures that casuistical analysis promoted and made directly available to literary discourse. The rivalry between Elizabeth I and Mary Queen of Scots epitomized the kind of crisis for which casuistical discourse was eminently well suited. Though the specifics of the case were exceptional, the underlying tensions were not. Here was a case that involved rival claims to political power and, behind those claims, a web of competing ideologies and competing discourses of legitimation that converged in the word "conscience." The first three chapters give a detailed picture of the circumstances that made the vagaries of the Scots case intelligible in the context of a broadly accessible tradition in the sixteenth century of casuistically inflected strategies of coercion and evasion. By way of introducing this picture, a few preliminary remarks are perhaps in order, to indicate the general dimensions of the frame in which I situate the Scots case.

Associated with the rise of auricular confession in the thirteenth century, casuistry had become, by the end of the sixteenth century, part of a common language, a widespread method of problem-solving by calibrating particular circumstances against general precepts. But casuistry's successful career would not have been widely understood to be a foregone conclusion at the beginning of the sixteenth century, given the protestations of the early reformers, who associated casuistry with the abuse of papal and ecclesiastical power in the Christian world. In "The Babylonian Captivity of the Church," for example, Martin Luther singled out and condemned one book, the *Summa Angelica*, a handbook of casuistry that enjoyed, as he remarked, a "wide circulation." [3] He had it publicly burned. English reformers followed suit.

That the science of casuistry, however maligned, did not suffer the fate so ardently desired by Luther and his English followers is probably due in part to the continued, not to say more urgent, need, as the century advanced, for a method of addressing and resolving problems of moral choice that arose from the "equal poise" of conflicting laws, obligations, and loyalties. Beneath this overt aspect of casuistry as an instrument of pastoral care lay a related but covert one—its apparent efficacy as an instrument of social and political control. The science of casuistry fostered an activity we might describe as spiritual colonization, the institutional absorption of marginal psychological and moral states—conditions of internal disorder— into ecclesiastically sanctioned or legitimized modes of thought and behavior. The presumed potency of its colonizing aspect may well have insured casuistry's place in the discourse of power in Tudor England, the unspoken premise being that what had worked for Rome might work as well for Westminster. As we shall see, the dissemination of casuistry in the central legal and political documents of the Tudor government and, finally, in the Anglican establishment makes explicit what is otherwise not immediately clear from the rather arid tomes of case divinity, whether "Romish" or Anglican: the continued association of casuistry with structures of power.

This association, however, was ambiguous—and intrinsically so, for casuistry had a third aspect, one that existed in a state of tension with the instrument of pastoral care and the colonizing agent. As an epistemological procedure, casuistry fostered a habit of dwelling on particularities and nuances of individual experience, a habit that resisted the putative purpose of casuistry: to reach a certain judgment of acts based on a clear definition of the boundary between culpability and innocence. To engage in casuistry, as every penitent did in the examination of conscience and in the interrogations of the confessional, was to arrive, ultimately, at the casuist Jean Gerson's appraisal of human complexity: "The diversity of human temperament is incomprehensible—not just in several men, but in one and the same man—and not, I say, in different years or months or weeks, but in days, hours, and moments."[4]

Casuistry thus contained an inherent duality, one that unfolded historically as a shift in emphasis between its opposing tendencies. From its origins in the thirteenth century to its "golden age" in the sixteenth and seventeenth centuries, casuistry revealed a gradual drift from the rigorous adherence to the law in directing consciences to a more supple interpretation of the law in the face of the "diversity of human temperament." The objective morality that had guided the first school of casuists—the "tutiorists"—in their search for truth and for a single resolution of a case was covertly challenged by the gradual development of a subjective morality that led a later school of casuists—the "probabilists"—in their search for verisimilitude and for multiple, probable resolutions, a search conducted under the aegis of the so-called "doctrine of benignity" and guided by the conviction that the "ways of virtue should be wide."[5]

An analogous duality informed casuistry in its manifestation as a discursive operation representing the relation of legal structures to the structures of human experience. Here the notion of historical drift recalls the myth of Babel. Casuistry—the discourse of conscience—began as a method of enforcing the hegemony of a single prescribed text, a *logos*, as the pattern for the narrative of a Christian life. Tutiorists characteristically invoked a clearly demarcated and impenetrable boundary between permissible and forbidden behavior; they instilled in the consciences under their direction a habit of interpreting human experience as an ongoing sequence of binary oppositions dictated by the strict observance or the unqualified transgression of ordained laws; finally, they implied that human experience could be made intelligible in these terms: as phenomena to be located on one side or the other—without involvement in the margins—of established boundaries. Here, where no negotiation was allowed, where the force of a taboo stricture obtained, casuists participated most obviously in the process of "naming," of categorizing and delimiting, the possibilities of human behavior by imparting to the conscience a set of controlling images, a semiotics, the authority of which was defined and validated by the reigning complex of theological and legal structures of thought from which casuistical discourse drew its own origins.[6]

But the introduction of the probabilistic school, in the midsixteenth century, gave prominence to the discourse of conscience as a precision tool for registering the vagaries of human experience, for producing multifaceted narratives of Christian lives, accounts of crises that resisted the imposition of a normative reading. The praxis of this kind of casuistry underlined the inscrutable character of conscience itself, which turned all secure, authoritative readings of a word, a gesture, or an event into provisional, unstable ones.

It would be misleading, though, to confine the duality of casuistical analysis to its historical representation, as a parable of entropy in which casuistry's successive transformations fragmented an initially unilateral interpretive apparatus. Whether at the tutiorist or the probabilist extreme, to read casuistically was by definition to engage in an interpretive project structured by an internal paradox. Put another way, to act as a casuist was to attempt a series of more or less adroit negotiations between, on the one hand, an idealized configuration of the Christian life (an ideal beset by its own internal conflicts, which the casuist had to address and resolve, in the nexus of divine, natural, and positive laws) and, on the other, a pragmatic, empirically based apprehension of Christian lives in the contingency of the moment and at the intersection of their other, competing, manifestations: Christians recognized as social and political beings.

Casuists ascribed a dualistic, and negotiatory, principle to the central locus of their practice: conscience itself, which they perceived not only as a place but as an ongoing activity, as a syllogistic dialog between *synteresis* (the passive and infallible storehouse of divine truth) and *conscientia* (the active witness, viewing particular cases in the light of the moral knowledge acquired from *synteresis*).[7] The description, which gave logical priority to *synteresis*, carried a prescriptive element: the internal structure of conscience, functioning as a perceptual and interpretive faculty, replicated and confirmed the hierarchical structure underpinning the *societas* of Christians in the commonwealth. But, in the praxis of casuistry, the internal structure of conscience belied the immanence of the patterns of order located in social, religious, and political institutions. For the prescribed negotiation between *synteresis* and *conscientia* did not completely mask the points of rupture in the frame for the Christian life that the word "conscience" produced. "Conscience," construed as an interpretive activity within a continually changing socio-political context, performed a covert deconstructive operation on the other, the dominant, property assigned to the word: "conscience" construed as the fixed locus of truth, as "a little God sitting in the middle of men['s] hearts."[8] That is, the very word that overtly referred to itself as the site of pre-existing and immutable meanings covertly referred to itself as the site of the production of meaning.

The duality of casuistical analysis, organically related to the dualistic structure of conscience itself, thus produced an ongoing, if implicit, tension—one that corresponds to what anthropologists like

Sally Falk Moore have observed as the underlying, contradictory impulses whose interaction characterizes the formation, and formulation, of "social reality." In this process, attempts "to crystallize and concretize social reality, to make it determinate and firm," by imposing a "fixed framework of rules or understandings," are modulated in the presence of countervailing actions that work "by exploiting the indeterminacies" in a given situation or "by generating such indeterminacies or redefining the rules or relationships."[9] During the latter half of the sixteenth century the implicit tension between these two actions became explicit, and explicitly politicized, within the discourse of conscience, a discourse that cut across the boundaries of religious, social, and legal structures.

The place of casuistical analysis in Tudor legal discourse, as I have suggested, was well established. Indeed, in a litigious society that fairly teemed with interacting and competing court systems, the invisible court of conscience held a privileged place: it was, as one judge put it, the "highest tribunall . . . wherein the power of the keys is exercised to the highest degree."[10] Since the Henrician Reformation (the Marian years excepted), the Tudor government had indicated its vested interest in establishing something like eminent domain over the *foro interno* of conscience, a project we find, for example, in Thomas Cromwell's reforms, which produced pamphlets that politicized the making of a moral choice, urging the consciences of Henry's subjects to follow the spiritual and temporal lordship that resided in London, not Rome. It is worth noting, in this context, that the practice of Tudor jurists in addressing anomalous legal cases was shaped by the casuistical discourse—the language of the *Angelica*—embedded in one of the most influential legal texts of the period, Christopher St. German's *Doctor and Student*, which explored the relationship between equity and common law. The official embodiment of conscience was the Court of Chancery, which defined itself as the visible locus of the related principles of equity and the monarch's conscience. The discourse of conscience, then, inhabited the Tudor discourse of power in its most exalted form, imparting a rhetoric of inviolability to the monarch that exemplified both the prerogative, in the *regnum*, of the *princeps*—whose conscience contained the *arcana imperii*, the secrets of state—and, in the *sacerdo-*

tium, the prerogative described by Paul, and appropriated by pontiffs and anointed princes alike, of the "spiritual man," who "judges all, but himself is judged by none" (1 Cor. 2:15).

But the discourse of conscience flourished, as well, outside its official legal and political arena. As the Jesuit Robert Persons observed, the itinerant priests in the English mission had to be "able to deal with all the cases of conscience that occur here and are very grave ones," cases representing the efforts of a people to delineate, with precision, the patterns of thought and behavior that would identify them as loyal members of two apparently irreconcilable societies: English and Catholic. And the *cura pastoralis* of Protestant casuists like Richard Greenlaw and William Perkins, though shorn of the abhorred legalism of Romish moral theology, was nonetheless directed toward a community for whom the scrutiny of conscience was assuming increasing importance—and not merely because of a peculiarly Protestant habit of introspection.[11]

The climate in which English subjects of the late sixteenth century lived, a climate of advertised religious and political strife, promoted the exercise of a casuistry, among Protestants as well as Catholics, that was directed both inward and outward. This kind of casuistry, at the pinnacle as well as at the margins of power, invited one to explore the premises of both private and social discourse while moving through the book of the world like the Anglican divine Joseph Hall's reader of the enigmas in the "deeps of Scripture": a reader "well ballasted, and well tackled, and skillful in the compass," in order to "escape a wreck."[12] In this climate, under the aegis of the discourse of conscience, the cognate practices of "honest dissimulation," equivocation, and "mental reservation" became common coin in the language of political and religious dissent. That Catholic recusants, steeped in the "Maeandrian turnings and windings" of Jesuit casuistry, habitually eluded their interrogators' probes with "sleeveless aunsweres . . . never aggreeing to any certayntie" passed for a self-evident fact: it was "what everybody knew," from the official Protestant pulpit and press, about popish heretics.[13] This knowledge deflected attention from another kind of knowledge: that of the Protestant community's own participation in such practices. To be sure, it might be observed that members of the radical fringe like the Family of Love would "for commodity . . . transform themselves into all colours and conditions," believing "it was good *Christendome* to lie, swear, and forswear, to say and unsay to any."[14] It was less convenient to observe that a mainstream, and popular, Protestant casuist like William Perkins (his Puritan affiliations notwithstanding) admitted the practice of the "good deceit" (*dolus bonus*), with the same kind of indeterminate qualification ("if there be reasonable cause") usually attributed to the casuistry of the Jesuits.[15]

However they might define or justify their particular brand of casuistical discretion, both Catholics and Protestants during the latter half of Elizabeth's reign had occasion to exploit the destabilizing effect of casuistry, evidently unwilling or unable to see that what they practiced for the sake of conscience and its nominally stable truths was producing a context of ideological and interpretive instability that might be beyond their power to contain. This was the climate in which the struggle between Mary Stuart and Elizabeth was both played out and displayed to the public for consumption. Elizabeth's two well-publicized speeches concerning the fate of Mary Queen of Scots, made to Parliament in late 1586, displayed her expertise in exploiting the procedures of casuistry. Informed by the controversial doctrines of equivocation and mental reservation, the narrative constituted by Elizabeth's speeches and her subsequent action against Mary reinforced the fiction of the monarch's inviolable power by establishing the royal conscience, which had been submitted under duress to public inquiry and judgment, as a self-effacing text destined to be misread.

This narrative, which I examine in the first chapter, resonated in a context represented by extant cases of conscience of the English recusants and church-papists, cases that sabotaged the implicit claim of the centers of ecclesiastical and political power to exclusive authority over the discourse of conscience. The cases, discussed in the second chapter, point up the generalized indeterminacies and the ethos of misreading that characterized the social texts generated in a regime plagued by widespread and often covert religious and political dissidence.

One of the most notorious cases of conscience, the focus of the third chapter, is that of Father Anthony Tyrrell, multiple apostate and double agent, whose career reached its climax in the priest's sensational, though unwitting, parody of a public confession at St. Paul's

Cross, little over a year after Elizabeth delivered her confessional
speeches at Richmond. Governed by the same motives of evasion
and concealment and implicated in the same discursive pattern of
mental reservation that informed Elizabeth's speeches, the Tyrrell
case collapsed the distance between two anomalous figures: the be-
leaguered monarch and the hunted dissident. The case challenged
the exclusive and uncontested right of the monarch to the privilege
of inviolability; and it raised implicit questions about the ways in
which norms in general achieve their objective status, their separa-
tion from social, political, and cultural processes.

Significantly, the scandal of the Tyrrell case was rewritten as a
triumph of Protestant orthodoxy and suppressed by the English
Catholic hierarchy: the potentially radical critique of the great doxal
texts of the sixteenth century was consigned to virtual unintelligibility. The second part of the study takes up this phenomenon of cultural aphasia, which marked the apologetic or polemical use of the
cases of conscience that laced the Elizabethan discourse of power.
My premise, drawn in part from commentaries and pamphlets on
the ethical and political dangers of mental reservation and the lax
conscience, is that the prospect of acquiring not only political but
also psychological and spiritual power (the sense of "being in the
right") furnished a sustaining motive to suppress, or to "misrecognize," the arbitrariness of one's own orthodoxy as well as one's secret
complicity in the legitimation of reigning structures of power. This
phenomenon undergoes critical interrogation notably in texts that
are defined as canonical: texts whose canonical status is related to
their rhetorical pose as the disinterested purveyors of truth, a status
underscored by internal references to conscience that have assumed
a merely conventional value. Two examples illustrate the point and
its implications for the production of visual and literary narrative:
the Pinacoteca "Siena Sieve" portrait of Elizabeth (ca. 1580) and
book 5 of Edmund Spenser's *The Faerie Queene*, which contains a
deceptively encomiastic—indeed, a conspicuously inconclusive and
self-censoring—representation of the fateful conflict between Elizabeth and Mary Queen of Scots. I show how the iconographic and
narrative anomalies that figure in each work, invoking the thematics
of conscience, transgressively reenact the processes through which

the social formation conceals from itself its complicity in the production and legitimation of norms.

The affinity between the destabilizing operation of casuistry and the deconstructionist theory of language may now seem apparent. Consider the central premises of deconstruction. Reversing the hierarchy of speech over writing, it "shows that language does not simply 'come after' the concepts it is supposed to represent, like some kind of delayed supplement or exposition." Deconstruction shows how language "ensnares and defeats rationality, rendering some of its fundamental categories—origin, presence, meaning—perfectly useless." Invoking a metaphysics of absence, it insists that "the precondition for meaning . . . is always absent, always elsewhere, like a horizon we can never reach. The moment of full meaning, the plenitude of presence, when the chain of signification will be reached, never comes: full presence is endlessly deferred, it is always 'in *différance*.'"[16] My readings of Elizabeth's speeches and of Spenser's "legend of justice," for example, indicate how the casuistry informing these texts appears to deconstruct prevailing assumptions about the coercive and normative uses of conscience in the mechanisms of power in Elizabethan culture—notably its role as the transparent locus of truth and as the guarantor of intelligible, and governable, words and behavior.

Yet casuistry is not the sixteenth century's royal road to a prospect from which "all discursive paths are dead ends or labyrinths which turn back upon themselves," as they turn out to be in the deconstructive enterprise.[17] "The trick of deconstruction," writes Allon White, "is to treat texts not as specific performances within a social discourse, but as abstract repertoires of competence. As soon as you do this, then all the terms of the repertoire become ambiguous and fall away from each other. They are no longer held together by the social motivations, functions, and uses of the discourse, but fall back into their plurality of potential."[18] I would venture to say that in the sixteenth and seventeenth centuries casuistry was uniquely equipped to redefine the relation between the two properties of texts that deconstructionist theory, in White's critique, sees as mutually exclusive. For it was casuistical analysis that described conscience itself as a relation between an "abstract repertoire of competence" (*langue* to Ferdinand de Saussure; *synteresis* to the casuists) and "specific performances within a social discourse" (*parole*; *conscientia*). The prospect that casuistry thus leads to is one from which the "trick" of deconstruction—the mythos of the text as the site of endless deferral—can be contextualized, read as a socially and politically motivated trope of language.

What I show, for example, in the speeches Elizabeth read to Parliament and had published as the official representation of her conscience is Elizabeth's deconstructive gambit undertaken in response to a specific crisis that threatened to alter the balance of power between monarch and subject. The gambit produced a text that defined itself not only as unreadable but also as authorless—and, therefore, as readerless, too. Elizabeth's representation of conscience had become a medusan text, inviolable not because it represented the "little God" within us issuing a command to be obeyed, to be read properly, but because it represented the impossibility of its being "read" at all. The text, in effect, cancelled itself out of the particularized, and ungovernable, relations of power between authors and a potentially indeterminate number of readers: between authoritative discourse and its various uses or interpretations. By situating the speeches in their historical context, then, we can demystify the paralyzing effects of "endless deferral" the speeches contain: we can ground such effects in Elizabeth's persistent refusal to submit to the contingencies of history that the dynamic between readers and authors implied, insofar as the act of reading the conscience of the queen empowered her readers to judge her responsibility in a particular case of conscience and, from that judgment, to determine the scope of her power and autonomy.

What the broader social practice of casuistry brings into focus—in the cases of conscience associated with religious and political dissidence—is a context that Elizabeth necessarily had no interest in acknowledging, a context that demythologized the mythic structure Elizabeth tried to create in her speeches. The cases indicate that the medusan text of conscience was not the inimitable property of authority. They indicate, further, that the ostensibly "pure and unmotivated" aspect of the text of conscience, its decontextualized pose, was inflected by a potentially limitless variety of motives and circumstances, including ones attached to social class and gender as well as political and religious affiliations.[19] This is not to say that the cases of conscience I analyze reveal the dissidents' conscious project to disable Elizabeth's power or the cultural norms associated with it. If anything, the cases reveal the dissidents' desire to achieve the kind of inviolability that Elizabeth enacted in her speeches and their desire to virtually negate the informing hand of circumstances in the text of conscience they presented to the world. Taken as an ensemble, the cases and Elizabeth's speeches reveal a generalized cultural anxiety, directed through the lens of conscience, in the face of the apparent limits of authorial intention in shaping the meaning of texts and, more broadly, in the face of the apparent collapse of a centralized, normative control of meaning. As the vehicle through which we can read this anxiety, the discourse of conscience, indeed, points up the evidence of this collapse. Not, however, because of an abstract, destabilizing power of textuality but because of textuality's necessary involvement in social practice, including the intentions and biases, both collective and individual, that form the context in which texts are produced and assimilated.

What the discourse of conscience points up in fleeting and fragmentary ways in the political documents and ephemera I have assembled, Spenser's narrative localizes in book 5 of *The Faerie Queene*. Producing something other than the sincerest form of flattery, Spenser imitates the medusan rhetoric of conscience but does so equivocally, providing two kinds of contextual information, which work in contradictory ways. The "legend of justice" demythologizes, more fully than the isolated cases of conscience could, the kind of casuistry that Elizabeth's speeches epitomized; but it also enacts the very social and political imperatives in Elizabethan culture that were likely to make Spenser's message unintelligible. What Spenser produced, in effect, was an evacuated polyphonic text, one whose contextual inflections both speak and are silenced through the agency of conscience.

Ultimately, the documents I use to illustrate the hermeneutics of casuistry can be seen as participating in the kind of novelistic enterprise that Mikhail Bakhtin described, in that the texts variously enact what Bakhtin saw as the signal characteristic of novelistic discourse:

an "eternal rethinking and re-evaluating" of a culture's structures of
order and privileged idioms.[20] For Bakhtin, novelistic discourse "is
always criticizing itself." This habit manifests itself, pre-eminently, in
the representation of a dialogic, as opposed to a utopian, orientation
of language and culture. The Word, as well as the ideology it contains, loses its firm outline, its absolutist character; in its place arises
a congeries of words, of interanimating languages that reflect a
"heteroglot conception of the world" rather than an "abstract system
of normative forms." Novelistic discourse represents the interaction of
these languages of heteroglossia, out of which words emerge not as
isolated, neutral objects with fixed meanings but as contextually saturated events: as utterances that point to a dynamic relation between
individual speakers and listeners, between social groups, between
cultures; utterances whose meanings therefore resist containment
within fixed boundaries. Like the chameleon, novelistic discourse itself is protean, and its mode probative: it absorbs other, both literary
and extra-literary, discourses and relativizes them, allowing them to
frame, comment on, and interpenetrate each other. Within its confines the privileged semiotics of all authoritative discourses is tacitly
discredited: truth is made to reveal its artifice, its contextual—its
social, political, and cultural—underpinning.[21]

Bakhtin saw novelistic discourse as an expression of the "disintegration of stable verbal-ideological systems," a phrase that captures as
well the destabilizing effect of the casuistical discourse that emerged
in post-Reformation England.[22] In part, the effect was extrinsic:
its appropriation by the competing centers of power—Rome and
Westminster—ultimately showed casuistry to be less a manifestation
of a stable, authoritative discourse than a barometer of the struggle of
such discourse to maintain its authority in a climate of religious controversy. It was, in fact, no coincidence that casuistry should flourish
in such a climate, where words like "heresy" and "orthodoxy," no
longer reflecting a single, controlling ideology, did not so much define the opposition of clearly demarcated conceptual categories—
and of clearly differentiated social groups—as suggest a concourse
of contextually oriented opinions. Casuistry itself, I argue, promoted
such a climate of moral and epistemological uncertainty, as an expression of the intrinsic metacritical structure of a discourse that resided,
by definition, in the interstices between the fixed framework of estab-

lished laws and the indeterminacies of lived experience. As such, the discourse of conscience possessed an ingrained dialogic character, a capacity to insinuate a polyphony of what Bakhtin called "internally persuasive" discourses into the structure of authoritative discourse. In short, the discourse of conscience possessed the capacity to "novelize" whatever representational or analytical structures it inhabited.

By "novelize" I do not mean the production of sixteenth-century proto- (or even para-) novels, if by "novel" one posits a canon of literary texts sharing specific formal attributes, texts from which one can extrapolate a taxonomy of rules for a genre that is called the novel. The novelistic genre defies such fixity (though the impulse, essentially logocentric, among narrative theorists to establish fixity certainly exists, as Tztevan Todorov's criticism of Bakhtin's "barely coherent" and finally "irrational" description of novelistic discourse suggests).[23] A given text that seems to us to invoke such generic traits is, in the words of Michael Holquist, "simply the most complex and distilled expression" of the impulse of novelistic discourse, whose particular *aporia* resides in its apparent self-definition as a genre that is anti-generic. "Novel," as Holquist puts it, "is the name Bakhtin gives to whatever force is at work within a given literary system to reveal the limits, the artificial constraints of that system. . . . Always it will insist on the dialogue between what a given system will admit as literature and those texts that are otherwise excluded from such a definition of literature."[24]

The discourse of conscience in sixteenth century England, then, does not so much illustrate a chapter in the development of the novel, qua canonical genre, as it does the diffusion—in texts both social and verbal, extra-literary and literary—of varieties of dialogism that will crystallize most strikingly in works that are conventionally called novels. Furthermore, by inhabiting, and eroding, a discourse of power charged with the presence of an authoritative Word, the discourse of conscience articulates the inherent capacity of the "novelizing" act to serve as a vehicle for political and ideological subversion.

The assemblage of texts I have used in this study indicates a complex of previously unexamined and problematic aspects of casuistry's career during what was arguably the period of its highest visibility in England. The shape of that career, I believe, effectively rewrites the premises governing the eventual manifestations of the discourse of

conscience in the literary culture of the eighteenth century, at a time
when casuistry, if it no longer commanded the kind of prestige (and
infamy) it had once known as an independent discourse, nonetheless
continued, cannibalized by other discourses, to exert its power—a
fate, one might argue, peculiarly fitting to casuistry. The project
this observation implies—of investigating the relations between casuistry and the narrative practices of a Daniel Defoe or a Samuel
Richardson, say, from the perspective I introduce—remains to
be done.

I do not, however, intend to situate my reading of casuistry in
the Renaissance solely as a pre-text for such a future investigation.
Casuistical hermeneutics played a pivotal role in the shifting relations of power between producers and consumers of texts within the
interwoven religious, political, and literary cultures of Elizabethan
England. I have tried to make the dimensions of this role, and its
impact on Spenserian narrative, intelligible primarily within the
context of religious, political, and literary problems that, together,
helped shape the edifice of Elizabethan culture as well as the politics
of interpretation that was the culture's scaffolding.[25]

Reading the text of casuistry in the Renaissance illumines the
pivotal, complementary processes of reading and writing the texts
through which Elizabethan culture defined itself—its texts of power,
its hierarchy of values and norms, its taboos, and its tacit or naturalized protocol for determining canonical texts and "good" readings.
Essentially, casuistry and the discursive structures it informed—
whether orations like Elizabeth's speeches, fragmented exemplary
biographies like Robert Persons's of the missionary Anthony Tyrrell,
or the Spenserian narrative on the vexed subjects of justice and
equity—point up the bond of complicity between the culture's
sacred mythology of conscience and its construction of scandal. The
arc that begins with the story of two rival queens and ends with a
dubiously commemorative legend of justice describes in its course
the scandal of textuality itself—the wild card in the game of power
in Elizabethan culture, ungovernable in its range of nuance and ambiguity and in the equivocal poise it insinuates into the relation of
canonicity and subversion.

PART I

Victims of Conscience In and
Around Elizabeth's Court

The Text of Casuistry in Elizabeth's Discourse of Power: Misreading the Conscience of the Queen

Much suspected by me,
Nothing proued can be:
    Quoth Elizabeth prisoner

           —after Holinshed, words etched by
           Princess Elizabeth in a glass
           window at Woodstock, 1555[1]

The Architecture of the Scots Case

In the middle of October 1586 Mary Queen of Scots was tried by a court of commissioners at Fotheringay Castle. Several months later, on the first day of February, Elizabeth signed the warrant for Mary's execution, which her secretary of state William Davison delivered to the lord chancellor to be sealed with the Great Seal of England. On February 8, 1587, Mary was beheaded. This is the public record of the events intended to resolve a crisis that had been simmering for fifteen years of Elizabeth's reign.

In 1579 John Stubbs included in his forthright denunciation of the Alençon match an eloquent description of the threat the Scots queen posed: she was "the only lodestone that should draw traitors together and rent our kingdom."[2] This passage from the *Gaping Gulf*, a book that aroused Elizabeth to fury and cost its author one hand, touched a matter the queen would have preferred to make as unutterable as the question it raised about her succession. Yet it expressed a widespread attitude, one certainly held among the vocal members of

Parliament. From the moment Mary, deposed queen and political refugee, took up residence in England until the axe fell at Fotheringay, Parliament pressed Elizabeth to remove the "favourite daughter of the Pope," who had come to symbolize the Catholic threat in England.[3] Elizabeth countered Parliament's hostility to Mary with protestations of concern for her "kinswoman" and with a sustained effort to stave off as long as possible any direct involvement in the proceedings against her sister queen, even after Mary, incriminated in the Babington Plot, had been brought to trial and found guilty of high treason. Mary's execution, she knew, was going to arouse controversy—as was her own hand in the matter.

From the first years of her reign, Elizabeth had sought to avoid the kind of exposure to the forum of public judgment that now seemed inescapable. She had skirted religious and political controversy, preferring not to antagonize the "mighty factions," as Sir Philip Sidney called them, that divided her realm, factions "bound upon the never dying knot of religion."[4] True, in the last ten years she had permitted increasingly severe pressures to be brought to bear against the "English hypocrite" and "Romish pharisee"—the puritan and papist factions.[5] But Elizabeth's overriding impulse had been to temporize, "not liking," it was said, "to make windows into men's hearts and secret thoughts, except the abundance of them did overflow into overt and express acts and affirmations."[6] The favor, she expected, would be returned.

This spirit informed the burgeoning *via media Anglicanae*, which under Elizabeth was more than a program for the reconstruction of the Church in England; it was a main artery in Elizabeth's system of royal power. The "sufficiently indeterminate" language of the Elizabethan Settlement mirrored Elizabeth's idealized relationship to her people: a sufficiently indeterminate power, whose overt effect, therefore, could not be precisely apprehended.[7]

When Elizabeth found herself before an anxious Parliament in the middle of November 1586, her first words conveyed that ideal, though her putative purpose was to express a relationship of a different order. "The bottomlesse graces and immesurable benefits bestowed upon me by the almightie," she began, " . . . have been so manie, so diverselie folded and imbroidered one upon another, as in no sort I am able to express them."[8] Just as the power of God confounded Elizabeth's soul with its "immesurable benefits," so must the royal power of Elizabeth, his ordained minister, confound her subjects: the image of Elizabeth's adorned soul reproduced itself in the glittering ornaments of Gloriana's court and, by extension, in the myriad manifestations of Gloriana's power throughout the body politic.

The cult of Gloriana signalled a wide range of responses—love, adulation, wonder, an undercurrent of fear—all directed toward the total effect of Elizabeth's words and actions. But the case of the Scots queen dictated two responses—sanction or censure—that threatened to undermine the efficacy of the cult. It was one thing to live under "the eies of manie"; such was the condition of monarchs, one Elizabeth usually knew how to exploit. It was quite another for a queen to subject herself, and her Crown, to public sanction or censure for a particular act that was better left enshrouded in the mysteries of monarchical power.

Sir Robert Naunton, secretary of state to James I, included in his reminiscences of the queen's reign a telling description of the hazard Elizabeth confronted in the winter of 1586–87: "If we search further into her intellectualls and abilities, the whole course of her government deciphers them to the admirations of posteritie; for it was full of magnanimitie, tempered with justice, pittie, and pietie, and to speake truly, noted but with one staine or taint."[9] Naunton duly recorded the official virtues of Gloriana as part of a seamless cloth of estate. It was the "whole course" of Elizabeth's reign that drew admiration; no distinct moment was to be singled out and judged better or worse than another—with the exception of Elizabeth's "treatment of the unfortunate Mary."[10] The stain of Mary's blood called attention to a specific act that left, in turn, a stain on Elizabeth's government and, if we consider the pronounced religious implications of the term, a "staine" of sin on Elizabeth's soul. Naunton did not openly condemn Elizabeth, as did many of the Catholic polemicists both in England and on the Continent. But, by inviting his readers to weigh the specific evidence of sin against the abstract commonplaces of royal virtue, he charted a relationship between queen and populace that exposed the limits of Elizabeth's power to shape and control her image as an inviolate ruler.

In contrast, *A Declaration of the ends of traytors*, written by one

"R.C." in the year of Mary's death, charted precisely the kind of relationship that Elizabeth sought to establish. He recalled a hidden *virtù* that emanated from her royal person. Conspirators of recent times, Elizabeth's would-be assassins, presented no real danger, he reminded her. She could rest assured that they would be warded off by her "graue, sage, and honorable Counsellers," whose insight was such that if "any thing hath beene purposed or meant, which might any way tende to the daunger of her Maiesties person, or to the trouble or perill of this state, that hath beene by them quickly espied, deepelie looked into, and with wisedome and pollicie in time preuented and auoyded, to their immortall fames, glories, and renownes for euer." But R.C.'s final consolation did not urge the queen to rely on her counsellors. Their acumen, rendered metaphorically as a condition of visual acuity and perceptive power, was fallible. The queen's, R.C. suggested, was not. Even if conspirators managed to come within striking distance of the queen's body, they would find themselves, mysteriously, immobilized in her presence, "so dismayed upon the sight of your princely person, and in beholding your most gracious countenance," that they would suddenly have "no power to per-forme the thing, which they hadde before determined upon."[11] Like all the heroic attributes of Elizabeth, her Medusa-like aspect, ad-justed to the exigencies of courtly praise, tapped a constituent part of the economy of power in Elizabeth's court, an imaginative projection of inviolability that served both courtiers and queen, particularly in 1587. It gave a model lesson to Elizabeth's subjects: how best to in-terpret crises that appeared to threaten the court and the queen. R.C.'s conspirators are not pursued, arrested, imprisoned, interro-gated, tried, executed, and, finally, memorialized in broadsides or excoriated from the pulpit and government presses. Instead they find themselves simply "with no power" at the sight of the monarch, whose gaze, invoked in the progressively narrowing focus on the queen's person and then on her countenance, instantly discovers and overpowers their own treasonous perspective. The actual administra-tion of the cumbersome and sometimes messy machinery of the Tudor penal system was translated by the fiction of the petrifying gaze, the localized medusan power of the monarch, into an unob-trusive, virtually invisible contest for power, from which Elizabeth, unfailingly, emerged triumphant, with no trace of conscious effort and without a murmur of approbation or disapproval from a judging body.

R.C.'s mythologizing of royal omnipotence through the allusion to the Medusa gave Elizabeth's subjects a particularly emphatic reading of the *arcana imperii* theme, which defined the monarch's right to withhold secrets of state from public scrutiny. R.C. conveyed Elizabeth's determination to brook no exceptions to the rule. The image of the petrifying gaze described Elizabeth's elimination of conspirators—in 1587 who would not think of Mary?—as an event that not only should not but could not be directly observed. No discrete act implicated Elizabeth in the destruction of her enemies. There was only a gaze, only a continuous emanation of power. While it was possible, then, to enjoy, or to suffer, the effects of Elizabeth's power, it was not possible to discern the means by which she exerted it. One might rejoice, or privately lament, that Mary was suddenly absent from the theater of the world; but one could not pinpoint the moment at which Elizabeth assured her going. Those who tried to probe into the mechanism of Elizabeth's power might consider the uncomfortable parallel R.C. left to be discovered between them and the conspirators. Like the conspirators, the curious would find that they, too, suddenly had no power to perform the thing determined upon. They would be impotent observers, automatically deprived of the capacity to scrutinize and judge Elizabeth's actions. On the one hand, all discernible traces of royal intervention in the crisis were eliminated; on the other, all eyes capable of discernment were bleared.

R.C.'s allusion suggested an impavid queen and an unimpeachable power. The allusion was embedded in a pamphlet that otherwise submitted Elizabeth to public scrutiny as a victim of circumstance, a woman "unwylling to take away the Queene of Scots life" but unable, finally, to resist the pressures of political necessity. The two images were not incongruous. Both expressed the high premium that Elizabeth placed on unaccountability. The Medusa figure may well have captured Elizabeth's most fervent hopes: to seal off from public scrutiny her own role in extinguishing Mary's life and to eliminate the very possibility of public approbation or disapproval. The image of a queen swept along by the tide of events, yet persisting in a valiant effort to impede the inexorable progress of Parliament and her ministers against Mary, shows us the direction she pursued in realizing those hopes.

The image was well publicized, buttressed by other details— the delays in bringing Mary to trial, the deferral of the proclamation against Mary, the prorogation of Parliament in the intervening months before Mary's execution—all of which took their place in the public record, all visible evidence of Elizabeth's frustrated attempts to break the chain of events that would lead to Mary's death. R.C.'s *Declaration* gave only a truncated account of Elizabeth's role in the controversy. His earlier pamphlet, *The Copy of a letter to the Earle of Leycester* (1586), gave far more complete documentation, including, notably, drafts of the important Parliamentary petitions to Elizabeth and of Elizabeth's two speeches to Parliament, which gave eloquent testimony of her reluctance to proceed against Mary. John Stowe reprinted the *Copy*, with Elizabeth's approval, in the second edition of *Holinshed's Chronicles* (1587). A French edition also appeared.[12]

Elizabeth clearly intended to make a virtue of necessity: that which could not be kept from the public eye should, then, be thrust before it, but qualified by an array of circumstances that would impede judgment of her conduct. I single out one event as emblematic of Elizabeth's entire strategy. The Fifth Parliament convened on October 29. Traditionally, the monarch opened the session with a verbal declaration, words that exemplified the performative power invested in royal authority. But Elizabeth did not open the Parliament whose energies, she knew, would be directed to bringing Mary to the executioner's axe. Three commissioners—John Whitgift, William Cecil (Lord Burghley), and Sir Edward Stanley (the Earl of Derby)— arrived at Westminster in her place. By delegating the authority to open Parliament, Elizabeth positioned herself at one remove from the performance of a necessary royal act. As a symbolic gesture, her absence signalled a shift from the active to the passive voice in the ceremonial language of authority.[13] "Elizabeth opened parliament" was to read "Parliament was opened." The message: an event had occurred without reference to a specific royal agent.

In the months that followed, Elizabeth repeated the message. Her words and behavior—including the two speeches, the signing of the warrant, and her vendetta in the court after Mary's death—followed the syntax of a rolling periodic sentence. Only after the last phrase was in place—her denunciation of Burghley and Davison—might the dissociation of agent and event, of subject and verb, be perceived as part of Elizabeth's own syntax of power. Thus in November it was not clear how things would turn out; it seemed unlikely that the crucial event—Mary's execution—would in fact occur. In her second speech Elizabeth had given an apt emblem of indecision, prompted, it seemed, by Elizabeth's aversion to the "taking of her [Mary's] blood": Elizabeth's "answer answerlesse" seemed to forecast a habit of retracting whatever she might say, or write, against Mary. On February 1, when Elizabeth finally took up her pen to sign the warrant, it seemed as if she had decided against Mary—but who knew how long she would abide by her decision?

Seven days later, Mary was dead. In the City "the bells announced the joyful intelligence, and numerous bonfires illuminated the darkness of the night." And Elizabeth erupted in an outburst of rage against the ministers who had proceeded with too great haste, she claimed, in carrying out the order for Mary's death. Davison, into whose hands she had delivered the warrant, suffered the ignominy of a grievous fine (ten thousand marks) and an indefinite term of imprisonment. Burghley, who had urged the Privy Council to send the warrant on to Fotheringay, despite Elizabeth's apparent relapse into indecision, suffered temporary banishment from the court.[14]

The apparent message: had Elizabeth's ministers properly interpreted the signing of the warrant, Mary would not have been executed. That is, the event had occurred as a result of their inadvertence, not as a result of Elizabeth's decision. In a letter to James VI, Elizabeth underlined the message: "I would you knewe (though not felt) the extreme dolor that overwhelmes my minde for that miserable accident, which (far contrary to my meaninge) hath befallen."[15] During the investigation of Davison's role in the "miserable accident," it came out that Elizabeth's apparent "meaninge" had been to produce something like a "warrant warrantlesse"—an official document intended to be kept secret, inactive until some future, unspecified event—perhaps an invasion—should force Elizabeth's hand.

An unofficial document—one she ordered written the same day that she signed the warrant, one her ministers were aware of—gives us a more precise picture of her meaning. Elizabeth had a letter sent from Francis Walsingham and William Davison to Mary's guardians,

Sir Amyas Paulet and Sir Drue Drury, asking them to take Mary's life without the warrant. The letter expressed the queen's discomfiture at the two men's apparent lack of initiative: "She doth note in you both a lack of that care and zeal for her service, that she looketh for at your hands, in that you have not found out some way to shorten the life of the Scots queen."[16] Elizabeth did not draw attention to the coincidence of the two documents. But they were in fact parallel texts, the letter articulating the primary "meaninge" behind Elizabeth's signing of the warrant. Elizabeth responded to the crisis by seeking to introduce circumstances that would produce a credible account of a "miserable accident," so that her signing of the warrant would not be the pivotal incident in determining Mary's death, as the law said it must. Either Mary's guardians would preempt the action of the warrant or Elizabeth's ministers would act "far contrary" to her "meaninge" by enforcing the warrant without due consideration of her intention in signing it. Elizabeth found that she had overextended her jurisdiction over her subjects by having the letter sent: Paulet grasped her meaning but refused to obey her, "to shed blood without law or warrant."[17] Elizabeth quickly recovered from the contretemps; she would no doubt have been relieved had the letter succeeded, but it is possible that it succeeded well enough in its capacity as a gloss of the warrant itself.

What she made explicit to Paulet in the letter she left implicit, but available to scrutiny, in her signature on the warrant. It was up to her ministers to read between the lines, to perceive that some way had to be found to dissociate Elizabeth from the scandal of Mary's execution—it was their responsibility to misread the warrant. Elizabeth had already conveyed the point in her two speeches, delivered in the Parliament that Burghley had wintrily called the "parliament of words," when it appeared doubtful whether the efforts of the Lords and Commons would ever come to anything.[18] During his banishment, he realized that Elizabeth's words were not empty but had a depth of meaning that, as she had suggested, would be difficult to plumb.

Burghley's private papers include a page of random phrases including the curious fragment, "Always not to be acquainted with the circumstances."[19] It is difficult to tell whether Burghley intended a declarative or an imperative statement. Was he lamenting his failure to understand the apparent meaning of Elizabeth's signature, or was he rehearsing a motto that conveyed her full meaning—the lesson that misreadings were inevitable, not to say desirable? Either statement would have been appropriate. Both echoed the complex message Elizabeth had insinuated into her speeches in November, in anticipation of the moment when she would find the warrant under her pen. Like Burghley's phrase, the speeches, too, were fragments, associative musings on her dilemma, ending inconclusively. More than that, their implicit theme was the fragmentary and opaque nature of human expression. Though she was "in the sight and view of all the world dulie obserued," Elizabeth cautioned her ministers and Parliament that no word or gesture of hers could convey inner folds of meaning with absolute fidelity. Like Burghley's phrase, the message described both what was and what must be.

John Lingard, the nineteenth-century Catholic historian, surmised that Elizabeth's elusive words and behavior exhibited a defect "in the constitution of her mind" that led her to a habit of irresolution and dissembling.[20] Attributing the events I have described to a psychological defect does not, of course, tell us much about the mechanism of Elizabeth's power in broader terms, as an emanation of cultural and social forces. Elizabeth's words and behavior in the winter of 1586–87 indeed reveal something about the constitution of her mind. They reveal an ingrained habit of problem-solving, of analyzing anomalous experiences, that was part of a common language, a communal "constitution of the mind," in the sixteenth century. The problem before Elizabeth invited the exercise of casuistry; and Elizabeth exploited its resources.

In 1586 the cult of Gloriana was invaded by the determination of Elizabeth's subjects to coerce her into making a moral choice. The crisis, "so weighty and unusual a cause," seemed to demand casuistical analysis. Among people and Parliament, Strype observed, "it was seriously debated whether it were lawful to cut off a queen, or to bring her into judgment."[21] The question summoned two opposing, irreconcilable jurisdictional claims, voiced respectively by Mary and by the Commons.

Throughout the proceedings against her, Mary claimed the pre-

rogative of royal majesty. The circumstance of her royal blood, she
argued, preempted the jurisdiction of English law: "God alone the
highest judge," she argued, had the right to pass sentence on an
anointed queen. Mary was warning her "most dear sister" of the ominous consequences of pursuing a queen to her death. Mary could not,
of course, speak directly to Elizabeth, for Elizabeth did not attend the
proceedings at Fotheringay Castle: she remained at Richmond. In the
Presence Chamber of Fotheringay Castle, where the trial took place,
there was only an emblem of absence, of royal self-erasure, one that
forecast Elizabeth's subsequent opening of Parliament: an empty
"chair of estate for the queen of England, under a cloth of estate."[22]
Undeterred by the physical, and moral, distance Elizabeth tried to impose between Fotheringay and Richmond, Mary invoked Elizabeth
repeatedly in her words before the commissioners. Her opening statement at the trial shattered the pretense of Elizabeth's uninvolvement.
By refusing to "prejudice her own royal majesty, the king of Scots
her son, her successors, or other absolute princes," Mary presented
herself as the guardian of a principle that Elizabeth was allowing
to erode.[23]

For fifteen years, Mary—willingly or not—had been associated
with papist insurgents and viewed as a constant threat to the safety of
Elizabeth and the entire realm. Now, incriminated in the Babington
Plot and soon to be found guilty of high treason, Mary inverted
the roles that she and Elizabeth had played. She professed herself willing to "die a thousand deaths" rather than forsake the
Pauline injunction upon which sixteenth-century monarchs, including Elizabeth, grounded their claim to royal sovereignty: "the powers that be are ordained of God" (Rom. 13:2). By discrediting Mary's
royal prerogative, by allowing Mary to be pursued under the terms
of English law, Elizabeth was betraying the divine right of monarchs
and therefore neglecting the superior jurisdiction of divine law—she
was endangering her soul as well as her royal estate.[24]

Elizabeth's act of treason would never be judged, of course, in
a court of the realm. But there was another court, in which "God
alone the highest judge" would review Elizabeth's conduct: the court
of conscience. Mary made no direct appeal to Elizabeth's conscience;
but she did not have to. Several times, before and during the
trial, Mary warned the commissioners to search their consciences.

Through them she spoke to Elizabeth. For what the commissioners did, they did in the service of a queen who possessed the power to obstruct the proceedings against Mary, as she had shown in 1572 by rejecting Parliament's demand for Mary's head in the aftermath of the Ridolfi Plot.[25] Mary's "immunity and majesty" had been repudiated in the external forum at Fotheringay, in the chamber that held the emblem of Elizabeth's attempt to extend the range of her own immunity—to dissociate herself from the administration of what Burghley called the "exact rule of Justice."[26] But Mary's words fastened a disturbing text to the emblem of the empty chair of estate: her defense of the royal prerogative, shot through with reminders of an internal forum that had greater significance *sub speculum dei* than the forum in which Mary was constrained to speak, belied Elizabeth's immunity in the court of conscience.

Before submitting to the trial, William Camden tells us, Mary advised the commissioners to "look to their consciences, and to remember, that the theatre of the whole world is much wider than the kingdom of England."[27] By conflating the topoi of the *foro interno* and the *theatrum mundi*, Mary evoked an image of a pre-Reformation society whose judgments mirrored perfectly the judgments of conscience. However divided the world might be in matters of religion, it would not remain so, she implied, in its judgment of Elizabeth. Mary saw a universal human community, a "whole world," united in a condemnation of Elizabeth for the judicial murder of an anointed queen. It behooved Elizabeth to consider the binding force of such a judgment within the internal forum of her own conscience.

The Protestant casuist William Perkins later defined the judgment of conscience as "nothing else but a beginning or a fore-runner of the last judgment."[28] Mary's words reminded Elizabeth that her sacrilege might produce more immediate, and politically devastating, effects. What Elizabeth, in Parliament and under the protection of English statute, did to Mary, others, perhaps in Parliament itself and with a similarly convenient legal apparatus, might one day do to Elizabeth.

After the trial, and after the sentence against Mary had been passed and made public, Mary's veiled warning became more explicit. Parliament now required only one act of Elizabeth: the signing of

Mary's death warrant. By that single act, Elizabeth would signal not only her assent to Mary's destruction but also her responsibility—in conscience as in the theater of the world—for an act that, whatever its legal justification, set a precedent for regicide. James VI, observing the crown that might one day be his, perceived the hazard. He responded to the proclamation against his mother with a cautionary letter to Elizabeth, a letter that reveals less his anguished filial sentiment than the acute perception of an anxious monarch. Appealing to her "rypest judgment," he urged Elizabeth to consider the risk she was taking: "Wuhat monstrous thing is it," he asked, "that souveraigne princes thaimselfis should be example-giveris of thaire owen sacred diademon prophaning?"[29] It was a compelling argument.

Mary's claim, then, was uncompromising, on religious, legal, and political grounds; but the opposing claim was equally so. The civil lawyers flatly denied Mary's royalty. She had been deposed by the "three estates of Scotland," they argued.[30] But they did not rely on this argument. Christopher Hatton, who as vice-chamberlain represented "the holy conscience of the queen," was perfectly willing to allow the circumstance of her royalty, because it was, in his view, insignificant, a "bootless privilege."[31] Parliament agreed. They countered the absolutist pretensions of Mary's claim with the rival claim of constitutionalism, emphasizing the jurisdiction of positive law over princes. Every person in the kingdom, as Burghley pointed out to Mary, was subject to the authority of common law and was "bound even by the latest laws." The "latest law"—the 1585 Act of Association—proved to be Mary's winding sheet. It asserted the power of English law to determine its own jurisdiction, especially in the "matter of Treason," a grave circumstance that, according to the civil lawyers, negated all "differences or privilege of the person suspected."[32] The Act engulfed the royal privilege, translating into statutory law the promise, made by all who had entered into the Bond of Association, to "prosecute, suppress, and withstand" all suspected enemies of Elizabeth, "of what nation, condition, or degree soever they shall be."[33]

The terms of the Act itself were not nearly so global. Without naming Mary specifically, the Act made it clear that she was its intended object. It tailored the "matter of Treason" to the volatile issue of Mary's claim to the English throne: "any person that shall or may pretend title to the crown of this realm" was liable to the charge of high treason for virtually all seditious acts against the Crown; and all evidence of sedition, according to the Act, automatically extinguished the pretender's claim to the succession.[34] The point was not to bring Mary, although a queen, under the jurisdiction of English law, but to do so precisely because she was a particular queen, a queen whose very existence, it was believed, threatened the sovereignty of Elizabeth and peace of the realm.

To prevent what they saw clearly as the imminent "ruin of the realm," Parliament devised an Act that came very close to legislating a model for the parliamentary deposition of a sovereign prince.[35] But if it gave an apparent edge to the constitutional impulse of Parliament, the Act equally gave testimony to the symbiotic relationship that existed between the monarch and Parliament in Tudor government. The opening words of the Bond of Association aptly described an attitude of submission to royal sovereignty: since "Almighty God hath ordained kings, queens, and princes to have dominion and rule over their subjects," it followed that "all subjects should love, fear, and obey their sovereign princes . . . to the utmost of their power."[36] With the Act, Parliament tested the "utmost" degree of its power, nominally as a pious service to a divinely ordained prince. In fact, Parliament was less concerned about the preservation of Elizabeth's sovereignty per se than about the preservation of the godly society, which would suffer yet another upheaval if Mary, the Catholic heir apparent, should succeed to the throne.

Mary denounced the Act before the commissioners. It had been made "to entrap her," she protested, "enacted directly and purposely against her." In the same breath she "appealed to their consciences": the Act, she implied, would have no jurisdiction in the higher court of conscience. Christopher Hatton, urging Mary to consent to the trial, countered her appeal by protesting that "all Justice would stagger, yea fall to the ground" if "such kind of offenses might be committed without punishment." As the terms of the Act had indicated, more than Elizabeth's sovereignty was at stake here. "All Justice" comprised the hierarchy of all laws, which stemmed from divine law; the jurisdiction of divine law itself was imperiled, he argued, by Mary's refusal to stand in judgment before the commissioners.[37] His rejoinder, while grounded in the traditional common law claim to supreme jurisdiction in England, echoed the Calvinist defense of political resistance to ungodly authority as a religious duty. The members of Parliament were Christian subjects and therefore sentinels of God's law in the Christian commonwealth. Should Mary succeed to the throne, the Christian commonwealth as they knew it would be demolished. They were therefore bound in conscience to safeguard the principles of justice that formed the ligaments of the commonwealth, principles inscribed in the positive law of England.

Furthermore, both the Bond and the Act of Association were couched in the language of religious obligation. The Bond was a solemn vow that called "to witness the name of Almighty God." And the text of the Act established its affinity to the Bond, as a legal extension of the vow that had been taken "in the name of God, and with the testimonies of good consciences."[38] The obligation extended to Elizabeth herself, as Parliament was quick to point out. They reminded her of her responsibility before God to preserve the realm from chaos. One message cast the argument explicitly as a case of conscience, predicting "the burden of her majesty's conscience, in being guilty of the universal harms that may follow, in not cutting off the Scotch queen."[39]

Elizabeth's evident reluctance to "cut off" her cousin later prompted Parliament to deliver two successive petitions, both of which raised again the issue of conscience. They weighed Elizabeth's conflicting loyalties, to Mary's disadvantage. True, Mary was Elizabeth's "kinswoman," but she had proved herself a "very unnatural sister": so much for the familial bond. They reminded Elizabeth of her primary loyalty to her true family—her people, who were her "children." As their sovereign, she had a responsibility to safeguard the consciences of the dutiful children who had sworn to protect her. Near the end of the second petition, Sir John Puckering, the Speaker of the Commons, described the moral dilemma Elizabeth would bring about by refusing to act:

Thousands of your loving subjects . . . cannot save their oaths if you keep her alive; for then either we must take her life from her without direction, which will be to our extreme danger by the offence of your law; or else we must suffer her to live against our express oath, which will be to the uttermost peril of our souls; wherewith no act of parliament, nor power of man whatsoever, can in any wise dispense.[40]

Elizabeth's subjects found themselves trapped in a case of conscience—between an "extreme danger" and an "uttermost peril"—that only Elizabeth could resolve. "It resteth in you," Puckering advised his queen, to insure that her subjects be "delivered from this trouble of conscience." Should she fail to deliver them, he warned, the consequences would be devastating: "Lastly, God's vengeance against Saul for sparing Agag, against Ahab for sparing the life of Benhadad, is apparent; for they were both by the just judgment of God deprived of their kingdom, for sparing those wicked princes, whom God had delivered into their hands of purpose to be put to death by them, as by the ministers of his eternal and divine justice."[41] It was left to Elizabeth to consider the ways in which God's wrath might deprive her of her kingdom.

The Royal Discourse of Conscience:
Elizabeth's First Speech

Both Parliament and Mary sought to impart a hierarchical order to the opposing jurisdictional claims by invoking the authority of divine judgment: both assumed the role of casuist. What both in fact achieved was a compelling statement of the contradictory positions informing the "burden of her majesty's conscience." Unlike Mary, however, the members of Parliament addressed the queen directly, spelling out in their petitions an ultimatum that demanded a public response, a sign of the queen's submission to the divine judgment embodied in the casuistry of her subjects. Neither of Elizabeth's two speeches, delivered in November of 1586, gave a direct answer to the petitions. They were bids for time, part of Elizabeth's familiar procrastination. But Elizabeth did take up the theme of her "burden of conscience." In both speeches she adroitly challenged Parliament's ultimatum. Parliament had "read" the conscience of the queen and had found potential guilt inscribed there, guilt for the "universal harms" that would follow if she chose to save Mary from the rigor of English law. Elizabeth's first speech corrected that reading; it provided a lesson in how to misread the queen's conscience.

On the surface, Elizabeth appeared to accept the casuistry of Parliament. The speech culminated in a statement that, without actually submitting to Parliament's demand, indicated the direction Elizabeth's resolution of the case would probably take: "I thinke it verie requisite with earnest praier to beseech his divine majestie, so to illuminate my understanding, and inspire me with his grace, as I maie doo and determine that, which shall serve to the establishment of his church, preservation of your estates, and prosperitie of this common wealth under my charge."[42] Her words echoed precisely the arguments voiced by Parliament in their first petition. By describing her eventual decision as the result of divine inspiration, Elizabeth appeared to recognize, however tacitly, that Parliament's and God's advice would be the same and that Elizabeth, for the safety of her conscience, would follow it.

Her acquiescence seemed even more probable in her subsequent recollection of the "oth"—the Bond of Association—which, she acknowledged, had been "taken and entered into upon good conscience." Elizabeth made it clear that she intended to respect their oath. It was "a perfect argument" of their "true hearts and great zeale"; it demanded a reciprocal expression from Elizabeth. She recognized her obligation: "So shall my bond be stronger tied to greater care for all your good," she proclaimed, recalling the oath she had taken at her coronation—her obligation before God to protect the commonwealth.

Elizabeth's speech, her own "perfect argument," did not reproduce an oath that would commit her to the answer Parliament anxiously awaited; but on two occasions it alluded to an equally privileged utterance, the confessional dialog. These allusions further strengthened the intimate bond Elizabeth sought to establish with her auditors. Her speech took on the rhetorical character of a confession, registering the condition of her conscience. Implicitly, Elizabeth invited Parliament to study her conscience: she accepted the role that Parliament had already assumed, acknowledging their right to scrutinize her conscience and to shape her behavior. Moreover, she offered them a guarantee that her words would not be mere excursions into political rhetoric designed to obscure her real purpose. Just as the oath taken by her loyal subjects was a transparent expression of their "true hearts," so her speech would be a transparent expression of her conscience. It would be, as St. Bernard had described the confessional utterance, *vera, nuda, et propria.*[43] As she neared the end of her first "confession," Elizabeth emphasized the point, recalling the penitent's examination of conscience: "For though I have manie vices, I hope I have not accustomed my toong to be an instrument of untruth." To allow even a grain of uncertainty to enter into her examination only emphasized her absolute integrity: what Parliament read in her speech could be taken as the truth of her conscience.

In the two confessional sequences, Elizabeth presented information appropriate to the exercise of casuistry: relevant circumstances in the case of the Scots queen. First Elizabeth revealed a secret correspondence between the two queens, in which Elizabeth, assuming her role as spiritual governor of the realm, had urged Mary to confess her role in "sundrie treasons." Elizabeth did not enter into the details of the correspondence. Instead she cited an array of circumstances that would have led her to "most willingly pardon and remit" Mary's offense. Elizabeth imagined how different—how much less serious—the case would appear to all if she and Mary were "but as two milke maids with pailes upon our armes" or if "there were no more dependencie upon us but mine owne life were onelie in danger, and not the whole estate of your religion and well doings." These were the circumstances, Elizabeth implied, that her conscience had duly considered—but each was contrary to fact.

On two counts, Elizabeth's bond, and her conscience, seemed assured: not only might Parliament rest secure in the transparency of Elizabeth's confession—they, too, believed such circumstances did not apply—but they might well hope to see Elizabeth remove her burden of conscience as they directed, given her professed concern for the safety of the "whole estate" of their religion and "well doings." Her second confession gave further evidence that she had settled on the resolution Parliament desired:

And even now could I tell you, that which would make you sorie. It is a secret, and yet I will tell it you; although it is knowne I have the propertie to keepe councell, but too well oftentimes to mine owne perill. It is not long since my eies did see it written, that an oth was taken within few daies, either to kill me, or to be hanged themselves: and that to be performed yer one moneth were ended. Hereby I see your danger in me, and neither can nor will be so unthankefull or carelesse of your consciences, as not to provide for your safetie.

Elizabeth alluded to the *arcana imperii* theme, according to which the monarch had the privilege of withholding secrets of state from public scrutiny—a privilege analogous to the confessor's with respect to the secrets of the confessional.[44] Here the *arcana imperii* theme served as a symbolic gesture of royal submission. Having embarked on a confessional mode, Elizabeth allowed her auditors access to the very heart of the royal conscience, where the secrets of state were stored. And she signalled that what she was about to confess—the imminent threat to her life—was not merely a private matter. It bore immense public and political significance: Parliament, she again implied, could rest assured that the conscience of the queen would submit to their resolution of the case. For any personal obligation to Mary or to other monarchs—indeed, even any private fears for her own safety—paled before her obligation to her people.

Burghley noted that Elizabeth's speech "drew tears from many eyes."[45] As well it might: although Elizabeth had not given a straightforward answer, she had given Parliament every reason to hope that she soon would. Touchingly, the queen had bared her conscience; she had confessed her loyalty to her good people and her determination to preserve the realm from ruin. "All Justice," as Christopher Hatton had put it, would be saved, to Elizabeth's everlasting credit. Parliament had successfully exploited, it appeared, the procedures of casuistry as a means of coercing the queen into action.

"Some few daies after," the chronicles report, Parliament received a message from the queen, "mooving and earnestlie charging them to enter into a further consideration, whether there might not be some other waie of remedie, than that they had alreadie required, so far disagreeing from hir owne naturall disposition." It was reported that the queen was "in some conflict with hir selfe what to doo in a cause so weightie and important to hir and the realme." Apparently, Elizabeth had not yet received the divine illumination necessary to resolve the case. As matters stood, she was caught between her "naturall disposition" and the opinion of Parliament, suffering from what any casuist would have identified as a "doubting conscience." To act with a doubting conscience was to sin.[46] The implication: if

Parliament forced her hand, the burden of conscience would be theirs. Elizabeth's message did not openly defy Parliament's judgment; nor did it retract her first speech. Instead, it offered Parliament a gloss that emended their probable reading of the speech. It reminded Parliament that they must not be too quick in predicting the queen's future actions or, for that matter, in pronouncing judgment on the state of her conscience before they had a firm grasp of all the pertinent circumstances. The message struck an appropriate coda to her first speech, as well as a fitting prelude both to her second speech and to the curious events that followed. It isolated the fundamental purpose of Elizabeth's casuistry during these critical months of her reign: to exploit dislocations between her words and actions and their perceived meaning. What was misunderstood could not, finally, be judged.

Elizabeth insinuated the point into both speeches. Although she addressed the fundamental, and well-known, circumstances of the case—the personal, legal, and political conflicts—she dwelled on incidents of misunderstanding and on distortions of meaning and of perception. These, too, she implied, were circumstances of paramount importance, not to be discounted in the exercise of casuistry. Discreetly, Elizabeth introduced an epistemological problem into the case Parliament had called her "burden of conscience." The case she herself admitted to be "rare, weightie, and of great consequence" posed, she implied, rare and weighty problems of perception. It would be difficult to perceive accurately all the circumstances of the case—difficult, therefore, to attribute blame or innocence to Elizabeth for whatever action she took.

She was urging Parliament to reconsider her own role as victim. Determined to be rid of Mary, Parliament and Elizabeth's ministers had repeatedly invoked Elizabeth's imminent fate as a victim of countless plots undertaken by seditious papists, all of whom had probably sworn in conscience to seize the throne for Mary.[47] Faced with Elizabeth's apparent intransigence, they had played their trump, warning her—not for the last time—of the spiritual ravagement she would face as a victim of conscience if she allowed Mary to live. Elizabeth graciously listened to their caveats, but the tenor of her speeches suggested the inadequacy of their insight. The point, she would have them know, was not to prevent but to insure her role as victim, though not the kind they imagined.

"I would (I assure you) not desire to live; but gladlie give my life," she told them, "to the end my death migyht procure you a better prince. And for your sakes it is, that I desire to live, to keepe you from a worse." It was possible that Mary would be sacrificed in the interest of maintaining an "ever prosperous and florishing estate." But Elizabeth was perpetually ready to give her life to the same end. These words, which closed Elizabeth's first "confession," permitted a view of the royal conscience in which the discrete acts of the prince—along with their physical and spiritual consequences—were obscured by the exalted image of the prince as passive, sacrificial victim.

Under the pressure of the crisis, Elizabeth was turning Gloriana into Iphigenia. It was an image partly intended to deflect attention in the theatre of the world from Mary's all too literal role as victim. Elizabeth, echoing Mary's words at her trial, later picked up the *theatrum mundi* topos, admitting that princes "are set on stages, in the sight and view of all the world dulie obserued"; it "behooveth us therefore," she noted, "to be careful that our proceedings be just and honorable." Even better: to insure that the proceedings, which stood little chance of being universally accepted as just and honorable, not be attributed to the "supreme governor" of the realm.

Exploiting the resonance of sacrificial violence in the idea of kingship, Elizabeth suggested that her own sufferings, like Mary's, would serve as the channel through which peace flowed.[48] The image of Elizabeth as victim in the exalted, ritualistic sense allowed her to diffuse the question of her ultimate responsibility for Mary's fate. It redefined, implicitly, her role in the proceedings against Mary. Elizabeth would be neither Mary's savior nor her murderer, because a victim did not act; a victim was acted upon.

As her speeches indicated, it behooved Parliament to learn that her particular fate, in this crisis, was to be the victim of repeated misunderstandings. Elizabeth's opening words in her first speech—her reference to the "bottomlesse graces and immesurable benefits" from God—made the point discreetly, setting limits to the transparency of the words that would follow. Just as the diverse strands of God's "wonderfull works and graces" could not be separated and perceived as discrete entities, so Elizabeth could not articulate them: "in no sort I am able to expresse them," she said. The inexpressibility topos, a rhetorical commonplace, can hardly have stunned her auditors into attention: this was the familiar, heightened language of the public oration. But given what was to follow—both in the course of Elizabeth's speeches and in the course of subsequent events—it established a discordant counterpoint to the confessional mode that Elizabeth seemed to have embraced.

Thus, when professing her own equanimity before the prospect of a violent death, Elizabeth allowed one fear—the fear that her own profession might be misjudged. "I hope you will not meerelie impute [it] to my simplicitie or want of understanding," she said, "but rather that I thus conceived, that had their purposes taken effect, I should not have found the blow, before I had felt it." When deliberating over the legality of the proceedings against Mary, she noted the inherent difficulty that observers would face in ascertaining the correct intention behind the Act of Association. It "was not made particularlie to preiudice hir," she maintained; indeed, it "was so far from being intended to intrap her, that it was rather an admonition to warne the danger thereof." Again, when reflecting on the decision now demanded of her, she warned Parliament of the ease with which her actions might be misconstrued:

But I must tell you one thing more, that in this last act of parlement you have brought me unto a narrow streict, that I must give direction for hir death, which cannot bee to mee but a most grievous and irksome burthen. And least you might mistake mine absence from this parlement (which I had almost forgotten) although there bee no cause whie I should willinglie come amongst multitudes, for that amongst manie some maie bee evill: yet hath it not beene the doubt of anie such danger or occasion that kept me from thense; but onlie the great griefe to heare this cause spoken of; especiallie, that such a one of state and kin should need so open a declaration, and that this nation should be so spotted with blots of disloialtie.

Elizabeth, we know, had broken off her speech just before this passage, leaving Parliament with the vaguely reassuring pledge that she would be "just and honorable" in proceeding against Mary. Resuming the speech at this point gave her next words the added luster of spontaneity, an encouraging sign that Parliament would be able to spy, untrammelled, into the conscience of the queen. Indeed, for the first time in the speech, Elizabeth referred openly to the case of conscience—the "narrow streict"—before her: she had reached the heart of the matter. Elizabeth exploited the moment. She countered Parliament's warning of the "burden of conscience" that would befall her if she did not give direction for Mary's death: to give such a direction created, as well, a "most greeuous and irksome burthen." This double burden drew attention to the fundamental impediment to her action in the case: her doubting conscience, of which all hopeful reading of her speech must run afoul.

But Elizabeth did not belabor the point. Instead of explaining why she would not be able to do what Parliament expected, she urged them to reflect upon a recent public event that had occurred without her direct involvement: the opening of Parliament. What role could be more negligible than that of absence? Elizabeth herself had "almost forgotten" it. Yet she reminded Parliament that even her absence was susceptible to misreadings. And she provided the correct interpretation of her absence: what they read as "doubt" of possible danger was "the great griefe to heare this cause spoken of." Through an adroit narrative displacement, Elizabeth was inviting Parliament to interpret a future event—Elizabeth's role in Mary's execution—in her revelation of the true shape of a past event. What must happen, would happen, with Elizabeth's role reduced to the vanishing point, with the inevitable misreading by those who would judge her, and with Elizabeth's subsequent revelation of the proper reading. Elizabeth was writing herself out of the future account of Mary's death by insisting that it would be virtually impossible to establish accurately the nature of her involvement in the event.

Each of Elizabeth's revisions made the same point: however transparent in appearance, the events "diverselie folded" around Elizabeth —her words, her actions, even the statutes enacted in her Parliament—contained hidden recesses of meaning, critical circumstances that invariably altered the significance of the events. Addressing those who would judge her, Elizabeth echoed the Thomist criteria for the casuistical judgment of an act: *materia licita, intentio recta, et debitae circumstantiae.*[49] Those who would play the casuist, she implied, must take care to understand the intention and circumstances surrounding an event before reading a judgment. Past judgments had proved dismally inaccurate; yet Elizabeth was not reacting with defiance, not removing her conscience from public scrutiny. She was acquiescing, a patient victim, to the inevitable, doing what she could, in her public revelations of conscience, to soften the abuses to which she was subjected. And, as her last revision suggested, she was instilling the idea that such abuses would continue—must continue—through the last stages of the current crisis.

In effect, Elizabeth's first speech turned the casuistry of Parliament on its head, repeatedly undermining the discursive premises on which their casuistry depended. Parliament had addressed their queen in the idiom of tutiorism, the mode of casuistical analysis that viewed the "probable" not as a function of commonly held opinions but as the reflection of an unchanging ideal—Christian heroism. Their petitions and letters to Elizabeth unfolded a "uniquely probable" account of the case—a narrative whose verisimilitude derived from its conformity to an objective moral order, an "exact rule of Justice."[50] Parliament had assumed the privilege not only of directing Elizabeth's conscience but of composing the privileged, "true," account of her actions.

Elizabeth replied in the same idiom, apparently guided by the question "what is the right choice to make?" Of course, the reference to her "burthen" signalled the presence of a doubting conscience, evidence of a certain resistance to the account Parliament had rendered. But it also signalled her effort to arrive, as well, at a "uniquely probable" reading of the case, one that would permit her to act without risk of sin. Thus the narrative of her speech contained the circumstances deemed credible by her auditors: Mary's duplicity, the evidence of Mary's "sundrie treasons," Parliament's oath to protect Elizabeth, Elizabeth's bond to her people, and so forth. These circumstances appeared to govern Elizabeth's narrative, advancing it inevitably toward the resolution imposed on her. Though her speech failed to deliver the expected resolution, her last words were nonetheless proleptic: whatever was necessary to maintain the realm, "that doo I assuredlie promise inuiolablie to performe," she said, "for requitall of your so manie deserts."

At the same time, Elizabeth's words conformed to the spirit of probabilism, the method of casuistical analysis that redefined the "uniquely probable" account as merely one of many, among which one was free to choose the most expedient. While meditating on the case Parliament put before her, Elizabeth analyzed a case of an entirely different order. "Which account of the case is to be chosen?" she asked, introducing circumstances that challenged the capacity, if not the right, of any observer to answer the question. The question indicated the metacritical impulse of Elizabeth's casuistry, which shifted the field of scrutiny from the matter of her innocence or guilt to the discursive premises framing the act of judgment. Under such scrutiny, even the privileged, confessional passages proved problematic. They were not, finally, what they appeared to be: they divulged pseudo-secrets. The first secret, she admitted, was "not unknowne to some of my lords here." And though the second, Elizabeth's revelation of the most recent plot against her life, might have been unknown to some of her auditors, it revealed nothing about her generally imperilled condition that Parliament did not already know.

More significantly, the conscience opened to them in Elizabeth's confessions registered only the defects of others. Elizabeth exposed the treasonous intent of unknown conspirators and, specifically, the duplicity of one whom she could not bring herself to name. Mary, her "neere kin," appeared as a woman whose own confession could not be trusted: "perhaps she would easilie appeare in outward shew" to repent, Elizabeth said. Later, when reviewing the Act of Association, Elizabeth observed that those who believed it was made to "prejudice" the Scots queen were merely projecting their own prejudice against Mary—their interpretive bias—in the case. As Elizabeth put it, such a motive might indeed be "suspected, in respect of the disposition" of those thus inclined.

While she was on the subject, she cited in particular the abusive disposition of the judges and the common lawyers. She wondered whether the judges had not in fact "deceiued" her with "false" books in their presentation of the case against Mary according to common law, the "ancient laws of the land." She wondered whether the common lawyers were sensitive, like herself, to the demands of equity.[51] It was doubtful, for they were "so nice in sifting, and scanning euerie word and letter, that manie times," she knew, they stood "more upon forme than matter, upon syllables than sense of the law." Those who, by nature or habit, missed the sense of the law were unlikely candidates to judge fairly the acts, much less the intentions, of others. When she finally broached the subject of her "burthen" of conscience, she defined her own disposition in the matter as "great griefe" not for a personal sin but for the "cause" at hand: Mary's crime.

Fifty years later the Protestant casuist Robert Sanderson, engaging in the kind of self-reflexive action characteristic of his profession, wondered whether the impenetrability of conscience was not an isolated, independent phenomenon but, rather, a reciprocal relation between an observed and an observing faculty:

> How then dare any of us undertake to sit as Judges upon other men's Consciences, wherewith we are so little acquainted, that we are indeed but too much unacquainted with our owne? We are not able to search the depth of our owne wicked and deceitful hearts; and to ransacke thoroughly the many secret windings and turnings therein; how much lesse then are wee able to fadom the bottomes of other mens hearts, with any certainty to pronounce of them either good or evil? [52]

Elizabeth conveyed a similar message to Parliament—and, through Parliament, to any who sought to "sift" and "scan" her conscience with legalistic precision and with impunity. A judgment of Elizabeth, they would find, necessarily constituted a judgment of oneself. It did so because, in the royal conscience, distinctions between "inside" and "outside," between the object and the act of scrutiny, were blurred—as "diverselie folded" as the graces that covered Elizabeth's soul.

Into the Intertextual Labyrinth: Elizabeth's Second Speech

Twelve days elapsed before Elizabeth delivered her second speech, a period marked by further evidence of her paradoxical attempt to preserve the artifice of Gloriana's inviolability by discrediting the medium—language itself—through which the artifice was preserved. Through Christopher Hatton the Commons received a preliminary message from the queen (who remained ensconced at Richmond), in which she referred them to the imperative embedded in her first speech—that she be held unaccountable for whatever happened in the resolution of the case. She expressed the desire to save Mary from the executioner's axe, but did so in language that in fact encouraged the Commons to reflect on the widest possible array of resolutions to her apparent burden of conscience. Ostensibly assigned the task of helping Elizabeth spare "the taking of her [Mary's] blood," the "Great Council of the realm," she let it be known, was expected to devise "any other means" of preserving "the safety of her Majesty's own person and of the state."[53] The words were well chosen: they echoed Parliament's own repeated arguments that Mary must in fact die, precisely in order to preserve not only the queen and the state but, as Puckering was soon to remind Elizabeth, also the consciences of all the faithful subjects who had taken the Bond of Association. The real issue, then, lay in the "other means" which Elizabeth advised the Commons to consider, means not necessarily coterminous with Mary's survival. If, where Mary was concerned, the machinery of the Tudor legal system pointed decisively to the scaffold—as it did— an equivalent solution might be achieved by unspoken "means" outside the law and, officially, beyond Elizabeth's control. In the absence of the willing hand of an assassin, there remained the avenue of finding "other means" of interpreting what seemed destined to happen within the law and under Elizabeth's eye. Appropriately indeterminate, subject to a virtual infinity of interpretations and misunderstandings, the very phrase stood as a locus for one of the implicit themes of Elizabeth's first speech: the "unaccountable," contingent relationship between her words and what they signified in conscience.

Elizabeth amplified this theme in her second speech. As before, she implied that the hopes of Parliament would not be disappointed, that she would accept their ultimatum. Twice in her opening words she referred to Mary's death. However oblique the reference (as usual, Elizabeth chose not to name her "iniurer"), and however qualified as an event over which Elizabeth claimed no control, Elizabeth allowed her auditors to picture the event as a given. It was an unfortunate "accident, that onelie my iniurers bane must be my lifes suretie," she complained; she later insisted on her "just cause to complaine," since "it is now resolved, that my suretie can not be established without a princesse end."[54] The two statements flanked an extended passage in which Elizabeth reminded the Commons where guilt, if it must be found, would lie. "But if anie there live so wicked of nature, to suppose . . . thinke or imagine," she began, going on to list a battery of false suppositions about her behavior that she suspected certain subjects of having harbored in their attempt to probe the secrets of the royal conscience. Those who might interpret her hesitation to act merely as a pro forma policy "to the intent to make a shew of clemencie" or as evidence that "the least vainglorious thought" prompted her were not only mistaken but were themselves liable to judgment in the *foro interno* before God: such people did her "as open iniurie as euer was doone to anie liuing creature, as he that is the maker of all thoughts knoweth best to be true." As Elizabeth had implied in her first speech, to spy the conscience of the queen was a hazardous, because self-incriminating, enterprise.

Moments later, she levelled a similar charge against the authors of the "manie opprobrious books and pamphlets" accusing her "to be a tyrant. . . . I beleeue, therein their meaning was to tell me news," she remarked, "and news it is to me in deed; I would it were as strange to heare of their impietie!" The underlying message of her ironic pun: it was the monarch's privilege to interpret meaning, to define the proper significance of a word, and to expose guilt. But Elizabeth did not dwell on others' propensity for guilt. Instead she set about redefining the case of conscience that had been put to her. Her opening words, a preface to the awaited case ("my iniurers bane" poised against "my lifes suretie"), signalled the shift in focus:

Full greeuous is the waie, whose going on, and end, breed cumber for the hire of a laborious iourneie. I have strived more this daie than euer in my life, whether I should speake, or use silence. If I speake and not complaine, I shall dissemble; if I hold my peace, your labour taken were full vaine. For me to make my mone, were strange and rare: for I suppose you shall find few, that for their owne particular, will cumber you with such a care. Yet such hath beene my greedie desire and hungrie will, that of your consulta- tion might have fallen out some other meanes to worke my safetie ioined with your assurance . . . as I protest, I must needs use complaint, though not of you, but unto you.

Elizabeth chose not to remind the "parliament of words" that Mary's fate hinged on Elizabeth's own words. She admitted that the moral choice besetting her doubting conscience—"whether I should speake, or use silence"—resided in a problem of language itself; but the problem, as she described it, had virtually nothing to do with the determination of Mary's fate. True, she implicitly acknowledged that if she used silence the sentence against Mary, too, would be dumb, as Burghley feared. But, in putting the terms of the case before Parliament, she implicitly rejected the corollary. The condition that she might "speake and not complaine" did not produce the acknowledgment that she would therefore speak in order to give permission for the sentence against Mary to be administered. For, as Elizabeth suggested moments later, Mary's fate was an "accident" that had "fallen out," one in which, Elizabeth implied, the power of the royal utterance was not involved. To "speake and not complaine" would identify the royal conscience, rather, with the act of dissembling—the mark of rupture, in language, between words and thought. The phrase, then, located the words of the monarch within the category of the untraceable, the secret.

Elizabeth, of course, was insisting that the secret within her conscience must exfoliate in the shape of a "complaint." It is worth noting that in the tradition of complaint literature the speaker does not normally adopt the self-reflexive stance associated with the searching out and articulation of secrets contained in conscience. To complain is not to confess—at least not to confess personal guilt. Rather, the speaker exposes the treachery located outside himself: the behavior of a fickle lover or, as Spenser's *Complaints* indicate, the movement of Time and Fortune, agents of "the Worlds Vanitie."[55] Elizabeth thus associated her speech with the genre that identifies the speaker as victim and his condition of interiority—the domain of conscience—as a representation of external, and often impersonal, actions over which he has no control. Once again, Elizabeth was implying that in the royal conscience it would be difficult to discover a record of her own role in the case of the Scots queen—difficult, that is, even when her words were transparent, without dissimulation, as she claimed her speeches were. But she was also speaking prophetically. In the "if" clause, the impending association between Mary's fate and Elizabeth's subsequent words—the written and spoken words that would release not a complaint but the "exact rule of Justice" against Mary— appeared as a "case" that would involve dissembling.

Elizabeth's second speech, if it did not already display the queen in the act of dissimulation, offered evidence that she was thinking about it. Her opening words presented an enigma—a manipulation of language that, like verbal dissimulation, exploited the dissociation of private meaning and public utterance. What was the "waie" whose "going on, and end" she described as "full greeuous" because destined to "breed cumber for the hire of a laborious journeie"? Given their cadence and place in the speech, the words resembled the announcement of the "theme," usually drawn from Scripture, that governed the homily.[56] Though not Biblical, the phrase resonated with echoes of devotional literature. "Waie," of course, evoked the way of divine providence, the Christian *via*, and the pilgrimage, in both literal and spiritual senses. In the spiritual landscape, a "greeuous" way filled with obstacles raised the spectre of sin. And a "cumber," which meant an obstruction or burden, was associated in proverbial lore with the guilty conscience: "Whose conscience is cumbered and stands not clean, of another man's deeds the worse will he deem." [57]

Conceivably, the "waie" to which Elizabeth referred was indeed hers. But it is doubtful that Elizabeth was confessing to a spiritual burden imposed on her conscience by the "waie," or course of action, she had chosen in the case of the Scots queen. She likened the "waie" that bred cumber to her own speech, her "mone," which imposed a burden on others—a burden of frustration before the intransigent queen, perhaps; but, even more to the point, also a burden of responsibility for the outcome of events and, equally, one of perplexity in the attempt to interpret and act on the queen's words. Like the inscrutable ways of the *deus absconditus* professed in the doctrine of Calvin, Elizabeth's "waie" defied the penetrating eyes of the curious. In the context of her first, enigmatic words, it was hardly necessary to spell out an alternative meaning of "cumber": to confound, to perplex.[58]

Barely into the speech, Elizabeth had already drawn a parallel between the indeterminate "other meanes"—or "waie"—that would, she hoped, "worke" her "safetie" and the "waie" represented by her speech itself: a "complaint" laced with exempla of dissimulation. The most celebrated—the "answer answerlesse" passage, habitually served up by Elizabeth's biographers as evidence of her evasive temperament—appeared as her Parthian shot, at the close of the speech. Elizabeth prepared the way for it in the body of the speech: she made two unobtrusive references to other, prior, texts that gave telling precedents for what was to follow, both in the speech and after.

Twice she mentioned her desire that "some other meanes" might have "fallen out" to resolve the case; the second time she conveyed the urgency of the desire by insisting that in such "meanes" she would have "taken more comfort, than in anie other thing under the sun." Unlike her opening words, the phrase "under the sun" was not likely to give pause. It was a commonplace; and, in a society actively engaged in the study of the divine Word, its precise origins were no less familiar. Elizabeth had borrowed the words of Ecclesiastes—of Qoheleth, the preacher, who was still generally associated in the sixteenth century with Solomon.[59] Through his words Elizabeth summoned an image of a world hospitable to her absolutist pretensions. No less emphatic than the Pauline injunctions to obey the sovereign was the command of Solomon: "I advertise thee to take hede to the mouth of the king, and to the worde of the othe of God. Haste not to go forth of his fight: stand not in an evil thing: for he will do whatsoever pleaseth him. Where the worde of the king is there is power, and who shal say unto him, what doest thou?" (Eccl. 8:2–4).[60] In her own speeches Elizabeth was in fact attempting to represent a world like Solomon's, in which the sign of the power that resided in the monarch's words lay in the incapacity of others to articulate words of scrutiny, to say, "What doest thou?" Such power, of course, was akin to God's and, as such, appropriate to anointed rulers.[61] But there was more. In Ecclesiastes, the mute, unreflecting submission to authority expressed an attitude born of necessity in the face of the unrelenting evidence "under the sun" that "all is vanitie . . . and vexacion of the spirit" (Eccl. 1:2;14). The principal vanity, the preacher-king repeated, lay in the search for wisdom and knowledge:

When I applied my heart to knowe wisdome, and to behold the busines that is done on earth, that nether day nor night the eyes of man take slepe, then I behelde [in the] whole worke of God, that man can not finde out the worke that is wrought under the sunne: for the which man laboreth to seke it: yea, and thogh the wise man thinke to knowe it, he can not finde it (Eccl. 8:16–17).

Solomon's survey of the vanity of human knowledge showed that one was likely to discover a perplexing lack of difference in the visible consequences of good and evil. "All things come alike to all: and the same condition is to the just and to the wicked" (Eccl. 9:1–2)—what this implied was the presence of an irreparable difference between human and divine knowledge; and, correspondingly, between thought and word, between truth and appearance—differences that necessarily clouded one's capacity to judge.[62] As the composer of the epilogue to Ecclesiastes pointed out, God alone would "bring euerie worke unto judgement, with euerie secret thing, whether it be good or evil" (Eccl. 12:14). Elizabeth made a similar point. "Although I maie not iustifie, but maie iustlie condemne my sundrie faults and sinnes to God," she said, "yet for my care in this government, let me acquaint you with my intents." The admission of error *sub speculum dei* was not to be confused with the words in which she would "acquaint" her auditors with the "intents" behind her actions in matters of state. But Elizabeth's quiet reference to Ecclesiastes reminded them that even those words might be unreliable vessels of secret knowledge. Like the Biblical treatise to which it referred, Elizabeth's "complaint" exposed a hostile climate for the scrutiny of another's conscience, especially the monarch's.

The "intents" she revealed did not appear out of the ordinary, given the judicial crisis facing Elizabeth and Parliament. She surrounded herself with an aureole of royal virtues: justice, temperance, magnanimity, judgment. And, discreetly, she attributed her evident procrastination in Mary's case to her careful exercise of justice and temperance:

This dare I saie; amongst my subjects I neuer knew a difference of person, where right was one: nor neuer to my knowledge preferred for fauour, whome I thought not fit for woorth: nor bent my eares to credit a tale that first was told me: nor was so rash, to corrupt my judgement with my censure, before I heard the cause. I will not saie, but manie reports might fortune be brought me by such as might heare the case, whose parcialitie might mar sometime the matter: for we princes maie not heare all our selves. But this dare I boldlie affirme, my verdict went euer with the truth of my knowledge. As full well wished Alcibiades his freend, that he should not giue anie answer, till he had recited the letters of the alphabet: so haue I not used ouer sudden resolutions, in matters that haue touched me full neere: you will saie that with me, I think.

Of a piece with the image of Solomon that she had evoked, Elizabeth's words drew on conventional and generalized attributes of the good prince. Both her procrastination and her eventual verdict, where Mary was concerned, were thus caught up in the official idiom of courtly homage, an idiom consonant with that of royal portraiture. Elizabeth's verbal self-portrait, like the visual productions of a Hans Holbein or a Nicholas Hilliard, invited a communal response to recognized and understood signals. The words "you will saie that with me, I thinke" conveyed, however demurely, Elizabeth's expectation that the response to her action in the Scots case be both univocal and exclusive: conventional adulation of the conventionally just and temperate queen, a chorus to be defined less by the particular cadence of choice accolades than by the absence of any controverting words of judgment against the queen.

In this context the verbal icon of Alcibiades, which graced Elizabeth's self-portrait, posed an interpretive problem. It was not likely that his name would have summoned a univocal response. The Athenian, who as a youth was the lover of Socrates and who later enjoyed a meteoric rise to power in the second Peloponnesian War, had acquired a celebrity that, however amply documented, was double-edged. In their biographies of Alcibiades, Plutarch and the Roman historian Cornelius Nepos dwelled on his physical beauty, military prowess, and eloquence. Plato and Thucydides, in the main, did not; they found such qualities eclipsed either by his unbounded ambition or by his dissolute habits.[63]

From Alcibiades, it seemed, one might expect both the worst and the best of which human nature was capable. In his infinite changeability, as Plutarch observed, Alcibiades surpassed even the chameleon—a figure that lent itself to disapproving moral commentary.[64] In the widely circulated *Emblemata* of Andrea Alciati, the chameleon appeared as the emblem of the dissembling and verbal subterfuge associated with the sycophant. The closing lines of the device told briefly what one might expect from the "adulator": "Et solum mores imitatur Principis atros, / Albi, & pudici nescius." In at least one edition of Alciati, the commentary on the emblem recalled Plutarch's Alcibiades.[65] So did Thomas Lodge when he began his *catalogue raisonné* of capital sins in *Wit's Miserie and the World's Madnesse* (1596). Alcibiades represented "Vainglory," the "first sonne" of the "fearfull race of Leuiathan," whose treachery Lodge identified as the "bait" of eloquent speech: "Were he examined in his owne nature, his courage is boasting, his learning ignorance, his ability weaknesse,

and his end beggery; yet is his smooth tongue a fit bait to catch
Gudgeons; and such as saile by the wind of his good fortune, become Camelions like Alcibiades, feeding on the vanity of his tongue
with the foolish credulity of their eares."[66] Ever the wit, Lodge managed to exploit a proverbial characteristic of the chameleon that had
not previously been brought up in portraits of Alcibiades. The chameleon, it was believed, fed on air.[67] So, too, the eloquence of an
Alcibiades, Lodge implied, was insubstantial, like air itself. And it
worked a terrible metamorphosis on the credulous, which turned on
the submerged image of a symbiotic consumption. Baited—and
taken in—by the "smooth tongue" of the chameleon, the prey, once
absorbed, became chameleons, too, sustaining the predator by continuing to feed on air—on the "vanity of his tongue."[68]

Lodge's witty, not to say grotesque, foray into natural philosophy
sharpened an already unambiguous, condemnatory, judgment of
Alcibiades, one he carried into the *foro interno* of conscience. From
one like Alcibiades, he warned, "you shall heare as many lies at a
breath, as would breed scruple in a good conscience for an age." For
Lodge, the figure of Alcibiades represented the invisible action of
conscience in its most elusive and ungovernable form, precisely the
kind of conscience Elizabeth had taken pains to disavow in her first
speech: what Perkins called the "seared" conscience, without scruple
and therefore able to adopt any word or action with impunity.[69]

In 1586 Elizabeth did not of course have Lodge's portrait of
Alcibiades in mind. But the implications he drew out would not have
been beyond her reach. She would have known his source: Plutarch's
biography of the hero. She had more than a passing acquaintance
with Greek and Latin historians. And she certainly knew another
text that contained a portrait of the Athenian: the popular *Consolatio*
of Boethius. In 1593 Elizabeth herself translated the work, which was
otherwise available to her in a number of existing translations, including the one that appeared in the 1554 edition of Lydgate's *Fall of
Princes*.[70] Lydgate's poem contained, as well, a portrait of the hero. It
gave a glowing account of Alcibiades as a model for "Noble pryncis"—
a man "Loued & weel fauoured for his gret fairnesse, / Famous in
knyhthod for his worthynesse"; a man destroyed by the malice of
"fals conspirators" at the height of his "glorie & gret honour"; ulti-

mately, a man whose virtues could not protect him from the "variant and unstable" action of "froward Fortune." There was much here that might have seemed appropriate, if not prophetic, to Elizabeth in 1586. In the *Consolatio*, however, it was the fabled beauty alone of Alcibiades that held pride of place, as the epitome of the vanities of the world—what Lydgate called the "tourn of Fortune." Even in its bloom, Lady Philosophy warned, his beauty carried hidden signs of inherent adulteration. The *pulcherissimum corpus* was merely a cipher for its opposite: the *turpissium* aspect, the viscera, that scrutiny would yield.[71] At once fascinating and revolting, Boethius's figure of antithesis, no less than the image of the chameleon, neatly exploited the legacy of ambiguity that surrounded Alcibiades, a legacy that cannot have been lost on the queen.

Why, then, did she choose to liken herself to a figure whose "qualities and properties," as Plutarch had indicated, seemed to display an equal propensity for good and evil; even, in fact, to shatter the distinctions between the moral categories of good and evil?[72] Elizabeth had taken a risk—a risk, nonetheless, by which we can measure the urgency of her desire to erase herself from the impending events destined to establish her responsibility for Mary's death—the proclamation of the sentence and the signing of the warrant. Elizabeth was perfectly aware of the censure that awaited her. Earlier she had admitted as much, in her tirade against the authors of "opprobrious books and pamphlets": "What will they not now saie, when it shall be spread, that for the safetie of hir life, a maiden queene could be content to spill the bloud, euen of hir owne kinswoman?" To forestall such scandal—that is, to preserve her kinswoman—meant to raise the outcry of other scandalized voices, already amply represented in Parliament, warning her that in the court of conscience she had neglected her duty. Alcibiades—a ruler in turn maligned and exalted, viewed as innocent victim and potential tyrant—in fact proved an appropriate icon for the queen in crisis. Appropriate not because she wished to be associated with the worst that might be said about an Alcibiades; and not merely because the name registered the queen's painful recognition of what was in fact going to be said against one who, like Alcibiades, had stood before the world as the model of the perfect courtier. The name constituted a *défi*. The ambiguity that had produced contradictory judgments of the hero also obstructed—"cumbered"—the formulation of any single, decisive judgment for or against him. When Elizabeth capped her representation of the "intents" in her conscience with the reference to Alcibiades, she invited her own would-be judges to discover the same message. Characteristically, she did not advertise it. Comparing herself to the student and lover of Socrates, she implied that her speech merely carried the traits of eloquence and judgment that the young Athenian was assimilating. She left it to the penetrating eyes of her would-be directors of conscience to perceive that the queen's words might have something in common with the chameleon.[73]

Elizabeth had closed her first speech with the heartening promise "inuiolablie to performe" that which was expected of her. By the time she reached the close of her second speech, she had given Parliament cause to suspect that what had been promised inviolably might also be performed that way—that is, beyond censure. The last words she uttered publicly in reference to the case of conscience resumed the theme she had articulated at the beginning of the speech: whether the queen "should speake, or use silence." Throughout the proceedings, Parliament had approached the queen expecting her to speak in accord with Christ's admonition: "But let your communication be, Yea, yea; Nay, nay: for whatsoever is more than these cometh of evil" (Matt. 5:37). While Elizabeth's "answer answerlesse," at the most perfunctory level, represented simply an elegant refusal to comply, it also represented a further meditation on the hazardous enterprise of expressing, and judging, the "intents" within her conscience. She had now abandoned the language of complaint; but she had still not quite taken up the announced alternative: dissembling. Rather, she spoke about dissembling, in words that described the indeterminate space between words and silence, where the queen's doubting conscience—her "doubtfulnesse"—resided:

And now for your petition, I shall praie you for this present, to content your selues with an answer without answer. Your iudgement I condemne not, neither doo I mistake your reasons, but praie you to accept my thankefulnesse, excuse my doubtfulnesse, and take in good part my answer answerlesse: wherein I attribute not so much to mine owne iudgement, but that I thinke manie particular persons maie go before me, though by my degree I

go before them. Therefore if I should saie, I would not doo what you request, it might peraduenture be more than I thought: and to saie I would
doo it, might perhaps breed perill of that you labour to preserue, being more
than in your owne wisedoms and discretions would seeme conuenient, circumstances of place and time being dulie considered.

This was not merely another bid for time. Parliament had demanded
an answer and she had given them one that defied their attempt to
coerce her into pronouncing the desired "yea." Elizabeth's answer
answerless presented a pattern of unaccountability in language: a
word that undid itself, making its meaning the very process of self-
erasure that Elizabeth had alluded to in her speeches. Her reply also
presented itself as a model of interpretation for whatever subsequent
"yea" or "nay" the queen might utter. In her closing words, Elizabeth
was arguing that such straightforward answers could not accurately
represent the inner folds of meaning necessary to grasp in resolving
the case. A "yea" or "nay" must in fact be read as a kind of answer
answerless as well, she implied, because neither was an adequate
reply, given, as Elizabeth put it, the weight of "circumstances."

William Warner, author of *Albions England*, gave prominence to
Elizabeth's "Aunswer Aunswer-lesse" as the key to the events of No-
vember 1586—and, implicitly, to the crucial ones that took place in
February 1587.[74] He identified her reply as the appropriate utterance
of Gloriana: it was one of the "Sweet Adumbrations of her Zeale,
Mercie, and Wit." He also identified it as the sign of her power—
power he associated with the manipulation of enigmas. "But with her
Oracle that bod them do, and doe it not," he wrote, "Play'd they as
Alexander did with King Gordians Knot." Warner's having Parliament
play Alexander to Elizabeth's Gordian knot was not intended, I think,
to announce prophetically the shifting axis of power between Crown
and Parliament—that is, to expose the danger to the Crown that lay
in the rising political aspirations of Elizabeth's Parliament. Rather,
his witty couplet represented the queen's attempt to preserve the
untarnished image of Gloriana by effecting a transfer of accountability in conscience for Mary's execution as a traitor. Alexander's subsequent mastery of Asia was less significant in Warner's simile than
the fact that the conqueror had not untangled but had instead cut
through the Gordian knot. He had not deciphered but had instead
violated the intricate inner mechanism of power that inhabited the

knot, replacing it with an ethos governed by swift, not to say impetuous, and unorthodox action—and by a refusal to attach significance to apparent ambiguities. A related ethos characterized the behavior of Elizabeth's ministers, notably after the signed warrant was carried out of the queen's chamber. What mattered was that the problem facing them be solved swiftly, without speculating or dwelling on the possible affinity between the warrant and the answer answerless—that is, on the possible hidden nuances of meaning, the mental reservation, with which Elizabeth had inflected her formal assent to the execution. In any case, had they decided to parse the royal statement implied in the action of signing the warrant, they were not destined to get very far, for Elizabeth had already given ample evidence in her speeches that such interpretive action, carving a passage to the queen's conscience, would be "cumbered." Nor were they likely to attempt such action, for the signed warrant represented, it seemed, a clear victory for Parliament—not a moment in which to consider whether the queen intended anything remotely like a "warrant warrantlesse."

Their solution to "King Gordians Knot," like Alexander's, arose from their refusal (or their inability—the difference mattered little) to maintain and puzzle through the idiom in which the problem had originally been couched. Thus, after Davison reported the queen's displeasure upon hearing that he had sent the warrant to be sealed, the Council, urged on by Burghley, decided not to keep the queen abreast of the further progress of the warrant [75] That is, once the warrant had been signed, they considered Elizabeth's case of conscience resolved; made a deliberate effort to prevent the continuing evidence of the queen's "doubtfulnesse" from having a direct bearing on the case; and, implicitly, agreed to assume responsibility for the execution. Not until Davison and Burghley faced the retribution of their angered queen, after Mary's death, did the issue of conscience resume its overt place in the discourse relating to the case—this time in Davison's and Burghley's protestations of their own innocence.[76] The Council's decision represented, then, the inadvertent fulfillment of Elizabeth's intention. As she had predicted in her speeches, they had misread the queen's conscience, disallowing its agency in her performance of the final action that would determine Mary's fate.

The Conscience of the Monarch's "Body Natural": A Medusan Text

The publication of Elizabeth's speeches on the fate of Mary Queen of Scots underscored the authoritative character of the message her words contained, a message now extended, in theory, to the entire body of the reading public. The official record of Elizabeth's words and actions during the critical period when the conscience of the queen was most susceptible to public judgment—both before and after the sentencing and execution of her cousin—provided ample evidence that any attempt to read, to scrutinize and judge, her conscience was destined to be frustrated by what appeared to be the inherent *aporia* of such an act. Elizabeth conveyed the message that to read the monarch's conscience was, by definition, to misread it; and, by misreading it, to affirm what the queen herself had not explicitly set up as a claim that might be disputed or subjected to critical interrogation: the inviolability of the monarch's conscience. In other words, Elizabeth tailored the deconstructive operation of the discourse of conscience in order to disable an implicit assault on a fundamental principle behind her divinely sanctioned, sovereign power. Elizabeth, we should recall, had not taken refuge in the royal prerogative by flatly proclaiming (as Mary had, in rather more desperate circumstances) that only God could be her judge. Nor had she explicitly identified the monarch's conscience with the tradition of the *arcana imperii*. That is, Elizabeth had not taken the route of open defiance in the face of public judgment. Rather, she had adopted the more disarming, and more convincing, pose of gracious submission, of metaphoric victimization, allowing her would-be judges to discover for themselves that the process of judgment within the discourse of conscience turned, imperceptibly, into one of self-judgment and, further, into an experience of epistemological uncertainty that made misreadings of the queen's conscience less an exception than a rule.

Implicated as well in this disorienting context was a fundamental distinction implied in Parliament's communications: the distinction between the public and the private conscience of the monarch. Of course, a public sense of conscience inhered in Elizabeth the queen just as, in the theory of the "king's two bodies," the king's eternal, public "body politic" expressed itself in his mortal, private "body natural." The king's two bodies, as Tudor jurists commonly pointed out, were "consolidated into one, and the Body politic wipes away every Imperfection of the other Body, with which it is consolidated, and makes it to be another Degree than it should be if it were alone by itself."[77] The "twin-born majesty" sheltered the idea of an inviolable royal conscience, which Blackstone suggested in his *Commentaries on the Laws of England*. The king, he noted, "is not only incapable of doing wrong, but even of thinking wrong: he can never mean to do an improper thing; in him is no folly or weakness."[78] Elizabeth alluded to the idea in her first speech when she attacked the common lawyers: unlike them, she possessed the "sense of the law." As supreme temporal and spiritual governor, she embodied an abstract principle of equity; she represented, in the language of sixteenth-century jurisprudence, the "conscience" of the realm.[79] At her coronation, the Spanish ambassador had alluded to this trait in his correspondence to Philip II, praising Elizabeth's demeanor as the image of conjoined opposites, "mildness with majesty"—both the spirit and the letter of the law. She had become, as one commentator has put it, "the image of the conscience that now resided in the common law and which would persist after her death as her most precious bequest."[80]

But Parliament, exercising its "utmost" power in the service of the law, had tacitly reminded Elizabeth that the king's two bodies, however "conjoined together," as the jurists argued, remained "distinct capacities"—as the jurists also argued. Parliament (like Mary herself) had chosen to address the "body natural," which was invested with a private conscience susceptible to the burden of sin. Accordingly, in her speeches Elizabeth did not insist on the inviolable—and invisible—attribute of her Crown. Such a response, however emphatic, would have left the specific charges of Parliament unanswered and their casuistry unchallenged. Elizabeth submitted her "burden of conscience" to public scrutiny. But what she revealed was a *camera obscura* that, poised between two received meanings of "conscience," recovered an image of royal inviolability.

In the sixteenth century, the word "conscience" implied two kinds of knowledge. *Con-scire* ("to know with") meant both to be conscious of one's own acts and thoughts and also to be conscious of what transpired in the outside world.[81] Elizabeth conflated these meanings. Her conscience reflected the secret acts and thoughts of others, observing and defining others' fears, misapprehensions, treacheries. Behind this reflecting screen lay a common metaphor that existed concurrently with the theory of the "king's two bodies" in Tudor political thought: the body politic of the realm, with the king as the head and the subjects as the members. Just as the king's two bodies were "conjoined" and yet "distinct," so, too, in the body politic the head and the members were distinct and yet indistinguishable.[82] Elizabeth exploited the ambiguity. The conscience of the body natural of the queen reflected the acts performed by the members of the body politic. And suffered for them. Enacting the role of victim-king, Elizabeth exploited the Christological references embedded within the interwoven images of the body politic and the *corpus mysticum*: she reconverted the spiritual ravagement associated with the guilty conscience into a paralyzing, quasi-divine "great griefe" for another's crime.[83]

In so doing, she dismantled a fundamental premise upon which both Parliament and Mary had constructed their ultimatums. Both had chosen to exploit the coercive power that resided in the word "conscience" as a mediating agent of divine wrath. They were echoing what was originally a Greek conception of the word: conscience as the parsing of spiritual pain. It articulated the idea of pain itself as the measure of one's departure from a norm, one's transgression of a boundary. Accordingly, it assumed a boundless aspect: it was not only the agent of pain but the faculty in which pain was felt and the very substance of pain as well. It mirrored the plenitude of a divine power whose wrath might not be escaped.[84]

This conception passed into the Christian world through Paul's dictum commanding obedience to the "powers that be": "wherefore ye must needs be subject, not only for wrath, but also for conscience' sake" (Rom. 13:5). Thus framed, the word gained a privileged place in the discourse of power wielded by ecclesiastical and secular authorities. The mere uttering of the word—ascribing one's position to "conscience"—held not only a referential but a performative valence: it anchored one's discourse to a body of truths presumed to be communal and sacred while obliquely calling down an anathema upon the potential speaker of any divergent discourse—and while obliquely warding off such anathema from oneself. It was a persuasive expres-

"Mala Conscientia," from Johannes Kreihing, S.J., *Emblemata Ethico-Politica*.
Courtesy of the Department of Special Collections, Stanford University
Libraries.

sion of self-effacing power: self-effacing because it defined authoritative discourse as the indistinguishable corollary of its opposite: the
discourse of one who, Scheherazade-like, must speak in order to
avoid victimization by divine wrath.

The Greeks conveyed the sacred and destructive resonance of the
word by identifying conscience as the internal, psychological manifestation of the Furies, the "embodiments of law" and "ministers
of Justice."[85] Emblem books of the seventeenth century testified to
the enduring impact of the association. It proved an apt metaphor,
notably, for the discourse of power in a state whose ruler shared
with the Furies the role of a revenger ordained, as Paul argued, "to
execute wrath upon him that doeth evil" (Rom. 13:4). Thus in the
Emblemata Ethico-Politica of Johannes Kreihing, S.J., the *mala conscientia* appears as an execution scene: a criminal, hanging from a

gallows in a public square, is tormented by hangmen, the agents of the ruler's vengeance, bearing snake-like hair and scourges—the iconographical properties of the Furies (see illustration).[86] One need only invert the dynamic described in the emblem to recover the premise that informed Parliament's and Mary's analysis of the crisis Elizabeth faced. Articulating their own position in the *foro interno* of conscience, both Parliament and Mary appropriated the accents of a potential victim of conscience in order to speak in a voice of judgment that preempted the ruler's. They implicated Elizabeth as a ruler who, by betraying her function as the official dispenser of justice, would find herself in the role of victim, tormented for her sin by the divinely ordained scourges of a guilty conscience. In her response—accepting the role of victim while problematizing the locus of guilt—Elizabeth in effect invited her would-be judges to discover a third interpretation of the *mala conscientia*, one yielding an image of Gloriana's conscience that anticipated the image R.C. would suggest in his *Declaration*. Ministers of justice, the Furies were also Gorgons—of the same family as Medusa, the figure who signalled precisely the immobilizing effect Elizabeth seemed determined to produce.

This strategy did more than deflect the focus of inquiry from her own role in the case. It allowed the queen to represent her conscience as a "corrupt" text, invariably distorted through the conduit of language, so that the crucial, inviolable character of her conscience—and, accordingly, of her power—seemed ultimately to be unrepresentable. In effect, Elizabeth disavowed not only her subjects' role in the production and maintenance of royal power but her own role as well. By a kind of *force majeure*, the monarch's inviolable power thus imposed itself as an objective, self-evident truth, precisely because neither its textual character nor its authorship could be located. Authorlessness emerged as the sustaining mythos of authoritative discourse.

The *Foro Interno* Outside Gloriana's Court: Honest Dissimulations in the Commonwealth

> But what man alive, what judge or justice, what Minos, Radamanthus, can carry his inspection into the Conscience? What evidence, what witness, or rack, can extort a discovery of that, which the conscience is resolved to conceal, and keep within itself?
> —Robert South, sermon on "Obedience for Conscience-Sake, the Duty of Good Subjects"[1]

Casuistry and Mental Reservation

One could without difficulty assign Elizabeth's behavior to the general category of dissimulation, well known in the Renaissance, that Tiberius had espoused. George Puttenham, for example, cited the emperor's maxim—*Qui nescit dissimulare nescit regnare*—as a necessary model of behavior for his readers: "not onely euery common Courtier, but also the grauest Counsellour, yea and the most noble and wisest Prince of them all."[2] By the mid-1580s, however, the precise verbal and gestural structures of dissimulation had gained currency from another source—the language of casuistry, to which Elizabeth had been subjected in the communications from Mary and from Parliament, and to which she had repeatedly made allusion in her two speeches, both of which might be subsumed in her prophetic "answer answerlesse," the phrase that announced her subsequent strategy of signing the warrant while silently disclaiming the force of the signature as the representation of her full assent or accountability. Both her words and her action showed the queen participating in the category of equivocation known as "mental reservation."

Neither equivocation nor mental reservation was the exclusive property of the upper echelons of power, as Puttenham's remarks about dissimulation suggested; and neither, of course, was the invention of the late sixteenth century. Raymond of Pennafort discussed their application in an early and seminal casuistical text, the *Summa de paenitentia et matrimonio* (ca. 1235).[3] Defenders of the doctrines commonly brought up the names of Aristotle, Augustine, and Thomas Aquinas, among others, in their search for precedents from the arguments of *auctores*.[4] Thus Henry Garnet's definition of mental reservation, which we may take as representative, provided not only a clear example but also an Aristotelian frame in which to locate it. Positing a case "beyng demaunded whether John at Style be in such a place," he proposed the following reply in *A Treatise of Equivocation*: "I knowinge that he is there in deede, do say neverthelesse 'I know not,'—reserving or understanding within myselfe these other wordes (to th'end for to tell you). Heare is a mixte proposition conteyning all this,—'I knowe not to thende for to tell you.' And yet part of it is expressed, part reserved in the mynde."[5] Garnet's particular understanding of the *oratio mixta*, or "mixte proposition," came from the sixteenth-century casuist Martin Azpilcueta of Navarre rather than from Aristotle directly; but it was Aristotle to whom Garnet attributed the logical foundation of the doctrine.[6] One learned "out of Aristotle" that "the essence or whole truth of every proposition . . . is in the mynde" and that "voyces and wrytinges are ordayned as instruments or signes to express that proposition which is in the mynde." From this premise it was possible to extrapolate the doctrine of mental reservation as one of several possible categories of discourse:

Therefore as I may express all in word or all in wryting, and the proposition of the mynde remayneth the same, so may I by an other kind of mixte proposition express part and reserve part, and yet the proposition of the mynde beyng not altered at all . . . onely this we affirme, that there is no lye; but as the altering of the signes which do express our mynde, partly speaking and partly wryting, alter not the verety of the proposition, so the expressing part and reserving part doth not make before God the proposition of any other condition than before.

Garnet later altered the title to read *A Treatise against Lying and Fraudulent Dissimulation*, no doubt in an attempt to refute, from the outset, the charges that had been levelled against equivocation in general and against mental reservation in particular. The title, which echoed Augustine's *Contra Mendacium*, located Garnet's argument in the established scholastic distinction, borrowed from Cicero and appropriated by the casuists, between lying and concealment: *aliud est celare, aliud tacere*.[7] The distinction occupied a central place in Augustine's definition of lying, which was based on the intention or the desire to deceive (*intentio fallendi* or *fallendi cupiditas*). Augustine had not specifically endorsed the practice of mental reservation, but the significance he attached to the intention, however unexpressed, behind a proposition lent an apparent cachet to the practice among its later apologists, who emphasized, as Augustine had, the integrity of the "proposition of the mynde" as the principal criterion for distinguishing "verety" from lying. It was possible, then, for casuists to condone the use of mental reservation, as Robert Persons did, in cases where one's "first and principall intention" was "not to deceaue the demaunder to his hurt" but to "deliver" oneself "by concealing a truth onely." To perform such an action was "to permit the other to be deceaued, and not properly to deceaue, or to have intention or cupidity of deceauing, as St. Augustine's wordes are."[8]

Garnet went so far as to attribute the judicious use of equivocation and mental reservation as a sign of virtue—virtue conceived within the Aristotelian frame he had erected for his argument. Given that "all vertewes consiste in a meane which is the avoyding of two extremes," it followed that the virtuous should not "rashely blabb out whatsoever they knowe." Nor, the argument went, did the strategies of concealment derive from the perusal of the *auctores* or the advice of casuists alone. "Who is there," asked Persons, "that naturally doth not seeke out some evasion, by answering doubtfully, but yet endeavoring to retaine some true sense in his owne meaning? . . . Worser myndes," he argued, made "no scruple to lye at all," whereas "amphibologies [i.e., mental reservations] & equivocal speeches" indicated "commonly the best mynds and most tymerous consciences," guided by "the instinct of nature it self." From the pulpit and the official press during the last two decades of Elizabeth's reign (and well into James's) English people learned to associate the doctrines of equivocation and mental reservation with the papists and, particularly, with the Jesuits—the "best mynds" and "most tymerous consciences" to whom Persons referred. Through this association both doctrines gained notoriety among Protestants as signs not of the scrupulous (Persons's "tymerous") conscience—not of an internal authority acutely responsive to the patterns of truth promulgated by the external authority of the church-state—but of a chameleon-like, politically subversive discourse, in which the uttering of truth seemed less an invocation of a stable referent than a representation of a vanishing point in language, subject to the modulations of circumstances perceived by the individual conscience.

In *The Whole Treatise of Cases of Conscience*, William Perkins briefly dismissed the practice of equivocation and mental reservation as "most impious"—a remark that hardly captures the intensity of the exchanges that arose between Catholic and Protestant controversialists in the last decade of Elizabeth's reign over the doctrines.[9] The catalyst: the deposition of a central witness during the arraignment of the well-known Jesuit priest and poet Robert Southwell in 1595. From Thomas Leake's relation we learn of "one Bellamies daughter, married to the keeper of Newgate," who reported under oath "that father S. tould them, that if in case anie should inquire for him and propose to them an othe whether they had sene him, that they myght deny it by oth; although they had seene him that same day; reserving this intention:—'Not with a purpose to tell you.'"[10]

Earlier in his career, lamenting the plight of his coreligionists, Southwell had written *An Humble Supplication* to the queen, in which he professed his inability to "sett downe the Laborinth of our afflictions," for "in which what way soever we goe, it is but a loosing of ourselves, and a winding us further into an endless course of Calamities."[11] No less labyrinthine were the arguments raised in the pamphlets and treatises written either to attack or defend the doctrine Anne Bellamie claimed to have learned from Southwell, the "impious" doctrine Perkins charged "Popish teachers" with having permitted papists to "practise in time of daunger, when beeing convented before the Magistrate, and examined."[12] At the forefront of the Catholic defense were the Jesuits Henry Garnet and Robert Persons. Their treatises—excerpts of which we have already seen—appear by turns as exercises in logical and legal disputation, Biblical exegesis, and historiography, in language by turns coruscating and tedious, the whole marked by a sustained effort, typical of casuistical analysis, to shape an argument that brought doctrine and lived experience together according to "circumstances of the place, tymes, matters, and persons."[13]

Recalling the juridical context of the Bellamie case, both Garnet and Persons addressed the legal "matters" that circumscribed the use of equivocation and mental reservation. Both emphasized that a subject being interrogated was bound "under paine of mortall sinne" to "confesse the truth without art, evasion, Equivocation, or other shift or declination, when soever the demaunder is his lawfull Iudge in that matter, and proceedeth lawfully, that is to say, according to forse of lawe, and equitie therein." But this obligation vanished "when the Iudge is not lawfull, or not competent at least in that cause, or proceedeth not lawfully"—in which case "they that are so required to answere against lawe, may and ought to use whatsoever amphibologie, or equivocation the usuall speach of men doth, or may beare, without a lye."[14] And without perjury: the oath—"the touchstone of truthe in matters of controversie"—had its legal perimeter as well.[15] Garnet reminded his readers that "in every oath is understood a condition that I will do or say so farr as I may lawfully do or say, or else the oath is uniuste and indiscrete." Somewhat indiscreetly perhaps— given his own subsequent failure to convince the prosecutors at his trial, in 1606, of his ignorance of the Gunpowder Plot—Garnet spelled out the implication of the restrictive condition. It was better to refuse to take an "uniust oath"; but if one took it, Garnet provided the appropriate formula, which amounted to a verbal pattern of infinite regress. One was to say "'I will aunswere whatsoever I knowe' [meaning] (for to tell you)." The hidden ambiguity turned on a point agreed upon by all moral theologians, he claimed: that "in matter of knowledge . . . the very propriety of the worde, 'I knowe,' or 'I knowe not,' hath a relation unto the utteringe of the same knowledge (or at least in such speeches one may lawfully retaine so much in mind)." Thus:

If the oath be ministred generally, lett hym admitte the oath with this intention, that he will answere directly and trewely (and if so they urge him), without all equivocation, so farre as he is assured, without all doubte or scruple, that he may or is bounde. And if they make hym sweare that he hath no private intention, or secreat meaning, lett hym sweare it also with that very same secrett understandinge, that he hath no such meaning to tell them. And with this generall meaning at the begynning whan he tooke the oath, lett hym not doubte but he shalbe safe from all perjury, although he answere trewly to nothinge, because in these cases he is bound to aunswere directly to nothing.

We do not need to guess what such words meant to the Protestant community. They were translated by Thomas Morton, author of exhaustive, and exhausting, attacks on the "more than heathenish" doctrine. "This is that monster which I called Hydra," he wrote, "in the which as often as one head was strucke off, immediately there sprung up another; signifying an endless businesse."[16]

He also remarked that "Hercules did impugne" the monster—Morton's attempt, perhaps, to define what he considered his own heroic role in a battle that was not confined to abstract and generalized legal discussions. To Persons, his principal adversary, he cried out, "You make all Protestant magistrates incompetent, with whom you may use aequivocation till you come to be tortured." It was an understandable reading of the casuists' position. Descending from the general to the specific, Persons acknowledged that "a Catholicke being examined whether he haue a priest in his house . . . may answere no, though he know he be there . . . (his whole meaning being) 'that I know no priest to be there as I am bound to utter him.'"[17] Implying as they did the wholesale immunity of English Catholics to laws enacted by a Protestant government, these were bold words to appear in print in 1607, in the wake of the Gunpowder Plot, which had seemed to confirm the hydra-like persistence of the "Romish iniquitie" in James's reign—and to warrant further and more severe measures "for the better discovering and repressing of Popish Recusants."[18]

But Persons was merely reiterating a tenet that had been established in the case-books for the English mission in the early 1580's, where the practice of mental reservation was offered as an available solution to priests undergoing an "enquiry [that] has no legitimate authority. . . . The whole problem," as the casuist put it, centered on the legal question of "whether ministers of the Queen have the authority to interrogate these priests." He had a ready answer: "It seems to me that an interrogation by them is never done by lawful authority." Among the explanations that followed, the casuist invoked the phoenix-like "benefit of clergy" (resurrecting the privilege of clerical immunity in the secular courts, which Henry VIII had done away with in 1547).[19] The other explanations, however, could apply as well to the Catholic laity. Like the missionaries, they were governed by a "heretic queen" who was therefore a "not legitimate queen"; a queen who, even if her legitimacy were granted, "in this matter at least does not conduct herself like a queen but exercises tyranny by persecuting religion"; a queen whose illicit exercise of power was mirrored in the judge, who was likely to proceed "in his judgment [against Catholics] from suspicion and often from insufficient conjectures which cannot be proved—and often from conjectures which he has as a private person—and not by the authority which he has as a judge." Indeed, when it came to advising "the Catholicke convented before heretickes" how to "answere without synne, either sworne or not sworne to the Interrogatores," the casuist affirmed that "all who are now in England under ecclesiastical jurisdiction" of the queen's government were "children without father or mother"—that is, subjects without a true prince and accordingly without legal obligation to answer the interrogatories administered under the prince's authority. The same advice thus applied to the Catholic who was "dragged before the heretics" as to the priest: "he can either refuse to take the oath (which is more prudent) or he can swear sophistically, or can reply sophistically to their individual questions."[20]

It did not take long for such advice to appear in printed antipapist propaganda. In 1582 Anthony Munday, a former Catholic, published a brief exposé of the casuistry employed by the Jesuits. The "rule and orders prescribed" in the manuals, he explained, taught papists "howe they should behaue themselves heere in Englande, and howe if they were demaunded of any thing, they should make aunswere indyrectlie: or to take the woorde it selfe, according as it is mentioned in the Booke, they must aunswere Sophisticae." Munday's own words described a model of verbal evasion that anticipated Elizabeth's at Richmond: steeped in the methods of casuistical discourse, the papists habitually gave "sleeveless aunsweres . . . never aggreeing to any certayntie."[21] In 1584 the Protestant controversialist Thomas Bilson furnished Elizabeth with an extensive exposé of "these hainous mysteries," this time in the form of a dialog between "Theophilus the Christian" and "Philander the Jesuite." The first alert came in the dedicatory epistle, in which Bilson acted the part of an official informer, making the queen publicly aware of the "secret instructions" circulating among the papists, which advocated the use of "anie pretence or policie," of "cavilling Sophismes & florishing termes," to "deface and traduce that right of your authority and bande of our obedience." In the dialog itself, a long and occasionally witty debate about the current religious and political turmoil, Theophilus reminds Philander of the notorious "cases of conscience, wherewith you furnished the Jesuites that came into Englande." Echoing the language of the casuists in the case-books, Theophilus accuses Philander of teaching "others, when they be called before such as you count hereticks; sophistice iurare, & sophistice respondere, sophistically to swear, & sophistically to answere, that is to mocke the Magistrate with a captious & cunning oth or answere."[22]

Neither Munday nor Bilson echoed the casuists' language precisely. Yet, notwithstanding their vested interest in presenting the most damaging interpretation possible of the "secret instructions," such discrepancies as occur between the hostile propaganda of Munday and Bilson and the case-books can be attributed in part to the frequently ambiguous language of the casuists themselves. Bilson, for example, had Theophilus argue that when a Catholic was asked whether the pope had the power to depose the queen the Catholic "must answere, not regarding any danger of death, I beleeue hee may," because "this question is a point of fayth, and requireth the confession of (our) fayth." The casuists indeed argued that equivocation and mental reservation—the "cavilling Sophismes"—were not permitted in responses to questions about "matters of faith," even if one had determined the governing context to be "unlawfull." But it was not always clear which questions, among those likely to be posed during the interrogatories or even in casual conversation with heretics, were to be understood as raising primarily a matter of faith. The questions fell, generally, into two categories. One might be led, like Bellamie's daughter, to inform against others, as royal proclamations and statutes throughout the period urged the queen's subjects to do.[23] Or one might be subjected to questions of a purely personal (and potentially self-incriminating) nature: asked whether one was a papist; whether one had recently attended church or received communion. And asked, as Robert Southwell pointed out, not only about one's "past deeds" but also about one's "future conduct," including what one "would be disposed to do under such and such circumstances."[24] Southwell was alluding to the "Bloody Questions," instituted in the early 1580s as a means of detecting the degree of the recusants' and priests' submission in conscience to the terms of the papal bull *Regnans in excelsis*, which excommunicated and deposed Elizabeth, released her subjects from their allegiance to the queen, and forbade them "to obey her orders, mandates and laws" under pain of excommunication. The questions included the point Theophilus raised—the deposing power of the pope—as well as the hypothetical case Southwell referred to, which usually took this form: "If the Pope or the Kinge of Spaine shall send an armye or any forces to invade this realme pretendinge to reforme religion, whether would you take parte with the Quene and the realme againste them to the uttermoste of your power or not?"[25]

A perusal of the case-books indicates that none of the above questions—from either category—amounted to an unequivocal "matter of faith." They contained an admixture of political and legal circumstances that defied resolution into a purely religious matter. The Bloody Questions were a case in point. William Allen argued that questions "which search of men's future facts or intentions, whereof themselves have neither knowledge nor rule beforehand" were "unnatural, intolerable, and to commonwealths most perni cious."[26] And, it appears, illegal, for their status in common law was arguable. It was "never part of the law of treason that a man could be punished for treasonable thoughts," Adrian Morey writes, adding that "in 1588 the Solicitor General warned the Council that refusal to answer these questions did not bring a man within the compass of the law."[27] Garnet later made the same point.[20] In any case, the obviously political turn of the questions established for the casuists the necessary distance from a straitjacketing "matter of faith": Catholics were allowed a certain range of options in shaping their responses to such questions. "He answers best who is not ashamed to answer all questions which concern faith and fact clearly," the casuist proclaimed, reminding interested and willing readers that "anyone who is killed because he confesses the faith is a true martyr." A subsequent, more pragmatic, analysis revealed that "not everyone can claim for himself the honour of being a martyr" and that, unless "necessity" compelled one to confess the faith, one was only obliged not to deny it. And permitted "to do anything he can—using equivocation, silence, returning the question, or any method he likes—to avoid making a reply" that would otherwise amount to a confession of secrets held in conscience. "Necessity," we should note, included the problematic circumstance of scandal; but its constraints appear to have been more theoretical than practical. While one was forbidden to "use pretence" in the presence of "rude and simple" Catholics who were "ignorant of the difference between pretence and lying," the manuals themselves contained precise models of verbal evasion to be assimilated by the Catholic population: evidence of the casuists' attempt to introduce preventive measures against scandal through proper instruction.[29]

The extant documents of interrogatories administered to convicted priests and recusants mirror the range of responses proposed in the case-books: everything from proclamations of loyalty to the pope (or to the queen "in temporal matters") to mental reservations of the kind described in an account of the trial of one Father Robert Freeman. Like his fellow missionary Father Ingram, Freeman "used discretion (according as God commandeth), serpentine and columbine simplicity, in matter, fit time, place, and person," with these results: "'Are you a Priest?' quoth the Justice. The martyr consideringe that yt was no denyall of his faith but only of his state, answered 'No.'"[30] Perhaps the best summary of the "cumbers" that the government had come to expect of the English Catholics by 1585 appears in a letter sent to the Privy Council by Richard Topcliffe, who had gained notoriety for his vigor in hunting down and torturing the dissidents whom Bishop Edwin Sandys castigated as "deep dissemblers, double-hearted, double-tongued, double-faced." Reporting the results of a recent examination of Catholic prisoners, he complained that "their answers are, they will not sweare, or els they will not answer, or els they knowe not." It did not seem possible for them, in fact, to give a clear answer: "albeit theie speak faier," Topcliffe continued, "yet they seeme to carrie fowle and traiterous harts."[31] The observation, of course, testifies rather more to Topcliffe's unsympathetic bias than to his acumen in reading the "harts" of his prisoners. It also testifies to the impasse erected between authorities and dissidents within the discourse of conscience. While Catholics were vulnerable to the projected hostilities, the potentially destructive misreadings, of their oppressors, their association with the casuistry of the Jesuits underlined the inscrutable character of conscience itself, which turned all secure, authoritative readings of a word, a gesture, or an event into provisional, unstable ones. "Is" habitually blurred into "seems," as even Topcliffe recognized.

Richard Spurstowe's responses before the Chester High Commission in 1592 offered further evidence that professions of loyalty within the discourse of conscience could not be made reducible to a single, transparent "yea" or "nay." To the Bloody Questions, administered without oath, he responded "directly and negatively," insisting, for example, that he "wold take parte with the Queene againste all the worlde coming to invade this realme, what surmise or matter soever they wold pretende." But when asked to surrender, under oath, such information as he possessed concerning the missionaries, he refused to take the oath—and was imprisoned. The already unintelligible distinction Spurstowe was attempting to draw—between political loyalty to the queen and religious loyalty to the mission—only proved more so by his refusal to take the oath. Here was a man unwilling to resort to mental reservations when it came to what he appears to have considered a "point of faith" made before God—a scruple that illuminated the enigmatic and unsettling aspect of the answers he was willing to give, within a different context, to the Bloody Questions.[32]

A month after his imprisonment Spurstowe escaped—a physical flight that followed the same trajectory as the verbal flight represented by mental reservation. Persons later invoked the parallel when he defended the doctrine as an instance of the lawful *fuga* that St. Athanasius "and other ancient Fathers" had recommended in times of persecution, following the advice of Christ and "the example of the Apostles themselves."[33] For John King, vice-chancellor at Oxford (1607–10), another precedent seemed more appropriate. In a sermon attacking the Jesuits, whom he held responsible for the spread of the doctrine in England, he turned not to Athanasius but to the even more venerable Augustine, who had written *Contra Mendacium*, he recalled, in order to discredit the Priscillianists, a fourth-century Spanish sect who justified lying "especially to conceal religious doctrines from strangers."[34] The Jesuits were nothing less than "the new Priscillianistes of our age, of whom St. Austin complained soli inventi sunt dogmatizare mendacium, the onlie men that are found to dogmatize and defend lying." King's complaint moved beyond questions of dogma to a more urgent question: the "declination of state." In his sermon, delivered on the second anniversary of the Gunpowder Plot, King defined the political threat of the Jesuits as a direct function of their skill in manipulating the discourse of conscience "with their Maeandrian turning & windings, their mentall reservations, their amphibolous, amphibious propositions, which live, as those creatures part in the land, part in the water, so these halfe in the lippes, halfe in the heart and conscience." Disclosed in its labyrinthine aspect, such discourse seemed to King a "deepe and dangerous vault" containing "a wicked and unsearchable heart"—or conscience—that was synonymous with "an endlesse and living veine of powder & salt-peeter, an everlasting burning Aetna, of rooted, engrafted, settled maliciousnes against Christ and his members."

The linguistic subversion of mental reservation, "engrafted" to the political subversion of religious dissidents, hinged on the intrinsic capacity of conscience itself to remain "unsearchable"—invisible, a power much to be desired and feared. It gave maximum protection from curious eyes while leaving would-be observers with the disturbing awareness that an unobserved eye might be watching them. It defined a space in the discourse of power where received distinctions between conformity and dissent might prove problematic, because unstable. Such was the property of the chameleon, to whom King did not fail to liken the Jesuits. "What means shal we find to encounter these changlings, Camaeleons?" he asked. It was a question that Elizabeth's government had been asking about the papists since the establishment of the mission some thirty years earlier, a question that the members of the mission echoed in their attempts to elude the government's intelligence network. The members of Elizabeth's Parliament might well have asked a similar question in the course of their frustrated efforts to probe the conscience of the queen, whose allusion to the chameleon-like Alcibiades—the forger of illusory words, of hidden and changeable meanings—epitomized the "unsearchable" character of her own words and actions during the months of crisis in 1586–87.

Casuistry in the English Mission

There is everywhere an immense number of papists, though for the most part concealed.

—John Cox to Peter Martyr (1562) [35]

During the first years of Elizabeth's reign, it appeared as though the consciences of English papists would not become a locus of political subversion, for the papists were gradually being absorbed into the Protestant community.[36] With the passage of time, it appeared, the habit of the old ways, along with any lingering spiritual and ideological commitment to Rome, was bound to diminish, following the attrition of the remaining Marian clergy. The 1559 Act of Uniformity further encouraged the absorption of the papists by imposing a penalty of twelve pence, "to be levied by the churchwardens," on those who did not "diligently and faithfully . . . endeavour themselves to resort to their parish church" on Sundays and holy days. By 1563 church attendance meant, necessarily, systematic exposure to official propaganda against the Romish church: one would hear denunciations from the *Book of Homilies* and graphic accounts of papist atrocities from John Foxe's *Book of Martyrs*. As Francis Bacon later observed, the government was proceeding in accordance with the queen's intention that consciences were "not to be forced"; they were, rather, "to be won and reduced by the force of truth, by the aid of time, and the use of all good means of instruction and persuasion."[37]

But in a single decade, from 1570 to 1580, a concatenation of events created the alarming—if grossly exaggerated—impression that the papists, far from being a vestigial and moribund element of society, were in fact a well-organized fifth column whose religious sympathies were being marshalled into subversive political action in the service of the papacy and the Spanish Crown.[38] Mary's flight to England, in 1568, had already given the English government the uneasy impression that disaffected Catholics might unite to place

Elizabeth's Catholic heir on the throne. The rebellion of the Northern earls, in 1569, and the Ridolfi Plot, uncovered in 1571, appeared
to confirm the impression. Had either succeeded, Mary's accession
would have been assured, though in fact they were isolated events,
neither well organized nor governed by religious zeal.[39] But the publication of the papal bull *Regnans in excelsis*, in 1570, lent credence to
the suspicion that a campaign to restore Catholicism in England had
been launched and given official sanction.[40] Four years later, a small
group of English priests, trained at the English college in Douai,
which William Allen had founded in 1568, arrived in England. This
was the beginning of the English mission, which, despite its members' repeated assertions to the contrary, was viewed by the government as the principal vehicle through which the political threat
expressed in the bull would be carried out. By the end of the decade,
the government perceived a rise in recusancy—that is, in the number
of papists who refused to attend church. Interpreted consistently by
the government as a political statement, a breach in loyalty to the
queen, recusancy was taken as a sign of the growing strength of the
mission. Its success seemed assured after the arrival, in the summer
of 1580, of Robert Persons and Edmund Campion, the first Jesuit
missionaries to England.[41] They galvanized the mission, attracted
much public attention, and, ultimately, provided an already anxious
government with the image of the Jesuit as the epitome of papist
treachery.

   Even if both men had been models of discretion, their presence
in England would have antagonized the government, for the mission
they joined had already begun to acquire an association with unmistakable acts of sedition. Only weeks after their arrival the government received a missive (a forgery, as it happened) from the English
ambassador in Paris, warning of a plan for an invasion instigated by
exiled rebels and traitors who had enlisted the support of the pope
and the king of Spain. In the form of a royal proclamation, the same
news was passed on to the English people.[42] The previous summer,
Dr. Nicolas Sanders—like Campion and Persons, a native son, a
sometime Oxford scholar, and an outspoken apologist for the old
faith—had become involved in the Irish rebellion, the ill-conceived
and ill-fated action instigated by Gregory XIII in the hope of creating a base from which to invade England. The rebellion, which was

quashed within months after the arrival of the two Jesuits, helped fix the hostile attitude of the government toward the activities of the English mission. It did not help Campion and Persons that Sanders, whose name for nearly a decade had been notorious for its association with vigorous religious polemic, should have participated in the rebellion, even though he had no direct affiliation with the mission. In subsequent pamphlet controversies and political texts of the sixteenth century, his name supplied a kind of synecdochic reference for the evident connection, in the government's view, between the *cura pastoralis* espoused by the missionaries and the treasonous action into which they would seduce the people of England. Burghley, for example, brought up the name of the "traitorous priest, Dr. Sanders" in 1583 when he wrote *The Execution of Justice in England*, a book intended to justify the fate of the missionaries—including Campion—who had "of late suffered death" under the 1352 Treasons Act. In the career of "the Pope's firebrand in Ireland," Burghley argued, one might read the underlying purpose of the mission: to enforce the papal bull, which was "the ground of the rebellions both in England and Ireland."[43]

Now, in the summer of 1580, Campion and Persons seemed to have inherited the onus that had fallen on Sanders. Like Sanders—indeed, like most propagandists—both men shared a keen appreciation for the value of the printed word. Shortly after their arrival a secret printing press, established at Greenstreet House under Persons's supervision, began to produce devotional and polemical works, supplementing the Catholic propaganda that was filtering into England from the Continent.[44] Neither the seizure of the printing press nor his own exile, after Campion's arrest, dulled Persons's commitment to the enterprise he had initiated at Greenstreet House. From the Continent he continued to direct and support the English mission; it was no coincidence that he also pursued his career as controversialist and author of devotional literature.[45] It was Campion's pen, however, that produced the first shock wave. Faced with the growing certainty of their eventual capture, both men had decided to write, in advance, an account of their purpose in England, to be held in safekeeping by their friends until their arrest, at which point the accounts were to be published in order to contradict the false confessions of treason that the government was likely to distribute. As

it happened, Campion's unsealed manuscript fell into the hands of
the bishop of London in rather short order; it reached the Privy
Council (to whom it was addressed) and provoked a blistering pamphlet controversy, in the course of which Campion's statement was
published, to an end neither Campion nor Persons had anticipated:
as incriminating evidence of a traitor still at large in the land.[46] The
controversy itself reflected the degree to which the "greate Bragge and
Challenge of M. Campion," as one pamphleteer called it, had fueled
the hostility of the authorities toward the Jesuits, in whom they now
located the main artery of the mission. Campion's "Challenge" testified more to his impetuous exuberance for spiritual reform, even in
the face of death, than to any intention to rouse papists to sedition.
Of course, reconciliation to Rome could not help but signal, to the
government, that one was "disposed naturally to sedition," particularly in an age when, with Bacon, Protestants and Catholics alike
found "the permission of the exercises of more religions than one"
to be "a dangerous indulgence and toleration."[47] There was, then, no
received idiom in which Campion could have persuaded his opponents of his apolitical purpose—not even the language of disputation,
which he offered to use "before the lawyers, spiritual and temporal" in
order to justify his faith "by the common wisdom of the laws standing yet in force and practice." Avowing that he had no other object
than "to instruct the simple, to reform sinners, to confute errors"
was begging the question, particularly when his very presence as a
missionary in England indicated a disposition to accept the jurisdiction of a body of laws other than English statute.[48] And particularly
when his defense of the Jesuits' pastoral care culminated in this kind
of expostulation:

And touching our Society, be it known to you that we have made a league—
all the Jesuits in the world, whose succession and multitude must overreach
all the practice of England—cheerfully to carry the cross you shall lay upon
us, and never to despair your recovery, while we have a man left to enjoy
your Tyburn, or to be racked with your torments, or consumed with your
prisons. The expense is reckoned, the enterprise is begun; it is of God; it
cannot be withstood. So the faith was planted; so it must be restored.[49]

   Campion intended these words to speak for him after he would no
longer be able to speak without government intervention; clearly, he

wanted such heroic language not only to eclipse whatever damaging construction the authorities might put on his words and behavior but also to console his flock and caution his enemies with the promise that the death of Campion would not destroy the "enterprise." Yet, even had it not reached the public precipitously, such language could not fail to be taken as adversarial. For one thing, the "Challenge" fostered the image of the Society as an infinitely renewable, encroaching presence in England. Though the number of missionaries—Jesuits and secular priests combined—never approached the vast army that the government seemed intent to ferret out, it was true that the priests accepted the peripatetic nature of their pastoral work. They were constantly on the move, driven by a dual purpose: to reach the scattered population of English Catholics and to escape the government's network of pursuivants and spies, whose search efforts had sharpened in intensity after the arrival of Campion and Persons.[50] And many of the priests approached their work with a heroic determination reminiscent of Campion's. One wonders what the public reaction would have been to the words of one young Jesuit, writing from Dieppe in anticipation of his arrival on the English coast: "And now at length with full Sail and couragious myndes most like unto Aeneas we will cutt the Surging Seas and make assault towards our foes."[51]

Preaching, of course, was a fundamental part of their mission as they travelled through the counties of England; so was the hearing of confessions—a practice that the authorities isolated as the wellspring of sedition. In Bacon's words:

[The priests] by vow, taken at shrift, reconcile her subjects from her obedience; yea, and bind many of them to attempt against her majesty's sacred person; and that, by the poison they spread, the humours of most Papists were altered, and that they were no more Papists in custom, but Papists in treasonable faction. . . . For it is to be understood, that this manner of reconcilement in confession, is of the same nature and operation that the bull itself was of, with only this difference, that whereas the bull assoiled the subjects from their obedience at once, the other doth it one by one. And therefore it is both more secret, and more insinuative into the conscience, being joined with no less matter than an absolution from mortal sin.[52]

It was not enough for captured priests to defend their confessional practice, as many did, by arguing that they were merely exercising spiritual jurisdiction *in foro conscientiae*, for the authorities were not disposed to accept such jurisdiction as an indifferent matter. In a society virtually bristling with interacting and competing court systems, the invisible court of conscience held a privileged place: it was, as one judge put it, the "highest tribunall . . . wherein the power of the keys is exercised to the highest degree."[53] True, the ecclesiastical arm of the government, maintaining its reformist position, had repudiated the recognized locus for the direction of conscience—auricular confession, which had been discredited by the early reformers as an instrument of papal tyranny. Nonetheless, the Tudor government had appropriated the essential dynamic of the confessional dialog by exploiting the coercive effect of the word "conscience" in the official discourse of the burgeoning church-state, which made the Pauline injunction—"wherefore ye must needs be subject, not only for wrath, but also for conscience' sake"—the touchstone for its authority.[54] As Bacon's words suggest, the apparent resurgence of auricular confession was taken as nothing less than a papal conspiracy to usurp the jurisdiction of the Crown over the consciences of English subjects. In *The Execution of Justice*, which enjoyed a wide circulation, the lord treasurer made a similar point. The itinerant priests possessed what must have seemed to Burghley the enviable power to "search and sound the depths and secrets of all men's inward intentions, either against Her Majesty or for her." But, given its affiliation with Rome instead of Westminster, such power was to be feared: by "striking many with pricks of conscience," the priests were producing a growing body of subjects who were "in their hearts and consciences secret traitors," an invisible society who "wanted nothing but opportunity . . . to be indeed arrant and open traitors." This argument, which was to recur without much variation in subsequent anti-papist polemic, suggests a growing sensitivity to the privileged place that casuistry occupied in the pastoral care of the missionaries.[55]

A few months after his arrival, Persons wrote a letter to the rector of the English College in Rome, emphasizing the need for future recruitments of priests with an expertise in casuistry. Among the "new draft of men of our Society" he asked explicitly for one "able to deal with all the cases of conscience that occur here and are very grave ones."[56] What kinds of cases of conscience was Persons referring to? It is of course impossible to reconstruct the confessional dialogs that took place between English Catholics and missionaries; but we do have access to a number of cases of conscience, written and compiled specifically for the English mission, that give us an idea of what Persons meant. Through them we have already discerned the point of entry of the doctrine of mental reservation into the discourse of Elizabeth's subjects. Through them we will now be able to locate the subversive impact of this doctrine as a function of a more global phenomenon: the production of verbal and social texts that illuminate what it meant to read casuistically in an ideologically divided culture, a culture embodying what I have already described as the inherent duality—the at once normative and destabilizing impulse—of casuistical analysis.

The cases covered a wide range of questions—about marriage, inheritances, rents, fasting, private prayer, churchgoing, and so forth. As an ensemble, the cases give us an externalized and politicized picture of the negotiatory dynamic between the two parts of conscience: between the fixed, idealized space of *synteresis* and the indeterminate, contextually oriented space of *conscientia*. The cases, and the contexts they summon, point to the operation of casuistry— the discourse of conscience—in the competing official idioms of ecclesiastical and political power that emanated from Rome and Westminster, idioms that made implicit claims to the status of *synteresis*, presenting themselves as verbal sanctuaries of received truths and as discursive models for defining and "healing," or reabsorbing, conditions of spiritual and moral disorder. But the cases also reveal the operation of the discourse of conscience in the idiom of men and women who, from the point of view of the Tudor government, represented the religious and political periphery: dissidents and disaffected members of Elizabethan society. Embodying the diverse actions of *conscientia*, the words and actions of these people echoed the discourse of conscience inculcated by their secular and spiritual authorities—an echo, however, that did not so much reproduce as dismantle the discursive premises of the controlling ecclesiastical and political structures in England.[57] Ultimately, the cases give us a picture of a casuistry that, as an interpretive regime governed by the same motives of evasion and concealment we observed at Richmond, redefined and enlarged the context that Elizabeth tried to fix within

the isolated sphere of monarchical *arcana*. The cases revealed a medusan rhetoric of conscience travelling, like Spenser's Blatant Beast,
through the hidden parts of the realm.

Throughout Elizabeth's reign, and well into James's, one of the
most controversial and politicized cases of conscience, provoking
contradictory judgments among casuists themselves, centered on the
issue of church attendance, as required by English statute. As one
historian of the debate has argued, an "official" judgment, which
dominated the published propaganda that circulated in the form of
pamphlets and treatises, unconditionally forbade church attendance,
while an "unofficial" judgment, which characterized the responses in
the unpublished case-books for the mission, espoused arguments
rendering occasional conformity morally permissible.[58] The inherent
duality of casuistical analysis is perhaps nowhere more sharply defined than in this protracted conflict, in which the very discourse
employed to define a signal characteristic of the English Catholic
contained a space that illuminated the possibilities of rupture or
alterability in the outline of any such definition.

As one might expect, the conflict was grounded in legal arguments. Advocates of recusancy invoked the authority of divine law,
which was found immanent in the principle, inscribed in canon law
and buttressed by an array of Scriptural passages, that forbade *communicatio in sacris* with pagans, heretics, or schismatics.[59] Recent pronouncements by the ecclesiastical hierarchy—the ruling of the Council of Trent in 1562 and, of course, the directive issued in the papal
bull *Regnans in excelsis*—had affirmed the principle for the English
mission.[60] The consequence of attending Protestant services was thus
outright schism.

The uncompromising, official reading of church attendance represented an attempt to preserve the integrity of a single vision of the
world, as defined and controlled by the Church (a model imitated
by the Tudor church-state). It betrayed, as well, the impulse in casuistry to assert the efficacy of a hierarchical legal code in shaping and
accounting for human experience, and, at a deeper level, to preserve
the category of the sacred, which included divine law as interpreted
by the Church, from implication as an artificial, perhaps mutable,
construct, one produced by the human community itself as a self-
regulatory device. This double act of preservation meant, fundamen-

tally, an act of exclusion: directing individual consciences to relocate the perspective of dissent under the sign of the outcast, mortal sin. Gregory Martin, author of *A Treatise of Schisme* (1578), conveyed the point through an image that Protestant apologists might well have bristled at. Catholics, who were "true branches" of Christ's "body mystical," cut themselves off from the mystical body, Martin wrote, by going to "schismatical service," and in so doing had "no more the life, graces and gifts of the Holy Ghost to merit life everlasting than hath the leg or arm cut off from the body the life of the soul, which only remaineth in the body."[61] Reappropriating for the Catholic cause a metaphor that had been naturalized by the English reformers and the Tudor government, Martin summoned an argument fundamental to the English mission: that the mystical and political bodies were not conjoined at Westminster; that the queen had merely temporal authority over her subjects. The argument had a corollary, branching from the discourse of conscience into that of sixteenth-century resistance theory, which lent further cogency to the legal grounds for recusancy: any human laws that seemed to countermand divine law (like the English statutes regarding church attendance) were unjust and not binding in conscience.[62]

Other voices—appearing in pamphlets advocating conformity and in the case-books, where occasional conformity was allowed—took the same language of resistance theory and, to borrow the apt phrase of P. J. Holmes, "turned it on its head."[63] They argued that the canon laws regarding recusancy, given their derivation from ambiguous Scriptural passages, did not in fact articulate divine law. They argued, further, that canon law was by definition human law and therefore subject to transformations and dispensations, particularly in cases where it conflicted with natural law, whose jurisdiction prevailed over that of human law.

The casuists who defended occasional conformity drew out the nuances to be inferred from this point; their solutions exhibited the more clearly negotiatory impulse in casuistry. One response in the case-books contained the admission that while the ruling of the Church did reflect a higher natural law, the application of the ruling in England was best left to the individual consciences of the queen's subjects, who might discern a countervailing directive imposed by the same higher law, which would absolve them from recusancy "in cases of necessity." Those "who have found out that they will be harmed by going to heretic churches are bound by the law of nature to avoid doing so," the casuist observed. But "there will not be many people of this sort," he added, emphasizing the weight of circumstances likely to minimize the harmful effect of occasional conformity. He was confident that "those who are physically present in these churches will not pay attention to what is said"; and that "if they do pay attention they will often be more strongly confirmed in the faith by hearing the nonsense of heretics." He supported the point by an appeal to what seemed "reasonable": "familiar conversation and normal social intercourse with heretics hurt more than public sermons, but familiar social intercourse with heretics has been made lawful, so it is much more reasonable to make listening to a sermon lawful."[64] Whatever its logical and theological flaws, the appeal reflected the kind of duality that casuistical discourse might yield in the appraisal of the context in which laws were to be applied. Having relied on a distinction between the physical and mental or spiritual presence of Catholics at Protestant services, the casuist now adopted the opposite strategy, invoking another distinction only to blur it: the distinction between secular and spiritual points of contact between Catholics and Protestants.

While maintaining that one should not practice regular conformity until the pope saw fit to grant a general dispensation, the casuist tacitly recognized the privilege of conscience, the internal authority, to grant its own dispensation in the light of "certain circumstances"— in this case, a context in which the spiritual consequences of attending church were absorbed and redefined by the secular consequences of refusing to attend. The "law of nature" that had seemed to prohibit attendance to avoid spiritual harm now allowed a space for occasional conformity to avoid physical harm, in cases where "just fear"—which included the fear of financial ruin—obtained.[65] It was essential, the casuist argued, to "safeguard especially the consciences of noblemen and gentlemen who cannot reveal themselves to be Catholics without great danger to their lives and without risking the utter ruin of their families." "Utter ruin" was not a certainty, given the erratic enforcement of the Tudor penal system. But addressing certainties was not the principal business of casuistry; addressing ambiguities and risks was. And risks existed: by 1581 a conviction for recusancy could lead to the considerable monthly fine of twenty pounds, to be divided between the Exchequer, the informer, and the poor of the parish; by 1587 failure to pay the fine could result in the seizure of all the recusant's goods and two-thirds of his lands.[66] Moreover, the risk of "utter ruin" was not limited to the purse or to the reputation of individual families; it extended to the English mission itself. Safeguarding the consciences of English Catholics thus included sanctioning behavior that helped preserve "noble and rich families in their former positions of honour and dignity, so that, after the death of the Queen, they can stand up for the faith with their full authority and protect it with their strength and power against the audacity of heretics," whose own strength and power, the casuist argued, could only be fortified by the financial drain imposed on the mission by the penalties for recusancy. The point nearly launched the casuist on a jeremiad: "It is incredible how bad it is for the Catholic religion when a noble is discovered to be a Catholic and is punished," he lamented, "for often as a result of his ruin some heretic is advanced and nearly all the Catholic's dignities and titles of honour pass to heretics, to the great detriment of the Church."

Alban Langdale's advice reflected this view: "Lett every wise man weighe his owen case," he wrote, urging his readers to direct their own consciences, to determine whether the jurisdiction of natural law prevailed in their particular situation—indeed, to do as "good menn and martirs" were known to do "in tyme of persecution," entering the temples of "Protestants and Idolators . . . without grudg of conscience . . . as circumstances moved them."[67] Behind his words lay the implication that going to church might represent primarily one's obedience to natural law—avoiding the penalty, which might bring on "utter ruin"—and only indirectly represented, if at all, a decision in conscience to obey English statute. Such language helped define the discourse of conscience as a main artery in the discourse of power conducted in the queen's commonwealth: the casuists, describing a context in which secular and spiritual considerations, the private and the public good, and political necessity intermingled, had constructed for a harassed English Catholic population a protective shield against the punitive action of the conscience embodied in the Tudor government.

Grounded on a legal debate in which the perspective of conscience alternately dominated and receded from view, the casuists' directives, when translated into the corresponding behavior of the queen's Catholic subjects, produced an opaque social text, precisely where the government had attempted to insure a transparent and uniform one: in the congregations assembled to hear the Word of God as channelled through the services and homilies approved by the church-state. The interpretive difficulty hinged on the internal controversy among the casuists themselves over the question of whether recusancy and conformity held spiritual or temporal significance. In Persons's *Reasons of Refusal* (1580), among the arsenal of arguments enjoining English Catholics to adopt the practice of recusancy, we find the claim that one's response to the statute produced a "signe distinctiue betwixt religion and religion"—that the "abstayninge from Churche" must be interpreted as "a proper and peculiar signe of a true Catholique" and the "yealding in the same" as "a flat and euident denyinge of God and of his faith."[68] It followed that recusancy was not to be interpreted as a political act, as a sign of disloyalty to the queen. Persons and other apologists for the English mission made the point repeatedly, as many of the recusants themselves did under interrogation—like Richard Waldern, a "citizen and salter of London," convicted for recusancy in 1593, who tried to depoliticize his action by professing his desire to "take the Quene's Majestie's parte soe farr as yt shall not be against his conscience."[69] In Langdale's pamphlet we find the opposite claim: that the "goinge and not goinge" was not a "signe distinctiue betwene C. & P." but, rather, a "signe distinctiue betwene a trew subject and a rebbell."[70]

Behind their opposing claims, both men were waving a banner that had been raised in the verbal warfare between medieval popes and emperors, a banner on which Christ's admonition, implying a clear distinction between spiritual and temporal power, was writ large: "Render, therefore, unto Caesar the things which are Caesar's and unto God the things that are God's" (Matt. 22:21). The distinction, made problematic by the rivalry between popes and emperors for the *plenitudo potestas* (the plenitude of power embracing both spiritual and temporal spheres), remained a source of contention in the mid-sixteenth century between anointed secular rulers and the enfeebled post-Reformation papacy. Caught between rival, global claims to authority, both Persons and Langdale, advocating opposite kinds of behavior, were asserting a distinction that in practice could not hold. The government authorities were not prepared to grant that recusancy was what Robert Southwell called a "meere matter of conscience," without political significance. Nor, in rebutting the Catholics' complaints of religious persecution, were the authorities able to maintain, despite Burghley's efforts, the argument represented in Langdale's pamphlet: that the pursuit of recusants was merely a political matter; that a recusant merely signified a "rebbell"— as if the threat of rebellion in the discourse of the Elizabethan church-state could be detached from the quasi-judicial and spiritual action of the *foro interno*. In the Act against Popish Recusants (1593), the presumed rebels were charged with using a "false pretext of religion and conscience"—but the very phrase represented an attempt by the government to impose an authoritative and politicized reading of the recusant conscience, which was believed to be under the direction of Rome instead of Westminster and therefore likely to hide "traiterous and most dangerous conspiracies."[71] And certain to be damned, as the words of the "Homily against Disobedience and Wilful Rebellion" indicated: "such subjects as are disobedient or rebellious against their princes disobey God, and procure their own damnation."[72]

No less than the word "conscience" to which they referred, recusants had become a "signe distinctiue" of ambiguity itself. This characteristic applied as well to their counterparts—the conformists, known as "church-papists," whose own connection to the recusants proved a source of ambiguity, especially where the practice of occasional conformity occurred. Christopher Haigh has observed that in parts of England there was indeed "no sharp dividing line between recusants and church-papists," citing by way of example the "large body of Catholics in the Fylde [in Lancashire] who were recusants for most of the year but who conformed for a few weeks before each assize to escape prosecution."[73] Nor was there a sharp dividing line between church-papists and Protestants in the congregations assembled in the parish churches. Langdale insisted that the church-papists could be discerned: "Yf I pray not with them, if I sett whan they knele, if I refuse theire (communion), &c be not these signa distinctiva and do not these factes shewe a dissent as well as express words." What such "factes" showed, Persons argued, was not the explicit dissent of a Catholic conscience but merely a difference subject to ambiguous interpretation. Refusing communion could indicate no more than that one was "out of charity with a member of the congregation," for which fault Protestants themselves could refuse communion. Sitting instead of kneeling could indicate illness. And neither the church warden nor the potential informer could claim the privilege of judging a churchgoer's silence as a sign of dissent instead of a retreat into private meditation. In any case, the advice given in the case-books did not require occasional conformists to advertise their position in conscience. One was allowed to participate "with heretics in prayers in which nothing is said against the faith"; if the conform-ist was an "uneducated person," the casuist urged him to avoid, "as far as he can, paying attention" to heretic sermons and to "[mourn] when he hears blasphemies against God, the saints etc." Arguably, clinging to the proscribed trappings of popular Catholicism—using a "papistical catechism," or carrying a rosary into church—might arouse suspicion. But it might be difficult, indeed, to distinguish the most placid Protestants from the church-papists who sat through a sermon with their ears stuffed with wool.[74] Such behavior reflected the tenor of the advice given in the case-books: to conceal the faith "as time and place require."

If anything, the church-papists magnified the ambiguity associ-ated with the recusants. While the physical sign of the recusant was absence—an absence that implied the flight of conscience from the scrutiny and authority of the Elizabeth church-state—the physical sign of the church-papist was a presence that masked (or seemed to) the same condition of absence. And while the recusant could escape detection through a variety of ways—not the least of which was the government's own inefficiency in documenting the recusant popula-tion—the church-papist embodied a means of escape that pointed up the irony of the government's attempt to enforce the Act of Uni-formity. The process of absorption implemented by the church-state was built on the premise that outward conformity, achieved through repetitive, ritual action within the community, would shape inward conformity—conversion.[75] By 1580 the premise had become prob-lematic. The dissemination in England of Gregory XIII's ambiguous qualification of *Regnans in excelsis*, releasing Elizabeth's Catholic subjects from their required obedience to the controversial papal bull "under present conditions" (*rebus sic stantibus*), merely gave a sharper definition to the subversive political context in which the government was habitually prepared to locate the papists generally, and with which most papists were understandably not eager to be associated—though their position was by definition contradictory and, possibly as much to themselves as to observers, unpredictable.[76] Many church-papists might gradually slip into "heresy," as some casuists feared; many, as some casuists hoped, might also emerge as the foundation of a realm restored to the Catholic faith. Marginal to a degree the recusants were not, the church-papists thus presented an enigma likely to disturb the official hierarchy of the Catholic Church as well as that of the Tudor government: were they participating in the construction of a uniform social text or were they defining its limits as a fictional construct, concealing its points of rupture?

The existence of the church-papists, unofficially sanctioned by the casuists, underlined the potential of the discourse of conscience to generate in effect a semiotics of social action in which "signa distinctiva" dissolved into a penumbra of interpretive "cumbers"—in which, to borrow the language of casuistry itself, the unquestioned, immutable truths contained in *synteresis* began to assume the contours of the continually questioned, changeable probabilities of circumstance filtered through *conscientia*. Through their inspection of the interstices to be discerned between acts, as one casuist put it, that "deny the faith" and those that "conceal it as time and place require," the casuists thus helped perpetuate a context of social indeterminacy—one that the church-papists incarnated, in what amounted to a behavioral equivalent of the verbal practice of mental reservation. (And, in some quarters, an equivalent as well of the lax conscience, which was believed to foster the analogous dissimulations of church-popery and mental reservation. "He would make a bad martyr and good traveller," John Earle later wrote in his character sketch of the church-papist, "for his conscience is so large he could never wander out of it; and in Constantinople would be circumcised with a reservation.")[77]

Commensurate with the "honest dissimulations" of the occasional conformists was the practice—for which the Jesuits were notorious—of physical disguise. The practice, advocated in the case-books, seemed a natural extension of the discourse of conscience into extralinguistic fields, as the description of one anonymous Jesuit suggests. Working in the Workshire district, the missionary "kept in store all kinds of dresses which he used to adopt according to circumstances;

appearing one while as a clown upon a pack horse, then, in splendid attire, entering the houses of the nobility, he made himself, like the Apostle, all things to all men that he might gain all."[78] Echoing the Pauline missionary ethos ("I am made all things to all men, that I might by all means save some" [1 Cor. 9:22]), this anonymous voice echoed, as well, the secularized, courtly equivalent that Lodge condemned in his portrait of the adulator: only in the indiscernible region of conscience, presumably, might the good missionary be distinguished from the Alcibiades-like courtier.

The parallel illustrates the significance of the missionaries' practice of disguise in destabilizing the semiotics of clothing and gesture in Elizabeth society. Take Campion's portrait of Robert Persons: both the author and his subject seem to have relished what was evidently an impenetrable disguise as a soldier. Persons was "such a peacock, such a swaggerer, that a man needs must have very sharp eyes to catch a glimpse of any holiness and modesty beneath such a garb, such a look, such a strut."[79] The disguises of another priest, Thomas Holford, realized the ethos of indeterminacy within the discourse of conscience to a remarkable degree. His flamboyant disguise as a dandy, which he adopted in Cheshire, did not save him from arrest; but after his arrest he refused to abandon his disguise: refused to acknowledge the distinction between the veneer and the grain of his role as missionary. After his escape he assumed a form that pointed up the absence of stable connections between language and meaning, a form that, paradoxically, implicated this condition of instability as the "signe distinctiue" of the missionary. In London he appeared "with white hose on one leg and a yellow stocking on the other"—a form so "grotesque," according to one account, that "a fellow Catholic mistook him for a madman."[80] Holford's behavior underlined a practical feature of the mission that the martyrologies, with their idealized, conventional portraits of long-suffering Christian soldiers, tended to ignore.[81] For Holford, success as a missionary, not to say survival, had become very much a function of his mercurial ability to elicit and to elude the practice of reading casuistically, to make of his appearance a disorienting, unreadable text.

In comparison to the matters of church attendance and clerical disguise, most of the cases treated in the case-books are rather tame affairs. Most do not exhibit immediate or obvious political connotations. What they do exhibit is the quotidian aspect of reading casuistically in a climate of political and religious controversy: the quotidian aspect of appraising the hermeneutic challenges that circumstances like "just fear" or scandal could generate. What was one to do, for example, if in the course of a journey one was served meat on a fast day at a table of heretics? One casuist concluded that it was "not a sign of heresy, constituted by the law or the custom of heretics, to eat meat on fast days." (Heretics "do what they do—for example, they eat meat—because they are accustomed to do so," the argument ran.) Nor was abstinence a sign of the loyal Catholic, for it had not been made "a means by which men were understood to profess their faith." Of course, if the heretic who offered the meat and the Catholic who accepted it had established that it would be eaten "in contempt of the Church," there was no doubt that the act performed in such circumstances was a mortal sin and, by implication, a virtual sign of heresy. This kind of argument had become axiomatic in casuistry: even the most virtuous act was subject to adulteration by the insinuation of a less than virtuous intention or purpose.[82] But in the absence of the specific intention to transform it into a "declaratory sign of heresy"—an unequivocal transgression of divine law—the act remained an indeterminate sign, on the margin between sin and non-sin, subject to a certain degree of drift into either category, depending on the presence of circumstances like "just fear" or scandal.

One solution to the case concerning fasting allowed that no sin would be committed "against the law of the Church" if one ate meat out of "just fear." "Just fear," which figured prominently in the polemics surrounding church attendance as well, appeared to obtain only under certain conditions, which were located within a hierarchically ordered pattern of domination and submission. For example, the casuist doubted whether an innkeeper who offered prohibited food was likely to inspire "just fear." First of all, because "just fear" never intervened in the communication with "inferior people who cannot frighten firm men." And because the innkeeper's offer was more likely to be motivated by greed than by the desire to lead a Catholic into contempt of the Church—to the casuist, the offer did not represent a conscious determination to create a context in which the jurisdiction of divine law obtained. It followed that, rather than submit to the perceived authority of the innkeeper, one could without risk avoid the occasion of sin by taking charge of the situation: inn-keepers, after all, could be "placated by being treated prudently, courteously and with liberality." On the other hand, "certain circum-stances" might give rise to "just fear"; the casuist singled out the presence of "pursuivants or similar people ready to arrest Catholics." "Just fear," elsewhere called "mortal fear," preempted the fast law because it evoked a fundamental natural law, according to which no one could be bound to place oneself in mortal danger. Yet even "just fear" did not create an absolute security against sin, as the casuist's final remark indicated: "even if there is 'just fear' a man should not eat prohibited food in public, because it would cause scandal unless he could inform ignorant bystanders of his reasons, which I think it would be difficult to do." The spiritual hazard of scandal eclipsed that of personal physical danger, for scandal struck at the edifice of divine law by threatening to turn the faithful into apostates. This argument, employed as well by the opponents of recusancy, had the effect, generally, of closing all discussion in matters of conscience. Or, rather, of indicating the speaker's desire to do so; for the argu-ment, deriving as it did from the appraisal of indeterminate circum-stances, was inconclusive.

Just as human laws, mirroring the mutable character of human society, were acknowledged to possess a certain degree of indeter-minacy—they required, as William Perkins observed, "restrictions, amplifications, and modifications of all kinds, with new readings and interpretations"—so, too, were the circumstances one uncovered in casuistical analysis.[83] To be sure, some circumstances—like the pres-ence of a known hostile government agent—were both easily discern-ible and attached to a fixed meaning. But others—like the intention behind the innkeeper's offer of meat, the threat of scandal, or the possible further applications of the concept of "just fear"—were not as easily codified. Elsewhere the casuist had reminded his readers that the mere appearance of anomalous behavior—including the de-parture from customs—might elicit the protean shape of scandal: "If you do not follow the custom of the area in which you find yourself, you do not know whether you cause anyone scandal, and others do not know if they scandalize you."[84] The casuist was referring to customs established in Catholic communities—in this case, to the custom observed in the North of England of abstaining from eggs as well as meat on Fridays. In the inn scene, however, one entered a world dominated by a heretic (i.e., Protestant) population; accordingly, the already difficult appraisal of scandal became more so. On the one hand, the risk of scandal caused by eating prohibited food in the presence of heretics appeared negligible. Heretics by definition were already outcasts, subject to what was known as "pharisiacal scandal," scandal caused by the misreading even of what in Catholic orthodoxy would be considered unimpeachable behavior, a misreading for which they alone were held responsible.[85] Heretics might indeed believe that a Catholic who ate meat on a fast day had apostatized, the casuist pointed out; but such an interpretation was a function of their own "ignorance and blindness," which prevented them from understanding "that it is possible to eat meat out of necessity." One might thus be free to consider the relative weight of a circumstance like "just fear" and, submitting to the pressure of a perceived hostile environment, virtually melt into the landscape.

On the other hand, this very argument suggested that the risk of scandal threatened to surface precisely at the point where one's interpretation of the case appeared most secure. One might not be able to distinguish a heretic from a "careful Catholic" among one's fellows in the inn, given the possibility that a "'heretic' in outward appearance" was perhaps "a Catholic at heart," who "would like to eat food which is not forbidden if it were served him, and only eats forbidden foods when they are served him to avoid revealing what he is." The observation, which figured unobtrusively among the casuist's remarks, contained a conservative edge, theologically. By summoning a circumstance that would prove difficult to discount absolutely, the casuist was offering a compelling reason not to eat the prohibited meat. The observation also contained an unsettling corollary, which moved beyond purely theological considerations. The perceived risk of scandal might turn out to be a cause for "just fear"—a presumed "Catholic at heart" might in fact be a heretic in the service of the government's intelligence network. This was the kind of epistemological quandary to which the "inn cases" led, enacting in the body politic the labyrinthine turns of conscience that Elizabeth represented as the monarch's privilege in her speeches.

THREE

Reading and Misreading the Body Politic:
The Conscience of Anthony Tyrrell,
Spy and Apostate

[Government authorities] have suborned such a number
of secret spies, who, under colour of Catholic religion, do
insinuate themselves into our company and familiarity,
and that with pretence of such zeal, sincerity, and friend-
ship, that it seemeth a thing almost impossible either to
decipher or avoid them. These men do give intelligence,
and inform our adversaries continually of all our actions,
sayings, and many times our secret intents, if they gather
by any sign or sinister suspicion of their own that we are
conceited otherwise than they would have us.

— "Father Richard Holtby on
Persecution in the North" (1593) [1]

Parallel Registers of Conscience:
The English Mission and
Elizabeth's Intelligence Network

By the mid-1580's, it might indeed have been difficult to discern
whether a probable context for "just fear" had arisen, given that
Walsingham's intelligence network had become, in reputation if not
entirely in fact, a formidable embodiment of the "conscience" of the
government, scrutinizing the body politic for recalcitrant papists and,
especially, priests. (When he wrote Walsingham's obituary notice,
Camden described the late secretary of state himself as "a most dili-
gent searcher of hidden secrets.") [2] The pursuivants ("lynx-eyed" men,
Robert Southwell called them) generally represented the most visible

branch of the network.[3] Under the supervision of local authorities, they were responsible for the actual seizure of the presumed traitors, an action likely to include pillaging as well. "Every their finger is a lime twig, and hardly faileth to catch one thing or another"—the quip came from one Yorkshire recusant who found the mercenary note poorly masked beneath a seedy chivalric display. "Before they search a man's house," he wrote, "the doughty champions send forth their scouts, place their spies at every door and window, appoint a guard before themselves, give the charge and assault. Then they enter the house with drawn blades, bent crossbows, and charged dags."[4] The more subtle business of detection, as the recusant's words suggest, belonged to what one historian has called a "floating population" of informers, spies, and *agents provocateurs*, whose numbers and activities remain, necessarily, difficult for us to establish.[5] But the uneven documentation of this sector of Elizabethan society presents a deceptive impasse. To confront the lacunae in the historical record is, from another perspective, to gain a sense of an underlying tension in the social discourse—where fact, hearsay, and speculation intermingled—of the queen's subjects themselves, who would not have had access to a central bureau's revelatory file of documents even if one had existed.

This space of underlying tension—where potentially dangerous anomalies, concealed cases of conscience, threatened to erupt—promoted the exercise of a casuistry that was directed outward as well as inward and that took nothing for granted. Particularly in a period of advertised religious and political strife, it behooved one to read the "book of the world" casuistically, whether in a public inn or in church or at home among one's friends and servants; to be equipped with the tools of casuistical analysis was to be poised to cut through the surface of an apparently uniform social text—like the one represented by the congregation assembled at prayer—in order to scrutinize the underlying network of shifting and often ambiguous relations between its constituent parts: the members of the social and political body.[6]

At this submerged level, Walsingham's intelligence network and the English mission converged. Both movements left indiscernible points of rupture, defying the integrity of perceived boundaries, within the commonwealth. Both movements articulated, on the plane of social action, the interpretive action that the practice of mental reservation epitomized in the discourse of conscience. Together, the largely unchartable body of Catholic dissidents and Protestant informers and spies pointed up the underlying metacritical aspect of reading casuistically. These people gave evidence that a case of conscience could only be fully apprehended through an interrelated process of empirical observation and conjecture, of scrutiny and self-scrutiny, a process that mirrored the dual perspective of conscience itself, which looked both inside and outside: inside, to secret knowledge as well as to received divine and moral truths; outside, to the theater of the world. They gave evidence that this interrelated process, while conducted in order to locate the precise jurisdictional boundaries of the obtaining laws, might well bring a heightened awareness of the imprecise boundaries of the case itself, which were subject to change according to the shifting weight of circumstances.

It is perhaps unnecessary to point out that not every Protestant was a spy, or even that the social and commercial bonds within many communities might indeed have belied the official antagonism between Protestants and Catholics.[7] Yet we know that the Tudor government, lacking an adequate police force, did rely on Walsingham's intelligence network, however loose its organization, in order to draw secrets from the conscience of the body politic; and that the success of the network depended on the ability of its members to sustain, like the missionaries and church-papists, a chameleon-like aspect of virtual invisibility. For example, one of Walsingham's spies, Thomas Rogers (alias Nicholas Berden) was so successful in assuming the guise of a priest that at one point, Conyers Read tells us, he was "hunted down by Justice Young, one of the most notorious of the searchers after priests, and was very nearly taken."[8]

It would have been odd, indeed, had the official press advertised the existence of such people—they were the secrets of the government's conscience. But the press, while keeping the public abreast of the periodic discoveries of assassination plots against Elizabeth, did help advertise the existence of papist spies (the term, in government propaganda, amounted to a tautology).[9] Also of double agents, who were even more notorious, inasmuch as they represented the destabilization of both Catholic and Protestant groups from within.

The execution in 1585 of the civil lawyer Dr. William Parry brought an end to the underground career, if not the infamy, of a self-proclaimed "true subject," privately reconciled to the Catholic faith, who had for several years sought advancement in the court by keeping Walsingham and Burghley informed—more or less unreliably, it appears—of the movements of his disaffected coreligionists abroad. (To Burghley he wrote in 1581 of his assurance "in few months to be well able to discover their deepest practices.")[10] By the middle of 1584, the "utterly dejected" aspirant to the queen's favor had "vowed to undertake the enterprize" of assassinating Elizabeth "for the advancement of Religion." According to the "voluntary confession" made after his arrest "in discharge of his conscience" (a confession he later claimed was extorted under threat of torture), Parry's doubt in the matter had been resolved by the "opinion of some learned divines," in particular by the resistance theory he found in William Allen's *Defence of English Catholics* and by a letter he received several months before his arrest from one Cardinal di Como, virtually absolving him in advance of sin if he should "bring forth the effects" of his "resolution."[11] As it happened, Parry vacillated for several months, long enough for him to be betrayed by a fellow conspirator.

"My cause is rare, singular, and unnatural," lamented Parry at his trial. His ultimate exposure did not mask the disturbing evidence that, whatever its other attributes, his cause was also Byzantine, as unyielding to the investigation of the queen's commissioners as it had proved unpredictable in the course of his apparent insinuations into the opposing Protestant and Catholic enclaves of power. For Catholics the Parry plot was an embarrassment; for Protestants it was further proof of papist treachery, and it was exploited as such. An account of Parry's "horrid treasons" was published after his death. Holinshed published details of the case in the *Chronicles*. Special prayers of thanksgiving for the deliverance of the queen "from the murderous intention of Dr. Parry" were composed to be read in churches. One prayer exalted the "vigilant eye" of providence for the "sudden interruption of his endeavour."[12] The passage contained an implicit reminder that the members of the Christian commonwealth—the particulars of Parry's case made it germane for both Catholics and Protestants—must acquire a vigilant eye as well: must gain an expertise in locating and interpreting ambiguous social texts in the book of the world, an activity of a piece with the examination of cases of conscience.

A more explicit reminder of the need for such expertise came in the discoveries of apostate priests who passed information about the mission to the authorities. They were not many; but it did not take many informers of this sort, given their particular association with secret knowledge, to arouse public attention. In his autobiography Father William Weston, the well-known exorcist, recalled that "nothing was more notorious in the mouths of all men." Weston was referring to the "public renunciation of the Catholic faith by Tyrrell the priest," scheduled to be made at St. Paul's Cross in January 1588.[13] It was neither the first nor the last recantation, though possibly the most spectacular, in the career of Anthony Tyrrell, whose multiple permutations in allegiance brought the intelligence network and the mission to a point of intersection in one of the most egregious, and enigmatic, representations of conscience in Elizabethan England.

The following examination of the Tyrrell case will take us a good distance, in some respects, from the written cases of conscience that circulated in the English mission. But it will lead us to a sharper understanding of the discourse of conscience as an expression of a cultural hermeneutics that extended beyond the confines of the mission, one that alternately seemed to mask and unmask the indeterminacies of the verbal and social texts produced in conjunction with the direction of conscience—whether at Richmond, at St. Paul's Cross, or at the local court of assizes. To study the Tyrrell case, ultimately, is to return to the casuists' elusive configurations of "just fear" and scandal in order to pursue the metacritical aspect of the very act of reading casuistically. And to discover the extent to which such an act was also subversive, especially against a background that included Tyrrell, the queen's "sorrowful and distressed subject," whose career by the end of 1588 had illuminated the destabilizing effect of the discourse of conscience within the discourse of power.[14]

Tyrrell's decision to become a spy for the government seems to have been prompted by his perception that neither he nor his career as missionary was likely to survive unless he took it upon himself to transform the context in which his association with the mission might be read by the government. It remains unclear whether Tyrrell's decision was governed by pragmatic, not to say cynical, motives or by a mis-guided sense of what he could accomplish for the mission in the long run; in any case, fear of implication in the Babington Plot—he was a close friend of John Ballard, one of the priests later executed for com-plicity with Babington—apparently led Tyrrell to enter into secret communication with Justice Richard Young (a man whom Tyrrell later called "a most cruel bloodsucker") and with the lord treasurer himself.[15] In one of his subsequent confessions, Tyrrell remarked that he had consented "to become a Judas in kind," disclosing more than he actually knew, a tissue of fact and incriminating fiction, about the movements of the Babington conspirators. This was the beginning of his government service, which he maintained while overtly pursuing his pastoral ministry. He reported information gathered during pe-riods of incarceration with recusants and other priests in the Counter in Wood Street and, later, in the Clink. After a time Justice Young arranged for Tyrrell to be released, enlarging his scope "to play the spy abroad." Already a number of Catholics involved in the mission had been apprehended as a result of Tyrrell's betrayals while in the Clink (it was "the only place to get good intelligences," he ob-served), including Henry Vaux, of the notable recusant family whose home at Harrowden would gain fame for its hiding-holes in which priests were sheltered.

Tyrrell appears to have exploited his privileged position in the mission to the satisfaction of Young and Burghley—even of the queen. Though otherwise preoccupied in the last months of 1586, Elizabeth followed Tyrrell's career with interest. She accepted letters from him and on at least one occasion sent him an encouraging mes-sage: "She willed me to tell you from her," reported Young in a letter to Tyrrell, "that you fear no man, for she hath, and will have, care over you." Young and Burghley, who maintained more frequent communication with Tyrrell, seem to have realized that periodic care needed to be taken, rather, of his conscience, which posed a more pressing threat than any external agent. The business of uncovering secret information and disclosing it to the government caused him, he wrote, "continual conflict and horror of my own conscience." The theme appeared frequently in his personal narrative; in his commu-nication with Justice Young he emphasized, advisedly, the anxiety that maintaining his role as priest caused him. ("Dissembling there so deeply as I did," he later recalled, required incessant vigilance, "as well in going to confession as unto the altar, and in all my talk and conversation.") In response, both justice and lord treasurer played the casuist, enjoining him to alter his perspective of the case in view of the circumstances. From Burghley, a hurried note: "Your dissimulation is to a good end, and therefore both tolerable and commendable. I pray you therefore persevere therein, as I will persevere in good will." Young, though he began on a note of exasperated pragmatism, remembered to tailor his advice to one trained in the care of consciences: "Dissemble, marry, what else, Mr. Tyrrell? Dissemble, and spare not, remember always the cause wherefore and why you do it. You can do God no better service than in hunting and deciphering out traitors."

What neither man knew was that Tyrrell's guilty conscience was spinning out a disturbing internal narrative that complicated his dissimulations. The priest who had gained notoriety, with Weston, as an exorcist now imagined himself caught up in an inverted repetition of the rite of exorcism: "Triumphing of their possession of me, and watching when they should carry my soul as their perpetual prey unto eternal damnation," a host of devils, he wrote, waited "with implacable hatred" to "afflict me in hell, that had so much here afflicted them." While Tyrrell was "deciphering out traitors," it was therefore possible that his behavior, if not his words, would release traces of guilt that his companions would be able to decipher in return.

Tyrrell in fact believed he had dissembled his "inward and secret afflictions" adequately, largely because the internal authority of his conscience had so suffused him with the sense of his own guilt that he was unable to conceive of his case in other than purely dichotomous terms—the arithmetic of the most rigorous casuist. He was damned; therefore his fellow prisoners were "innocents": "innocent" readers of their environment who incarnated an idealized, objective moral order and projected it in a mirror reversal of Tyrrell's own perspective. In Tyrrell's words, they "suspected neither fraud or guile, nor occupied their minds upon other thoughts but how they might please and serve Almighty God, receiving their present afflictions with great patience, and wholly relying upon His blessed will and pleasure for their release." He was wrong.

Before considering his companions' discovery of his secret, let us recall the location of the group: the prison. A brief word about prisons, I think, will help illuminate the underlying social context in which their discovery was made. The organization of sixteenth-century prisons in England, notwithstanding the unsavory conditions in prisons like Bridewell or Newgate, was more fluid than rigid (just as the penal system, while terrifying in its official language, was sporadic in its enforcement). Some prisoners were able to circulate with relative freedom both within and without the prison walls. Recusant prisoners frequently congregated surreptitiously in cells for masses and devotions (behavior not unlike that which took place in recusant homes). And Tyrrell's experience indicates that the transitory population of the prison made it a marketplace for news.[16] Such features illustrate the point Foucault made in his general appraisal of the prison structure: the prison reproduced the mechanisms found to exist in the social body.[17] One notable parallel emerges between the prison and conscience, both of which were conceived of as regions with hidden recesses where disorder—sin, crime—was punished. (William Perkins made the parallel explicit in *A Discourse of Conscience*: he instructed his readers to consider the "evill conscience" as "the Jaylor to keepe man in prison in bolts and yrons, that hee may be forth comming at the day of judgement.")[18] The "pricks" and "wounds" of conscience, both probative and punitive devices, charted degrees of spiritual pain while the rack, the "wall," the "scavenger's daughter," and other instruments of torture within the prison exploited physical pain: in both cases to analogous ends. The application of pain led, under ideal conditions, to the disclosure of secrets—the confession of personal sin to an ecclesiastical authority or of a criminal act (or pertinent information) to a secular authority.[19]

The parallel is useful, not because it points to the literal experience of Tyrrell's companions (they exerted neither spiritual nor physical pressure on him) but because it suggests the premium placed on an attitude of watchfulness by both ecclesiastical and secular institutions in their society, by both external and internal courts of law.[20] In the *foro interno* of conscience Tyrrell found himself condemned; his companions in prison, while not systematically employing the investigative procedures of casuistry to discover his guilt, proved keen observers of his behavior, engaged in precisely the kind of scrutiny that would have been required in the formal analysis of a case of conscience. From Weston's account of Tyrrell's stay in the Counter we learn how his companions noticed in "the manners of the man" certain "symptoms of vacillation."[21] For example, it was not considered a "good sign that he received so many visits from heretics, and conversed so much with them." Certain books found in his possession—a vernacular Bible, John Calvin's *Institutes*—presented a "circumstance" that "strengthened much further their opinion that his courage was waxing feeble and faint." To this circumstance they added more perplexing ones: "when there was no call or necessity for so doing, he always retained his secular dress"; at table "he could not be induced to say grace" when it seemed appropriate that he should do so—that is, when he was "the only priest among many secular Catholics"; nor did it escape them "that the book marks in his Breviary, that indicated the Office for the current day, were not rightly placed."

The careful observations of Tyrrell's companions uncovered, as did casuistical analysis, an array of circumstances to be weighed against a normative pattern of behavior. The "declaratory signs" of the ministering priest—for example, the masses said and confessions heard by Tyrrell—were eroded by the accumulation of the other, incongruous, signs that belied the apparent transparency of Tyrrell's words and actions. The inner disturbance of his conscience had produced, in effect, a destabilized discourse: "talk and conversation" that did not quite signify the unambiguous priest or the unambiguous apostate. Accordingly, his companions arrived at a suspended reading, contingent on the discovery of conclusive evidence—"declaratory signs"—of his betrayal; as Weston observed, they found "from every side tokens and signs that there were just grounds for suspicion."[22]

Tyrrell's public recantation at St. Paul's Cross—after having rejected his "abominable course" in the service of Protestant heretics, returned openly to the Catholic faith, and, shortly after, resumed his former, Protestant, association—hardly settled the matter. The event was set up to be a sermon in which Tyrrell delivered a retrospective exposé of his past crises of conscience, viewed from a position of recovery and security in the bosom of the Protestant faith. In particular, his "masters and managers" had instructed him to "unsay" his recent confessions, written and "spread throughout the whole realm by his own request," in which he denounced his "spiery" as well as the queen's ministers who had brought him into "their new religion—to wit, dissimulation, spiery, knavery, and all abomination." As insurance against further vagaries, they had also placed Tyrrell once again in prison—this time, as Robert Persons noted, to safeguard his conscience: "to the end no Catholic man might come at him to work remorse or scruple of conscience in him."[23]

The "fame" of Tyrrell's impending sermon, Persons recalled, had spread "over all of London and over most parts also of the realm," so that, when the announced day arrived, "there wanted not concourse of people" at St. Paul's Cross "from all parts, nor of all sorts, and many of the Council and nobility were also present to hear so rare a comedy." Calling it a comedy captured, first, the anticipated element of spectacle that was part of the architectonics of St. Paul's Cross: an open space, governed by a pulpit, that recapitulated the dynamic between pulpit and nave, between preacher and congregation, within the adjacent interior of the cathedral. In this case the term conveyed, as well, a Dantesque sense of comedic narrative (however ironic from Persons's perspective): the crowd that assembled to hear Tyrrell embodied the diversity of human experience brought into and contained within the transparent revelation of divine truth. Indeed, Tyrrell's words were to be taken as transparent evidence of the single truth that resided in the "upright conscience." From Persons's account of the event we learn that Tyrrell was preceded by a preacher who gave the congregation an "earnest exhortation to be attentive to what the other should say and to believe him."[24]

We also learn what in fact transpired: a public representation of Tyrrell's "symptoms of vacillation," which provoked a startling breakdown in the authoritative discourse of the church and the state government. Moments into his sermon, Tyrrell announced his true intention: to affirm his loyalty to the Catholic faith and to denounce, again, the purpose and practices of the Protestant heretics. One phrase from the printed text of Tyrrell's sermon, culled from one of his former confessions, summarized his message: that "my heart and conscience was never with them, but that only their negotiations, the devil's conceits, and my sin induced me to feign myself to be of

their side and to accuse others." It is not certain whether Tyrrell ever
reached the end of the phrase, since he was quickly pulled down
from the pulpit by his mentors in the midst of a great tumult and
carted off to Newgate. Persons recorded the scene: "All was in mar-
vellous hurly and burly at Paul's Cross, where the people had heard
three sermons in one hour, all contrary the one to the other; the first
of the preacher in praise and credit of Tyrrell; the second of Tyrrell
himself in derogation of the preacher; the third of Justice Young
threatening death to those that should believe Tyrrell."

Joseph Hall, the seventeenth-century Anglican casuist, once described the function of the sermon in a way that underlines what
went wrong at St. Paul's Cross the last Sunday of January 1588. "To
preach," he wrote, "is to divide the word aright; to apply it to the
conscience of the hearer, and in an authoritative way to reprove sin
and denounce judgment against sinners."[25] Taking as their theme the
word inscribed within Tyrrell's conscience, the three preachers at St.
Paul's Cross produced a patchwork of competing interpretations of
the word. Issuing from a single, physical locus of authority—the
pulpit—the sermons exposed the potential for subversion that lay
within another locus of authority—conscience—lodged within the
ecclesiastical and political discourse of the realm. Individually, each
sermon identified itself as a text in which words were pronounced as
authoritative and stable in meaning, a text to be applied (like the
formulations stored in *synteresis*) to the "conscience of the hearer."
Together, the sermons created a destabilizing context that uncovered
the aleatory connections between words and their perceived, and
received, meaning; together, the sermons enacted the kind of vacillation associated in casuistry with the loss of authority of *synteresis*:
with its usurpation by the doubting conscience, the *motus indifferens
in utramque partem contradictionis.*[26] St. Paul's Cross had become,
momentarily, something like a Bartholomew Fair of language sub-
tended by the operations of a radical casuistry: within the pivotal
space of the pulpit/conscience, words like "heresy" and "orthodoxy,"
"truth" and "opinion" intermingled at the frontier of established
jurisdictions of meaning. St. Paul's Cross had also become a parodic
inversion of Elizabeth's spectacle of the monarch's conscience, represented in the two speeches she delivered to Parliament a little over

a year before Tyrrell mounted the pulpit. Tyrrell's spectacle of conscience showed the rhetoric of the authorless and impenetrable text of conscience to be something more than a textual strategy that fit hand in glove with the *arcana imperii*. Indeed, in Tyrrell's spectacle, the rhetoric showed itself to be not so much the product of the hidden, suasive intentions of a given author (whether monarch or dissident) as the effect of the ungovernable social practice of casuistical hermeneutics, in which authorlessness and impenetrability emerged as tropes of the collision of rival, mutually unintelligible discourses of truth between observed and observing consciences and of the collision of mutually disputed claims to "possess" the text of conscience by virtue of an authoritative perspective.

Conscience as Reader, Conscience as Text: Reconstructions of the Tyrrell Case

Several months later Tyrrell, repenting his "furious madness," delivered the sermon required of him by the Protestant authorities; the text was published, advertising the "recantation and abjuration" of one who was now "by the great mercy of God converted and become a true professor of His Word."[27] From this point Tyrrell began a long career as a Protestant minister, determined, it seems, to abide by the promise he made in a letter to Burghley shortly after delivering his second sermon at St. Paul's Cross: "Henceforth you shall not hear of me so much as a light suspicion either of treachery, hypocrisy, or dissimulation."[28] It is not certain what sort of reputation he gained as a "true professor" of God's word in the Protestant community. Among Catholic apologists, Robert Persons's response is instructive, for it illustrates a casuist's attempt to establish a purposeful misreading of what had emerged, finally, as an unreadable conscience.

Persons tried to attenuate the "foul scandal" of Tyrrell's perplexing career by redefining it as an effect of divine providence. Faced with an anomaly, Persons responded as a proper casuist, searching out the point at which the scandalous narrative of Tyrrell's life might sustain interpretation as an edifying one. "Foul facts of themselves in respect of those that commit them" might be "very loathsome and abominable and worthy to be suppressed," he wrote; but such facts, "though never so evil of themselves," might be "most profitable . . . to be conserved in memory" if understood "in respect of God's most sweet and holy providence that permitteth them and directeth them ever . . . to some good end for the profit of many, beyond the intention of the doers or procurers." In the adjustment of ablative conditions we can perceive the casuist's hand, uncovering one perspective, then another. And privileging the divine perspective by participating in a divine (and Adamic) activity of naming—in this case, of renaming, of making the absence of edification itself an edifying sign.[29] Thus, in "The Fall of Anthony Tyrrell," Persons invited his readers to "consider the dissolution that crept into this man little and little, and brought him at length to so dangerous a shipwreck" and, with Tyrrell in mind, to "better look into themselves"—in particular, "to proceed plainly, simply, and sincerely in matters of conscience." In the preface he invited them, implicitly, to recognize the parallel between the casuistical dilemma he had faced as a writer, trying to decide whether "to publish or to supress" and let "die in oblivion" the "roll of papers"—Tyrrell's personal narrative and letters—that eventually became part of "The Fall," and the quasi-judicial procedure that would be required of readers of the book if they were to interpret it as a source of edification. Like Persons, they would have to weigh "with some attention . . . not only the things themselves, but also the time wherein they happened, the horrible and bloody effects that ensued thereupon, and the persons that had been actors and authors therein, with the manner of their proceeding and other such circumstances."

Reading Persons's catalog of reasons for publishing Tyrrell's confession, we learn that his own reading of the case did not arise exclusively from a transfiguring construction of an evident scandal. He was construing the man's "dissolution" retrospectively, from what he perceived to be its clear intersection with a secret providential plan— that is, he was construing Tyrrell's narrative from the redemptive point of closure in what emerged as a harrowing trial of conscience. Persons made it clear to his readers that Tyrrell's confession—the confession announcing his return to the Catholic faith, written before his first sermon at St. Paul's Cross—established the cumulative meaning of all that had come before, in a moving illustration of the power of a "scruple of conscience." Tyrrell's personal narrative, he wrote, "cannot but confirm greatly any reasonable man in the truth and comfort of the Catholic cause which works these effects."[30] Such was Persons's intended message in "The Fall," which concluded with his account of Tyrrell's *volte face* at St. Paul's Cross. Persons did not dwell on the disturbing implications of the "hurly and burly" that marked the episode; what mattered was that Tyrrell's sermon, showing him "to be so earnest in this point," had recapitulated the confession and confirmed, Persons believed, the "pure force of truth and conscience."

It was a fitting conclusion to Persons's book. Of course, as we have seen, it was not the end of Tyrrell's wavering. The news of Tyrrell's second St. Paul's Cross sermon, followed by the rapid publication of the text, effectively put an end to Persons's own revisionist effort: he did not publish "The Fall of Anthony Tyrrell." His immediate reason for not doing so had something to do, no doubt, with the fact that it was no longer possible to claim, triumphantly, that the "pure force of truth and conscience" had restored Tyrrell to the Catholic faith. What, then, had become of Persons's determination, as casuist, to explore the hidden, edifying meaning that might be extracted from what seemed now to be an incontrovertible scandal?

Persons's decision not to publish "The Fall" had less to do, I believe, with Tyrrell's most recent decampment to Protestantism than with the interpretive crisis posed by Tyrrell's continuing vacillation. The second episode at St. Paul's Cross, which underscored the inscrutable aspect of Tyrrell's conscience, as well as the limits of authorial intention in dictating the meaning of what was said or written in the name of conscience, made it virtually impossible to assign a point of closure to Tyrrell's narrative; made it impossible, as well, to see his "scruple of conscience" as a source of anything other than a condition of perpetual contingency. And made it possible to see objective meaning—for example, the corpus of truths held to be immanent in conscience and articulated in the language of casuistry—as a malleable construct, a category of subjective meaning. For Persons, these perspectives seem to have implied a *rapprochement* between Persons's own voice, as represented in "The Fall," and those of the three preachers at St. Paul's Cross. Persons's decision not to publish his manuscript represented a choice not to contribute to what might have proved an endless monument, in more ways than one, to the verbal, theological, and political subversion implied at St. Paul's Cross.

I have discussed the case of Anthony Tyrrell at some length because it epitomizes the kind of *mise en abîme* that the praxis of casuistry could generate in the interpretation of cases: it points to a discursive ethos in which the indeterminate perimeter of circumstances like "just fear" and scandal and the multivalent aspects of conscience itself figured as constituent parts of a metacritical apparatus for reading casuistically, an apparatus that exposed the contingent and dynamic relation between social and verbal texts and their readers. To follow the Tyrrell case meant, necessarily, to treat conscience both as text and as reader: as the object of scrutiny and as the lens through which scrutiny was conducted; and it meant to perform this action while traversing the spectrum, drawn by the casuists, that identified the types of adulterated consciences, each of which corresponded to a particular "cumber"—what Kenneth Burke would call a "terministic screen"—in the appraisal of circumstances.[31]

Let us consider again the "just grounds for suspicion" (a circumstance analogous to "just fear") raised among Tyrrell's companions in prison. Their grounds for suspicion, we should recall, represented the accumulation of several anomalous signs, none of which, either alone or in any prescribed array or number, could be read conclusively as a sign of treachery. What the anomalies did signify was the very imprecision of a circumstance like "just fear" or suspicion, which depended, in part, on the vagaries of the scrutinized conscience. Tyrrell's passed only incompletely for what the governing context— his role as priest and political prisoner—dictated: the good conscience. As much as anything, it was the elusive sense of incompleteness or *reticentia*, of something missing or withheld, that lent a disturbing edge to Tyrrell's "talk and conversation." Covertly, he was giving voice to the "continual conflict and horror" of his conscience, a peculiar amalgam of the doubting and the guilty conscience: doubt (or "conflict," noted by his companions as "symptoms of vacillation") about his current, and future, course of dissimulation; and guilt (or "horror," what he called his "inward and secret afflictions") for his past dissimulation. In effect, his conscience had introduced stumbling blocks, points of discontinuity, into the heroic Christian narrative in which both Tyrrell and his companions were participating (i.e., the selfless priest ministering to his flock in the shadow of death). In response, his companions made an effort to provide the missing sense of coherence, an effort that led one of them to a physical act of reconstruction. The pieces of torn letters (the communications between Tyrrell and Burghley), discovered after a careful search of Tyrrell's room, were "arranged upon a gummed sheet of paper that they might be read"—an action that mirrored the interpretive effort of Tyrrell's companions to make sense of the anomalies in his behavior. The restoration of the letters produced what the casuists would have called a "declaratory sign" of the secret that burdened Tyrrell's conscience. It now appeared possible for his companions to restore Tyrrell's good conscience, to reaffirm his place in the heroic narrative destined to culminate in salvation and, possibly, the martyr's crown: they drew a confession of guilt from Tyrrell and "persuaded him to return to his former profession as soon as possible."

But the larger arc of Tyrrell's career, which traced the continued destabilizing effects of the doubting conscience, only betrayed further regions into which "just grounds for suspicion" might extend. In particular, Tyrrell's repeated reversals attached a problematic significance to confession. The locus of transparent discourse, from which Tyrrell's companions as well as Persons had sought evidence of the "pure force and truth of conscience," yielded a text of unbounded self-reflexivity: invited a perpetual questioning of its own premises. Were transparent meaning and truth primordial categories, emanations of divine language and knowledge, or were they the positis of human culture, reflections of its needs and desires? Was confession an act of revelation, through which the immanent "truth of conscience" might be articulated, or was it, as well, an act of concealment, a verbal structure that, by virtue of its own existence, tacitly suppressed the very questioning of categories like the "truth of conscience?"[32] The Tyrrell case relocated such categories within the jurisdiction of "doubtfulnesse" in the reading of conscience. Confession, the alpha and omega punctuating the narrative of the Christian life (in Pauline terms, the outward expression of *convertio*, the end of the old man and the beginning of the new), thus seemed to have joined the array of signs that populated the category of mutable circumstances, like suspicion or "just fear," attending a case of conscience. The episodes at St. Paul's Cross contained, finally, not so

much a succession of confessions as a parodic representation of the
confessional utterance—a demythologizing of the *logos* from within
the discourse of conscience itself.

Tyrrell's subsequent baring of his conscience to Burghley—the
letter in which he disavowed his future association with acts of dissimulation and, accordingly, with the problematic circumstance of
suspicion—illustrated further interpretive "cumbers," this time in
connection with what was known in casuistry as the "lax" conscience. In the taxonomy of consciences, it was the lax conscience,
rather than the guilty, that stood in direct opposition to the good
conscience, despite the habitual eschatological projection of the
guilty conscience as "a litle hell within us" corrupting an internal
Edenic state in which, as Perkins wrote, "everie man is as Adam, his
conscience . . . his paradise."[33] And despite the articulation of what
the "litle hell" was like.

In the literature of casuistry it was common to find, as we do
in Perkins, vivid memory images of the guilty conscience, images
that give us an idea of its coercive power. In addition to what were
arguably its most potent manifestation—the avenging Furies—and
its most explicit political cognates—the hangman and Perkins's "Jaylor"—there were the "wild beast" with "fierce eis" that "flies into a
mans face, & offers to pull out his throat" and the ravenous, "gnaw-
ing and grabbling . . . worm of conscience that never dieth." Horrible as the chimeras of the guilty conscience might be, such images
evoked the "generall goodnesse" implicit in the action of the guilty
conscience. By accusing those "which are justly to be accused" before
God, it served as "an instrument of the execution of divine justice"—but also of divine mercy, insofar as the torment it caused
prepared the way for the "reformation of conscience." The lax
conscience (known variously as the "dead," the "benumbed," the
"seared," or the "false") was considered the sovereign evil precisely
because it did not accuse: "though it can do nothing but accuse,"
Perkins observed, "yet commonly it lies quiet, accusing litle or nothing at all."[34] It produced a silence that signified the suppression not
merely of guilt but even of the knowledge of guilt; a silence, engendered by the habit of sin, that reproduced the tranquility of the good
conscience and undermined the coercive effect of conscience in
general.

When St. Bernard of Clairvaux warned against the danger of the
lax conscience, he called attention to its mimetic capacity. "Only at
the top and at the bottom" of the Christian *via*, he wrote, "is there
a free and effortless course, upward toward life or downward to
death. . . . Perfect love or complete malice cast out fear. Security is
found in truth or in blindness."[35] The "free and effortless course" of
spiritual blindness—elsewhere St. Bernard called it the "false perspective" of the "eye of the heart"—was itself the product of an imperceptible metamorphosis. In his sermon "sur la fausse conscience,"
Louis Bourdaloue, one of the most celebrated Jesuit preachers of the
seventeenth century, emphasized the point. Nothing was more easy
and natural, he wrote, than to form what he described, in Pauline
terms, as a "conscience cauterisée," given the "ascendant malheu-
reux" that the twin forces of desire and personal interest could assume "insensiblement sur notre esprit."[36]

Once acquired, the lax conscience, while virtually mirroring the
good conscience, betrayed what the good conscience concealed: the
subjective bias that the faculty of conscience was capable of introducing into what had been conceived of as the objective, the "invari-
able et inaltérable," character of divine law. Augustine had captured
the sense of mutability implied by this action in the phrase *quod-
cumque volumus, bonum est*, where *bonum* did not so much refer
to the *lex domini immaculata*, an absolute category, as to the interpretation of divine law by the conscience—which was capable, as
Perkins warned, of judging "evill good, and good evill", capable, as
Bourdaloue warned, of establishing "la paix dans le péché, et le péché
avec la paix."[37]

What made the reversibility of terms as dictated by the lax conscience particularly insidious was, ironically, the weight of the Thomist tradition in moral theology, according to which the judgments of
conscience, even those of the *conscientia erronea*, possessed a normative value. One was always bound to follow the dictates of one's
conscience, even when doing so led one into an act considered
by moral theologians to be "objectively evil." Thus the celebrated
"double bind" codified by St. Thomas: *stante erronea conscientia,
quidquid fiat, peccatum non vitatur.*[38] To escape this dilemma, in which
sin appeared inescapable, it was necessary, according to the Thomist
tradition, to free oneself from the error that had corrupted one's

conscience—that is, to cultivate a good conscience. Such an action implied that one was, in the language of moral theology, "vincibly ignorant" of truths one was obliged to know—able to exert sufficient effort to discern, and to accept, the distinctions between good and evil as established by natural, divine, ecclesiastical, and civil law. But it was possible for the lax conscience to have become "invincibly ignorant"—to have arrived, imperceptibly, at a state inaccessible to the kind of perspective from which the conscience might recognize itself as lax rather than good. To borrow Bourdaloue's phrase, the lax conscience fostered an ingenious, eventually an ingrained, habit of self-deception, which produced a "morale étroite qui ne le soit pas." Whether or not one was therefore morally responsible for a given sinful thought or act—invincible ignorance generally made one inculpable—one was in any case held responsible, and therefore culpable, for having reached such a state of laxity, for having formed a conscience that sanctioned something very like a condition of infinite unaccountability.[39] Arguably, this kind of pronouncement represented an attempt to affirm, in theory, the integrity of the boundaries between established moral categories precisely at the point where, in practice, the erasure of boundaries had already taken place.

In this light, the Biblical text that Bourdaloue chose as his opening theme in the "Sermon . . . sur la fausse conscience" was strangely appropriate: he likened his voice to that of John the Baptist, the "voice of one crying in the wilderness."[40] To address the lax conscience meant, in effect, to speak in a wilderness, in a discursive context that posited the existence of an unavailable, indiscernible subject, one that could be only represented as a textual figure by an external authorial voice. It could not be directly addressed, made to speak in its own voice. An Elizabethan might well have called it a conscience conscienceless. St. Bernard called it the *conscientia quasi abyssus multa*. He was referring to the numberless sins it could contain; but to call it an abyss was also to recognize tacitly that, whatever the theoretical virtue of the censures placed on it, the lax conscience suggested an untraceable presence in the moral universe. For two reasons: because, as an experienced state, it did not recognize itself as lax; and because, unless exposed in an evident crime, it was therefore virtually indistinguishable, as an observed state, from the good conscience.

It was thus the lax conscience, pre-eminently, that blurred the distinctions between moral categories and upset the stable denotative character of language as a vehicle through which truth might be apprehended. It was the lax conscience that epitomized the art of dissimulation in its most thorough, penetrating, and subversive aspect. St. Bernard conveyed the disorienting power of this *locus* by conflating two distinct images to produce an enveloping context of indeterminacy: the lax conscience, he added, was also like an imponderable sea filled with numberless reptiles (*Mare magnum ac spatiosum; illic reptilia, quorum non est numerus*). So, ran Bourdaloue's commentary, we should understand the imperceptible but pervasive presence of sin in the conscience of the reprobate.[41]

His image of sin as a reptile "qui s'insinue et se coule subtilement" evoked, fittingly, the Old Testament strictures against unclean animals, a category that represented, as Mary Douglas has pointed out, an attempt to stave off the threat of apparent anomalies—animals whose movements or physiognomy departed from a perceived norm, such as reptiles who, unlike fish, "have not fins and scales in the seas" (Lev. 11:9–10).[42] By the same kind of regularizing process that underpinned the official exploitation of casuistry, that which could not be accounted for became itself a received category that accounted for what it contained, defining and delimiting what was to be recognized as the unclean—and the sinful. It is therefore not surprising that we should find among the characteristics of the unclean animals in Leviticus not only the incongruous movement of the marine reptile but also the imperceptible movement of all "creeping things that creep upon the earth" (Lev. 11:29)—the very movement associated with the subtle dissimulations of the lax conscience; the very movement commonly attributed, in anti-papist propaganda of the sixteenth century, to English Catholics and missionaries. (Burghley, for example, described the Jesuits as having "warily . . . crept into the land"; and Catholics, in the words of the 1593 Act against Popish Recusants, were believed to "secretly wander and shift from place to place within this realm, to corrupt and seduce her Majesty's subjects, and to stir them to sedition and rebellion.")[43] Nor is it surprising that one of the "creeping things" under anathema in Leviticus should be the chameleon, the figure of dissimulation.

Let us now return to the key words in Tyrrell's letter to Burghley, written at the threshold of the priest's career as a Protestant preacher: "From henceforth you shall not hear of me so much as a light suspicion either of treachery, hypocrisy, or dissimulation." How was Burghley to take these words, coming as they did from a man whose career in dissimulation Burghley himself had helped launch? Perhaps the words contained a smoothly concealed dissimulation, a mental reservation designed to protect one who had secretly returned to the English mission, for which cause, as Perkins later warned, "Popish traitours" might do or say anything "without checke of conscience." The erratic aspect that had marked the recent events of Tyrrell's career—signs of a doubting conscience—could have raised a further doubt in one prepared to judge his words: perhaps Tyrrell had by now reached a point where he failed habitually to recognize his own dissembling. François De La Rochefoucauld, the French moralist, would later devise a maxim that described the metastasis of spiritual blindness it was possible to infer from Tyrrell's letter: "Nous sommes si accoutumés à nous déguiser aux autres, qu'enfin nous nous déguisons à nous-mêmes."[44]

Both texts—the letter as well as the maxim—exhibit the underlying metacritical structure of the discourse of conscience. They invite unqualified interpretation as truth statements, making an implicit claim for the language in which they are couched as a transparent medium. Yet under scrutiny they yield a countervailing interpretation, one shaped by the indiscernible presence of the lax conscience. Once deployed, the lax conscience dislodged truth statements from their category of immanence by implicating them as silent parodies of the very idea of truth statements—that is, by insinuating a contextual bias into the uttering of apparently objective truths. In so doing the lax conscience pointed up the implicit problematic in the act of reading casuistically. The meaning of Tyrrell's words, for example, was more than a quantity to be drawn out, by a relentless process of exegesis, from an unyielding and isolated text. It was a function of the text as reconstructed by the reader within a perceived context—a context shaped by the bias not only of the observed conscience but of the observing conscience as well.

Thus at the height of his service in the intelligence network Tyrrell found it puzzling that Burghley showed himself willing to pursue any lead Tyrrell offered, apparently without suspecting that the priest's dissembling might work both ways. Tyrrell later recalled that Burghley was not "so simple but that he might perceive how that in many places I lied grossly; yet all passed for truth, even in matters most weighty of men's lives, states and utter overthrow." For Burghley, Tyrrell's individual statements "passed for truth" insofar as they corresponded to his appraisal of the global truth concerning the papists, which he had expressed in *The Execution of Justice* when he decried their "wicked and dangerous, traitorous and crafty course."[45]

As for the good faith Tyrrell later expressed in his letter, there is no evidence to show whether his words provoked in Burghley even a "light suspicion" of the priest's possible dissimulation. But if we may take the gap in the historical record as a reflection of the lord treasurer's willingness to suspend disbelief, we may take it also as a sign of his evident understanding of the context in which the letter was written. Whatever the state of Tyrrell's conscience, whatever secret knowledge Tyrrell's conscience infiltrated into his discourse, Burghley was not Tyrrell's only reader, even though the letter itself probably remained private. There were other readers—the English Catholic population—whose response to Tyrrell's cumulative behavior provided the context that would impart a virtual transparency to his words. Tyrrell's career in the Clink had come to an end because after his discovery the prisoners, as he himself put it, were "standing in fear" of him. Even before the notorious St. Paul's Cross episodes, according to Father Weston, the "rumour of this scandal [Tyrrell's apparent embrace of the Protestant faith] had been spread far and wide." After St. Paul's Cross, the members of the English mission were unlikely to engage the services of a man who could no longer be believed without risk, whose career had disclosed the potentially scandalous aspect of the very claim to truth-telling. If, then, upon writing to Burghley, Tyrrell indeed harbored a secret intention to exploit his position in the Protestant community to the advantage of the English mission—and whether or not he was fully aware that the intention had germinated in his conscience—the circumstances of "just fear" and scandal that persisted in the consciences of his sometime flock militated against the effective truth of any such secret discourse that might be contained in the letter. The difference between the truth that might lie concealed within Tyrrell's conscience and what

"passed for truth" in the consciences of those whom he addressed
had, in effect, been erased—erased because the difference ceased to
matter. The meaning of Tyrrell's words had become a function of
the meaning that a man in Burghley's position (a position shared
by the Protestant community Tyrrell now promised to serve) would
be able to construct from a perceived context in which those who
stood to benefit from Tyrrell's possible dissimulation—the papists—
themselves identified Tyrrell as the very embodiment of dissimulation. Paradoxically, Burghley could believe Tyrrell's disavowal of
"treachery, hypocrisy, or dissimulation" precisely because Tyrrell was
a known dissembler.

Within the English mission, Robert Persons's evaluation of Tyrrell's career, in "The Fall of Anthony Tyrrell," carried a tacit acknowledgment that the observing conscience itself was a circumstance to
be included in the interpretation of a case. Persons was illustrating
the compositional art of the casuist in his role as an observing conscience, directing the consciences of other readers of the case toward
a privileged perspective in which the dimensions of a "foul scandal"—
the scandal it was possible to read into circumstances like Tyrrell's
apostasy and apparently unrestricted capacity for dissembling—faded
before another, edifying, reading. Persons was, in effect, exploiting
the resources of casuistry in order to remove the "cumber" (etymo-
logically, the word *scandalum* referred to an obstacle or stumbling
block) that threatened to invade the interpretation of the Christian
via as represented by Tyrrell. Behind Persons's action lay the argument from moral theology that scandal would not obtain in the
presence of impervious witnesses, who were either secure in their
faith or already entrenched in the habit of sin—that is, good or lax
consciences.[46] Persons's own argument in "The Fall" thus represented an attempt to confirm a reading body of good consciences.

His suppression of the book represented a tacit admission that such
a body could not be confirmed, particularly in view of the subversive
effect that Tyrrell's continued vacillations had on the very concept of
the good conscience. Persons was doing his utmost not to aggravate
the scandal by publishing a book that his readers might find scandalous as well, were they to associate Persons's own text with the
unrestricted dissembling embodied by its subject. In the gospel ac-

cording to Matthew, Christ warned his disciples that, despite the inevitability of scandals in the world, woe would come "to that man by whom the offense cometh" (Matt. 18:7). Symbolically, Persons was suppressing words that risked serving as a vehicle through which such opprobrium would fall on his own head. In addition, he was following the course of action that Christ urged upon those who would avoid scandal: "And if thine eye offend thee, pluck it out, and cast it from thee" (Matt. 18:9). The symbolic gesture of casting out a text that might offend extended to the offending subject as well: Tyrrell himself, whose confessions formed the heart of Persons's book. The priest who had gained a certain fame in the casting out of evil spirits and who now seemed to contain one—the contamination of language itself—was being symbolically cast out as the offending member of the *corpus mysticum*. As with his earlier decision to publish "The Fall," Persons's ultimate decision to "let it die in oblivion" reflected an argument posed in moral theology, according to which any action that furnished a probable occasion of sin to an observer— even if sin or "injury to the faith" did not in fact occur—made the agent of the action guilty of scandal, regardless of the motive that had prompted the action. Among the contributing circumstances in the interpretation of a case, therefore, one had to allow a space— which might not be filled—for the perception of scandal by an observing conscience.[47]

Such caution had its Scriptural resonance as well. In the first epistle to the Thessalonians, Paul warned the "children of light" to "abstain from all appearance of evil" (1 Thess. 5:5, 15). The message was amplified in Paul's first epistle to the Corinthians, in which he addressed the question of whether the faithful might eat sacrificial meat that had been offered to idols. Paul's solution evoked the category of the *adiaphora*, which had arisen in the philosophy of the cynics and stoics and which would later prove a buttress to the anti-papalism of the English reformers as well as to the purified ecclesiastical structure they envisioned: the category of things indifferent, things remaining in themselves neither good nor evil. It did not matter whether the faithful ate meat that had been offered to idols, Paul said, for the faithful understood the indifferent nature of such an act: "Neither, if we eat, are we the better; neither, if we eat not, are we the worse"

(1 Cor. 8:8). (To borrow the idiom of the casuist in the English cases, eating sacrificial meat was not a "declaratory sign" of heresy.) But Paul added a caveat, one that both medieval and post-Reformation casuists were to elaborate in their discussions of the *adiaphora*: he emphasized the vital role of context and the observing conscience in determining the significance of acts otherwise deemed indifferent. "But take heed," Paul warned, "lest by any means this liberty of yours become a stumbling-block to them that are weak . . . when ye sin so against the brethren, and wound their weak conscience, ye sin against Christ" (1 Cor. 8:9–12).[48]

Still another fold in the already dense texture of casuistical interpretation had emerged from the Tyrrell case: the bias of the weak—or the scrupulous—conscience in extending the perimeter of circumstances like "just fear" and scandal. In one of the Tower works, *A Dialogue of Comfort against Tribulation*, Thomas More conveyed the bias simply and vividly. The scrupulous conscience was the "nightes feare," the "dowghter of pusillanimite," which engendered a "hart evermore in hevynes unquiat & in fere, full of dout & of dulness without comfort or spirituall consolacion." In other words, the scrupulous conscience mirrored the doubting and the guilty conscience, just as the lax mirrored the good. One of the casuist's responsibilities, of course, was to cure the scrupulous conscience, a point More did not omit. In another Tower work, the *De Tristitia*, he referred with admiration to the skill of Jean Gerson, the late medieval casuist, as "a most gentle handler of troubled consciences" who used "certain palliatives which are analogous to those medications which doctors use to relieve bodily pain and which they call 'anodynes.' "[49] The fate of Persons's book illustrates its author's radical solution to the inherent difficulty in determining the effect of a textual "anodyne" on the spiritual constitution of those for whom the palliative was intended—readers whose observing conscience might have become, in the words of Jeremy Taylor, "an undiscerning, undetermined faculty."[50] For such readers Persons created what became literally an unreadable book.

Ultimately unreadable, as well, were the official texts inscribed in English statute for the purpose of creating in the commonwealth a uniform body of good consciences. The Act to retain the Queen's subjects in obedience (1593) attempted to induce conformity by allowing convicted recusants to be "clearly discharged of the penalties imposed" on the condition that they make a "submission and declaration of conformity," in words clearly designed to represent the submission of an erring *conscientia* to the controlling *synteresis* lodged in the church-state. The prescribed language of the presumed rebels recalled the penitent's in auricular confession: "I . . . do humbly confess . . . that I have grievously offended God in contemning her Majesty's godly and lawful government and authority, by absenting myself from church." The abjuration, to be made in church "before the sermon or reading of the Gospel," further obliged one to "acknowledge and testify in . . . conscience" that henceforth one would "obey and perform her Majesty's laws and statutes" concerning church attendance—words that amounted to a public baring of a reformed conscience, its transparency assured by its place in the service, as a proleptic announcement of the divine Word. And silently undermined by the inescapable parallel of the entire procedure to the Tyrrell case.[51]

As if in an effort to arrest the verbal anarchy contained within the discourse of conscience, the government required the would-be conformists to promise obedience "without any dissimulation or any colour or means of any dispensation."[52] But, as the Tyrrell case (and, from a distance, Elizabeth's speeches as well) had shown, the discourse of conscience exposed the potential of such words to undo themselves, to engage interlocutors in what we might call an infinite spiral of language, a process not only of questioning the use and abuse of words but of confronting the underlying network of social and cultural conditions that frame the very questions posed. What, indeed, did a promise not to dissimulate mean, when at the farthest reaches of the inner mechanism of language—its conscience, if you will—truth emerged as a supreme artifice and artifact of the human community; not as the distinct opposite of dissimulation but as its guileless twin? What did a promise not to dissimulate mean when, to pose the problem in terms of a topical issue, truth was fragmented and obscured by the practice of mental reservation? As Tyrrell's career suggested, mental reservation was, indeed, the silent, indiscernible scrambling of the code implicit in the very idea of a common language of a society: the code that affirmed the efficacy of verbal contracts like the "submission and declaration of conformity" and the promise to speak "without any dissimulation"; the code that affirmed the efficacy of the primordial verbal contract of the commonwealth—the oath—by defining it as a "religious act which bindeth the conscience"; the code that amounted to the deployment by ecclesiastical and secular authorities alike of seigneurial rights over the discourse of conscience.

PART II

The Discourse of Conscience in the Elizabethan Canon

The "Siena Sieve" Portrait and Book 5 of *The Faerie Queene*: Vanishing Points, Aphasiac Readers, and the Rhetoric of the Lax Conscience

As we have seen, the social and political context of Elizabeth's response to the crisis of 1586–87 was freighted with signs that neither the monarch nor the church-state could control the operation of the discourse of conscience as a *de jure* means of legitimating and perpetuating the inviolable status of the discourse of power. Catholic recusants provided recurring evidence of the pivotal role the discourse of conscience played in legitimating a competing structure of orthodoxy. But the threat posed by the recusant conscience was limited, for reasons that had less to do with the recusants' own words (under interrogation, we may recall, they often minimized the extent of their dissent) than with a matter of numbers and the implication of numbering. In theory, the number of recusants could be counted. They could be physically located, perceived as a discrete body, and conceptually cordoned off by the establishment as the Other, the Unorthodox, the Heretic. That is, while the existence of recusants challenged the establishment's claim to orthodoxy, it did not challenge the principle upon which orthodoxy itself, indeed all authoritative discourse, rested: what we might call the principle of absolute difference. The notion of a fixed boundary separating orthodoxy and heresy, truth and falsehood, good and evil, justice and injustice remained unquestioned, as did the objective, authorless status of the categories thus demarcated. The church-papists, who by definition could not be counted, posed a more serious threat, precisely because it was possible to construe from their existence a challenge to the principle of absolute difference, a challenge implicit in the much-

advertised practice of "honest dissimulation," or *dolus bonus*, and in
the motions of the lax conscience that the church-papists evoked. To
formulate the challenge would be to question whether absolute differences might prove relative, a function of context; to question
whether all the great doxal texts of the sixteenth century—all that
was taken for granted as objective, self-evident, and authorless—
might be constituted by a subjective order and naturalized by a collective, self-effacing authorship.

The discourse of conscience empowered those who participated
in it to produce such questions. But, to borrow Pierre Bourdieu's
terminology, it also furnished a powerful motive to suppress them,
to "misrecognize" the arbitrary, socially constructed nature not only
of the doxal "universe of the undiscussed" but of the boundary separating that universe from the "universe of things that can be stated,
and hence thought."[1] The motive for such misrecognition was, in a
word, self-interest. That is, the very act of engaging in the discourse
of conscience typically implied an interest in legitimating one's own
discourse—and, therefore, in maintaining a habit of "learned ignorance" or "practical knowledge" that screened out, by a kind of reflex action, the processes of legitimation themselves.[2] For example,
Robert Persons's self-censorship—his decision not to publish his account of the scandalous career of Anthony Tyrrell—was ultimately
an act of misrecognition in the face of a potentially radical critique
of the principle of absolute difference and of the corresponding
doxal texts to which Persons was committed. So, too, the analogous
critique posed by the mere existence of the church-papists, by the
practice of "honest dissimulation," and by the chameleon-like character of the lax conscience was generally misrecognized, even by the
most ardent opponents of such phenomena, precisely because to
draw out the full implications of the critique would mean to recognize the arbitrariness of one's own orthodoxy as well as one's secret
complicity in the legitimation of the very category of authoritative
discourse. Insofar as the discourse of conscience contributed actively
to the discourse of power—not only political power but psychological and spiritual power, the sense of "being in the right"—it was the
only game in town.

In other words, being in the throes of a case of conscience (which
we may assume of at least some of the religious and political dissi-

dents, including Tyrrell), or having a specific motive for appearing to be (which we may assume of Elizabeth), or, more generally, simply making an appeal to "conscience," whether for a polemic or an apologetic purpose, put limits on the kind of interpretive project that the discourse of conscience might be said to accomplish. As if by a mute consensus, the heuristic function of casuistry controlled, if not entirely preempted, the metacritical.

This paradoxical state of affairs accounts for the apparent aphasia represented in the social texts we have examined: the persistently inexplicit character of the interrogation that the discourse of conscience directed at the principles of objective order sustaining the discourse of power. To realize the metacritical operation available in the discourse of conscience, one would have to locate oneself, conceptually, outside the social formation. One would have to be not merely marginal; one would have to perceive oneself, if only provisionally, as being beyond marginality. One would have to assume sufficient interest in adopting, and sustaining, a pose of disinterestedness in the rules of the game (including the very rule defining marginality and centrality as terms corresponding to an objective schema of the world) in order to represent the nexus of social, political, and cultural practices that formulate and legitimate the rules themselves.

Such a representation, of course, could never be more than partial, if only because the pose of disinterestedness could never be more than a pose: no text exists in isolation from social and cultural processes, in isolation from what Raymond Williams has called the "structures of feeling" that characterize and shape the social formation in which texts are produced.[3] But not all texts are bound merely to represent what is dominant in such structures; certain texts may represent what is emergent as well. In the Elizabethan period, it is the texts that do not betray an imperative motive for exploiting the discourse of conscience—texts that appear to have thoroughly assimilated and naturalized the pose of disinterestedness—in which we find textual substance being given to what is emergent in the discourse of conscience: its metacritical and destabilizing character. What this means is that the critical interrogation of the principles presumed to be self-evident in the discourse of power occurs in texts that are defined—and, further, that define themselves—as canonical.

The very texts that advertise themselves as major participants in the repetition of "what everybody knows" are the texts that stand the best chance of representing—and, as it were, simultaneously dismantling—the mechanisms sustaining the indisputable character that informs such cultural givens. Precisely where the dispensation of misrecognition would seem to prevail, it is relaxed. To put the matter in casuistical terms: nowhere can the scope of the lax conscience be more fully realized than where the good conscience is known to obtain.

Two examples will illustrate what I mean: the "Siena Sieve" portrait of Queen Elizabeth (ca. 1580) and book 5 of *The Faerie Queene*. Each work announces its unambiguous participation in a canonical genre (the royal portrait, the epic poem) and its consequent status as an authoritative discourse. In the portrait, the suavely draped figure of Elizabeth is surrounded by icons of royal power and virtue; in the fifth book of Spenser's epic, the proemial invocation of the "Dread Souerayne Goddesse, that doest highest sit / In seate of iudgement, in th'Almighties place" inaugurates a sequence, one might say a phalanx, of allegories of the queen's "great iustice praysed ouer all."[4] Each work, not coincidently, also offers cues indicating its relation to the discourse of conscience, a relation assigned the status of the unproblematic, the inert, and, in effect, the tautological. In each work, images of "conscience" assume the neutral, self-evident character of indices pointing to what is already known, taken for granted, beyond question—to a repository of absolute and authorless principles that cohere around the variously articulated signs of the queen's sovereignty. Sovereignty is not merely legitimated; it presents itself as not even needing legitimation.

At the same time, in each work there is evidence that such images, taken as the last word on the subject, are something of a red herring. Each work exhibits a range of anomalies that elicit recognition of the processes of legitimation. This is not to say that the anomalies constitute an explicit statement of what was inexplicit in the social texts relating to the English mission or the spy network—in the ephemera of the discourse of conscience. Neither the portrait nor the poem redefines itself through its anomalies as an unambiguous exposé of the cognitive and normative structures legitimating the monarch's sovereign power. Merely to expose, to exchange one perceived truth for another, as one does in composing a satire or in uttering what the establishment knows to be blasphemy, would be to perpetuate the process of legitimating the corpus of absolute and authorless referents upon which authoritative discourse itself depends. Instead, the anomalies advertise the necessity and the implication of making choices in the act of reading the portrait or the poem. They furnish tangible textual evidence that to suppress what is perceived as a misreading is also to participate in the construction of what is perceived as its authorless opposite. Yet they do not so much discredit the mythos of authorlessness, or of any of the doxal texts invoked by canonical genres, as provide the information that the choice to do so exists.

Through the anomalies, then, both portrait and poem at once reveal and conceal the metacritical operation of the discourse of conscience as their organizing principle. What occurs, consequently, is a representation of the process of misrecognition, or cultural aphasia, through which the social formation conceals from itself its complicity in the production and legitimation of norms. This representation is also self-referential, in that the process is analogous to the one through which the "finished product" of the portrait or poem, endowed with an objective, "correct" meaning to be received by the presumably passive viewer/reader, silently enjoins the viewer/reader to forget her or his active participation in the production of meaning. In this light, the "Siena Sieve" portrait is to the art of royal portraiture as book 5 of *The Faerie Queene* is to the composition of the epic—the *effigiem justi imperii*—in the Elizabethan court and commonwealth.⁵ Each work has as its subject not merely the queen as virtuous sovereign or quasi-divine judge but the recipe for the canon in which she is inscribed: each work constitutes a text about the processes through which portrait and epic, as well as the principles and norms that underwrite them, are produced and maintained.

Let us turn now to the "Siena Sieve" portrait (see frontispiece).⁶ The figure of Elizabeth, as one might expect, dominates the canvas, establishing the queen as the particularized, historical embodiment of the eternal verities that the icons signify. Not uncharacteristically, the icons themselves are polysemous—which is not to say they establish, at the outset, an element of ambivalence or interpretive discord in the painting, for their various significations are orchestrated around the sovereign presence of the queen, who constitutes the physical and thematic center of the painting. The most luminous space—the white ruff encircling the queen's head—serves as the compositional paradigm for the icons: the globe partly hidden behind the queen's left arm, the round sieve dangling from her left hand, and the oval medallions incrusted on the pillar rising behind her right arm. An interpretive homology follows the visual, as if in obeisance to the authoritative gaze of the queen, whose eyes, lying along the invisible transecting line of the ornamental ruff, assume a quasi-ornamental, impersonal character, at once all-seeing and sightless. The various significations of the icons, in the context of the empty gaze, assume its irreducible aspect: they constitute the self-evident principles to be read in what lies behind the gaze: the monarch's conscience.

The most prominent icon—the sieve in the foreground, reputed to be the favorite device of Elizabeth—alludes, in fact, to the thematics of conscience.[7] In iconographical literature the sieve represents the act of discerning good from evil. Thus, in George Whitney's *Choice of Emblemes* (1586), we find under the title "Sic discerne" the engraving of a sieve in which chaff is being separated from grain, with the moral point indicated in the last lines of the accompanying motto: though "harde it is, the good from bad to trie," the "prudent sorte" should "have suche judgement founde, / That still the good they shoulde from bad descrie: / And sifte the good, and to discerne their deedes, / And weye the bad, noe better then the weedes." However difficult the act of discernment, it is assumed as a matter of course that the task can be accomplished. The doxal character of the principle of absolute difference remains inviolable, as it does in the normative practice of the discourse of conscience, where the contextual bias supplied by *conscientia* in the act of discernment is subordinated to that which admits no bias, the divine truths contained in *synteresis*. An equivalent message appears in the inscription engraved on the rim of the sieve in the portrait: *A terra il ben mal dimora insella* (the good falls to the ground, the bad remains in the saddle).[8] One of the purposes of the sieve, then, is to associate the queen's sovereignty with her official status as the inviolable "conscience" of the realm.[9] Another is to isolate a specific dimension of the queen's inviolability: her chastity. As most commentators on the portrait have pointed out, the sieve alludes to the story of the Vestal Virgin Tuccia, who proved her chastity by carrying water to the Tiber in a sieve. Apart from its timeliness (a number of "Sieve" portraits appeared after 1579, when it was becoming evident that a particular virtue, chastity, had to be made out of a particular necessity, the passage of the queen's childbearing years), the allusion is apposite on at least two other, related, scores.[10] It emphasizes the sacral and hieratic resonance of the virtue (the monarch as high priestess). And, by illustrating the virtue in the context of an ordeal, or *judicium Dei*, the allusion defines the queen's chastity as a miraculous event—as the point of intersection between two distinct spheres, the eternal and the temporal; as a truth manifested through a divine rather than a human agency.[11] In short, as an unquestionable, objective reality, a doxal text.

The architectural ambiance of the portrait emphasizes this message (the queen is standing in repose, idol-like, within what appears to be a temple), a message to which the icons flanking the queen contribute further refinements. The pillar denotes a spectrum of virtues to be found in the monarch's conscience—fortitude, chastity, constancy—as well as the ethos of imperialism that galvanizes them.[12] The globe, reiterating the ethos of imperialism, defines as well through its motto, *Tutto vedo e molto mancha* ("I see all and much is lacking"), the relation of the conscience of the monarch and those of her subjects. The monarch's exercises an omniscient specular power that is directed entirely outward, seeing and judging all, and is therefore itself seen by the consciences of her subjects not so much as a potential object but as the sempiternal agent of scrutiny and, it follows, as the ubiquitous locus of truth. The globe and its motto thus echo the mythos of authorlessness that authoritative discourse—including the portrait—promotes: authorlessness manifested through the absolute character of that which is globally, consensually known, as Spenser's narrator will define the justice of Gloriana: "From th'vtmost brinke of the Armericke shore, / Vnto the margent of the Molucas . . . / Those Nations farre thy iustice doe adore"(5.10.3).

The medallions on the pillar, which depict the story of Dido and Aeneas from the *Aeneid*, invite a similarly univocal reading. The founder of Rome provides both a genealogical and a typological reference, signalling the noble ancestry and imperial legacy of the Tudor monarchs as well as the array of virtues with which they are to be identified. The depiction of Aeneas's passage through Carthage, of his triumph over the distractions of love, establishes a particularized narrative equivalent of the schema of virtues denoted by the pillar (the pillar thus providing not only the physical but the thematic frame for the narrative). Dido herself does not merely define the context in which Aeneas's constancy is confirmed—that is, she does not remain at one remove from the schema of virtues shared by Aeneas and his illustrious avatar, Elizabeth; she contributes directly to it, largely through the associative power of her name. "Dido," Camden observed in the *Remaines*, was a "Phoenician name, signifying a manlike woman."[13] An appropriate name for the woman who, possessing something of the vision of Aeneas, founded Carthage and established a reign of prosperity. An appropriate name, in turn, to be invoked in a visual tribute to a monarch whose gender promoted a whole discourse of accommodation, manifested perhaps nowhere more thoroughly than in *The Faerie Queene*, a poem whose interanimating male and female paragons illustrate the complementary acts of mythologizing the traditional female attributes of the queen's "body natural" and the traditional male attributes of her "body politic." The figure of Dido, in fact, appears to be well integrated into this discourse, embodying the heroic and princely—and, accordingly, "manlike"—character of chastity. Dido had another name, "Elissa" or "Eliza" (an appellation not lost on panegyrists of Elizabeth), which invoked the pre-Virgilian accounts of the chaste widow of Sychaeus, who had never met Aeneas and whose suicide was a personal triumph rather than a self-betrayal, an act through which she preserved her imperilled chastity from violation rather than an act of despair provoked by an uncontrolled passion. It is this chaste Dido, for example, who appears in the final procession in Petrarch's well-known *The Triumph of Chastity*, where she is preceded by none other than the Vestal Virgin Tuccia.

The poem adumbrates the particular iconographic syntax of the portrait, which locates the sieve and the figure of Dido, along with the other icons, in what appears to be a reflexive, and ultimately tautological, relationship. To read the portrait following this syntax is, then, to "invent" it, in the sense of discovering or coming upon a self-contained, self-perpetuating system of resemblances whose components, infallibly in phase, both refer to a corpus of stable, pre-existing meaning (located in iconographic manuals and/or traditional lore) and reconstitute, endlessly, the mutually reflecting facets of that meaning.[14] Referentiality and self-referentiality converge, just as the icons cohere physically around the royal figure, who provides their telos, as though time, history, and the mutability of signification itself were arrested in a *pax anglicana* sustained by the conscience of the queen.[15] The apparent stasis extends to the viewer/reader, whose own conscience, reading the portrait, discovers that it has no other apparent function than to witness and absorb what it already knows: the truths encoded within the authoritative discourse of *synteresis* repeat those encoded within the closed, parthenogenetic system of the portrait. The mythos of authorlessness that this system invokes may thus be adduced from the status of the viewer/reader as well, whom the portrait addresses as a global, collective presence—that is, as *synteresis*, the *scintilla conscientiae*, the repository of what everyone is believed to hold in common, of what no one can therefore be said to have "invented," in the alternative, the productive and performative, sense of the word.

Like a kind of contraband, this sense nevertheless enters the portrait, most noticeably in the area illuminated by a source of light different from the one that gives definition to the queen's ruff and the surrounding icons. In the background, partly hidden by the queen's drapery and the curved outline of the globe, two courtiers, at the head of a procession, stand in a shaft of light emanating from behind an abstract black rectangle, possibly an arras or simply the end of a wall. This rectangular space marks the point of rupture between the dominant, flat, visual plane of the portrait and the severe perspective that the shaft of light introduces, drawing the eye toward a vanishing point in a distant penumbra, the perspective itself delineated by the double configuration of receding Doric columns and foreshortened courtiers standing in file. The perspective suggests a compositional superfluity: it serves no clear organizational function in the portrait, for the portrait, like most Elizabethan works of art, does not exhibit what Roy Strong has called the "homogeneous geometric totality" characteristic of works governed by the Albertian laws of perspective; it does not assert the "notion that a picture's surface should encapsulate a given viewpoint at a single moment in time."[16] The perspective does have a thematic function, however, as a citation of a way of ordering experience, of constructing reality, that represents a syncope in the closed circuit of the presumably authorless, denotative iconographic codes dominating the portrait. Norman Bryson's analysis of what he calls the "Albertian regime," instantiated in perspective painting, is apposite here. The Albertian regime "assumes the viewer not simply as an ambient witness . . . but as a physical presence; and in this sense the vanishing point is the anchor of a system which incarnates the viewer, renders him tangible and corporeal." This system yields a "logic of representation which changes the viewer himself into a representation, an object or spectacle before his own vision. In operating the codes of monocular perspective the viewing subject creates a self-definition as this body approaching the image in this space."[17] The "Siena Sieve" portrait, by citing this system, accords it the status of an icon: legitimates its signification. Paradoxically, the painting covertly identifies the viewer/reader as a specific body—and authoring presence—participating in the construction of a work that, by definition, denies that presence.

I will flesh out shortly the implications of this paradox, as a constitutive part of the process of misrecognition that the discourse of conscience infiltrates into the portrait. For the moment, let us consider how the portrait, in the light of the unobtrusively cited perspective, invokes the authoring presence of the viewer/reader and how it thereby cites the contextual arena defined by *conscientia* as the ground of its own premises. The placement of the sieve is a case in point. Occupying an ambiguous threshold space in the foreground of the portrait, and thus marking the point of transition from the represented world of the painted subject to the world of the viewer/ reader, the sieve betrays its double function within the thematics of conscience. It is at once the ceremonial property of the queen and the representation of the viewer/reader's own faculty of discernment; at once the invocation of a corpus of timeless and impersonal iconographic texts, out of which the portrait arises, like Athena from the head of Jove, and the invocation of particularized interpretive contexts that give rise to and perpetuate such texts. It provides at once the proof of the inviolable character of the portrait's message and the

circumstantial evidence suggesting that the proof is in fact constituted within the social formation and not passively received from
some transcendent objective realm.

The sieve itself is anchored to a particular episode in the life of
Elizabeth that is instructive here: the period of her imprisonment on
a charge of treason during the reign of Mary Tudor. "But such was
the innocency of that lady," one account reads, "as she wrote in the
windows of her lodging in the Tower yet to be seen, and in other
places, with a diamond: Many things have been objected against me,
but nothing proved can be. So she gave for her Device a Sieve, for
she had been sifted and fanned with all curious devices, but no chaff
found."[18] The sieve, we should note, entered Elizabeth's personal
iconography as a kind of *défi*, much like the speeches she would compose during the last months of Mary Stuart's imprisonment, a period
when Elizabeth's conscience was again the object of public scrutiny
and judgment. In the sieve, then, we find an allusion to a specific,
politically charged "sifting" process begun outside the perimeter of
authoritative discourse and appropriated by the sovereign, its metacritical impulse arrested, so that retrospectively it might be adduced
as a divinely plotted manifestation of "innocency"; ritualized into the
emblem of a miraculous ordeal, like Tuccia's; assigned the glacial
atemporality of a canonical, iconographic text. The figure of inviolability, the sieve also names itself the figure of the rhetoric of inviolability, redefined in its immediate historical context as a human construct manipulable as much by the social and political body—a body
that includes, of course, the viewer/reader—as by the queen.

Once recognized as the emblem of the very act of discerning the
portrait, the sieve invites the viewer to sift the "good" from the
"bad" readings of the portrait and, further, to discern that such dichotomous cognitive and normative categories themselves are not so
much discovered as produced and defined, according to what the
casuists habitually described as the circumstances of time, place, and
person. The representation of Dido, directly opposite the cited perspective, furnishes the principal occasion for these related interpretive actions. We have already observed how Dido participates in the
iconographic homology that appears to govern the portrait: how she
reiterates, for example, the virtue of chastity associated in the portrait with the inviolability of the royal conscience. In this context it

is hardly even appropriate to speak of the image of the chaste Dido
as contributing to a "good" reading of the portrait, insofar as such a
qualification raises the possibility of producing a competing, "bad"
reading: given the ostensible pre-lapsarian status of the portrait as
an authoritative discourse, all readings, presumably, will be good
ones. Yet, the embedded Tuccia-Dido synapse notwithstanding, the
chaste Dido is patently not the Dido who is portrayed on the pillar.
The medallions specifically cite Virgil's Dido, whose automatic identification with chastity can be maintained only by a considerable
wrenching both of the text and of its subsequent allegorical lacquer,
through which the victim of a ravaging sexual passion took on the
aspect of a temptress, a "mere Circe."[19] This Dido represents, at best,
chastity compromised, not to say consumed; she represents an un-
anticipated lapsus in the corpus of absolute, doxal texts to which the
chaste Dido refers, a lapsus that redefines the absolute as a function
of historicity, of context, of the weight of alterable circumstances.
(Virgil's Dido herself, preparing her funeral pyre, laments the "interruption" of Aeneas in what would otherwise have remained the
serene, unchanging, and unchallenged story of the faithful widow
of Sychaeus.)[20] This Dido introduces, in short, the possibility of a
"bad" reading, or rather—given the plenitude of meaning to which
the portrait, viewed as a canonical text, lays claim—the possibility of
what will likely be an unintelligible, an impertinent, one.

The profile of such a reading emerges when one locates the portrait in its historical context. Dated around 1580, the portrait coincides with the period of Elizabeth's controversial courtship by the
Duke d'Alençon. The prospect of the "French Marriage" presaged,
to English Protestants, a dangerous union with the house of Guise,
which, it was believed, would usher in a reign of political intrigue,
aggravate the problem of the succession, and bring the realm once
again under the yoke of popery. In short, the prospect of Elizabeth's
succumbing to Alençon's charms (he was reputed to be "a most
choice courtier, exquisitely skilled in love toys, pleasant conceits and
court dalliances") spelled both a private and a public disaster for the
queen.[21] It also prompted open criticism of the queen, notably in
the publication of John Stubbs's *Gaping Gulf* (1579). Responding to
the perceived crisis, Stubbs abandoned the fiction of the inviolable
sovereign and dispensed, instead, brutally frank admonitions to a

woman of 46 about to lose her head over "the old serpent himself in the form of a man," who had "come a second time to seduce the English Eve and to ruin the English paradise."[22]

The well-known fate of the book and its author does not need to be rehearsed. What bears noting, in consideration of Elizabeth's swift retaliation, is the evident incompatibility of Stubbs's rhetoric and the rhetoric of sovereign power. In Stubbs's discourse, despite his honorable intentions (indeed, partly because of them), there was the scent of an implicit demythologizing of the mythos of author- lessness upon which Gloriana's indisputable authority rested. That the queen-as-icon could be shelved at the discretion of the con- science of an avowedly loyal subject intimated the power of the queen's subjects to author—to produce, maintain, and modulate ac- cording to circumstances—the battery of doxal texts subtending both Crown and commonwealth. The intimation was suppressed in the case of the *Gaping Gulf*, the author discredited as a criminal and the texts burnt. But it emerged in the "Siena Sieve" portrait, local- ized in the visual reference to the queen of Carthage, who had made a bad marriage with the Trojan hero and had paid for it—as would the queen of England should she commit herself to an unpopular foreign marriage. Like Ovid's Dido in the *Metamorphoses*—"herself betrayed, she then betrayed her life, her home, her country"— Elizabeth, too, might precipitate the undoing of her claim to invio- lable power.

Through the ambiguous figure of Dido, the portrait thus memo- rializes a recent crisis and insinuates a message to be reconstituted in future ones. Dido speaks to Elizabeth: showing her how she will be read by her subjects if she chooses a bad match; showing her, fur- ther, how the absolute principle of her sovereignty may be remolded or even dismantled if in the exercise of power she makes what the weight of consensus deems a bad choice. Dido speaks as well to the viewer/reader of the portrait, who must choose, in interpreting the Carthaginian queen, whether to observe the paradigmatic homology of the icons, which sustains the work as a canonical portrait, or to observe the syntagmatic coherence of the narrative constituted by the medallions, which implicates the work as an anti-portrait.

Neither choice will eclipse its alternative, since Dido herself oc- cupies the juncture of the two opposing contexts. The portrait defines Dido, in effect, as the insoluble figure of choice, the locus of contingency in which the fixed boundary between objectively "good" and "bad" readings breaks down. Dido's own post-Virgilian textual history provides ample precedents. Literally, this history consisted of attempts to eradicate (with one striking exception) Virgil's representation of Dido; to restore, as it were, her original luster. What these attempts produced was a third Dido, whose identity resides in the very process of forging a Dido from the not-Dido.

In *The Triumph of Chastity* it is not enough that Dido be praised as the chaste widow of Sychaeus. Petrarch insists that his heroine not be confused with the lover of Aeneas; and, to emphasize the point, he brings her into the pageant not once but twice. At her first entrance, with Juno, she is immediately renamed:

> Not that Dydo that men doth wryte,
> That for Eneas wyth death was dyte,
> But that noble Lady true and juste
> for Sychen her joye and hartes luste.

When she reappears following Tuccia, Petrarch repeats the message. The woman he sees is the one

> That for hyr husbande was content to dye—
> And not for Eneas, so affyrme I.
> (Let the vulgar people then holde theyr peace!)
> It is that Dydo that I do here rehearse,
> That honest love broughte unto an ende,
> And not vayne wanton love that dyd her offende.[23]

The point, it would seem, cannot be made too often; Petrarch's own description of the unwanted Dido helps explain why. That Virgil's name should not appear as the contaminating agent indicates more than deference to the author whom Dante called the "glory and light of other poets" (*Inferno* I.82). It indicates that the contaminating agent can no longer be defined or contained. It is now "men" in general who give credence to the account of Dido that Petrarch disavows; it is the "vulgar people" who have swallowed what "men" have written. Virgil's account has passed into the realm of "what everybody knows" about Dido. Accordingly, Petrarch's account is in danger of being taken as a misreading, even of being unintelligible, unless it undertakes to establish its veracity by repeatedly showing how what has passed as the indelible imprint of truth can be traced to the slow, silent incrustation of consensual opinion.

This project, of course, begs the question of its own objective, authorless status, Petrarch's affirming "I" arbitrarily defining itself as an impersonal witness to a primordial, atextual Dido, a Dido whose represented truth appears exempt from the bias of subjectivity and context. A similar crux arises in two earlier, not unknown, representations of Dido. A poem by Ausonius "on her picture" (included in Sandys's commentary on the *Metamorphoses*) passes for an epitaph composed by the defunct queen herself. She protests:

> I Dido was . . . not of suche a minde
> As Maro feigned, to furious lust inclin'd:
> Me Troys Aeneas never saw; . . .
> But flying outrage and Iarbas; I
> By death secur'd my spotlesse chastity.
> This thrust the sword through my undaunted brest:
> not rage, nor injur'd love, with griefe opprest.[24]

Telling her own story, Dido cannot merely announce her "spotlesse chastity"; she must supplant Virgil's account, her presumably unmediated, autobiographical voice tacitly discrediting Virgil's. (The message: who, indeed, but Dido can speak for Dido, reveal the truth of her conscience?) Dido tells her own story again, but from a different perspective, in Ovid's *Heroides*. At the end of her epistle to Aeneas, she addresses Anna (and, through Anna, posterity), composing her epitaph and delivering it in a brief speech filled with the magisterial power of a dying person's last words:

Anna my sister, my sister Anna, wretched sharer in the knowledge of my fault, soon shall you give to my ashes the last boon. Nor when I have been consumed upon the pyre, shall my inscription read: Elissa, Wife of Sychaeus; let this brief epitaph be read on the marble of my tomb: FROM AENEAS CAME THE CAUSE OF HER DEATH, AND FROM HIM THE BLADE; FROM THE HAND OF DIDO HERSELF CAME THE STROKE BY WHICH SHE FELL.[25]

Even more baldly than Petrarch's pageant, which will not claim to enjoy such direct access to Dido's own words, each epitaph presents itself as the authorial, authoritative account of the Carthaginian queen. That the two accounts, coincident in their autobiographical frame, should memorialize diametrically opposed truths merely underscores the crux latent in the words Dido herself speaks (as it will be found in Petrarch's words): how is it that the authoritative discourses accruing around the figure of Dido can absolve themselves from the critical interrogation they enjoin their readers to perform on all discourses claiming such status? Indeed, the words voicing their own authority, defining the space of an originary "I," simultaneously voice the motive of authority, the need to create the image of such a space in human discourse. The legitimating, autobiographical, apparatus of Dido's "I" implicates itself, finally, as just that: an apparatus, a ventriloquizing machine whose own source of sound is an echo of an echo, unable to distinguish itself absolutely from the potentially indeterminate series of its textual simulacra.

The Dido in the "Siena Sieve" echoes this message. She, too, will always be caught up in the suspicion of the encroaching not-Dido, the truth of her chastity measured by the truth of her sexual passion. Conjoined, both readings evoke the influx of a relativizing context, a context that belies the claim of either reading to being the last, the unassailable, word on the subject of Dido and of her function in the portrait. Indeed, her "true" significance does not descend *toute faite* from some iconographic pantheon, the house of received knowledge, since the substance of her message is to let slip what such knowledge, with its attending self-evident status, conceals behind a blind spot: the evidence of its being not merely received but first constituted and shored up by consensual arrangement. Through Dido, who articulates this ongoing process of constructing, choosing, and legitimating the absolute, the principle of absolute difference yields the truth of its own arbitrariness.

Even to follow the narrative of Dido's story as it is distributed on the pillar is to encounter an analogous metacritical cue. The medallions are intelligible only if they are read in a sequence that moves "from right to left up the pillar."[26] In other words, they are backwards, in the wrong order, and must be mentally redistributed so as to conform to the correct, the normative, order, the one that reigns in Western scribal and painterly composition: downward from left to right. The apparent anomaly encourages the viewer/reader to take

cognizance—to "have conscience"—of the fact that the "right" order is merely the conventional one, the product of a tradition that
the viewer/reader, no doubt unthinkingly, has been helping legitimate, as she or he has been doing with regard to other truths believed to be ordained by divine fiat.

Through Dido, the sieve, and the cited perspective, the portrait
implies the arbitrary and contingent nature of its own parthenogenetic system, identifying the viewer/reader synecdochically as the authoring presence behind the book of norms in which Gloriana's inviolable sovereignty is written. Yet—and this is the final curve in its
deconstructive operation—the portrait, Cassandra-like, also indicates why such an announcement will be, if not disbelieved, forgotten or suppressed. It indicates why, for example, the figure of Dido
will be either unintelligible (the implications of her "wanton love"
banished from the portrait as an incongruity or an indiscretion, leaving a figure who is merely part of the furniture of Aeneas's story, a
figure to be valued, at best, as the anti-type of Elizabeth) or banal
(Dido's chastity, integrated into the iconographic homology of the
portrait, placidly corroborating the inviolability of Gloriana's conscience and power).

To read this message we must return to the perspective drawn in
the upper right corner of the portrait. We must repeat, in effect, the
very movement of the viewer/reader's eye, which is repeatedly drawn
from the iconographically rich center of the portrait toward a decen-
tered vanishing point   a vanishing point that, in fact, lies outside
the frame. The authoring presence that the vanishing point in the
perspectival system invokes is withheld, made absent. In other
words, the viewer/reader's complicity in the construction of the
world represented in the portrait cannot be recognized without a
price: exclusion from that world. By no coincidence, the cited perspective is filled with doubles of the viewer/reader: with courtiers
waiting on the sovereign, with members of the body politic whose
access to power, whose anticipated visibility in the monarch's gaze,
is contingent on their misrecognition of the contingency of the
norms upholding the discourse of power from which they have everything to gain. In the courtiers, the figure of the cultural poesis
behind the queen's sovereignty collapses into the figure of the cultural aphasia that is required if the objective identity of the cognitive

and normative systems generated by such poesis is to pass muster. In the courtiers—the aphasiac, amnesiac authors of this objectivity—Dido's chastity and Elizabeth's inviolable conscience are at once chosen and received as truths for which the problematics of choice are suspended. So, too, the physical trajectory of the viewer/reader's eye, returning from the indistinct periphery of the portrait to the luminous center, reenacts this process of misrecognition. As if by default, in the interval before the cited perspective once again exerts its gravitational pull, the monarch's impersonal gaze establishes its mandate as the miraculous center, the official conscience, of the portrait and of the world.

From this standpoint the "Siena Sieve" portrait "works" as a portrait: it substantiates the canon. But it also works, in the totality of its composition, as a meta-portrait, inviting the viewer/reader to discern how canonical texts are constituted: how, notably, they participate in the conspiracy of silence, in which monarch and subjects alike are engaged, enshrouding the arbitrariness of the absolute. The "Siena Sieve" portrait thus gives textual substance to the kind of *aporia* that the discourse of conscience engenders through the insistently self-muting voice of *conscientia*, which at once says and un-says what it knows will be unintelligible: the truth of the field of contingency that belies the immutability, authorlessness, and determinate boundaries implicitly claimed by all truths. In other words, to read the "Siena Sieve" portrait is to enter the vertiginous discursive space defined by what the casuists knew as the movement of the lax conscience, a space harboring the notorious practice, observed elsewhere in this study, of mental reservation. In this space, imperceptibly, the absolute difference between a portrait and its parody, as between truth and feigned truth, collapses: this is the forbidden fruit of the act of discerning in the discourse of conscience.

"Tempering by just proportions good venims from evill": The Secret Pharmacy of Equity in Spenser's Narrative

Book 5 of *The Faerie Queene*, the "Legend of Artegall or of Iustice," constitutes a verbal equivalent of the "Siena Sieve" portrait, marking the poem's entry into the discourse of conscience. Early in canto 1, the narrator invokes this discourse in his account of how the goddess Astraea nurtures the young Artegall, instructing him in the "discipline of iustice." The discipline, as it turns out, involves the same kind of heuristic practice that casuists (as well as their secular counterparts, the jurists, in Tudor courts of chancery) employed in resolving the problems of moral choice in cases of conscience. Artegall learns "to weigh both right and wrong / In equall ballance with due recompence, / And equitie to measure out along, / According to the line of conscience" (5.1.7).[1] These words may be taken as a statement not only of the mission Astraea imparts to Artegall but of the official interpretive project of the book as well, which is to present a canonical record of the timeless, irreducible truths and normative patterns of justice and order embodied in the actions of Artegall and his peers, Arthur, Britomart, and Mercilla. This record represents a narrative rendering, as it were, of the "line of conscience," with "conscience" understood in the sense dictated by *synteresis*—as the repository of divinely ordained, universally held, and therefore objective moral precepts, to be identified in the poem, pre-eminently, with Gloriana's "great iustice praysed ouer all," of which Artegall is the principal "instrument" (5.proem.11).

Of course, the sense of the word "conscience," as I have noted elsewhere, was double.[2] "Conscience," understood in this double

sense, both referred to a corpus of inviolable norms and provided a
self-reflexive conceptual frame capable of yielding an image of conscience as something more than a repository or guardian of such a
corpus: as a participating agent in the unobtrusive discursive operations through which a particular culture constitutes its norms and
enforces their objective status. As in the "Siena Sieve" portrait, it is
this double sense of the word that serves as the organizing principle
of book 5. It is this double sense of the word that gives the book its
metacritical edge, so that the apparent anomalies or incongruities
that punctuate the narrative emerge as a functional element of the
book's message, assigning to the legend of justice an equivocal perspective on its ethical and literary premises. Thus the legend, maintaining the Sidnaean profile of the epic poem, "teacheth and moveth
to the most high and excellent truth," notably the truth of Gloriana's
inviolable, quasi-divine system of justice.[3] At the same time the legend qualifies both that truth and the epic structure that claims to
instantiate it, showing their limits and their ideological underpinning as well as the social and political economy that makes misrecognition of such knowledge necessary. This dual enterprise informs the
three episodes that I want to examine in book 5: Britomart's passage
through Isis Church, Artegall's return to Faerie Court after beginning the reformation of Irena's "ragged common-weale" (5.12.26),
and the trial and judgment of Duessa in Mercilla's court. These episodes are at once central to the book's official purpose and yet shot
through with anomalies to which Spenser's narrator—whom I take
as the official model of the good scribe and the good reader of Gloriana's "great iustice praysed ouer all" (in other words, as the textual
equivalent of the courtiers in the "Siena Sieve" portrait)—fails to
attach significance.[4] The discrepancies I call attention to between the
narrator's statements and the implications of the narrative action and
structure will illustrate how the narrator comes into focus in the text.
As I see it, the distinction between the author and narrator in book
5 is not arbitrary but is, rather, a measure of Spenser's involvement
in the politics of the discourse of conscience. The very word "conscience," let us recall, was a dialogized construction between a privileged, authoritative discourse (*synteresis*) and a host of subordinated,
not to say suppressed, discourses (*conscientia*), discourses that contextualized what *synteresis* held up as indisputable, pointing up the

social and political mechanisms behind *synteresis* through the very tensions and conflicting circumstances they insinuated into the word "conscience." Spenser establishes his narrator as the embodiment of *synteresis*, a voice that presents itself as the virtually unmediated channel of the "divine" discourse of equity (the "righteous doome") that the "Dread Souerayne Goddesse" speaks (5.proem.11). But *conscientia* speaks its demythologizing discourse on the claims of *synteresis* through the discrepancies and gaps that punctuate the narrative and that represent the necessarily fragmented and opaque character of discourses that have been marginalized. The design of the narrative, as my reading shows, is informed primarily by the action of *conscientia*, which subsumes *synteresis* and thus inverts the traditional hierarchical arrangement of the two parts of conscience. In other words, in book 5 Spenser is imagining the emergence of a discourse capable of legitimizing the perspectives that, under the parallel regimes of *synteresis* and Gloriana's "divine" discourse, will be read as scandalous.

Spenser also seems to suggest that the relationship between the intentions of the author and the author's product, the written text, is to be understood in terms of *conscientia* as well—not, that is, as fixed and transparent but as indeterminate, changeable, fragmentary, subject to the bias that the reader or the particular context of reading can introduce into the text. In this regard, Spenser's legend of justice can be read as an elaborate trope of Elizabeth's medusan rhetoric of conscience. It can be read as an "authorless" text, on two counts: superficially, through the narrator's self-identification with the voice of "Iustice" and "simple Truth," a gesture that gives logical priority to the tale over the teller, who simply reports "what is"; and, more problematically, through the text's silent undermining of the narrator's status and its implicit references to an authorial presence and project, beyond the narrator's, that remain indistinct, hard to pin down. But, as we shall see, the legend does not trope the medusan rhetoric uncritically. Employing a fuller register of contextual details than Elizabeth could afford to admit into her speeches, it relocates the source of the petrifying effect of conscience in the social body rather than in the "bottomless graces" divinely bestowed on the monarch.

An Excursus into the Problem of Equity

The episodes I want to examine illustrate the demythologizing effect of the relationship between narrator and author on the subject of Gloriana's "great iustice," which the narrator professes to represent without equivocation. They also invoke the most frequently cited index in the book to the discourse that informs the subject of Gloriana's "great iustice": not "conscience" itself but a related term, "equity," which was popularly known as the "intent of the law" and as "a ruled kind of justice . . . allayed with the sweetness of mercy."⁵ Each of the heroic figures in the three episodes appears as a personification of this principle: Mercilla, whose "Dealing of Iustice" (5.9.36) furnishes "Royall examples of her mercies rare" (5.10.5); Britomart, whose passage through Isis Church establishes her association with "That part of Iustice, which is Equity" (5.7.3); and Artegall, whom Guyon explicitly identifies as "our iudge of equity" (5.3.36) and whose entire career as a justiciar measuring out equity "According to the line of conscience" implies a certain convergence of equity and conscience.

Indeed, the two terms did converge in Tudor legal discourse. Because of the prominence Spenser gives the concept of "equity" in book 5, particularly at the junctures I have singled out, let us pause to investigate some of the pivotal passages from this discourse, passages that indicate how equity picked up and amplified the destabilizing potential of the discourse of conscience.⁶ To begin with, the terms "equity" and "conscience" shared a precise physical locus in the maze of the Tudor law courts. William West, author of the *Symboleography*, a well-known legal treatise, was merely repeating a commonplace for his readers when he noted, in the 1594 edition of the work, that equity was the "court of conscience, which with us is called the Chancery," Chancery of course referring to the court system that was associated in English medieval jurisprudence with the discretionary juridicial power of the monarch and that during the sixteenth century came to provide, as a court of appeals, a "channel through which the plaintiff might hope for a greater measure of moral justice than that which the regular law courts [i.e., common law] afforded."⁷ Thus we find it noted in a 1589 case involving the Earl of Oxford that the function of Chancery, the court of judicial equity, was to act, in effect, as the "conscience" of the common law courts. Specifically, the office of the chancellor was "to correct men's consciences for frauds, breaches of trust, wrongs, and oppressions, of what nature they be, and to soften and mollify the extremity of the law, which is Summum Jus" (and which, as West put it, "oftentimes precisely regardeth the very letter and words of the Common Lawes").[8]

All of this seems laudable rather than subversive; yet, as with conscience, equity played an ambiguous role in the discourse of power. Simply put, the action of equity in relation to the law virtually replicated that of *conscientia* in relation to *synteresis*, a parallel that, as we shall see, apologists of equity had good reason to de-emphasize. Let us look first to West's matter-of-fact discussion of the proper business of equity, in which we can observe the parallel obliquely. The "matter whereabout this Equity must occupy and busie her selfe," West wrote, was "the affaires of men, infinite as they fall out," so that, necessarily, equity promoted "a mitigation, or moderation of the law written, in some circumstance, either of the things themselves, of the persons, or of the times."[9] Equity, then, had something of the maverick about it, an inherent deregulatory aspect. (As John Selden wryly observed in his *Table Talk*, equity was "a Roguish thing.")[10]

To be sure, the deregulatory aspect of equity was itself mitigated by the insistence, among apologists of the principle, that only a positive law might be altered by the action of equity, since only such a law—that is, one recognized as a mutable, human artifact—might be said to be "defective in some part, by reason of the generality of it."[11] This was the kind of law that Christopher St. German referred to in *Doctor and Student* (1530), his seminal book on the role of conscience and equity in common law, when he observed that "Laws couet to be rewlyd by equytye."[12] Indeed, for St. German the virtue of equity depended on the assumption that its scope, by definition, did not extend to the corpus of divine and natural laws, of which equity was held to be the uncritical sentinel. Thus, in his definition of equity, St. German could insist that the principle was "no other thynge but an excepcyon of the lawe of god / or of the law of reason / from the generall rewles of the lawe of man" and that the action of equity "taketh not away the very ryght / but only that that (semeyth to be ryght by the generall wordes of the lawe)."[13]

In this, historians of English law tell us, St. German was both following and improving on Aristotle.[14] In the *Ethics*, Aristotle had sought to establish the jurisdictional limits of equity by insisting that the principle was not "generically different" from justice, a point that turned on the ambiguity of the word "justice."[15] Equity was indeed "in some circumstances better than justice" but it was "not better than absolute justice." In other words, equity might be invoked as an intervening agent only insofar as the justice in question was that "of the law courts"—justice as codified in positive laws, which, by taking "no account of particular cases," were susceptible to "the possibility of error." "Absolute justice," on the other hand, was immutable and inviolable—and, in Aristotle's formulation, coextensive with equity.

It was also left at a level of abstraction that provided a very imprecise index of the perimeter it was presumed to designate. In St. German's formulation, the "absolute justice" dictating the action of equity took on a more precise character, referring to the corpus of laws—the "lawe of god" and the "lawe of reason" (i.e., natural law)—that informed conscience itself. Or, rather, *synteresis*: the double sense of conscience was not lost on St. German, but it was *synteresis* alone, the "naturall power or motive of the rational soul . . . mouynge and sterrynge it to good and abhorrynge euyll," that he indicated as the *primum mobile* of equity, of which it might therefore be observed, as of *synteresis*, that it "neuer synneth nor erryth." St. German's linkage, which located and defined the "governing moral principle" of equity in *synteresis*, furnished precisely the kind of *pièce justificative* that St. German needed for his immediate project, to adduce the shared intrinsic rightness and ultimate compatibility of equity and common law.[16] But the linkage also evinced the kind of internal paradox that discussions of equity, beginning with Aristotle's, seemed to engage.

The Aristotelian imprimatur relied on the introduction of a circular argument according to which the touchstone of equity—"absolute justice"—was itself an arbitrary, self-legitimating figure. The incorporation of the term "conscience" in St. German's treatise was no less problematic, insofar as his manipulation of the term could not be sustained without contradiction. In the interest of securing his argument to a fund of presumably unassailable premises, he was obliged to ignore the evident connection between equity and *conscientia* that his own definition pointed to, notably in the admission, which opened his discussion of the principle, that the function of equity was to consider "all the pertyculer cyrcumstaunces of the dede" or case in question.

A seemingly innocuous statement, certainly a conventional one (Aristotle had said as much), but one that could not, finally, be reconciled with the tenor of St. German's argument. First of all, the statement acknowledged that equity, like *conscientia*, was a discrete act rather than, like *synteresis*, a "universall prynciple that neuer erryth." As such, equity was capable of error—like *conscientia*, which, being "concerned with particulars," as St. German observed, "may or may not err." But the paradox of equity was not merely that it appeared both capable and incapable of error; the principle itself was equipped, by definition, to observe the arbitrariness of the terms of its own definition, including the implicit jurisdictional boundary cordoning off its deregulatory action from the corpus of absolute laws it was supposed to enforce. In other words, the disposition to examine, presumably without restriction, all the circumstances of a case lent to equity (as it did to *conscientia*) a power of critical interrogation that ultimately acquired a self-reflexive cast, so that the very ground rules of equity—the self-evident premises, whether known as "absolute justice" or as *synteresis*, that were believed to dictate, infallibly, the profile of objective truth and error—might themselves be perceived as subjectively constituted, shaped by the interests and needs of human society. It was, of course, in the immediate interest of the apologists of equity precisely not to articulate or pursue the implications of such knowledge. Again, a paradox: the very appeal to equity generally indicated a desire to invoke a system of final arbitration and a corresponding atemporal, objective reality rather than pursue the kind of interpretive action that equity itself pointed to, according to which the particular circumstances that established the need to produce such fixed categories within a society might be recognized.

Theoretically, then, equity defined an interpretive procedure that enabled one to dereify social reality—to take cognizance of the collective human agency installing and legitimating objective patterns of order.[17] Practically, it was more likely that the mere employment of the procedure would itself constitute a preemptive circumstance, a blind spot cut to the dimensions of the truths supplying one's own motive for employing the procedure. Equity thus participated in the expression of a power that we have observed in the discourse of conscience, a power that could be both destabilizing and self-censoring: Medusa-like, as the rhetoric of Elizabeth's royal presence and her Parliamentary speeches indicated.

Not surprisingly, it is the remarks of those who would put the principle itself on trial that immediately betray signs of the dereifying potential of equity, though, to be sure, the signs are announced as evidence serving another, to us a more limited, purpose: to decry the contaminating, hubristic potential of equity. For Richard Eedes, who delivered a sermon "of the difference of Good and Evill" to Elizabeth in the Lenten season of 1596 (the same year that Spenser's poetic treatment of equity and conscience appeared), it was inconceivable to doubt whether good and evil were absolute, divinely ordered moral categories.[18] Yet his allusions to the dubious action of equity and the lax conscience—cautionary words adumbrating those of Bourdaloue in the court of Louis XIV—suggested the kind of discourse in which the inconceivable might be articulated. Thus he insisted, on the one hand, that "the generall rules of good and evil" were palpably clear, discernible by "the conscience of good and evil," which was the "incorrupt both witnesse and judge of all our actions." He acknowledged, on the other hand, that conscience had another, a problematic, face, from which the idea of an incorruptible witness and judge might be seen to emerge as a function of context, so that the very need for such an idea might be seen to engender the idea and, completing the circuit, efface its human authorship. Eedes himself, participating in the act of effacement, gave the derogatory name "opinion" to this face of conscience. Opinion, because of the "wantonnesse of this disputing age," engendered not the "incorruptible" truth but a "desperate madnesse" that in fact illustrated the metacritical action of the discourse of conscience, a madness "that presumeth to call the grounds of truth in question."[19] Eedes amplified the alarm when he broached the subject of equity, taking the time-honored Aristotelian metaphor of the Lesbian rule and bending it to his own purpose:

It were beyond all credit, if it did not offer itself to all eyes, how many sleights this witlesse wittie, and learnedly unlearned age hath devised to make the rules of good and evill like that leaden rule of Lesbia, pliable to purposes, and to serve turnes: how many pleas iniustice hath found out to iustifie it selfe out of iust lawes; how many shadowes ungodlinesse to shroud it selfe under the law of God.[20]

Eedes's revisionist rendering of the metaphor represented, of course, an attempt to expose and thereby to contain the perceived sophistry of equity.[21] But the attempt accomplished perhaps more than Eedes intended. By discrediting the privileged position of equity as the unmediated and unbiased channel of "absolute justice"—by presenting that position as a mere rhetorical device or "sleight" that masked the particular bias of the agents administering equity—Eedes problematized his own discourse as well as the corpus of truths to which it referred. His discourse implicitly supplanted that of equity; in so doing it occupied the same discursive space and left itself open to the same kind of critical interrogation it had directed at equity, thus producing the same prospect of self-reflexivity that equity and the discourse of conscience harbored. Eedes could not sustain his argument without passing in silence over the paradoxical position it led him to: that of claiming for his own discourse the very status he had decried as a pose.

Unlike Eedes, William West was a perfectly uncritical exponent of equity, reproducing passages verbatim from the standard sources (notably Aristotle and St. German) in the *Symboleography*. Yet even this text, as we have seen, betrayed signs that equity, like the discourse of conscience, might represent something of a Pandora's box smuggled into the pantheon of absolute truths. Consider, then, his cursory description of "the materiall cause of Equity" as "the Law of Nature, the Law of Nations, and good manners."[22] On the one hand, the description evoked an image of cosmological plenitude: equity was the lens through which the structure of order underlying the universe might be perceived; concomitantly, if we consider the syntactical arrangement of West's "mixture," equity was also a kind of Jacob's ladder, evoking a vaguely Platonic system of correspondences that descended from the realm of the absolute, authored by God (i.e., by no human agent) to that of the conventional and the contingent, authored by the human community. On the other hand, the description tacitly challenged the assumption upholding such a system: the assumption that the absolute and the conventional were discontinuous, qualitatively different categories, however much the two categories might intersect in a single discourse (as in the case of the cited *ius gentium* or "Law of Nations").[23] To West, let us recall, equity was the product of a "mixture." As such, it signified a discursive site where the distinguishing marks of intersecting components dissolved: where the subjective human agency and the ethos of contingency that shaped the discourse of "good manners" might be construed as constitutive parts of the objective and immutable configuration of the "Law of Nature."

West had at hand another metaphor for equity, one that conveys even more tellingly the implications of the "mixture" to which he referred. Equity was

an Apothecaries shop stored with all kind of drugs, fit for all the maladies & diseases of men. Which notwithstanding, in case they should be unskilfully compounded together, would in stead of healing, work present death to the patient that should receive them: for it requireth the industry and exquisite art of a good Physitian, to make a right composition, discerning and tempering by just proportions good venims from evill.[24]

The appearance of the *pharmakon* in West's treatise underscores the correspondence that emerges at certain points between the irreducible ambiguity of equity and, according to the Derridean prescription, the ambiguity informing the *pharmakon* of writing itself. Jacques Derrida's well-known reading of the *pharmakon* does not need rehearsing in detail here; let us recall, briefly, that the *pharmakon* in Plato has the ambiguous property of being both a remedy and a poison, an instrument that at once differentiates speech from writing and subverts the possibility of such differentiation.[25]

It is no wonder that the *pharmakon* should infiltrate the dossier on equity (or vice versa), for the two exist in virtually the same relation to the logocentric scheme of the universe. To begin with, the relation of equity to the law is equivocal. One theory advances equity as a supplement to the law (hence the axiom "equity follows the law"); another advances it as a source of the law.[26] (As we shall see, Spenser exploits this ambiguity in book 5 of *The Faerie Queene*.) In either case, its credentials lie in its apparent power to embody the unchanging ideal of "absolute justice," though, paradoxically, it also embodies an opposing principle of alterity, since its operation cannot be made to fit into an absolute, unchanging profile—as its governing image of the Lesbian rule suggests. Another paradox: designated as the inexhaustible process that fills in the gap left by the generality of the law, equity itself admits only the most general and abstract of paraphrases to serve as its definition. Indeed, one might say that equity can never be adequately coded in language, that it cannot be precisely written down—which is another way of saying that equity (like the *logos*) is fundamentally different from writing. Yet it performs the very movement of writing through the act of instantiating, and therefore replicating or repeating, "absolute justice," an act that gives rise to the very ambiguity it claims to dispatch, since it betrays the imperceptible drift between tautology, which participates in the mythos of an unmediated discourse of truth, and surrogation, which falls under the demythologizing sign of dissimulation, producing varieties of mediated, "contaminated," discourse: good mimesis and bad mimesis; good deceit and bad deceit. Thus we find equity's unobtrusive, *pharmakon*-like operation infiltrating West's discourse: the standard virtue of equity (and, of course, of the discourse of conscience in general)—the power to discern good from evil—turns up as a power of a different order, that of "discerning and tempering . . . good venims from evil." The absolute opposition of good and evil has been supplanted by the relative and unstable distribution of different kinds of venoms, of poisons. Only the "exquisite art of a good Physitian" will produce the difference between good and evil, a difference not absolute but contingent on the physician's skill in determining what constitutes a "right composition" in view of the circumstances of the medical case addressed. The pivotal role of the mediating physician in West's description reiterates the dereifying potential of equity and the discourse of conscience: their shared capacity to reconstitute the traces of a human, subjective authorship in what is generally accepted as the authorless, objective order of things.

To be sure, the art of the physician may be redefined as that of a mere charlatan—as a false semblance of the physician's true art—and thus discredited; that is, the metacritical act of reconstitution may infold, turn in on itself, registering the needs and self-imposed restraints of that human authorship to misrecognize its own pivotal role in the construction of the cultural ground rules that must seem to have written themselves, or to have been passively received, as eternal verities. What emerges, then, from the *pharmakon* of equity and of the discourse of conscience is a perspective that resists neat categorization: a misrecognition that both is and is not cognizant of its own operation. The "Siena Sieve" portrait, as we have seen, furnishes a pictorial example of this phenomenon, articulated around the ambiguous icon of the sieve. Let us now return to the "Legend of Artegall or of Iustice," which points to the same phenomenon, this time articulated around the various representations of equity that punctuate the narrative and that implicate the discourse of conscience as an organizing principle of the work.

Profaning Isis Church: Equity and the Contingencies of Time, Place, and Person

The most sustained discussions of equity appear at the beginning of canto 7 and canto 10: first in the description of Isis Church, the temple of equity, and later in the narrator's philosophical argument, patterned after Aristotle, on the relationship of equity and justice. Despite their initial positions in each respective canto, both discussions, we might note, represent ruptures in the narrative scheme. The Isis Church passage comes as an interruption in the narrator's account of Britomart's quest to rescue Artegall from Radigund; so, too, the narrator's subsequent inquiry into the ontological status of "Mercie" intrudes into the account of Duessa's trial, arresting the momentum of the scene just as Mercilla is about to deliver her judgment. To be sure, interruptions and displacements are not uncommon fare among the narrative procedures of the romance/epic tradition out of which Spenser wrote. But they acquire particular force in the context of book 5, whose episodic structure echoes the official—the heuristic and the teleological—motives of the discourse of conscience.

With few exceptions, the cantos follow the structural paradigm represented in the first canto by Artegall's Solomon-like judgment of the suit that Sir Sanglier and the Squire bring to him, each disavowing responsibility for the fate of the lady whom Artegall finds beheaded at the Squire's side, "In her owne blood all wallow'd woefully," and each claiming possession of the surviving lady, who has been carried off by Sir Sanglier. This is merely the first of several stylized representations of a case of conscience: the predication of competing claims to what is just or true and the ensuing resolution by an authoritative voice, whose "doome" is accepted universally (by the represented participants as by the narrator) and given the cachet of finality by virtue of its coincidence, generally, with the close of the canto.[27]

The Isis Church and Mercilla passages are instructive precisely in the way they complicate this paradigm. While repeating the heuristic and the teleological motives of the discourse of conscience evoked in the paradigm, they also provide a frame for the critical interrogation of such motives, describing in the name of equity a pattern that, writ large, will give the book as a whole its equivocal relationship to its stated theme. While invoking equity as a principle presumed to represent the ethical and conceptual center of gravity of the book and of the social reality that the book represents, both passages enact the deregulatory and ultimately metacritical aspect of the principle. Both suspend closure and, in so doing, introduce a supplementary space into what would appear otherwise as an unbroken narrative. Occupying this space, both passages momentarily lift the dispensation of a battery of cognate values on which the narrative is predicated: the expectation of closure itself, as well as the self-evident character of its teleological ethos and of the related principle of absolute difference, which assures the intrinsic discreteness of things (as the sieve in Elizabeth's portrait implies)—at least of things pertaining to the realm of moral theology, like good and evil, truth and falsehood, justice and injustice.[28] Both passages, echoing the thematics of choice we observed in the figure of Dido, invite the reader to consider the implications for a text (as for the world it represents) in which these values are not automatically assumed as prior givens.

To put this phenomenon in terms of the casuistical model of interpretation that informs the text, both passages may be said to exemplify the narrative's recurrent exploitation of the insight that *conscientia* yields. Reading these passages involves a practice analogous to the interpretive action of Anthony Tyrrell's fellow prisoners: paying attention to the indeterminacies and contingencies of context—to the way the circumstances of person, place, and time (the explicit determinants of cases of conscience) problematically inform

Spenser's case-derived narrative and inflect the contours of the narrative context, including the narrative's intertextual dimension. Of the two passages, the narrator's digression near the end of Duessa's trial is perhaps the more transparently problematic, insofar as it occupies a prominent place in an episode already filled with anomalies and incongruities—an episode, indeed, that seems to parade its own inadequacy as a representation of the historical record (the trial and execution of Mary Queen of Scots) and that at the same time implicitly questions the criteria according to which the episode may be said to have "failed" in such an enterprise. I want to defer discussion of this second passage, however, since what I have to say about it will be more pertinent later on, when we take a closer look at the peculiarities of the episode as a whole. For the moment, then, let us return to the first passage, which will give us an idea of how the metacritical bias of the discourse of conscience is signalled by an apparently innocent citation of equity.

The "innocence" of the citation has to do primarily with its disarming effect of attenuating—or of justifying—the breach that has been made in the narrative to accommodate the citation. The narrator's excursus into "That part of Iustice which is Equity" takes the reader, as it does Britomart, into a temple, a circumstance of place that signals the primacy of eternal verities and of an immutable principle of order over the diversity of human opinion and the mutability of time (as of narrative) itself.[29] The symbolic resonance of the temple, then, emphasizes the identification of equity, "absolute justice," and closure. Like the temple that shelters its corporeal image (in the Idol Britomart pays homage to), equity is implicitly defined as a locus where questions will be met with answers, a locus mirrored by a text whose digressive potential will be turned inside out, as it were—made to reveal its proleptic power, anticipating rather than encumbering closure. Thus Britomart's perplexing dream is given an authoritative reading by the "greatest and the gravest" priest of Isis, who tells Britomart the meaning that the "immortall Gods" have embedded in the hallucinatory sequence, which depicts a spiral of violence and sacrilege: the temple, besieged by flames, is saved from devastation by a flame-devouring crocodile who, in an access of pride "of his owne peerelesse powre," threatens to devour the Idol as well but, once subdued by the Idol, possesses her sexually instead, producing "a Lion of great might." The priest's translation, in turn, maps out a network of correspondences—between equity and *ius strictus* (here called "clemence" and "cruell doomes"), the Idol and the crocodile, Isis and Osiris, Britomart and Artegall—to produce a political allegory that forecasts and legitimates the sovereign power, the "just heritage," that will belong to the dynasty founded by Britomart and Artegall (who, it goes without saying, announce Elizabeth's own "just heritage").

There is yet a further correspondence, underscored by the narrator's observation that Britomart has been attentive "unto the end." As though the coordinates of space and time had momentarily collapsed, Britomart's passage through Isis Church—through the lens of equity—has brought her closer to the glorious end that awaits her, the end projected by a divine agency, the end that Britomart, her identity and mission confirmed, now sets out to realize. So, too, the dilation in the narrative, culminating in the hieratic prophesy, appears to confirm the underlying sense of a telos that informs the official project both of equity and of conscience—and of Spenser's narrative itself, which through this episode announces its own glorious end in the court of Gloriana.

The disruptive potential of the Isis Church episode, however, is not simply cancelled out, not simply absorbed into the book's official project, like the flames into the crocodile's "gaping greedy wide" mouth. Rather, the potential remains precisely that· potential, its evidence passed over without comment in the text. Indeed, it is this kind of *reticentia* that indicates how the episode enacts the metacritical bias of equity and conscience, evincing the expected norms or truths while not entirely effacing the evidence of the processes of selection that shape them—evidence, it is implied, that must remain ignored or misrecognized.

Consider, in this light, the narrator's observation, at the end of the episode, that Britomart "much was eased in her troublous thought" at the priest's interpretation of her dream. To be sure, the news she hears is good. The point, though, is that it is good in two ways—not only in the sense that it reinforces Britomart's heroic destiny but also in the sense that it passes as a perfect translation of the dream, a "good" substitute. The hieratic voice conveys the impression of having uttered not only the truth of the dream but all of the truth: no lacunae. It has, literally, the last word on the subject (as all authoritative discourse claims to have). The reader is left, then, to contend with certain disjunctions between the dream and its translation; to observe, in particular, one part of the dream that the priest has nothing to say about and that neither Spenser's "Championesse" nor his narrator has paused to note. One source of the dream's terrifying aspect is the way it plays out, through the image of a temple threatened with desecration by tempest-fanned flames, a cosmic battle between good and evil. The battle loses none of its terror in the priest's reading, where it reveals its immediate, political significance: the temple of Isis-Britomart-Britain's Crown will be assailed by "raging flames," by the injustice and treachery of Britomart's "many foes," the Crown's enemies. What is lost in the translation is the evidence of the dream's subversive action on the very premise that the dream, as well as its official translation, appears to have confirmed. The dream does not sustain the absolute difference between good and evil; rather, it erodes the difference, introducing spatial details that confuse the boundary between inside and outside. The "outragious flames" that "all the Temple put in ieopardy / Of flaming" do not penetrate the temple from the outside; they are "kindled priuily" by the action of the wind on the "holy fire" (in a kind of parodic inspiration) within the temple itself. It is no wonder that this detail does not find its way into the prophesy, for its obvious rendering in the political allegory—as the threat posed by treasonous apostate-spies (a William Parry or an Anthony Tyrrell) near the center of power—would also be obviously inadequate, a transparent distortion of the dream's symbolic language. In the dream, devastation does not arise from a point merely proximate to, yet nonetheless distinct from, the sacred locus; devastation and the sacred locus appear as alternate facets or phases of a single, ambiguous element: fire, whose "good" and "evil" nature is a function of context, of proportion.

Enacting the metacritical property of equity, the principle to which the temple and the "holy fire" itself are dedicated, the dream sequence thus suggests how the potential for dislodging the truths of authoritative discourse from their absolutist standing resides within the very structures presumed to be under the dispensation of the sacred and the canonical. That the sacred locus of the temple

nearly undoes itself in Britomart's dream is an implicit bid to consider the context(s) in which such a locus came into being and acquired the status of an absolute in the first place. This is the kind of
bid Spenser will make repeatedly throughout book 5, which, as a
canonical text in the cult of Gloriana, nearly undoes itself as well.
But, like the temple of Isis, only nearly; and the bids remain implicit.

The lapse in the priest's reading of the dream—his refusal, or failure, to make sense of the "holy fire" that grows "unwares" into "outragious flames"—is apposite here. He cannot afford to make explicit
what the anomalous detail suggests: to do so would be to undermine
the unassailable position claimed by the nexus of ecclesiastical, legal,
and political power that he alludes to in his reading and that his own
discourse, as a hieratic utterance, participates in. Nor can he afford
to smuggle the detail into his reading, *in cognito*, as a passing polemical shot at the "many foes" who have penetrated and contaminated the power structure: to do so, as we noted above, would be to
risk advertising the gap between the language of the dream and that
of its official translation; that is, to risk implicating the translation, if
caught in its subterfuge of glossing over the anomalous detail,
merely as a further contamination of a text that, in any case, is already contaminated from within. The truth of the official translation
would be thus marked with the evidence that the act of representing
the unbiased truth is an act with an inherent, though concealed, bias,
one that the discourse of conscience, unleashed, would be apt to
subject to its contextual machinery: scrutiny according to the circumstances of person, place, and time. The priest, then, to maintain
his privileged role as the channel of the truth of the "immortall
Gods," the truth that endorses the "just heritage" of the mortals
claiming sovereign power, must edit out from the dream whatever
betrays the contingency of such truth. To be sure, this very enterprise
betrays the priest's complicity in the construction of the pantheon of
absolute truths represented by his prophetic utterance and by the
sacred locus in which he resides. But the enterprise is ignored in the
text. Both heroine and narrator accept the priest's authoritative discourse as the unmediated "truth" of the dream; both participate in
the fiction of authorlessness that shores up the objective status of the
truths encoded in such discourse.

The message: progress in the narrative (and upward mobility in the world it represents) depends on the maintenance of such an ethos of misrecognition; that which is impolitic must remain, officially, unintelligible. This message, which we may infer as coming from the operation of the text, derives specifically from the text's problematic inflection of the circumstances of place and person, so that both the sacred locus of the temple and the array of privileged readers who fill its "arched" space may come under suspicion as being clandestinely informed by the angularity, the bias, of historical and political contexts.

The narrative enacts such an economy of disingenuous misreading in the episode that represents a time frame roughly parallel to Britomart's visit to Isis Church: the account of Artegall's physical entrapment by Radigund (canto 5). The action centers, in fact, on an entrapment of a different order: the "subtill nets," the irreducibly equivocal nature, of language itself, which unfold when the social or political context of writing and reading is foregrounded. The exquisitely turned verbal impasses described in this episode demythologize two premises that underwrite the entire narrative—the transparency of speech and the universality of received meaning among interlocutors in an enclosed community. Radigund, Artegall, and Clarinda represent an enclosed community hierarchically arranged (the triumphant Amazon, the disenfranchised hero, the trustworthy servant); a community whose network of communication is—as hierarchical arrangements tend to be—shot through with the accents of frustrated and covert desire. The seventeenth century might well have found in this episode all the elements of a Racinian deadlock; we can find a transgressive rewriting of the dynamic in Elizabethan England between monarch and subjects and of the enabling role that the production of an authoritative discourse performs in that dynamic.

Stock images of love's bondage—Radigund's ambivalent desire to possess Artegall, to bind him metaphorically by literally "unbinding" him, without losing the appearance of her own "happie freedom"; and Artegall's desire to repossess his freedom without giving the appearance of a "cancred will" or "obstinate disdaineful mind"— reconstitute the counterpoint of subtle submission and aggression that informed the relationship between Elizabeth and her subjects in court and Parliament. More pointedly, Radigund and Artegall's mutual discourse of "free entreatie," which is marked by an imperceptible grain of equivocation, discloses the covert interrelation of speaking or writing and the destabilizing movement of the lax conscience in the politics of truth-telling that characterized a culture where to be utterly transparent (rather than to cultivate the illusion) was to be utterly vulnerable, trapped in another person's vision of one's place in the stratified channels of social and political power. For Radigund, authoritative discourse involves saying less than one means—what the casuists would have recognized as the scaffolding of a mental reservation. Thus to her confidant, Clarinda, who is to mediate between the Amazon and her prisoner, Radigund issues the command to "win him any way / Without discouerie of my thoughts pretence" (5.5.33). This is no idiosyncrasy of degenerate authority. Sensing from the context that the probability of gaining freedom will increase if he not only curries Clarinda's favor but also fuels the servant's nascent desire to possess him, Artegall speaks in Radigund's idiom. "Faire words" turn out to carry a qualification his interlocutor is unaware of: submitting not to Radigund's person but to the casuistical inflections in the discourse of power, he speaks "faire words, fit for the time and place, / To feede the humour of her maladie" (5.5.55).

The figure who most fully thematizes the covert primacy assigned to equivocation and secrecy in this discourse between rival powers is Clarinda, the figure who ostensibly signifies the act of communication itself, the channel through which writing and speaking—acts of deferred and immediate dialog—occur. Her very name suggests the public associations such discourse invokes. Clarinda: *clarus*, clear, transparent. A mediating yet neutral, imperceptible presence; or, to borrow a metaphor that will become decisive in the Mercilla episode: a blank space. How appropriate that this cipher should yield a related association: Clarinda as the site where the ruler's conscience may be spied. Clarinda is Radigund's "nearest handmayd, whom she most did trust"; and it is to Clarinda that Radigund entrusts the utmost secret of her conscience ("Unto her selfe in secret she did call" [5.5.29]). Radigund furthermore invests Clarinda with a power to penetrate Artegall's cell that is couched in terms alluding to the imperceptible movement of conscience. Clarinda receives a ring, reminiscent of Gyges' ring in mythology, which made its wearer invisible; Clarinda's gives her "passage free" into the secret regions of Radigund's castle, regions guarded, apparently, by the mysterious figure of "old Eumenias," whose name evokes the Eumenides, the ancient Greek embodiments of conscience. In the figure of Clarinda, then, the channels of discourse through which power speaks present themselves as undistorting mirrors.

As the narrative unfolds, we learn that the channels realize their function as the faithful handmaids of power when, paradoxically, their apparent transparency serves as the screen for occulted desire (Radigund's "thoughts pretence"). Clarinda's essence, in fact, lies in the impersonation of the *clarus* aspect her name implies. The further complications of the episode—that Clarinda's dawning desire for Artegall should be "secretly retayned / Within the closet of her couert brest" (5.5.44) and should lead her to distort the already distorted discourses that pass under cover of "faire entreatie" and "faire words"—represent differences in degree but not in kind from Clarinda's original function. Clarinda's pivotal role helps focus the episode's allegorical rendering of the pivotal, if implicit, space between the theory and the practice, the idealized and the contextualized visions, of language—the space where the contingencies of desire inform the image of words as the creations of pure ideation.

In this light, the text may be said to constitute Clarinda as the scandalous personification of the narrator himself and of the canonical utterances he produces. Like Clarinda, both the narrator and his product serve as the conduit or site of exchange between an authoritative discourse and its designated audience; both occupy the conjoined space of mediation and self-effacing equivocation that Clarinda epitomizes. Clarinda's pivotal role in maintaining the hierarchical disposition of the status quo matches the narrator's; and her skill in issuing reportages so imperceptibly fictionalized that she herself becomes enmeshed in her own "subtill nets"—"So cunningly she wrought her crafts assay / That both her Ladie, and her selfe withall, / And eke the knight attonce she did betray" (5.5.52)—evokes the regime of selective vision that the narrator, principally, betrays in the text (an issue we will return to in a later chapter).

These resemblances recall one of the insights fundamental to casuistical analysis: that the teller—and the inflection of personal bias that the teller may bring to the tale unawares—is part of the tale, part of the informing context. There is a difference, then, between what the narrator defines explicitly as the episode's context of perpetual "bondage" and what the text, which subsumes the narrator and his canonical readings, conveys through the same detail. The represented "bondage" indicates the narrator's edifying attempt to differentiate Radigund's world from Artegall's (an attempt undermined by Radigund and Artegall's evident commonality of discourse). In other words, the narrator's appraisal of the dynamic of power supposedly peculiar to Radigund's world connotes, among other things, his misrecognition of the hierarchical ethos that the two worlds share, an ethos in which the idea of bondage lies, covertly, on a continuum with its canonical cognates, the order and stasis publicly associated with the cult of Gloriana. The word also implies the metaphoric bondage that "good" readings obliquely represent in such an ethos, in the sense that "good" readings depend, as they do in Isis Church, on a habit of responsiveness to the culture's authoritative signals—to what we might call an encoded authoritative fantasy of generalized conformity to a hierarchical weighting of circumstances of time, place, and person.

Through Clarinda and the narrator who mirrors her, the integrity of a "good" reading, the interpretive and narrative enactment of the clear (*clarus*) conscience, is thus problematically identified with a covert ethos of misreading that masks an underlying confusion of desires and allegiances and that, ultimately, sustains the received relations of power. The "good" reader, too, the text implies, will presumably follow the signals, echoing the pattern of equivocation in which the text itself engages, at once confirming and belying its place in the canon of authoritative discourse, where truth, justice, and Gloriana are one.

The text keeps ushering in evidence of this pattern, as though the destabilizing action of equity and the discourse of conscience, once tacitly acknowledged (if not explicitly articulated) in the text, could not be suppressed (in the manner of the hydras that the Protestant controversialist Thomas Morton invoked, we may recall, in his attack on the practice of mental reservation). The Isis Church episode, as we have seen, ritualizes equity's power to demythologize the circumstance of person, notably through the misreadings generated by the priest in the temple and symbolically imported from the temple into the nominally canonical space of the text itself through the mediating narrator. The episode also ritualizes the interrelated, systemic nature of such contextual factors. Just as the circumstance of "person" will generally emerge in a case of conscience as a function of spatial and temporal circumstances, so, too, in Spenser's narrative. The perspective the narrator brings to the cases he relates, for example, turns out to be enmeshed in considerations of temporality.

Consider the very opening of the episode, in which the narrator traces the origins of the temple, in a brief sequence that advertises his erudition regarding the customs of the "antique world," a sequence indebted, as is well known, to Plutarch's treatise *Isis and Osiris*. The narrator's ethnographic survey represents something of a departure from one of the stated givens of the proem, which defines the entropic vision of book 5, its comparison of a past "golden age" and a present "stonie one" that "being once amisse growes daily wourse and wourse." Here the narrator appears to assume, as a matter of course, a fundamental commonality between the contemporary and the antique world, a shared cognitive and normative reception of "true iustice" as the *ne plus ultra* of the moral (and political) universe: "Nought is on earth more sacred or diuine," intones the narrator at the beginning of the canto, defining the inviolable status of a principle adored equally by "Gods and men," by the pagan as well as the Christian world, and preserved within "Princes hearts." One is already in the shadow of the temple, where, to borrow William West's words on equity, a "just proportion" appears to have been found between what the narrator has otherwise found to be irreconcilable: the "state of present time" and the "image of the antique world" (5.proem.1).

In his actual account of Isis Church, however, the narrator employs a methodology liable to incommode the serene picture presented thus far: his summary of the careers of Osiris and Isis is a piece of euhemerism.[30] The narrative parvis, as it were, before the temple of equity coincides with a demythologizing analytical procedure reminiscent of equity and the discourse of conscience insofar as it equips one to relocate that which claims its point of origin in an atemporal, "sacred or divine" realm within a particular historical context. In its own long history (from the third century B.C.E. well into the Renaissance), euhemeristic interpretation acquired a variety of functions tuned to the changing contexts in which it was employed: it began as a weapon of early Christian polemicists *adversus paganos*, an assault on the pagan gods; then became an "auxiliary to historical research," a means of raiding the pantheon of pagan gods for evidence of pivotal figures of antiquity who contributed to the development of civilization; and eventually took on an important political dimension, as part of a discourse of legitimation employed by national groups and dynasties to validate their claims to prestige and power. (What better credentials, indeed, than to be able to trace one's ancestry to persons of such distinction that they were commemorated as gods or demigods—an Aeneas, a Hercules?)[31] Yet, regardless of its history of metamorphoses, euhemerism remained unchanged in one fundamental aspect: in the way its demythologizing capacity worked as an instrument of myth-maintenance.

Let me put this another way. Debunking the pagan gods served to reinforce the truth of the Christian religion; discovering the historicity of mythological discourse advanced the truth-telling claims of historiography over mythology; inversely, the elaboration of a discourse that traced the heritage of a dynasty, through the perceived historical fund of mythological lore, to a civilization of ancient heroes lent to the Crown's sovereignty the cachet of a divinely sanctioned truth that preempted the more mundane truth of the political strategies or contingencies behind the assumption of power. To engage in euhemeristic analysis, then, was to enter an economy with a fixed rate of exchange between rival absolutes. Devaluing one system of truth served to elevate the status of another (the one the euhemerist had a stake in) rather than introduce a climate of critical inquiry into all such systems. In other words, the demythologizing mechanism of euhemerism was delimited by the same self-censoring misrecognition that characterized the apologetic or polemical use of the discourses of equity and of conscience—the same misrecognition that Spenser's text thematizes and brings into the pale of visibility.

That the narrator's excursus into equity should itself include an excursus into euhemerism seems appropriate; the coincidence emphasizes the deregulatory yet equivocal character of Spenser's text in relation to the norms or givens it appears to represent unproblematically. A case in point: let us consider again the status of the "antique world" as represented in the opening stanzas of the canto, particularly in regard to the narrator's suggestion of the underlying commonality between the past and the Elizabethan present—their shared acknowledgment of the divine sovereignty of "true iustice." Couched in the discourse of euhemerism, this kind of suggestion raises questions about further possible commonalities that the narrator, it appears, must ignore. Indeed, only if the past is assumed to be informed by an ethos fundamentally different from that of the present can the narrator describe how the eternal fountainheads of justice and equity acquired their divinity at a particular historical moment by the action of human society. It is no longer merely a matter of returning to the classical model of gradual historical change through decay (the passage from the "golden age" to the "stonie one") but of invoking the transfiguring change of the Christian dispensation, from which perspective the deifying actions of the "antique world" may be viewed as the constructions, the necessary fictions, of a society that, as Sidney put it, "had not the light of Christ," a society using its resources to make up for the truth it has not yet received and does not yet know it lacks.[32]

The narrator's homage to "highest Ioue, who doth true iustice deale," at the opening of canto 7, has precisely the effect of such an invocation. To be sure, the homage is conventional; but it also suggests that the euhemeristic discourse to follow will obtain within a passage whose referentiality is exclusively pagan. In what follows there is, then, the scent of an archive of alien mores that has been opened and that remains at odds with the sense of connectedness between the present and a prefigural past, which the passage also suggests. This ambiguous poise informs the narrator's euhemerism, making it difficult to gauge and delimit the implications of the account of how the "antique world" commemorated the virtue of Osiris and Isis, two mortals "of the race / Of th'old Aegyptian Kings" (5.7.2), by transforming the couple into gods.

Isis herself is described unequivocally as having been "made / A Goddesse of great powre and souerainty" (5.7.3). Such a frank admission appears reassuring, from a certain perspective. It is as though the information were being transmitted from across the "dark backward and abysm of time," representing a society that not only authored its deities, norms, and absolutes but recognized its authoring role, a society where poesis functioned undisguisedly as a

surrogate for revelation—in other words, a society framed and dis-
tanced by the ethnocentric perspective that the text embodies in its
own role as an authoritative discourse, as the repository of the corpus of "real," authorless truths, which are unavailable in their plenary
form to the society in question and therefore not implicated in the
kind of poesis that the text describes.

Isis's description, we should note, follows Osiris's—and appropriately so, not only because the pattern observes a legal commonplace, which the narrator voices (Isis representing "That part of
Iustice, which is Equity"), but also because Isis's description appears
to justify the deregulatory capacity of equity. It rewrites, and alters,
the text that precedes it, erasing the implied evidence in that text
of the applicability of euhemeristic discourse to the mythopoeia of the
present as well as of the remote past.[33] The key word in the account
of Osiris's apotheosis is the verb that is rewritten in Isis's description
as "made." "Well therefore," the narrator affirms, "did the antique
world inuent / That Iustice was a God of soueraine grace" (5.7.2).
The text has it both ways, playing on the ambiguity of the word
"invent."[34] It adduces the perspicacity of a society able to discern, to
discover, the objective reality, the absolute, normative character, of
"true iustice"; at the same time it adduces the ingenuity of a society
skilled in preserving and legitimating the truths it values by constituting their objective reality. The primary meaning of the word "invent" in the phrase is presumably the latter, a meaning reinforced by
the narrator's subsequent choice of "made" in his treatment of Isis.
Similarly, its primary temporal reference is presumably to the remote
past. But that the ambiguous word should appear at all indicates that
such neat categorizations may be themselves an artifice, made rather
than discovered, masking the truth of what the opened archive of the
Egyptian past may hold as a mirror to the Elizabeth present.

I am not speaking here of the traditional fourfold allegorical bag-
gage that can be brought to bear on the "invention" of fictions, pagan or otherwise, saving their appearances, as it were, in a kind of
textual proselytization that attests to the immanence of a unitary corpus of truths discoverable through the media of human poesis. (I am
not speaking, then, of Spenser's official project, as announced in the
Letter to Raleigh, to compose a "historical fiction . . . clowdily en-
wrapped in Allegorical deuises.")[35] At issue, rather, is the inversion

of such proselytization. The narrator's brief, and dissolving, reference to the truth-sustaining allegorical method is apposite in this context. Commenting on the Egyptians' elevation of Osiris to the rank of a "God of soueraine grace," he observes that with "fayned colours" they shaded "a true case." The "true case" appears to be a tropological projection. The making of Osiris into a god follows the discovery of an atemporal moral verity—"true iustice"—in the pattern of his life (poesis merely repeating, tautologically, a prior truth imprinted in the human soul). But this projection overlooks the latent ambiguity of what the narrator defines as the "true case": "For that Osyris, whilest he lived here, / The iustest man aliue and truest did appeare" (5.7.2). The "true case" is, first of all, a historically verifiable incident rather than an eternal verity. To be sure, the case is to be read as the historical incarnation of an eternal verity. But the truth of the case is not simply discovered; it is made. Osiris's identity, as well as the profile of the virtue of which he "appeares" to be the "truest" avatar, emerges as a function of a cultural poesis, a consensual arrangement imposing a hierarchical structure on human behavior (as evinced in the superlatives attached to Osiris's name). That is, the changing value attached to Osiris's name attests to the collective action of a society "inventing"—in the sense of constituting and maintaining—its norms and rewriting them as "invented," discovered, quantities.

Under the aegis of the combined critical apparatus of euhemerism, conscience, and equity, the ambiguity of the word "invent" thus implicates poesis not only as the surrogate or the channel for revealed truth but as a factor in the genealogy of what is received as revealed truth. It invokes the ethos of a world whose received truths are held to be discovered, either through revelation or through the instrumentation of human poesis, and it introduces the trace of poesis into the sanctuary of these discovered truths. It implicates a subjective authorship behind the perceived objective realities of the "state of present time." Furthermore, the parallel accounts of the myth-making procedures of the "antique world," resulting first in Osiris's and next in Isis's apotheosis, are liable to give pause precisely because together they approximate the mechanism of misrecognition that persists in the world now ruled, as the proem states, by the "Dread Souerayne Goddesse" Gloriana "that doest highest sit / In seate of iudgement in th'Almighties place" (5.proem.11), an authority whose power is attributed not to a human but to a divine agency, in accord with the rhetoric of the conjoined discourses of power and of conscience as exploited by the Crown.

This kind of insight, of course, would amount to sacrilege if applied to the received spiritual and moral truths of Spenser's Protestant culture. But it is not necessary to locate the author on the radical, atheistic, fringe of his culture in order for the metacritical apparatus of book 5 to be plausible. Subversion need not be sweeping in order to exist, though its potential to be so may be perceived as ineradicable. For example, the invocation of "highest Iove," unambiguously signalling the narrator's immersion (however conventional) in an obsolete, pagan frame of reference, may be said to act as a surrogate for the deity the author himself is not willing to bring under the jurisdiction of euhemerism. As such, the invocation carries the trace of scandal that the text cannot be said to have entirely suppressed, since what the text represents here, as in the replacement of "invent" by "made," is the very attempt to curtail the network of correspondences between the closed archive of the past and the open, living present. The text, in short, betrays the author's own process of misrecognition in the face of certain truths that he will not permit himself to articulate, since to articulate them in this particular temple would be to dismantle them, to ground them in the cycles of human poesis.

But the text is less equivocal about the narrator's evident misrecognition, which represents what the author is willing to implicate as values whose contingency the narrator is shown to ignore. Thus, while the narrator describes the mechanism that produced the deities of Osiris and Isis, he fails to repeat the exercise on the other entities he has presented in the text as being inviolable. The invocation of "highest Iove" figures here again, not in its role as the author's own surrogate for the absolute that, as noted above, he withholds from the text at this point but, rather, in its more conventional role as a disguised, fictional construction of the absolute in the "antique world" (and in texts that, like *The Faerie Queene*, claim to reconstitute elements of that world), a construction that the reader is tacitly invited to perceive as such, without drawing implications for the "state of present time."[36] The accompanying citation of "Princes" (to whose hearts "highest Iove" reveals his "righteous lore") is more problematic and more daring, since the connotations of the word are clearly not exhausted by the depicted, limited, referentiality of the "antique world," despite the word's syntactic ligature to "highest Iove." Through this citation, the text slips out of the represented archival past, signalling the narrator's simultaneous participation in an extra-textual, contemporary world dominated by the rule of a prince whose sovereignty and "true iustice" hinge on the authoritative discourse that reveals in (i.e., imparts to) the prince the character of an *imago Dei*. The text thus invites the reader to observe how the ethos of misrecognition sustains the objective truth not so much of the Christian deity (whose status remains exempt from scrutiny) as of the Christian monarch's discourse of power. The lapse in the narrator's euhemeristic activity when it comes to the rule of princes alludes to the lapse that the monarch's subjects must repeatedly make—ignoring their role in the publicly sanctioned conversion of the rhetoric into the truth of a divinely sanctioned power—if they are to participate, to become visible, in the court of Gloriana.

Self-Cancelling Cases of Conscience: Britomart, Artegall, and the Transgressive Simile

The interrelated careers of Artegall and Britomart constitute a narrative enactment of equity's power to disclose, through the episodic "cases" the heroic figures encounter, the layers of contingency that envelop Gloriana's regime. The narrative recurrently implicates issues related to the process of reading in this thematics: the couple's independent reading strategies, as well as the reading strategies the text shows them to be the objects of, produce a disingenuous account of how *not* to observe that the process of determining what constitutes a case of conscience depends very much on the perspective of whoever is asking the question, and on what "fits," what becomes visible or is deemed pertinent, through that perspective.[1]

No less than Britomart's, Artegall's career helps define the narrative's equivocal poise, equivocal insofar as the narrative shows itself, in plotting Artegall's career along an axis in which evidence of an interpretive filter—the narrator—intermittently intrudes, to be constituted by two coextensive yet mutually exclusive projects. An overarching, official project of affirming the self-evident, universally observed coincidence of equity, conscience, and Gloriana's power is shadowed by a metacritical project of representing such a coincidence as the effect of a particularized perspective, one seized in the process of establishing its gaze as the privileged channel of the authentic, the real, the true. This operation (a narrative rendering of the introspective power of conscience) belies its own implicit claim to the adequacy of its resulting vision by the evidence it leaves in its wake: by the presence of incongruities and gaps that do not fit into the governing perspective, other than as detritus.[2] These recurring pieces of apparently insignificant information hint at the possibility of other contexts, other perspectives, gaining prominence—other interpretive regimes equipped to redefine the limits of what is perceived as insignificant. To hint at such a possibility is not, however, to announce or decry the limits and contingencies of the obtaining interpretive regime (in this case, of the book's official project). It is—perhaps more disconcertingly—to enact what the instauration of such a regime requires: an invasive silence that reduces apparent anomalies (potential sites of divergent discourses) to the condition of meaninglessness.

What is disconcerting about this phenomenon is that the resulting text, while it does not embrace heterodoxy (it advances no explicit critique of the norms that shape the official occasion of its composition), does not quite sustain its status as a transparent vehicle for an equally transparent, a divinely ordered and thus indisputably true, orthodoxy. If anything, it takes the rhetoric of transparency too far (too far, that is, if we assume the orthodox point of view). Leaving a trail of narrative details that must be made meaningless, or superfluous, in order for the whole to "work" ("work" in the sense of realizing the adequacy of the orthodox vision with which the book nominally identifies itself), the "legend of justice" shows too much. It shows that there is, in fact, work involved in establishing, among other things, the serene face of Gloriana's "great iustice"—work that includes a habit of not seeing, in effect, what doesn't "work" in (or fit into) the composition. Yet to show this is, paradoxically, to show virtually nothing: the book thematizes its own blindness. Even so, to show this much is already to have become, imperceptibly, something other than merely the pious legend of justice it claims to be. It is also to have become a book about and yet not about the hegemonic economy of interpretation brought to bear in the production of pious legends of justice, a book about and yet not about the necessary trade-offs—about what must get left out of the picture—in order to induce the falling into innocence that such legends depend on and perpetuate: the innocence implied in the mythos that poesis begins only at the moment of re-presenting prior givens.[3]

Chameleon-like, echoing the evasive speeches of Elizabeth to Parliament in the winter of 1586, this particular legend, then, proves relentlessly equivocal about its own status in the very canon it helps define; equivocal, too, about the relation between its readers and itself. It implies that the act of endorsing the values inscribed on its surface (as the narrator does and as the legend's readers, through the narrator's example as "reader" of the events represented in the text, are presumed to do) is to participate in an ongoing yet self-erasing process of constructing the fiction of permanent and universal values memorialized in canonical texts and embodied in the figures of authority that such texts serve. Ultimately, Spenser may be said to parody the myth of authorlessness that fueled Elizabeth's system of power; through parody, Spenser's text exposes the rhetoric of authorlessness—rewrites authorlessness as a cipher for a multiple, complicitous authorship whose action the text symbolizes. In this context, the text itself implicitly claims not to be responsible for its "meaning." Indeed, it appears to have no meaning, if one construes the term as a thing fixed in amber.

To read this particular legend of justice is to find the narrative equivalent of justice—the "just" or "true" interpretation—represented as a shifting relation of particularized relations of power. The relations center, principally, on two facets of a single but complexly organized political and social arrangement. Through the course of Britomart's and Artegall's careers, the text represents the problematic instauration of the female body as the locus of authority and the ambivalent instrumentality of a predominantly male aristocratic body. More generally, as the figurative agents both of Gloriana's rule and of the cultural processes that produce it, Britomart and Artegall lead us through a covert allegory on the subject of the transgressive, demythologizing potential implicit in all acts of mediation—and especially in those that pass, like Artegall, as the transparent or innocent "instruments" of an inviolable text of power.

Britomart, Equity, and the Problem of Female Power

Equity's demythologizing regime informs the two principal events that follow Britomart's passage through Isis Church, events that bring canto 7 to a close, as though sealing the rupture of the Isis Church episode, and that appear to demonstrate the officially sanctioned power of equity to bring about "absolute justice." First,

Britomart slays Radigund, an act that appears without doubt to be just. In describing their battle, the narrator emphasizes Radigund's association with evil and Britomart's with good. Radigund delivers blows that are "unmercifully sore"; and, though "proud," she exhibits the dishonorable, the unchivalric and morally suspect, dimension of pride, lunging at her weakened opponent with "fell despight"—with something like cruel contempt.[4] The single reference to the virtue of courage belongs to Britomart (she withstands Radigund's blows "with courage stout"), as do the references to nobility and, as we might expect, to equity. After Britomart has decapitated Radigund, the narrator dubs Britomart a "noble Conqueresse" and he illustrates her ability to temper the "wrothfull" spirit she has shown in slaying her opponent. Britomart stops Talus's "piteous slaughter" of the defeated Amazons, an action that implies her ability, in effect, to distinguish between intrinsic evil (Radigund), which must be destroyed, and the mere extensions of evil (Radigund's followers), which may be said to belong to the category the casuists called the *adiaphora*, the things indifferent, without an intrinsic, inalterable, moral valence.[5] The elimination of Radigund, then, appears to enjoy unqualified sanction in the text, as though it were part of a dramatic, and reassuring, realization of "That part of Iustice, which is Equity."

It also offers conspicuous evidence that what the conscience of the "noble Conqueresse" deems just or equitable is identical with what appears necessary, since by eliminating Radigund Britomart is able to free Artegall from bondage. She thereby advances the expected narrative fulfillment of the book, enabling Artegall to fulfill his primary objective, to rescue Irena from the tyrant Grantorto and "reforme" Irena's "ragged common-weale" (5.12.26). Indeed, the canto ends with the promise, in the form of the narrator's retrospective vision of the event, that Irena's case will be resolved: Artegall "Went on his way; ne euer howre did cease / Till he redeemed had that Lady thrall" (5.7.45). Britomart's other notable action, at the end of the canto, underscores this prospect of closure. Adumbrating the reformation, the *pax Gloriana*, that Artegall introduces in canto 12, Britomart changes "all that forme of common-weale" of the Amazons, restoring them "To mens subiection," to a patriarchal norm of order. Again, the narrator provides the official, the "correct," evalua-

tion of Britomart's action: she "did True Iustice deale," as she ap-
pears to have done in slaying Radigund. Like the priest's authoritative utterance in the temple of equity,
both evaluations turn out to be equivocal, framed by qualifying cir-
cumstances that take shape only to be passed over, misrecognized, in
the text. The deregulatory aspect of equity remains in force outside
Isis Church. And it acquires a significance that was only implicit in
the narrator's account of the female deity Isis. Now, in the person
and actions of the "noble Conqueresse," the hidden, threatening side
of equity is associated with femaleness. Conflated, equity and the
female gender constitute a demythologizing agent in the cultural system that book 5 represents, a system that by the 1590's had built up a
mythological discourse around Elizabeth's femaleness to accommodate the presence of a female sovereign in the prevailing patriarchal
and phallocentric structure of power, a discourse designed to supplant the kind of ideological objection most startlingly represented,
perhaps, in the tract by John Knox, which was published, rather
incommodiously, in 1558: the *First Blast of the Trumpet against the
Monstrous Regiment of Women.*[6]

Indeed, that Britomart should receive the title of "noble Conqueresse" at this point in the text testifies, arguably, not to the deregulatory but to the doctrinaire aspect of equity, its place in the
machinery of accommodation. But such a reading is problematic, if
only because, as we shall see directly, the arc of Britomart's career
suggests the contingency of what it purports to justify: the acquisition and exercise of power by a female. This is not to say that Britomart's actions can be pigeonholed as a testimony to the ultimate,
objective truth of the phallocentric vision of authority; that is, the
text does not simply betray the suppressed discomfiture of a society
governed by an anomalous female sovereign, a society privately
wishing the circumstance of her femaleness away. The demythologizing service to which Britomart is put, in the closing passages of
canto 7, cuts two ways. It invites the reader to take cognizance of the
supplementary, and ultimately dispensable, status of Gloriana. And
it extends the prospect of this cognizance, opening up to scrutiny
the normative status of the very structure of authority—the phallocentric ethos—that the cult of Gloriana has presented itself as having
assimilated and replaced.

In Britomart, female *virtù* and equity are conjoined in a figure that enacts the process through which the norm of authoritative (and nominally male) discourse comes into being and naturalizes itself by enjoining a collective misrecognition of the process. Accordingly, this figure maintains an equivocal status in the text, since part of its metacritical operation is to point up the passage into aphasia of the insights it is likely to yield. The text, in other words, records the erasure of the destabilizing capacity that it shares with the discourses of conscience and equity. To reintroduce a legal analog, the text records the erasure of the aphorism, captured in the oneiric representation of Isis standing over the crocodile, that equity precedes the law, an aphorism that, in dilated form, assembles equity, the association of power and femaleness, and the indeterminacy of the opposition good/evil as cognate elements preceding the law, male sovereignty, and the attending conviction that the natural order grows out of the absolute discreteness of good and evil. The text thus at once attests to and belies the primacy of this last triumvirate.

With this in mind, let us return to the confrontation between Britomart and Radigund, which represents, presumably, a particularization of the confrontation between good and evil. As we have seen, the narrator furnishes evidence to support such a connection. It is worth noting, however, that such discrete allocations emerge only after an initial moment, signalled by the "Trumpets sound," when the two opponents, coming together, cannot be distinguished from one another. They "together run / With greedy rage," and "through great fury both their skill forgot, / And practicke use in armes" (5.7.29). In the simile that follows, the characteristics of the two competing predators converge as well: the "Tygre" and the "Lionesse" (it is not absolutely clear which signifies Britomart and which Radigund) share an "equall greedinesse." The levelling power of mutual violence here duplicates the deregulatory power of equity, its power to suspend culturally encoded, received notions of good and evil, inviting one to discern, metacritically, how the fixity of such notions is constituted out of a pool of initially indeterminate, not easily bracketed, experience. The text does not, then, contradict its ensuing evaluation of Britomart's actions as good or just. It simply, and momentarily, belies the self-evidence of the evaluation; it opens to inquiry the assumption that Britomart, as the channel of "absolute justice" and its authoritative discourse, cannot be other than good or just. And it suggests the political and ideological imperative to eradicate this insight.

We will have occasion later, in examining the trial of Duessa, to return to the political dimension of this imperative, which registers the political hazard of resurrecting, in the dynamic between text and reader, the very dynamic between the conscience of the monarch and those of the monarch's would-be judges that Elizabeth tried to obstruct during the controversy over Mary Queen of Scots. For the moment, let us consider the broader ideological imperative behind the political. The text enacts the effort of a dominant phallocentric system of power to preserve the objective truth of its status by disabling the kind of critical inquiry likely to point up evidence of the means through which such normative systems of power are produced and reified—the kind of inquiry embodied in the discourses of conscience and equity, here associated with the articulation of female power. Notice, in this light, the first target during the initial moment of deregulated attack, with the "practicke use in armes" suspended:

> [They] spared not
> Their dainty parts, which nature had created
> So faire and tender, without staine or spot
> For other vses, then they them translated;
> Which they now hackt and hewd, as if such vse they hated.

(5.7.29)

The two warriors give the highest priority to the task of eradicating the visible signs of their own femaleness, an action that proves relentlessly problematic in the text. First of all, the action begs the question of what is and is not "natural" (i.e., in accord with the law of nature, to which the narrator alludes). The mutual hacking and hewing, after all, amounts to a mutual mutilation, producing literally denatured women. It also suggests, paradoxically, that they are most fully themselves, as figures of public authority and military power, when they are desexed (even to the point of hating, it appears, the proper, the "natural," use of their "dainty parts"). Evidently there is no place for signs of femaleness (of that which is, as the narrator puts it, "faire and tender") in the system of phallocentric power.

There is, conspicuously, not even a place for a discourse of accommodation: the "translation" of what "nature had created . . . / For other uses" is simply the act of eradication itself.

Though the depiction of self-cancelling femaleness seems, oddly, at once unnatural and natural, it does not explicitly challenge the received truth of the "natural" order of male authority. But it does import the prospect of a similar problem of signification into this "natural" order. On the one hand, for example, the passage points up the ostensible authorlessness of this order, which appears to have no direct agency in the violence: what the warriors do, they do to each other, as though in tacit acknowledgment of the objective truth of the phallocentric perspective. On the other hand, by invoking the thematics of self-cancellation, the passage reconceives, if only fleetingly, the "natural" order itself not as an authorless truth but as a socially constructed, self-legitimating system of power that sustains its atemporal, parthenogenetic aspect by eradicating any countervailing, contaminating, evidence—evidence that would arise through the channels of conscience, of equity, of the female. The depicted eradication of femaleness thus suggests the very processes through which the mythos of a "pure," indisputable phallocentric order constitutes and naturalizes itself by eliminating signs of its contextuality, of its generation in circumstances that include the not-male (and that include, in legal terms, that which is outside the text of the law, the *ius strictus*).

The predatory simile gives further definition to this process, notably by rewriting the "hackt and hewd" parts as "some hungry pray" torn apart by the two animals. Femaleness is no longer something that must be disfigured (and thus misrecognized) and cut off. It is now, by definition, something inherently apart, like the prey, which is implied to be neither tiger nor lion but to belong to a different genus altogether. (It turns up a few lines later simply as "the beast.") In the simile the warriors' femaleness has become reified and its destruction naturalized: the anomaly of self-mutilation has been redefined as a natural process, in accord with "what everybody knows" (and takes to be inalterable) about the law of nature as manifested in the animal kingdom.

In accord with the metacritical bias informing the episode, the simile also contains a measure of ambiguity that belies the adequacy of such a neat redefinition as the final, "true" statement about the natural order. While the phrase "hungry pray," for instance, may connote the sense of otherness that phallocentrism would attribute to femaleness as well, it also belies the absoluteness of that sense, in ways that suggest precisely the motives behind the depicted phallocentric fantasy of a self-eradicating femaleness. First of all, consider the ambiguity of the adjective "hungry," which describes the prey in terms of a characteristic that applies to the predators.[7] The distinction between subject and object, between dominator and dominated, has been blurred. The word "pray" itself, even without the adjectival cue, invokes this ethos of indeterminacy, blurring the distinction between inside and outside, since it is in the nature of prey not to remain other but to be assimilated by another body and, literally, to sustain that body (as it is in the nature of the "dainty parts," the breasts of the female, to nourish and sustain life).[8] What the text thus makes available for scrutiny through the simile is the "inside" of the image of the warriors' mutual mutilation, reconstituted as a phallocentric fantasy of parthenogenesis. The eradication of that which ostensibly has no place in the reigning mythos is rewritten as the consumption and assimilation of an element whose place in the reigning mythos is pivotal, insofar as the element signifies that which nurtures and produces. It is precisely this kind of signification, which belies the authorlessness of male sovereignty and the written text of the law, that the reigning mythos cannot afford to recognize. And it is precisely the attempt to install a condition of misrecognition that the text, under the jurisdiction of equity, enacts at this point, encapsulating its metacritical account of the motive behind the depicted eradication of the "dainty parts" within a simile whose ostensible purpose is merely to measure the violence of the female warriors.

Further signs of this represented aphasia are scattered throughout the remainder of the canto, in the form of anomalies that the narrator passes over without comment. Take the simile that follows the predatory one. There is a characteristically gory account of the battle between Britomart and Radigund, in the midst of which the narrator observes

> that all the grassie flore
> Was fild with bloud which from their sides did flow,
> And gushed through their armes, that all in gore

> They trode, and on the ground their liues did strow,
> Like fruitles seed, of which vntimely death should grow.

(5.7.31)

The paradox of the spilled blood that engenders "vntimely death" is conventional enough not to require comment. But the simile it frames warrants attention, insofar as it translates the paradox into one bespeaking a confusion of genders that is apposite under the deregulatory regime of equity and conscience. As the mutilated female warriors approach the ultimate corporeal transformation—from life to death—the simile invests them with the sign of a transformation of a different order, representing an attempt to give a final, a "perfected," form to the thematics of the eradication of femaleness. The comparison of the lifeblood of the female warriors to "fruitles seed" defines their potential biological productivity as an act of insemination—that is, as an act conceived in male terms. And as an act burdened with the evidence of its own impossibility: that the "seed" should be "fruitles" announces both the imminence of death and, self-referentially, the evident failure of the depicted phallocentric fantasy to reproduce and sustain itself. Both translations of the female warriors—into the not-female and into the dysfunctional male—are conspicuously imperfect translations of the plenitude of male authority. Both constitute textual evidence that belies the immanence and universality of the phallocentric regime. And both, conforming to the ethos of misrecognition that informs the text's potentially subversive moments, enter the narrator's discourse free of explicit cues pointing up their anomalous character. The message: to read the text is, of necessity, to misread it, to find (i.e., to make) unintelligible or banal that which might otherwise leave one, like Britomart in Isis Church, "doubtfully dismayed" about the truths that the text, in its guise as an authoritative discourse, appears to represent uncritically.

Such gestures of self-censorship, as we have seen elsewhere, are part of what the metacritical bias of the discourse of conscience is all about, part of its aporetic nature: to show rather than tell—and, moreover, to show equivocally—that which must remain officially misrecognized.[9] This ethos calls attention to itself most flagrantly (and paradoxically) as the canto approaches its close, with the rehabilitation of Artegall and the reformation of the society of Amazons. Invoking male authority as an unshakable tenet of the natural order, the narrator equates "True Iustice" with the "repeale" of the "liberty of women," who are restored to "mens subiection." As if to corroborate the equation, he reintroduces the thematics of the self-eradication of female power. The voices of the Amazons are indistinguishable from the men's in approving the suppression of their own "forme of common-weale" as the restoration of "True Iustice." Not only the Amazon culture but what we might call "Amazonness" itself—the possibility of a competing ideology—vanishes, constituting in its very absence a mute testimony to the absolute truth of phallocentric power.

This discretionary, self-censoring procedure repeats itself at the culminating moment of canto 7, with Artegall's substitution for Britomart as the sovereign authority over the Amazons. The act, let us recall, is engineered by Britomart herself; it is her principal achievement during her reign. And, associated as it is with "True Iustice," it stands, officially, as the perfect embodiment of the action of equity that Britomart has come to represent since her passage through Isis Church. This account of the proper direction the rule of a chaste female should take would seem to be impolitic at best, particularly when measured against the narrator's previous articulation of the norm of "lawfull soueraintie" in canto 5. Lamenting Radigund's victory over Artegall, the narrator voices a received socio-political commonplace.[10] Not only does he pronounce the "libertie" of women "licentious," contrary to "all rule and reason," and even to the dictates of "wise Nature," but indisputably so, as evinced by the accord of "vertuous women," who "wisely understand, / That they were born to base humilitie, / Vnlesse the heauens them lift to lawfull soueraintie" (5.5.25). Through the final concessive clause, the represented norm dilates, as it were, to include a space for Gloriana/Elizabeth: the discourse of accommodation itself, bearing a divine imprimatur, takes its place as a valid part of the norm—indeed, as a manifestation of equity in its doctrinaire aspect, rewriting an apparent anomaly as the fulfillment of what God intends by "lawfull soueraintie." (And, moreover, as a manifestation of the kind of entrée into the phallocentric norm that Elizabeth herself exploited. Witness, in the celebrated "Golden Speech" of 1601, her disingenuous admission of her "sexly weakness," which dissolves into an irrelevance, given its place in a passage governed by the higher truth that God had made Elizabeth "this instrument to maintain His truth and glory.")[11]

Yet when the chaste Britomart, her nomenclature now augmented with the titles of "Princess" and "Goddesse," finally assumes a position of "lawfull soueraintie," administering (like the "Dread Souerayne Goddesse" to whom the book is addressed) the "True Iustice" associated with such power, there is no longer a place for the discourse of accommodation. It is the one piece missing in the final picture. Or, rather, it is turned inside out. Britomart tropes the inverse of the discourse of accommodation. Her assumption of power—not for the first time—acquires the quality of a facsimile of the real thing, of the phallocentric norm. Neither her military prowess in canto 7 nor her judicial skill (her "wisedome" and "loring" in the commonwealth of Amazons) directly challenges Artegall's, since the former appears in his absence (indeed, in his service) and the latter only temporarily, as a kind of regency. (While the members of the Amazon state "admire" Britomart's wisdom, they "swear fealty to Artegall"; the difference between the two actions suggests the difference between honorific and actual power.)[12] Thus the figure of equity, even in the nominally mythologizing service of Gloriana's sovereign power (a power that Artegall himself, of course, is officially designated as being subordinate to), implicates the female sovereignty of Elizabeth/Gloriana as a figure of surrogation for an absent male sovereignty.[13]

None of this fits very well, of course, into the cult of Gloriana, in which book 5 ostensibly participates. But the text disingenuously posits the event of its coming under attack—of its being read as a censurable text—as remote; indeed, as virtually unimaginable. First of all, Britomart's act of self-abnegation, capping the cultural dissolution of the Amazons, reinforces the objective status of the norm to which she yields by furnishing a utopian model of self-censorship. The very figure that has come to epitomize the deployment of female power—and that therefore invokes the principal locus outside the text from which the arm of censorship might extend—silences itself, publicly recognizing its own contingency. Disarmingly, the text rewrites the image of petrification that R. C. in 1587 applied to the power of the monarch's gaze over would-be conspirators. Now the monarch's Medusa-like power willingly becomes self-reflexive. That is, it becomes self-cancelling in a context governed by an inviolable Other, by the phallocentric norm that a female sovereign, it is implied, can approximate but, in her "sexly weakness," cannot, and would not choose to, preempt.[14]

Britomart's self-abnegation, in effect, allows the text to equivocate about its own status as a canonical entry in Elizabeth's discourse of power—partly because it suggests that the provisional and supplementary character of female power is so indisputable that the book's prominent figure of female power herself enjoins uniform assent to this perspective. Yet Britomart's self-abnegation also belies even as it engineers the broader metacritical vision that the closing stanzas bring to bear on the presumably inviolable norm in which, by way of the discourse of accommodation, the cult of Gloriana has carved a niche for itself: the norm of a socio-political hierarchy based on male authority. That Britomart should be responsible for Artegall's assumption of power indicates that the normative structure he represents is itself contingent on the participation and complicity of the culture in which it achieves its transcendent aspect. Britomart thus articulates the deregulatory and contaminating power of equity, its power to illuminate the context in which the mythos of a self-evident norm is produced. Through Britomart, the image of female sovereignty becomes a vehicle for rethinking the absolutist premises behind sovereignty in general.[15]

I use the word "rethinking" advisedly, because the text does not allow a space for articulating the kind of insight that such thought might produce. That Britomart's pivotal role in the establishment of Artegall's power should coincide with her own act of self-abnegation reintroduces the ethos of misrecognition into the scrutiny of the norm that the text invites. Once again, the text furnishes evidence of the inherent *aporia* it shares with the discourse of conscience. Through Britomart's self-abnegation it at once perpetuates and dismantles the normative status of authoritative discourse, exposing the premises of such discourse to a critical interrogation that, paradoxically, articulates the process of installing a condition of aphasia where a critical voice might sound.[16]

Canto 7 closes on a note that will reappear on the two principal occasions promoting scrutiny of Elizabeth's power: Artegall's return to Faerie Court and the trial of Duessa. There, as here, Spenser's text stands at one remove from an unambiguous interrogation of the monarch's pretensions to inviolability. It occupies an indeterminate, equivocal discursive space, appropriating for itself what it exposes: the instauration of the aphasiac regime. And, through the proleptic image that closes the canto, it indicates the political motive that shapes this regime. The reference to Artegall's redemption of Irena ("that Lady thrall") announces the final curve in Artegall's peregrinations, his return to Faerie Court. His return, though problematic (as we shall see in the next section), is defined by the narrator as "his right course." Indeed, the text indicates, his return cannot be defined otherwise, despite the textual evidence to the contrary. Artegall's return to Faerie Court signals his reabsorption—literally, his implication—into a norm that is coextensive with Gloriana's system of power, a system on which Artegall's status and very identity depend, a system whose incongruities must therefore be misrecognized. This, too, is the final curve of the text's metacritical operation in canto 7. To make an anachronistic frame of reference: it is as if the text were reproducing the syndrome of the "Emperor's New Clothes," intimating that to represent the norm under the rubric of equity is to betray its artifice and yet at the same time to recognize the imperative to eradicate such insight.

Artegall's Return to Faerie Court

Marked by the self-referential and self-critical character that we have seen elsewhere in texts invoking the thematics of conscience, the final sequence of canto 7 alerts us to the equivocal position the book as a whole takes toward the truths, the pre-texts, on which the "legend of justice" is ostensibly predicated. The sequence does not simply reaffirm Artegall's rightful place as Gloriana's instrument of equity. In depicting the collusion of Britomart and the narrator in rendering Britomart's association with Artegall innocuous, not to say banal, it suggests that Artegall's place—and by extension the "absolute justice" with which Artegall, equity, and the domain of conscience are officially identified—is secured by a cultural and political imperative to misrecognize the signs of a material authoring presence behind what pass for authorless truisms.[17]

How appropriate, in this light, that the final image of Artegall in the canto should evoke a godlike agency performing a redemptive act. Artegall is the one who, the narrator points out, "ne euer howre did cease / Till he redeemed had that Lady thrall" (5.7.45). The narrative context permits us to read what the narrator does *not* point out: that the prolepsis has a retroactive resonance; that it constitutes the finishing touch in the rewriting of the episode in which Artegall, himself enthralled, had to be "redeemed"—refashioned, let us say, in his heroic garb; and that it is conspicuously a finishing touch, a detail that is not produced by the logic of the narrative at this point but introduced from without. This detail, we should note, militates against the absoluteness of Britomart's effacement by indicating the continued presence of Britomart's surrogate, the narrator, who knows how things will and must turn out for Artegall and whose perspective is both guided and limited by his conviction of possessing privileged information. As it happens, the information is true— Artegall does rescue Irena, in canto 12. But the information is also biased—it coincides with the narrator's allusion to his particularized vantage point, from which he announces where the true knowledge he possesses will "fitly fall" in his construction of the narrative. The narrator, advertising his power to withhold such information, to defer telling all until the appropriate moment arises (in "another Canto"), speaks in a context in which it is already apparent that the truth being unfolded about Artegall is the narrator's truth. That is, the narrator speaks in a context that shows the truth, which is necessarily mediated, to be necessarily the correlative of a certain subjectivity. To read the concluding sequence to canto 7 is to observe how this subjectivity, however evident (as shown in the narrator's self-conscious shaping of the canto's final events), is nevertheless destined to be misread, its presence rendered unintelligible (as Britomart's is), so that the distance between the marketplace of opinion and what Donne called the "Cragged, and steep" mountain sanctuary of "Truth" will continue to be seen as impassable—like the distance separating Britomart and Artegall.

The book's conclusion ostensibly fulfills the promises made in canto 7: it gives us the rescue of Irena and Artegall's return to Faerie Court. Reduced to tabloid simplicity, the narrative at this point tells a story about a homecoming, about the anticipated closing of the distance that separates Artegall and Gloriana. Bringing plot and theme together, the narrative appears to exploit the mythic power of the notion of the hero's return as a reinstatement and validation of the values obtaining in the world to which the hero returns. The narrative's heuristic and linear progression appears ultimately to be inscribed in a circular movement, in a narrative evocation of the conquering timelessness—the "stedfast rest of all things, firmly stayed / Upon the pillours of Eternity" ("Mutabilitie Cantos" 8.2)—of which Gloriana's reign, through the canonical perspective at least, affords a glimpse.

The tensions that complicate this reassuring vision, and the ways in which the tensions are treated, remind us that wherever the action of equity—Artegall—takes us (even into Gloriana's court), reassuring visions are likely to turn problematic. Resuming his career, we can observe how the contradictory associations of *synteresis* and *conscientia* are conflated in Artegall, who is both the book's exalted figure of equity (equity considered as the sentinel of stable norms) and the recurring locus of equity's dislocating power, its power to summon the contextual information (i.e., the circumstances of time, place, and person) that enables equity itself (like conscience) to assume its official and timeless or decontextualized pose, to appear outside rather than inside a culture-specific continuum of interpretive construction.

Let us look again at Artegall—first, at the narrative details that contribute to Artegall's official status as the icon of equity.[18] Gloriana chooses Artegall as her "Champion of true Iustice" (5.1.3) because he is already so designated: the goddess Astraea has instructed Artegall from his infancy in the "discipline of iustice" (5.1.6). What better credentials, indeed, could be produced? No human hand, not even a privileged, royal one, has made Artegall what he is. Gloriana's choice merely recognizes the incontrovertible, because divinely chosen, identity of the hero, who is not only Astraea's disciple but, after her return to the heavens, her surrogate on earth as well. Through Artegall, equity thus appears as the trace of the divine mind in human affairs and, specifically, in the courtly social structure to which both Artegall and his sovereign belong.

As the privileged medium through which the now-absent Astraea will perpetuate her divine discourse or "discipline of iustice," Artegall delivers judgments that have the authority of a divine pronouncement. In his first case, the "doubtfull cause" between the Squire and Sir Sanglier, Artegall offers to resolve the conflict with a decorous modesty that does not prevent him from invoking the context in which his forthcoming judgment is to be received. His gracious request that the contenders let his words end their quarrel follows a summary of the other available options:

> Now sure this doubtfull causes right
> Can hardly but by Sacrament be tride,
> Or else by ordele, or by blooddy fight,
> That ill perhaps mote fall to either side;
> But if ye please that I your cause decide,
> Perhaps I may all further quarrell end,
> So ye will sweare my iudgement to abide.
>
> (5.1.25)

In this speech, Artegall locates his role as judge within a series of other, culturally sanctioned, heuristics: the hieratic utterance of the confessor; the ritual of the ordeal, with the outcome to be read as the *judicium Dei*; and, push coming to shove, the recourse to physical battle.[19] Artegall's suggestion that the kind of solution he offers would represent a marked improvement over the last option carries with it a more general, and more important, implication: what he offers is also not to be doubted as an adequate surrogate for the "Sacrament" and the "ordele" and should be received as such—as it is in the case of Amidas and Bracidas in canto 4. After hearing the terms of the dispute that has set the twin squires at odds, Artegall merely observes that the case would be easily solved if they submitted it to "some righteous man" (5.4.16). The squires have no difficulty perceiving that Artegall himself is such a man: they spontaneously vow to accept the terms of Artegall's judgment (and faithfully do so once the judgment is rendered). Enjoying the unsolicited recognition of his power and privileged place as the guardian of justice, the knight of equity has, it would seem, an epiphanic presence. To borrow the Scriptural touchstones, we might say that where Artegall appears the mythos of the Transfiguration rather than of Emmaus obtains. Artegall's quasi-divine status cannot, it would seem, go unrecognized.

This is not to say that Artegall's judgments and status are never disputed. Spenser's legend of justice, committed as it is to examining the state of entropy that Gloriana's "great iustice" must be shown to arrest, admits into its canvass the agonistic character of Artegall's progress through Faerieland. Indeed, the narrative is punctuated by verbal or physical challenges to Artegall's authority, challenges that, in the main, follow the pattern established in Artegall's first case: the knight of equity is tested so that the nature and extent of his power may make itself manifest. In canto 1, after Artegall has decided the case in favor of the Squire, Sir Sanglier refuses to accept Artegall's judgment. But his resistance is short-lived. No sooner has the challenge arisen than Talus, the "yron man," Astraea's groom whom Artegall has inherited, takes his first opportunity to serve his master. He enforces Artegall's word; he enacts its performative power, literally subduing the renegade word of Sanglier (who had sworn to follow Artegall's judgment). Talus, the text reads, "represt" Sanglier's "pride," so that Sanglier "saw it bootelesse to resist" Artegall's authority. In Talus, the mechanism of Artegall's authority, we encounter a force akin to that of conscience. "Immoveable, resistlesse, without end," Talus embodies the hegemonic and coercive agency associated, as in the Pauline epistles, with the analogous retributive actions of conscience and divine wrath.[20] Talus exhibits, as well, a perspicacity that recalls the omniscient power of conscience.[21] It is Talus who keeps a "nightly watch for dread of treachery" in Artegall's pavilion before the knight's battle against the Amazons, a service he later repeats for Britomart when she prepares to vanquish Radigund.[22] It is Talus who enables Artegall, when he finally undertakes the reformation of Irena's land, to administer "True Iustice" against the enemies of state ("those that used to rob and steale, / Or did rebell gainst lawfull government"), for it is Talus who has the power to "reueale / All hidden crimes" (5.12.26). Talus—monolithic, omniscient, swiftly avenging—epitomizes Artegall's own role as the embodiment of conscience in the realm: like *synteresis*, Talus appears as the unerring "true guide" of Artegall's "way and vertuous government" (5.8.30).

Thus endowed, Talus personifies one of the legitimizing functions of the discourse of conscience. He personifies the principle of absolute difference, which we have observed in other texts. This principle posits the inviolable integrity of the truth that conscience holds; it draws a kind of conceptual *cordon sanitaire* around the truth of conscience, relegating all that is not truth to an unambiguously demarcated zone whose regions are known to the arbiter of conscience and manifested by the "pricks" and other sensitizing and coercive actions of the guilty conscience. Articulating this principle, the discourse of conscience, in its official, normative usage, participates in the cultural phenomenon of constituting the Other, an action that defines what is to be perceived as intrinsically different, separate, and, as though in natural consequence, aberrant (an action represented in part by discourses detailing, and discrediting, the salient characteristics of the heretic, the pagan, the monstrous, and to a certain degree the female sex). We can see this principle being played out in one of Artegall's early triumphs in book 5, his agonistic encounter with the Egalitarian Giant, which culminates in the Giant's failure to "iustly weigh the wrong or right" on his scale—because it cannot hold right and wrong at the same time. The scale, the objective measure, corroborates Artegall's claim that the two qualities are essentially incompatible (a view that the narrator also voices, interrupting his description of the Giant's frustrated effort with the comment, "by no means the false will with the truth be wayd" [5.2.45]).[23] By no means, either, it would appear, are the Giant's egalitarian politics—the monster's monstrous program—to be mistaken for the truth, which must therefore be located, as though with a mathematical rigor, in Artegall's pious invocation of the hierarchical scheme underlying Gloriana's divine-right monarchy (as well as his own authority): God himself "maketh Kings to sit in souerainty; / He maketh subiects to their powre obay" (5.2.41).

   This kind of ideological polarization receives an even more compact treatment in the representation of Adicia's fate, in cantos 8 and 9. After her husband, the Souldan, has been destroyed in combat against Arthur, Adicia goes on a rampage of neon-like intensity, outstripping in the violence of her rage not only the most infamous cases of degenerate (and female) criminality—"raging Ino," Medea, and Agave—but the epitome of "crueltie and outrage" in the animal world as well, the tiger. She in fact becomes a tiger; and her transformation from human to beast is mirrored, as she is transported by her "franticke passion," in her passage from the world of human commerce to the "wyld wood," two regions that the narrator, in his gloss of Adicia's transformation, contrasts as absolutely as the opposing gestalts of right and wrong. In the figure of the tiger stalking in the wilderness, he remarks, we are to read the danger of "wrong, when it hath arm'd it selfe with might," a danger mitigated by the fact that wrong thus unleashed is at least visible, subject to universal censure, and, as the case of Adicia shows, subject to exile from the human community. Wrong, like the tiger and Adicia, is

> Not fit mongst men that doe with reason mell,
> But mongst wyld beasts and saluage woods to dwell;
> Where still the stronger doth the weake deuoure,
> And they that most in boldnesse doe excell
> Are dreadded most, and feared for their powre;
> Fit for Adicia there to build her wicked bowre.
>
> There let her wonne farre from resort of men,
> Where righteous Artegall her late exyled;
> There let her euer keepe her damned den,
> Where none may be with her lewd parts defyled,
> Where none but beasts may be of her despoyled.

(5.9.1–2)

The "saluage woods" appear as nothing less than the realm of otherness, of all that is constituted, in spatial terms, as "farre from resort of men," of all that is conceived of as intrinsically alien to human society. Like the transformed Adicia, the passions of bestial existence and government by brute force are represented as having, both literally and figuratively, no place in the profile of human society, a society governed, as the narrator sees it, by reason and righteousness.[24]

The self-evidence of the principle of absolute difference is not the narrator's perception alone, however. When Adicia takes what appears to be her proper place in the "wyld wood" she merely gives a final, spatially realized dimension to the otherness that has characterized her at her entrance in the book. Her very name makes the point morphologically. "Adicia," the Greek word for "injustice," is formed from two distinct, opposing, and irreconcilable parts: a substantive, which implies the ontological priority of the named concept, and the antithetical prefix, which identifies the semantic region of all that can never be assimilated into, or confused with, the originary concept.

Adicia herself contributes to the integrity of this polarized state. That is, she is represented neither as being subjugated by a distorting ethos nor as sabotaging the received order of things by staking a claim for her own character and actions as the epitome of a rival system of justice. Indeed, we learn early on that Adicia "her selfe professeth mortall foe / To Iustice, and against her still doth fight" (5.8.20). No less than the presumably objective measure of the scales, Adicia helps legitimate the principle of absolute difference on which Artegall's authority depends. In the clarity and rigor with which she corroborates this principle, she is to Artegall's enemy in canto 8, the Souldan, what Talus is to Artegall throughout the book. As the presiding spirit of the Souldan's "cruel tyranny," counselling him "To breake all bonds of law and rules of right" (5.8.20), she mirrors Talus's role as Artegall's "true guide," enacting in negative relief the differentiating function of Talus's iron flail, with which he "thresht out falshood, and did truth unfold" (5.1.12).

Talus's flail provides an apt emblem for the text's own nominal purpose of making visible an unchanging, unambiguous system of order underlying the apparently mutable and interchangeable identities of things. Like the flail, which belongs to a cycle of seasonal activities, to a natural order, the text participates in the propagation of what is known to be "natural," what appear as the unbiased facts, in the world Spenser represents—specifically, the association of truth and justice with Artegall, Arthur, Britomart, Mercilla, the various avatars of the "Dread Soueraigne Goddesse" Gloriana/Elizabeth in Faerieland, and the association of falsehood and injustice with figures like Adicia and the Souldan.

But, like the flail, the text has a double valence. It has the status both of an icon, a receptacle for timeless truths, and of a tool constituted and employed by the human community to meet certain needs, whether physical or symbolic.[25] It is in this latter capacity that the text, while exhibiting its normative, iconic function, implicates that very function as a product of a cultural practice, a practice that promotes belief in a corpus of unbiased truths through an economy of interpretation according to which the signs likely to problematize such a belief, signs pointing up the constitutive role of bias and context, are perceived as inconsequential—are relegated, one might say, like Adicia to a realm defined as having no points of correspondence

with the human community. In other words, the plenitude of meaning associated with the articulation and generalized reception of
categories like the unbiased truth, the Spenserian text implies, arises
from a selectivity of perception.[26] To follow Artegall as well as the
narrator, whose filtering role periodically becomes apparent, leads us
to observe how the act of representing a norm in the legend of justice
includes the act of erasing, or misrecognizing, the circumstances that
violate the mythos of a normative value as a thing received rather
than produced. The very status of norms thus becomes implicated as
a function or effect of a process of erasure, of selective vision. We
have already seen how Artegall's iconic dimension appears in the
text; we can now look more closely at this representation from the
perspective of the demythologizing contexts that, like a minefield,
surround the book's hero and the narrator who records his exploits.

Near the end of book 5 Artegall serves up what will turn out
to be his last major hieratic statement. Once again assuming his
designated role as judge of equity and director of conscience, Artegall chastises an unrepentant Sir Burbon for having fallen into the
"greatest shame and foulest scorne" by abandoning his shield in the
course of his attempt to recover his lady Flourdelis from her cap-
tors. In Burbon's estimation, the act is defensible on several counts,
all of which appear either inadmissible or unintelligible to Artegall.
For one thing, his action was prompted, Burbon argues, not by his
"will" but by the "inforcement" of circumstances—notably his perception that without the shield he would stand a better chance of
gaining access to Flourdelis. His action, he argues, amounts to a
necessary, but not a permanent, concession to the particular constraints of his case:

> When time doth serue,
> My former shield I may resume againe:
> To temporize is not from truth to swerue,
> Ne for aduantage terme to entertaine,
> When as necessitie doth it constraine.

> (5.11.56)

Here is Artegall's response:

> "Fie on such forgerie!" (said Artegall)
> "Under one hood to shadow faces twaine:

Knights ought be true, and truth is one in all:
Of all things to dissemble fouly may befall!"

(5.11.56)

Despite the apparent ease with which Artegall rejects Burbon's position, this is not an easy moment in the text. The absolutist rhetoric informing Artegall's words loses something of its integrity under scrutiny. To be sure, Burbon's representation and defense of his behavior evokes the kind of perceptual bias associated with the lax conscience: the collusion of self-interest and desire (to borrow Bourdaloue's terms) producing in the lax conscience a virtually impenetrable, because self-deluding, masquerade of innocence.[27] No doubt it is possible to see in Burbon's words, as Artegall appears to, a cunning imitation of a good examination of conscience—particularly in view of the political allegory that makes Burbon a figure for Henry of Navarre and Burbon's behavior, mirroring Navarre's notorious conversion to Catholicism, a metonymic enactment of what might be expected generally, by the 1590's, of the Catholic population at large, a population widely believed to be trained in the casuistry of the Jesuits and thus to be the epitome of the "forgeries" of the lax conscience.[28] No doubt, too, it is possible to see in Artegall's words the corrective to the laxity that might be ascribed to Burbon. Artegall, we might say, benefiting from his insight into the shape of absolute justice, sees Burbon's case from the proper, the objectively true, perspective and is able to see what Burbon, apparently, cannot: that the impulse to attain a desired goal—even, perhaps especially, a praiseworthy one—can be treacherous, insofar as the impulse can blind one to the larger ethical issues at stake and can convince one of the integrity of one's own motives even as one, pursuing the impulse, embraces an unethical course of action. No doubt this kind of reading meshes with the official position of book 5 as a tribute to the divinely inspired insight of Gloriana and her selected representatives in the administration of justice. But, as elsewhere in book 5, this kind of reading requires a certain blindness to the evidence in the text that the argument in which Artegall and Burbon appear pitted against one another cannot, in fact, be reduced to neat polarities.

To begin with, we should note that Burbon's action thematizes the casuistical principle of *dolus bonus*, the good deceit, which by definition blurs the strict conceptual boundaries demarcating truth and falsehood and, accordingly, problematizes the sieve-like role of conscience as the discerner of good and evil. So, too, with the social and political arena in which the principle was employed: while the *dolus bonus* might be docketed in Spenser's England as a popish (and therefore traitorous) practice, it was not the exclusive property of the alleged enemies of the state. True, both the physical and verbal evasions of the recusant population lent themselves to interpretation, among Protestants, as evidence of the moral degeneration to be found among papists and in the casuistical reasoning associated with popery. But, of course, by the 1590s it was also evident that casuistry was becoming a useful heuristic method in the pastoral care of the Protestant community, a method that, however "purified" of alleged Jesuitical excesses, did not exclude the *dolus bonus* from the protocol of permissible practices, as the casuistry of William Perkins, for example, indicates.[29]

Consider, too, Burbon's apparent self-deception—the way he appears to have hit upon an utterly persuasive (to himself if not to his audience) rationale for his behavior. If the insidious action of the lax conscience betrays itself here, it nevertheless cannot be said that such action is essentially a function of an immersion in popish casuistry. Shakespeare's Bolingbroke, in *2 Henry IV*, speaks the same self-protective language as Burbon when he reviews before Warwick the circumstances of his ascent to Richard's throne: "God knows," he avers, "I had no such intent, / But that necessity so bowed the state / That I and greatness were compelled to kiss" (3.1.72–74). No less than the Lancastrian's, the Bourbon monarch's capacity to engage in what might be construed as a kind of verbal fade-out before issues of moral responsibility cannot merely be consigned to the either/or frame of the sixteenth century's ongoing religious polemic. What the two Henrys have in common besides (and, surely, more significantly than) an association with the Catholic world is a deep, perhaps a blinding, involvement in the business of dynasty-building—and a fascination with the boundless extension of the self's jurisdiction, both spatial and temporal, that the acquisition of such authority and power promises.[30]

I will return to this point directly. For the moment it is worth noting that, if we can briefly suspend Artegall's condemnation of Burbon's "forgerie" (as well as Artegall's tone of indisputable moral superiority), the difference between the two men need not be ethically charged. Their respective positions indicate, among other things, two different ways of viewing and understanding experience. For Artegall, the shield in question is the irreducible equivalent of its symbolic meaning, of the code—the "honours stile"—inscribed on its surface. Thus conceived, the shield does not merely represent Burbon's honor. To borrow Artegall's own language, like a physical vessel it "contains" Burbon's honor; in effect, constitutes it. In Artegall's words we can see the hegemony of a programmatic allegoresis, the pure externalization and reification of intangibles, like personal honor. We can see, moreover, the implicit self-definition of Artegall's reading as the only possible reading (i.e., if "honour" itself—rather than its representation—is at stake, it will not do to interpret the shield according to other lights). Indeed, Artegall's reading, once seen as the only possible one, looks very much like not a reading at all: Artegall presents himself as merely articulating the single existential fact of the shield.

Burbon's words, in contrast, suggest the shield's polysemous character and the related possibility of multiple interpretations of the shield (as of Burbon's decision to lay it aside). For Burbon, the shield is as much a cherished testimony to the spiritual kinship between him and Redcrosse as it is a symbol of his own "honours stile." But it is also a physical object, a thing on which symbolic meaning has been conferred, a meaning that, for all its power, does not entirely efface the sheer literal substance of the shield as a mere "bloodie scutchin . . . battered sore." Burbon's words speak of the possibility of admitting more than one perspective onto an object or event under scrutiny. Such an approach yields a complex, rather than a reductive, vision of the act of reading casuistically. It recognizes, for one thing, the circumstances of interiority and intentionality in the profile of the determining issues in a case: Burbon's sense of honor may well appear slippery, sliding toward a nominalist, not to say antinomian, bias; but it is nevertheless Burbon's words, not Artegall's, that posit honor as having a private dimension, as being not merely a measure of *fama*, not merely a function of the collective interpretive powers of others. Implicitly, Burbon's position challenges the assumptions—of the exclusivity and plenitude of meaning and of a cosmos of static correspondences—that lie behind Artegall's hieratic pronouncement. None of this means, of course, that Burbon's view is therefore justified and that Artegall's is not. The abuses liable to accompany Burbon's interpretive method are evident enough. What Burbon alerts us to, besides an alternative, if problematic, way of reading the "hard case" of the shield, is an alternative way of reading Artegall as well. That Burbon's rule of conduct ("To temporize is not from truth to swerue") does not appear a "forgerie" to Burbon himself makes it possible to see how what one construes as an objective reality may derive from an imperceptible, self-legitimating subjectivity. This insight applies to Artegall's rule of conduct as well, which shares with Burbon's the cadence of a gnomic utterance and the implicit claim to being the unbiased impression of a general truth. In other words, once the thematics of the lax conscience are admitted into the picture, the convenient polarities break down; and they do so in ways that do not necessarily respect the official pieties recorded in the text. Artegall's words are not therefore discredited; they are, however, dislodged from their position, as words ultimately deriving from a divine agency, of *necessary* immunity to critical scrutiny.

Artegall's fleeting intersection with Burbon, and with the attending thematics of the *dolus bonus* and the lax conscience, does not bear alone the burden of problematizing the integrity of his position. It does not because Artegall's position is burdened with its own internal contradictions. First of all, there is something "immoveable, resistlesse, without end," something Talus-like, in his response to Burbon that points us away from the tempered justice of equity—which Artegall, of course, is supposed to embody—and toward the unmitigating rule of *ius extremis*. That is, Artegall's air of intransigence opens up his position to interpretation as part of a symptomatology of a sclerotized justice, one so hardened against the possibility of error on the side of permissiveness that it risks erring on the side of severity and, as William Perkins observed, risks betraying its original purpose: *summa ius, summa injuria.*[31]

Moreover, even if one accepts Artegall's position unquestioningly, the context that frames it continues to problematize it. It is Burbon, not Artegall, who has the last word in the dispute; and it is the priorities implicit in his words that prevail in determining the action that Artegall subsequently takes:

> "Yet let me you of courtesie request"
> (Said Burbon) "to assist me now at need
> Against these pesants which have me opprest,
> And forced me to so infamous deed,
> That yet my loue may from their hands be freed."
> Sir Artegall, albe he earst did wyte
> His wauering mind, yet to his aide agreed,
> And buckling him eftsoones unto the fight,
> Did set vpon those troupes with all his powre and might.
>
> (5.11.57)

Burbon maintains to the end the distinction between the infamy of a deed and the innocence of the agent. In this he introduces nothing new into his argument, nothing that can be said to effectively disable Artegall's scrupulousness. Yet Burbon succeeds in enlisting Artegall's aid. That is, he persuades Artegall to risk the infamy that could redound to Artegall himself as a result of his public association with an apostate and criminal. (This official view of Burbon, evident in Artegall's response to the knight, appears entrenched in the narrative. Witness the narrator's catalog of criminals at the beginning of the next canto: Artegall's concession does not save Burbon from being cited with Gerioneo and Grantorto, two of the book's notorious villains, of whom it cannot be said that Artegall is willing to risk the scandal of befriending.) The key to Burbon's success, perhaps, lies in the secular considerations he introduces, invoking a shared practical calculus of values that alters if not displaces the unyielding moral geometry to which Artegall had, theoretically, committed himself in chastising Burbon. Making his request "of courtesie" for assistance in putting down the rebellious "pesants," Burbon tacitly reminds Artegall of their aristocratic commonality and of the implications for Artegall of discounting it: the onus of transgressing the social code of "courtesie" and of contributing to the assault on the received social order that the behavior of the peasants represents. Acquiescing to Burbon's request, Artegall in turn tacitly admits that the abstract code of virtue he so ardently defended must yield, *de facto*, to Bur-

bon's. That Artegall should consent to join Burbon on the field belies, in effect, the adequacy of his own vaunted perspective, in contrast to Burbon's more nuanced one.

In any case, this is not the first time that Artegall's behavior has
been caught up in a web of contradictions. As we shall see in a moment, one of the central stories that unfolds in book 5 is that of the
narrator's attempt to occlude the details of Artegall's career that
threaten to contaminate his iconic aspect, including the evidence of
Artegall's own dissembling. Indeed, it is the very ethos that admits
the logic of dissembling—the *dolus bonus*—that pervades the narrative, in apparently contradictory ways. What appears on the one
hand as an object of censure, as in Artegall's decrying Burbon's "forgerie," turns up on the other hand in the actions of Artegall and the
narrator himself as an innocuous practice consonant with the text's
canonical status. This feature illustrates how the thematics of the
dolus bonus, an inherently maverick affair to begin with, betrays the
ambiguous status of the text. To focus the question in terms of Burbon's and Artegall's physical convergence on the field, the text invites
us to speculate about the apparent justification of Artegall's decision
to associate himself with Burbon. Is the decision justified because of
the motive prompting it (a motive, we should note, not made explicit in the text)? If so, Artegall remains in the contradictory position of condemning Burbon's ethos, which recognizes intentionality
as a pivotal circumstance, while apparently appropriating that ethos
when the time comes for him to act. Or is the decision justified in
some absolute sense? If so, the text does nothing to dispel the ensuing suspicion that such assurance derives less from the intrinsic quality of the act in question than from the received status of the agent:
are Artegall's actions exempt from the judgment of conscience because it is Artegall who performs them? The reticence of the text on
this point is itself unsettling rather than reassuring, insofar as it suggests that questions of this sort must generally be deemed irrelevant
(not to say unposable) because they are, to say the least, impolitic.

In other words, as Artegall approaches the scene of his triumph
over Grantorto the text insinuates a demythologizing perspective
into the background of the event, a perspective through which it
becomes possible to read the "True Iustice" that Artegall embodies
as a cipher for the relations of power that lie outside the text, in the

Elizabethan church-state, and that constitute a dissimulated bias informing the received profile of such absolutes as "True Iustice."[32] In this context we should note that what finally impresses the narrator about Artegall's behavior in the Burbon episode is not the cause of justice he nominally serves but the sheer force with which he acts. The knight of equity "Did set upon those troupes" not explicitly to preserve, say, "truth and right" but rather in a demonstration of "all his powre and might." Artegall's sweep across the field represents something more than the force of nature, though that is, no doubt, the primary sense of the comparison the narrator draws between Artegall and "wrathfull Boreas." Just as the wind is both invisible and penetrating, so is the hegemony of the politics of interpretation that secures the iconic status of Gloriana and her "instruments" in Elizabethan culture.

The text drives the point home in the culminating episode, the moment of Artegall's long-deferred and, as it turns out, equivocal triumph. Having dispatched Grantorto, Artegall seems at last to realize equity's restorative power. "His studie was true Iustice how to deale," we learn, and "How to reforme that ragged common-weale" through the agency of conscience, Talus, "which could reueale / All hidden crimes" (5.12.26). It should come as no surprise at this stage that such a vision of "true Iustice" is no sooner articulated than problematized:

> But, ere he could reforme it thoroughly,
> He through occasion called was away
> To Faerie Court, that of necessity
> His course of Iustice he was forst to stay,
> And Talus to reuoke from the right way
> In which he was that Realme for to redresse.
>
> (5.12.27)

We never learn why Artegall's mission is interrupted. The clues available in the narrator's words reveal very little; and what they reveal are mostly signs of a strained effort to suppress a heterodox reading of the event. To report that Artegall was called away "through occasion" is more than a piece of evasion, though on that score alone the remark would be damaging enough. The connotations of the word "occasion" cut two ways. It can be a neutral term, signifying a

"juncture or condition of things, an occurrence, fact, or consideration, affording ground for an action or a state of mind or feeling." It
can also be a sign of duplicity: "a pretext; an excuse."[33] The word
appears in book 4 manifestly endowed with the latter sense. One of
the impediments to Venus Temple, which Scudamour must vanquish, is the figure of Delay, "Whose manner was all passengers to
stay, / And entertaine with her occasions sly" (4.10.13). It is hard not
to see this sense of the word resonating in the description of the
aborted reformation of Irena's land, where the notion of delay is
triply appropriate. The interruption itself effectively delays the instauration of "true Iustice"; the narrative context indicates that Artegall's most recent exploit—the encounter with Burbon—danger-
ously delayed his mission, to the extent that, for the first time in the
narrative, the passage of time itself appears as a circumstance that
Artegall must strive to conquer (leaving Burbon, Artegall "to his
voyage gan again proceed; / For that the terme, approching fast,
required speed" [5.11.55]); and, finally, the referential scope of the
word invokes the staying hand of the monarch over the actions of
her ministers and courtiers—in particular, the characteristic temporizing and equivocal gestures of Elizabeth, which marked her behavior in the historical event generally read into the Grantorto episode,
the protracted course of taming Ireland.[34]

Whatever the circumstances—the "occasion"—of Artegall's re-
moval from action might be, they are rendered suspect by the second
evasive detail. The narrator's drumming up the "necessity" argument
tells us less about the occasion itself than it does about the ostensibly
imperceptible pressure to read Artegall canonically at all costs. The
narrator, of course, has appropriated Burbon's self-justifying argument, the very argument that Artegall condemned (remember his
outburst: "Fie on such forgerie!" [5.11.56]) and that Artegall himself
later implicitly embraced by joining Burbon's cause. In other words,
the elliptical account of Artegall's return begins by importing an image of Artegall—of equity—and of the "good" reader of the canonical text as related figures of embedded contradiction, of conflicting
values and allegiances. It is not surprising, then, that the account is
framed by two contradictory judgments. Leaving Irena's "ragged
common-weale," Artegall must "reuoke" Talus from "the right way";
yet moments later, as he continues his retreat, passing through the

obstacles of Envie, Detraction, and the Blatant Beast, Artegall is described as unswerving from "his right course." That Artegall's particular "right course"—obeying the monarch's most recent command—should mean departing from the "right way"—administering "true Iustice"—tells us something about the nature of the double bind, or the case of conscience, that Artegall's return evokes. To disobey Gloriana's command would be, of course, to question the inviolability of her authority and to envision a moral hierarchy not stabilized under the gaze of the monarch's conscience. But to obey Gloriana's command, as the legend describes such action, is not to proclaim the identity of the monarch's conscience and "true Iustice." It is to show this identification asserting itself in the face of evidence suggesting divergent, possibly rival, readings of what constitutes "right." It is to show how reading the text of "true Iustice" means submitting to the politics of interpretation that the casuistical weighting of circumstances enacts: to show how the equitable, Lesbian rule of "right" lies not so much in the monarch's word as in the social and political context that brings the word and its readers together, forging a bond predicated on a naturalized cultural disposition to read incongruities as inessential parts of the fabric of truth.

In this moment of closure that shows the artifice of closure in both written and social texts and that demythologizes the notion of an "innocent" or unbiased reading, the legend of justice posits itself as the image of a kind of Ur-text of power. In the narrative's anticipated space for resolutions and final answers, the legend shows itself to be neither submissive to an external authority nor scandalously, explicitly insubordinate. It fits neither the mold of the text that rigorously observes the generic constraints of the canonical encomium nor the mold of the polemical or heretical text. It resides, along with the discourse of conscience that informs it, in the utopian space of equivocation, of unstable and ungovernable significations.

The text illustrates this elusive discursive function in the image of Artegall's snake bite. Passing unperturbed through the obstacle represented by the hags, Envie and Detraction, and the Blatant Beast, Artegall is bitten by Envie's "cursed Serpent," a creature whose description evokes a liminal and indeterminate condition: "half-gnawen," it "was not all so dead / But that some life remayned secretly" (5.12.39). The snake arguably transmits its condition to the discursive power that Artegall—and the text itself—represents as the ambiguously situated instrument of Gloriana's authority. Consider the kinds of discourse the text situates outside Gloriana's court. On the one hand there are the multifarious voices of rumor—the Blatant Beast's "hundred tongues"—and the conspicuous "false sclaunders" of the two hags: these are the wellsprings of verbal anarchy that appear to remain active in the commonwealth, beyond Artegall's power to contain, though their own power, at least as represented by the unsavory trio, appears limited to the region of "woods and rockes," the periphery of Gloriana's world. On the other hand there is the discourse of bondage and submission, the articulation of the fantasy of absolute power, enacted in the dynamic between Artegall and Talus: Talus, we learn, would have "chastize'd" Detraction had not Artegall "him forbidden" and Talus "his heast observed." Clearly there are limits to this kind of discourse, limits that have to do, in part, with the apparent necessity of the reader's (Talus's) willingness to submit to the interdictory word issued to him.

But the text indicates another, a more problematic, limit. The discursive model represented by the exchange between Artegall and Talus does not pass into the jurisdiction of Faerie Court alone. Artegall's body represents a third kind of discourse, one secretly implicated in the dynamic shown to operate between Artegall and Talus. The snake bite, irreverently tattooed on the hero's buttock, presumably (Artegall is bitten "behind"), reminds us of the *pharmakon*-like power that Artegall, the figure of equity, possesses and now bears the mark of, a "marke" that "long," as the narrator observes, "was to be read." Artegall's body, about to be reabsorbed into the center of the body politic, becomes the site of an indelible and, as it were, "legible" yet inscrutable text. All the narrator observes about the "marke" is the length of time it is able to be read, not how it is to be read. Does the mark merely indicate Artegall's native immunity to the contaminated discourse of his adversaries, or does it announce the breakdown of the polarized vision that imagines conditions of immunity and contamination to be stable and unrelated states? Does it announce a break in the seamless envelope that surrounds the idealized corpus of the instruments—conscience, equity—of the discourse of power? What the narrative action shows, and does nothing to dispel, in charting the reentry of the mysteriously marked hero into Faerie Court, is the image of a canonical discourse modeled on the image of the lax conscience, a discourse that does not proclaim or, more disturbingly, appears not to know—to have no "conscience" of—the extent to which its word may work, imperceptibly, like a venomous agent on the body of the culture's sacred myths.

Transgressive Similes; or, The Hierarchies of Circumstances

Much of the destabilizing power of Spenser's text derives from the ways in which the narrative context—the sequencing and juxtaposition of images and, on a larger scale, even episodes—points up a denser, more ambiguously poised, range of signification than would be apparent from a passage read in isolation or read solely in the light of the book's explicit and official project. This power of the text, I have been arguing, has a diffused discursive model in the procedures of casuistical analysis, which represented historically an effort first to contain and later to exploit the evidence of tension between the irreducibly complex and shifting relations among the circumstances of a case, as well as the conflicting perspectives a case might generate, and the unilateral discourse of truth into which the circumstances—the contextual information—were supposed to be subsumed.

In Spenser's text, the most concentrated instance of such tension, and of the reading problem involved, lies in the simile. The appropriateness of its epic associations aside, the rhetoric of the simile finds a resonant chord in the book's heuristic function. The simile's power to adduce the resemblances of apparently disparate things, and the proximity of apparently distant things, participates in the rhetoric of the all-encompassing power that emanates from Gloriana's court, into which all parts of the commonwealth must converge. Furthermore, the simile represents, in a kind of shorthand script, the narrative's own nominal power to collapse its spatially and temporally divergent elements into the circular movement that Artegall's return to the court inscribes in the text. This movement defines closure not as the figurative discovery of a new land but as the recovery of the point of origin, as though the narrative were able to conquer or negate the linearity and temporal flux that narrative itself embodies. But the image of closure in this legend, we have seen, is a misreading, a façade. At pivotal moments in book 5 the simile, too, leads to transgressive vistas. The reading problems it raises have mainly to do with the centrifugal force of the intertextual space it introduces. Through its allusive extensions into other texts, into "foreign" interpretive regimes that remain at odds with the narrative context, the simile suggests the arbitrariness of the canonical perspective officially promulgated in the narrative. The vision of interpretive plenitude invoked by the simile's participation in the circular movement of the narrative is a vision won, the simile suggests, by a corresponding movement of interpretive elisions.

Book 5 begins, we might note, by signalling the privileged role that the production and reading of similes will play in the narrative. The primary mediator and "good" reader, the narrator, construes his activity on the model of simile making, bringing disparate and distant things together. Thus his opening words: "So oft as I with state of present time / The image of the antique world compare . . ." (5.proem.1). This activity is at once central and problematic: it does not yield a harmonious whole but a vision of irreducible conflict and incompatibility: "Such oddes I finde twixt those, and these which are, / As that . . . / Me seemes the world is runne quite out of square / From the first point of his appointed course" (5.proem.1). The first simile in the book follows, as if to illustrate what we, the readers, are to take as a model of the problematic of interpretation that will be variously exploited throughout the book. Pursuing the argument of entropy, the narrator observes that in the current "stonie" age, the human community is no longer "form'd of flesh and bone" but is "now transformed into hardest stone; / Such as behind their backs (so backward bred) / Were throwne by Pyrrha and Deucalione" (5.proem.2). The myth of Pyrrha and Deucalione is, of course, more than a story about creation; it is a story, like the myth of Noah, about the miraculous redemption and rebirth of the human community after a disaster and near extinction. It is a story about the defeat of entropy. Yet, rather than appearing near the proem's close, when the narrator asserts the godlike, restorative "soueraine powre" of Princes, the simile turns up here, garbled, absorbed into the entropic ethos, its message distorted—"backward bred"—through the interpretive lens the narrator has embraced at this point. The Pyrrha and Deucalione simile, misplaced and misread, does not so much testify to the universality of the redemptive ethos associated with the "state of present time," as idealized and given ritual shape in Gloriana's court, as it testifies to the ongoing bias, the interpretive hierarchies, that readers, like the narrator, project onto texts and that determine, according to measures not always obvious, what is to pass into intelligibility.

Barely into the proem, the initial simile invokes an imported text and a scale of values that the narrator misreads, as though in tacit admission of the intrinsic power of the simile, like the power of equity itself, to test the limits of the interpretive regime governing the text it is written into. The questions it raises—What are the boundaries of a "correct" reading? What forces determine such boundaries?—acquire more specific, more politically attuned, dimensions in the two cases we will examine next, the one taken from a pivotal moment in Britomart's career, the other from one of the signal triumphs in the book, Arthur's over the Souldan.

Even before she undertakes the business of reformation in the land of the Amazons at the end of canto 7, there is a prodromal sign that Britomart's association with power is about to evaporate. Given the metaphoric adulteration she has thus far been subjected to, it is not surprising that her own "great wonder and astonishment" upon discovering the imprisoned, transvestite Artegall should be couched in a simile that likens her to the "most chast Penelope," who failed to recognize Ulysses upon his return to Ithaca after "long travell of full twenty yeares" ("She knew not his favours likelynesse," the narrator recalls, "But stood long staring on him mongst uncertaine feares" [5.7.39]). Through the simile the narrator invokes the thematics of misrecognition, which resonates on several registers. We are invited to grasp a dynamic that the text allocates not only to the represented couples but, self-referentially, to its own procedure as well. Penelope misreads Ulysses. So, too, her chaste counterpart misreads Artegall. So, too, the narrator misreads Britomart and Artegall, invoking Penelope, the figure of female passivity and domesticity, as the typological model for Britomart and Ulysses, the figure of unbounded heroic pursuit, for Artegall. This event occurs, notably, at a moment when, through the direct contrast of the triumphant, kinetic (and, unlike Radigund, noble) figure of Britomart and the subordinate, passive figure of Artegall, the mythos of an infallible, self-generating male supremacy appears susceptible to revision. Framed in this context, the simile at once inscribes the text of the phallocentric "truth" as the interpretive touchstone of the episode and reinscribes that text as a text of patent incongruity. In particular, it associates that text with an economy of exchange that has no place, officially, in the self-presentation of authoritative discourse as a transcendent reality. Artegall's gain is measured out precisely according to Britomart's loss. His reinstatement as a figure of epic proportions appears as a function of Britomart's own translation into a figure that represents a male fantasy of what femaleness should signify and that denies the complexity and range of Britomart's identity. And, needless to say, that denies her role in reinstating Artegall. In other words, the passage from the narrative context to the simile—Penelope's substitution for Britomart—enacts the process through which authoritative discourse denies its own contextual background, rendering unintelligible what it deems incongruous: the destabilizing implications of femaleness, equity, and conscience. Paradoxically, then, the simile, by articulating the instauration of the regime of misrecognition in the text, posits its own contextual incongruity as unintelligible.

And, it would seem, as inevitably so. Even before Britomart herself abdicates (making what appears to be a conscious choice), an external voice, the narrator's, announces her abdication. In the simile the narrator sets up the limits of intelligibility that Britomart's rehabilitative actions—dispatching Radigund for Artegall, getting him out of his "uncomely" transvestite role, and restoring his "dreadfull manly looke" and heroic stature—can achieve in a world not disposed to dwell on the implications of recognizing the contingency of the norms that the heroic Artegall embodies. Indeed, at the end of the canto it is the mythic configuration of the simile rather than Britomart's recent personal history that provides the lens through which the narrator reads her. Both Artegall and Britomart leave the land of the Amazons, in a parallel action that emphasizes the gap that now imposes itself between the two figures. Artegall, resuming his quest, not only leaves Britomart; he leaves no trace of any connection, of any debt, to her. Britomart's "noble Lord" appears as an entirely self-contained, autochthonous force, whose basic character-istic is unstinting devotion to the rule of order he embodies: he "Went on his way; ne euer howre did cease / Till he redeemed had that Lady thrall" (5.7.45). He has been so completely rehabilitated, one might say, as to betray no signs of any prior need of rehabilita-tion. Britomart's culminating action is radically different from Arte-gall's. We learn that after Artegall's departure she

> continu'd for a certain space,
> Till through his want her woe did increase:
> Then hoping that the change of aire and place
> Would change her paine, and sorrow somewhat ease,
> She parted thence her anguish to appease.   (5.7.45)

It would not be entirely true to say that Britomart drifts aimlessly. Her movement is specifically motivated; but, unlike Artegall's im-plied purpose, which is oriented toward the resolution of a public crisis, Britomart's is entirely private. To be sure, the cure of private psychological or emotional disease in sixteenth-century culture was not dismissed as an enterprise of little consequence; in part, the cul-tivation of stoicism, for example, and, of course, the discourse of con-science itself grew out of a perceived need to attend to such matters. A quest pursued merely to appease one's anguish, however, did not quite fit into the heroic mold, an incongruity about which Spenser's narrator does not mince words. Britomart suffers, he observes, from "womanish complaints." Through this kind of detail we can see that Britomart and Artegall are separated at the end of canto 7 by an ever-widening distance that is not merely geographic. It is symbolic as well—a figural trace of the ideological imperative that dissociates the received profiles of justice and equity from their specific enabling conditions, from their historicity.

That Britomart, through her abdication, should silence herself amounts to, in this context, a virtual tautology. Britomart's indi-vidual voice, together with the message it might articulate about the mechanisms determining Artegall's status, is in effect muted in ad-vance by the narrative context. Muted, that is, by another voice: the narrator's. This voice does not so much rival Britomart's as consti-tute the interpretive frame—the collective, governing vision—of the world Britomart inhabits, a world whose bias is such that the *sine qua non* of Britomart's character can be read—indeed, generally will be read—in the image of Penelope, a figure embodying the very condition the narrator ascribes to Britomart: "woe" induced by "want" of her man yet attenuated by "hope of his successe." ("Tempered" and "represse," themselves indicative of muting, are the verbs the narrator uses.)

Given this bias, Britomart's abdication acquires an equivocal significance typical of events brought into the purview of equity and the discourse of conscience. The gesture that, officially, displays Artegall's innate right to sovereignty also leaves room, as I noted above, to be read as a complicitous act in the engineering of that right as an inalterable truth rather than a rhetorical pose. The narrative context of Britomart's gesture suggests, further, that the complicity in question is perhaps less a matter of the individual's particular actions or choices than of ones belonging to a more general order: the obtaining communal habits (one might say the reflex acts) of perception or reading that characterize the ambiance in which particular actions or choices are played out and their significance channelled (as the recurring shape of the Penelope/Ulysses simile indicates) into a ruling perspective on the "facts." The representation of Britomart's abdication, then, is also an enactment of the process according to which such a gesture is "naturalized" in context, its problematic aspect eclipsed by its evident compliance with what has been established within the narrative as an interpretive norm.

Britomart's abdication, coming as it does at the height of her promising career as a figure of public authority, appears as something of an anomaly; but it dovetails with what the narrator has chosen to isolate, in the simile, as the index of Britomart's identity and status. It becomes an appropriate—indeed, a predictable—gesture, part of a coherent profile of a figure that the text depicts in the process of being reconceived—being, in effect, normalized—on the model of Penelope. That the model itself should be imported by the narrator into the scheme of things at the eleventh hour, as it were, calls attention to what neither Britomart nor the narrator, who are both caught up in the narrative's official, and epic, project, is in a position to articulate: the constructed nature of the norms on which the authority of the represented figures of power rests. Indeed, nowhere is this insight made explicit in the text. It appears as a function of the phrasing of narrative details, notably in the cumulative effect of the sequence that begins with Britomart's rescue of the transvestite Artegall and that ends with her wandering off inconclusively (never to reappear in the narrative, incidentally), leaving Artegall as the sole heroic figure left on the horizon—and as the sole catalyst for the narrative itself. Not only is Britomart written out of the very narrative in which she has achieved prominence. She is, we might say, written into another narrative—a narrative at once projected and summarily dispatched by the narrator in the brief, final image of an improbable odyssey, undertaken not by the "noble Conqueresse" but by the new Penelope with only a private realm to conquer; a narrative in which the possibility of Britomart's memorializing (or repeating) her role as participant in Artegall's rehabilitation would be unimaginable.

The climax of canto 8 is arguably Prince Arthur's victory over the Souldan. On the surface, an unproblematic dichotomization: good, in the person of Arthur, the embodiment of Aristotelian "magnificence," triumphs over evil, in the person of the Souldan, in whose figure several faces of evil converge. The traditional political allegory renders the Souldan, the avowed enemy of Mercilla, as Philip II or the pope; the Souldan's repeated attempts to "subvert" Mercilla's "Crowne and dignity" as the much-advertised and much-feared Spanish and papist plots against Elizabeth; and the Souldan's ignominious end as the rout of the Armada. More broadly, the Souldan represents a spectrum of cultural and political anathemas (images of the Other), conveyed by his generic names: "Pagan" and "Tyrant." So indisputable is the polarity evinced by the prince and the tyrant that the narrator permits himself the luxury of pointing out the one characteristic they appear to share: "like fierce minds." As it turns out, the narrator exploits this detail to show just how ingrained the polarity is, enlisting the kind of casuistry—the attention to motive and to the condition of interiority—that will emerge in a later episode as the implied point of correspondence between Burbon and Artegall. Through the narrator's insight, we learn that Arthur and the Souldan have "like fierce minds, but meanings different," meanings that indeed substantiate the dissimilarity of the opponents: the

Souldan, we learn, is "presumpteous," "insolent," intent only on "slaughter and avengement" through "tortious powre and lawlesse regiment"; Arthur, on the other hand, seeks only what is laudable: "honor," "right," "truth."

The narrator further enlists a sequence of similes to round out the portrait of the Souldan. In his design to dismember Arthur, the Souldan, we learn, is like "the Thracian Tyrant" Diomedes, notorious for killing his guests and feeding them to his animals; later, in the wild flight of his "firie-mouthed steeds" retreating in panic from the sight of Arthur's "sunlike" shield, the Souldan is compared to Phaeton. Each of the similes contributes to the unambiguous ambiance of censure that surrounds the Souldan, whether by associating him with Diomedes' unnatural parody of civility or with Phaeton's transgression, the sin of arrogance, which, as Natalis Comes observed in his commentary on the myth, "more than anything brings down great calamities upon men."[35]

But the cumulative impact of these similes is blunted by the simile that follows them. The Souldan's demise appears to illustrate, appropriately, the dangerous effect of uncontrolled passion. Just as the ambitious Souldan has been mastered, psychologically and morally, by an ethos of "tortious powre and lawlesse regiment," his steeds are mastered by their "furie." They go out of control—"all obedience both to words and deeds / They quite forgot, and scorned all former law" (5.8.41)—and they precipitate the grisly accident in which the Souldan is so mutilated that "no whole peece of him was to be seene, / But scattred all about, and strow'd vpon the greene" (5.8.42). His fate seems doubly appropriate: not only is a lawless ruler destroyed by the lawless action of his creatures; he is destroyed in a way that echoes the fate of the tyrant to whom he was first compared (Diomedes, the narrator reminds us, was "torne in pieces by Alcides great"). All the more curious, then, that the final image the narrator presents of the Souldan should be dominated by a simile comparing the "Pagan hound" to Hippolytus:

> Like as the cursed sonne of Theseus,
> That following his chace in dewy morne,
> To fly his stepdames loues outrageous,
> Of his owne steedes was all to peeces torne,
> And his faire limbs left in the woods forlorne;

That for his sake Diana did lament,
And all the wooddy Nymphes did wayle and mourne:
So was this Souldan rapt and all to-rent,
That of his shape appear'd no litle moniment.

(5.8.43)

It is, of course, easy to see the points of correspondence between the two deaths, which bear a visceral similitude in the horses' rampage and in the victims' virtual obliteration. It is less easy, I think, to account for what looks like the narrator's fatal attraction to an illustrative text that, despite the vividness of the visual analog, works against the doctrinal point (the unmitigated evil of the Souldan) for which the narrator has presumably been marshalling evidence. Here, in the last words the narrator will have to say about Arthur's nemesis, his argument, like the Souldan's horses, appears to go out of control. It dwells precisely on the incongruous, and therefore problematic, aspects of the simile. Notice, to begin with, the narrator's fascination with the reception the death of the youth meets: grieving, Diana and the "wooddy Nymphes" introduce an elegiac note that jars in the context of the event the simile is supposed to resemble. Another dissonance: both a pagan and a tyrant, the Souldan presumably bears the onus of a divine curse, which is implicitly fulfilled by the quasi-miraculous effect of Arthur's shield on the Souldan's horses; but the "cursed sonne of Theseus," as the narrator's allusive remarks suggest, bears no such onus. The word "cursed" denotes the admittedly potent but misplaced anathema that falls on him, pronounced not by an omniscient god but by his father. Indeed, Hippolytus is a figure of maligned innocence, victimized by the abusive actions of Phaedra—both her incestuous passion and her subsequent dissimulation of her passion, which distorts Hippolytus's role in the scandal and prompts Theseus's curse.[36]

The Hippolytus simile, then, links the Souldan's fate to a story with a theme about the limits and concealed biases of authoritative discourses. The unremarked dissimulation of a source presumed to be transparent (Theseus believes Phaedra's charge) produces a patriarchal and authoritative utterance (Theseus's curse), one that, like all performative acts (as in the confessor's absolution or the monarch's signing of a death warrant), makes things happen. And it makes things happen even when it happens to be a misreading, as it patently is in the simile. Indeed, taken as part of the problematic of representation that the simile suggests, the pathos registered by the figures of Diana and the nymphs is the pathos borne of the recognition that a misreading has displaced the true perspective; not merely displaced it but simulated it so well as to have challenged the viability of the distinction that preserves the integrity of a single "true" reading against its competing simulacra. Though innocent of Phaedra's charge, Hippolytus nonetheless meets a brutal end. And if his death is an anomaly in the divine scheme of justice, this insight commands recognition not, say, in a public forum but in the "woods forlorne"—in a place, as described in the ensuing Adicia episode, "farre from resort of men." The lament of Diana and the nymphs—in a sense, their corrective vision—is both a futile and a marginated response.

We can deduce that it is so by the absurd prominence it acquires in the narrator's perspective at the end of the simile, immediately before the narrator returns to the image of the Souldan "all to-rent." In a word, the functional irrelevance of the scene is corroborated by the way the narrator sees its pathos: atomistically. Unconnected to the question of the inequity of Hippolytus's fate; unconnected, as well, to the image of the Souldan that mirrors and frames the simile; incoherent, in effect, like the torn bodies that litter the landscape. What we see, in turn, through the representation of the narrator's disjunctive perspective is at least a partial response to the questions the simile raises: why, at this climactic point, does the narrator choose not to pursue the Diomedes simile (which contains the wanted visual parallel of a body "torne in pieces," and, though missing the equine details, has the compensatory attraction of the hero/tyrant polarity); and why, having abandoned Diomedes for Hippolytus, does the narrator develop the chosen simile in a way that appears to belie the self-evidence of the Souldan's role as the antithesis of Arthur?

The point is that such hazards are defused through the narrator's interpretive bias, which does not permit potentially subversive insights to become intelligible. What the text gives us, not for the first time, is the narrator as an index of the hegemony and performative power of authoritative discourses. The text gives us, too, an immediate source of such a discourse. The patriarchal word in the simile is mirrored outside the simile in the actions of the prince after the Souldan's demise, as reported by the narrator:

> Onely his shield and armour, which there lay,
> Though nothing whole, but all to-brused and broken,
> He vp did take, and with him brought away,
> That mote remaine for an eternall token
> To all mongst whom this storie should be spoken,
> How worthily, by heauens high decree,
> Justice that day of wrong her selfe had wroken;
> That all men, which that spectacle did see,
> By like ensample mote for euer warned bee.   (5.8.44)

The narrator's words describe, in effect, the political condition that makes it virtually impossible for him, in his self-styled capacity as royal scribe, to draw out the implications of what he has observed. There is, conceivably, more than one "storie" to be construed from the Souldan's effects; but they are not ones that can be recounted in this legend of justice, as the narrator's words indicate. What the narrator describes is the process through which a royal authority in the ascendant insures its dominion by establishing an interpretive regime that is both coercive and overdetermined (as the ecclesiastical and political hierarchies in Elizabethan England exploited, for example, the discourse of conscience). Out of the Souldan's broken gear Arthur fashions both a "spectacle" and an accompanying "storie" that fairly bristles with the rhetorical arsenal needed to deter prospective readers and audiences ("all" of them) from coming up with divergent readings of his encounter with the Souldan.

Ascribing the defeat of one's enemy, as Arthur does, to a divine plan ("heauens high decree") and defining one's own victory as evidence of an avenging justice ("Justice that day of wrong her selfe had wroken") are, perhaps, verbal weapons conventional enough to be numbing, even by the standards of sixteenth-century polemics. Yet we should not underestimate their potency as truth-statements charged with an imperative not to be disbelieved. Behind Arthur's claim to supernal backing lies a claim at least as imposing. Arthur's "storie," we learn, is more than an edifying yet isolated "ensample"; it is a warning that both spectacle and story will repeat themselves "for euer," and become self-legitimating, through a terrestrial agency: the promulgated official discourse about Arthur's exploits. Thus the Souldan's demise will be inscribed in the chronicle of Arthur's triumphs, which is already depicted in the text as enjoying the prestige of originating in Arthur's own authorial and eyewitness account. Let us note, further, that the narrator describes the vestiges of the Souldan as having virtually no meaning—certainly no decipherable one ("of his shape appear'd no litle moniment")—until Arthur reenters the picture to seal his victory by defining (by making an "eternall token" of) what has just transpired. Arthur enacts what we might call an Adamic fantasy of hermeneutic sovereignty: naming as controlling. Implicitly, Arthur controls and delimits not only the range of constructions to be placed on the Souldan's demise but also the significance of his own verbal action, which is absorbed into the rhetoric of a divine rather than a human emplotment.

The impact of Arthur's words appears through the collusion of the narrator, who reads the point he himself makes of the prince's decisive intervention—Arthur's transformation of the "raw material" strewn on the field into a cautionary tale of divine justice—as a nonevent, a mere vehicle through which the truth manifests itself. The implication: to read the event otherwise would not necessarily be to violate the truth but to violate the prince's authority—and, by extension, the cultural and political norms associated with such authority—as the gauge of what is to be taken as the truth.

I am not suggesting that the Souldan is supposed to win our allegiance but, rather, that the prospect of imagining the Souldan through a perspective other than the one that Arthur defines (and that the narrator perpetuates) is represented as a dead end. Within the simile itself there is no "eternall token" to memorialize or disseminate what Diana and the nymphs know and do. Their lament—associated, oddly, with icons of innocence and chastity, implying that theirs is a "true" perspective—remains physically and conceptually beyond the pale, relegated to a sylvan landscape whose resemblance to Shakespeare's woods, the locus of moral healing and nurture, is qualified by the fact that Spenser's woods, unlike Shakespeare's, are not part of a circuit leading back to court and society. To adopt the perspective that Diana and the nymphs share is, in one sense, to enter into a world that will never intersect with the prince's—a world that must therefore meet with the kind of audience that the narrator represents: uncomprehending and aphasiac.

It would not be enough, however, to read the simile merely as the recognition and containment of a threat to the normative stance that the narrative seems to embody and to encapsulate in Arthur's victory speech. The price of reading the simile as an integral part of the narrative is that the very subject of the narrative thereby turns into something more damaging, potentially, to the official order than a mere attack on, or ironic reversal of, Arthur's word. The issue at stake is not the truth or falsehood of Arthur's word. What the text suggests is the inadequacy of his word. His word is not inadequate in the sense that it fails to adequately counter or even censor a distinctly impolitic association of the Souldan and an ill-fated innocent. It is inadequate in the sense that it fails to address the full extent of what the Souldan comes to represent in the course of the stanzas that record his demise. Part of what the Souldan represents grows out of the movement itself of the narrative into the simile: the movement that, imperceptibly, collapses the convenient polarities of good and evil and of guilt and innocence on which not only Arthur's triumphant pronouncement but the official message of the entire book is predicated. The perspective that the simile introduces—showing guilt to be "like" innocence—elicits, without openly endorsing, a radical rethinking and reordering of the cultural ground rules that sustain both the prince's authority and the commonwealth's sense of "being in the right."

The final word in this episode, then, is not Arthur's, and certainly not the narrator's; it is, rather, the text's. And the text's word is, necessarily, not a "word" at all: not a pronouncement that rivals the prince's and accordingly leaves itself (and its author) susceptible to disabling arguments or censorship. The text's "word" is the narrative enactment, through the disjunctive simile, of the kind of cultural and political nemesis that the movement of the lax conscience signals to normative systems of thought and behavior. Confounding the *a priori* distinctions between good and evil, the lax conscience makes suspect the stability and normative value of what is believed to be good or just. What is more unsettling, it does so while eluding detection as an agent of subversion—as, indeed, it must, because under its regime stable definitions of what constitutes subversion or the identifying marks of subversive agents no longer hold. This, too, is the impact of the intertextual transgression of the Hippolytus simile, which, like the Penelope simile, localizes the narrative's recurrent movement toward interpretive instability.

On Not Representing the Queen's "Answer Answerlesse": The Politics of Dissimulation and Allegory in the Trial of Duessa

One of the most glittering manifestations of the "Dread Souerayne Goddesse" Gloriana/Elizabeth in *The Faerie Queene* occurs in cantos 9 and 10 of book 5: the Mercilla episode. Notably, the descriptive set piece of the enthroned Mercilla (5.9.27–31), attributing to her an iconic status, renders in a verbal medium the kind of pictorial homage to the monarch that court painters accomplished in the royal portraits.[1] The description, then, identifies the narrative that coheres around it as a canonical text, as part of the cultural discourse of royal power. What we have seen throughout this study, of course, is that the discourse of power was inextricably caught up in the problematic ambiguities of the discourse of conscience; it is therefore no coincidence that the episode at hand, which celebrates and asserts Elizabeth's absolutist pretensions in the figure of the apotheosized Mercilla, should at the same time conduct, as a textual operation of the gaze of conscience, one of the most penetrating and destabilizing "anatomies" of the economy of the Elizabethan structure of power.

The thematics of conscience does not directly invade the descriptive passage of the monarch itself, but it does resonate in the episode's general preoccupation with the physical progress of Arthur and Artegall through a sequence of obstacles and spectacles toward a particularized place. The familiar casuistical preoccupation with the configurations of time, place, and person turns up, in this case, as a narrative progression toward the physical and symbolic center of royal authority, a "stately pallace" that encloses the very heart of that authority, Mercilla's court. What the episode discloses, among other things, is the ambiguous character of the word "court" and of its referents in Elizabethan culture. Mercilla's court is at once a place of royal spectacle (where Mercilla sits as the focus of the circuit of specular power: "on high, that she might all men see / And might of all men royally be seene" [5.9.27]); a royal court of justice in which "affaires of common-wele" are litigated; and—if we recall the Elizabethan designation of the monarch's juridical function as the channel of equity—a court of conscience as well. To be sure, the triune court Artegall and Arthur enter echoes the official rhetoric of the Elizabethan church-state; but it does not do so neutrally, without registering the corrosive effects of conscience when alloyed to the presumably inviolable conceptual constructions—like the metallic luster of Mercilla's palace and court—of the discourse of power. Indeed, the Mercilla episode conducts, arguably, the most searching examination in Spenser's poem of the paradoxical status of the discourse of conscience in Elizabethan culture, a discourse we have seen to be of capital importance both in the legitimation of the mechanisms of royal authority and, as assuredly as the interconnected referents of the word "court," in the erection of a vantage point from which to speak the unspeakable—to articulate equivocally the shaping role of historicity and contingency in the very processes of legitimation that produce the social and political context in which poems like Spenser's are generated. To borrow the allusion that penetrated the texts surrounding Elizabeth's adroit vanishing act in the case of Mary Queen of Scots, the Mercilla episode offers an extended representation of what it means to survive Medusa's gaze, to survive the petrifying effects of both desiring and being unable to escape from the naturalized artifice of the Elizabethan structure of power.

As with other episodes in book 5, a counterpoint of textual anomalies accompanies the otherwise conventional, not to say banal, and episodic *exempla* of Gloriana's justice. Unlike other episodes, the Mercilla episode goes beyond the representation of aberrations in the factors of time, place, and person in the narrative. It explores the relationship between fiction and historical discourse as one of interanimating doubles rather than of absolute opposites. And, in the course of its revisionist inquiry, the episode demythologizes two conventional and analogous premises in the production of allegory (the central textual artifice, it goes without saying, to which the poem's narrative strategies themselves refer) and of the historical record (notably the accumulation of politically significant events occurring outside the text, which the text absorbs). It demythologizes, on the one hand, the presupposition, which valorizes allegory, of an atextual, ahistorical, and apolitical realm of eternal truths; and, on the other, the presupposition, which valorizes the textualization/ writing of history, of a pool of historically grounded facts whose meaning can be stabilized, reduced to an indisputable, unequivocal reality.

Like the action of conscience itself, this kind of operation looks both inside and outside; and it suggests the relation between the two spaces—the text and what lies outside the text—to be like the two parts of metaphor. Just as in metaphor apparently different terms are brought together, dialogically, as it were, the textual auto-criticism that invades the Mercilla episode stands, obliquely (and necessarily so), for a radical cultural critique as well. In this sense, too, what the episode has to show, generally, about the interrelatedness of fictional and historical discourse enlarges on the counterpoint of its specific textual anomalies. Whether in its selection or phrasing of concrete narrative details or in its metacritical allusions to unstable generic boundaries, the Mercilla episode raises more problems and questions than it provides answers to.

Before turning to the problematized generic issue, let us locate some of the more easily identifiable textual anomalies through which the episode indicates this condition of malaise without conveniently defining the source of trouble. Can the trouble be traced merely to a text insufficiently under control? To a breakdown in the cultural scaffolding that the text arises from and that the text cannot help betraying? To a skillful, and intentional, interrogation of the cultural norms that the poem overtly professes to endorse? As with the other episodes I have examined, the Mercilla episode generates such questions, here to such a degree that the questions themselves, and the virtual impossibility of locating unequivocal answers, arguably come to constitute the final message of the text.

The actual depiction of the "Angel-like" Mercilla sitting in "royal rich estate" provides, apparently, a reassuringly (that is, unambiguously) encomiastic moment, though Thomas Cain's astute reading of this passage has shown that unsettling ambiguities intrude even here into the poem's official project.[2] Without rehearsing Cain's observations, we should note that part of the description's finally unsettling power has to do with a concatenation of related details leading up to and including parts of the description itself. A "glistering" palace whose towers and terraces "with their brightnesse daz'd the straunge beholders eye"; a porch guarded by the imposing figure of Awe followed by that of Order, with the implication from the allegorical configuration that awe is a prerequisite to order; the entrance to the court designated by the spectacle of the severed tongue, "Nayled to a post," of an indiscreet poet: a chilling assertion of the presumed coercive ability of the political hierarchy to delimit the meaning and the production of "bold speaches" and "lewd poems," to control the terms of discourse passing to and from the center of power; finally, the enthroned Mercilla who includes among her arsenal of royal icons a rusty sword and a growling lion, suggestive of her unlimited reserves of power: in the sword that she can "sternely draw" a display of untapped martial power not to be challenged, in the lion's ominous murmuring an equivalent display not only of physical but of verbal power (the mere sounds of royal disapprobation—the legitimized "salvage choler"—cancelling out the "salvage choler" of rebellious factions)—these details, among others, evoke the other monumental and deceptively reassuring locus in the narrative: Isis Church.

Both places, centers of a hieratic authority claimed by Elizabethan ecclesiastical and political organs alike, irradiate an ambiguous light on their conventional premises. Both show the spontaneous production of awe and silence before recognized ministers of divine authority as admitting a contravening, though necessarily silenced, interpretation: awe and silence as the product of a complex cultural system of occlusion that, covertly as well as overtly, turns avenues of critical investigation into dead ends. The light that virtually blinds Artegall and Arthur as they enter the palace is not unlike the aphasia that overtakes Britomart and the narrator in the temple; and, appropriately, it is not unlike the light their own armor seems to generate as they enter the court, producing an effect among the throng that recalls their own response to the gilded towers, architectural symbols of Mercilla's power: bedazzlement, "unwonted terror," and the cessation of speech (the crowd "ceast their clamors upon them to gaze") that bespeaks a complicitous relationship between the silencer and the silenced. The interrelated images of apparently spontaneous blinding and muting are, indeed, not unlike the spectacle of the literally muted poet that immediately precedes the description of Mercilla. In the context of such images, this spectacle (about which I will have more to say later) stands not merely as a case of a singular crime punished and transformed into a public caveat to other would-be blasphemers of the monarch. It stands as an exacerbated enactment of the generalized aphasia, or Medusa effect, that insures the illusion of stability and permanence in both court and commonwealth and in the culture they derive from and sustain.

In any case, this brief survey of the nodal point of the Mercilla episode indicates what we can expect from the episode as a whole: an enactment of the kind of misreading—the aphasiac regime of the lax conscience—we have observed elsewhere in book 5, here given a more pointedly political dimension as the narrator proceeds into the book's most transparent—and most risky—representation of the historical record, the trial of Mary Queen of Scots.

Considerations of place, as I have suggested, are central to the episode; by no coincidence, I think, as central as they were to Elizabeth's navigations through the last climactic months of the Scots case (consider her conspicuous absence, for example, from the trial at Fotheringay). The refractive character of Spenser's text in relation to the queen's behavior will become particularly noticeable as the narrative itself reaches the climactic moment when Mercilla, delivering her judgment, must assume her role as the inviolable conscience of the realm—a place in the narrative I want to give specific attention to. More generally, shifts in place, and the attending shifts in perspective regarding Mercilla, determine the very structure of the episode, which consists of three sequential yet interrelated parts. Each part—the journey of Artegall and Arthur to Mercilla's palace, their audience in the royal court, and the royal court transformed into the court of equity for the "tryall of a great and weightie case"—participates in an incremental problematization of the text as it nears its representation of the royal word and act that annihilate Duessa.

The Knights' Journey to Mercilla's Palace

Canto 9 begins on a prophetic note. Relating Artegall's exile of Adicia, the Souldan's wife, "farre from resort of men," the narrator voices a theme that announces the ostensible purpose of Duessa's trial: the elimination of the contaminating agent, the evil Other. The account of the exile also sets up a model of narrative stability and control against which to measure the forthcoming episode. Through the narrator's confident dispatching of the unambiguous personification of "wrong" to an appropriately "wicked bowre" at the opening of the canto—of a piece with Adicia's self-proclaimed identity as the "mortall foe of justice," introduced in the previous canto—the text enacts a ritual purge of the potential agents of narrative disruption, as though it were mirroring a realizable—and, as the official record of the Scots case would suggest, a fully realized—cultural practice. In other words, the canto opens with a metonymic celebration of the official canonicity of the entire book that the Mercilla episode will presumably corroborate.

Of course, the narrator's remarks about Adicia are, principally, the property of another context: they form the conclusion to one of the most potentially destabilizing episodes in the book, Arthur's triumph over the Souldan. Part of the book's message, of course, is that such moments must be eclipsed, silenced. In this sense, too, the narrator's culminating remarks about Adicia are to the point. The reassuring implication they contain of order restored reminds us of the official function of equity: to act as a *pharmakon*, the agent that, of course, includes the action of a purgative.[3] So, too, the Mercilla episode will invoke the issue of equity. Not only is Mercilla depicted literally in the process of administering equity (an action the narrator calls attention to, taking some three stanzas to praise); the episode presents itself as a narrative enactment of the restorative power of equity, though not without exploiting the inherent ambiguities of equity. At the conclusion of the Souldan episode, Artegall and Arthur are free to resume their journeys—in Artegall's case, to accomplish his mission (rescuing Irena) and to return to Gloriana's court. As with Isis Church, Mercilla's court functions both as a proleptic marker, anticipating Artegall's eventual return to Gloriana's court, and as yet another rupture in the course of the hero's progress, yet another deferral of the central heuristic narrative project, and, accordingly, yet another opening onto new (and not necessarily officially sanctioned) perspectives on the book's official function in the economy of Elizabeth's power.

The business of getting to Mercilla's court in the first place shows itself to be problematic. From one perspective, clearly, the knights' decision to take the detour does represent a fantasy of the magnetic pull of the monarch's power. What complicates the decision is that Mercilla both is and is not a figure for Gloriana/Elizabeth: more precisely, in the knights' progress toward Mercilla's court the text charts a process through which a substitute focus of authority gradually assumes total identity with the presumably central focus. Personification and impersonation are, bewilderingly, interlocked.[4] Another complication: the action that elicits the knights' decision. Anticipating an issue that the Burbon episode will provoke in a later canto, the lady Samient's plea to the knights invokes a potentially rival cultural order to Gloriana's absolutist regime. Samient "woo'd" the knights "by all the meanes she might" and the knights succumb, "ouercommen" by her "entreatie." Here the seductive power of rhetoric is associated with the voice of the female—Samient as siren—and, further, with the discourse of courtly love. The knights' submission to the female voice cuts two ways. It mirrors the absorption of the culture of the courtly love tradition into the Elizabethan court culture; but it also signals the tension underlying that hybrid state. Insofar as the status of Mercilla herself is ambiguous at the outset, Samient's successful wooing of the knights stands as a projection of the inarticulate desire of the aristocratic order, represented by the two knights, to assert its autonomy without destroying the political advantages to be gained from maintaining the posture of unstinting devotion and obedience to Gloriana/Elizabeth's commands.

The knights' submission also echoes the thematics of choice central to the discourse of conscience and variously exploited in the poem, notably in the recurrent representations of characters' or the narrator's convenient aphasia or of their always politically correct misreadings of potentially subversive events. The knights' choice is, of course, "rescued" by the allegorical flexibility of Mercilla. But the narrative itself goes on to exhibit another choice, one that invokes still another dimension of the text of conscience. In contrast to the condition of stability and predictability associated with *synteresis*, we will recall, *conscientia* asserts one of shifting hierarchies of value, of indeterminacy and instability. So, too, the immediate outcome of the knights' decision turns out to be yet another narrative rupture. As the narrator puts it, "and by the way / (As often falles) of sundry things did commen, / Mongst which that Damzell did to them bewray / A straunge aduenture" (5.9.4). The narrator's nonchalant parenthesis is a way, to be sure, of framing a rhetorical question: what else are we to expect from a narrative evidently indebted to the procedures of romance? Admitting the debt to the discourse of romance does not of course eclipse other debts or interconnections; indeed, given the overt preoccupation of book 5 with issues of conscience, it is possible to read the procedures of romance themselves as the enforced stylization and taming of the destabilizing insight of *conscientia*, a relocating of the finally uncontainable and ungovernable aspects of texts and their interpretations into the supposedly reassuring arena of free play, what in another time C. S. Lewis called the "robust tranquillity" of Spenser's allegory.[5]

In any case, the instability of the narrative has once again been invoked in the implication that the "straunge aduenture" about to be related is merely one of an undefined number of interruptions on the way not to Gloriana's court directly but to Mercilla's. Accordingly, the text constituting the episode assumes the character of a fragment, with parts chosen to be edited out, excisions made according to apparently arbitrary criteria. The circumstance of place, here lent what the casuists would have called a virtually "indifferent" status, is the one criterion that the narrator identifies: twice he mentions that the adventure he is about to relate occurred "not farre away," as though the other, undisclosed, adventures were reduced to invisibility and insignificance through the sheer function of distance. This looks like a minor detail; but despite its apparent innocuousness, it indicates the thoroughgoing engagement of the text in the thematics of suppression, constructing narrative blind spots and representations of aphasia, evidence of the regime of the lax conscience. Furthermore, as the discourse of conscience should remind us, even a slight adjustment in perspective can affect the significance of a circumstance. Viewed from a different place in the text, from the perspective of Duessa's trial, the spatial detail, as we shall see, will no longer appear quite so innocuous.

In the immediate context, the arbitrariness of the process that gives visibility to the digressive adventure appears to serve a canonical function. The knights' encounter with the "wicked villaine" Malengin, master of guile, works spatially in the narrative to indicate the nature of the hazards that exist outside the sanctuary of Mercilla's court and that constitute obstacles to reaching the sanctuary, obstacles to be overcome and, as it were, symbolically banished from the text. In a word, Malengin's sphere includes what Mercilla's excludes. Yet the Malengin episode also works as a spatial pun (appropriately so, given Malengin's role as personification of duplicity), a pun suggesting that the canonical reading does not exhaust the interpretive range of the passage. Just as the prefix "anti" bears an etymological kinship with "ante," Malengin's territory stands ambiguously in relation to Mercilla's court: both as figurative antipode and as anteroom.[6]

Consider the central physical detail of Malengin's territory: he lives in a rock. What, indeed, could be more opposed to the glittering "stately pallace" that houses Mercilla's court? The juxtaposition of the two images seems to demarcate absolutely the limits of the "savage" and the "civilized" world. Yet as the text amplifies its description of the rock, the demarcation begins to blur. Malengin's rock, we learn,

> Is wondrous strong and hewen farre under ground,
> A dreadfull depth, how deepe no man can tell,
> But some doe say it goeth downe to hell:
> And all within, it full of wyndings is
> And hidden wayes, that scarse an hound by smell
> Can follow out those false footsteps of his,
> Ne none can backe returne, that once are gone amis.
>
> (5.9.6)

The unremarkable natural object turns out to be the surface appearance, literally, of an intricate and ingenious architectural design, a parodic version of the artifice that surrounds Mercilla, realized in the palace's terraces and towers and in the ornaments and protocol of the court. Moreover, just as the physical aspect of Mercilla's world articulates figuratively the complex network of courtly etiquette and politics, so the rock's subterranean network gives concrete expression to Malengin's quintessential but elusive behavior:

So light of hand, and nimble of his pace,
So smooth of tongue, and subtile in his tale,
That could deceiue one looking in his face . . .
Well knowen by his feates, and famous ouer all.

(5.9.5)

Together, the descriptions of Malengin's behavior and the dwelling that embodies it invoke the critical point of intersection between Malengin's and Mercilla's spheres. To move from one description to the other is to reconstitute in the process of reading not a Manichean vision of warring opposites but the two faces of a single, and politically timely, discourse: the discourse of conscience. In Mercilla's sphere the normative, stabilizing rule of conscience is displayed, principally in its connection to the action of the monarch's equity. In Malengin's sphere the dark side of conscience gains prominence, principally through the image of the labyrinth—a recurrent image in the rhetorical trappings of conscience—and through Malengin's behavioral profile, which closely resembles the action of mental reservation, itself widely perceived to be the product of the lax conscience.[7]

In this light, it is appropriate that the Malengin episode should represent what the lax conscience was notorious for: the imperceptible breakdown of order, of stable principles of difference between opposing propositions. Such a collapse is conveyed through recurrent instances in which the depicted behavior or imagery governing the knights and their most recent enemy is made to intersect. Thus it is entirely predictable that Talus should end up in hot pursuit of Malengin, implacable as ever in his single-minded mission of destruction, inevitably defeating Malengin's attempts to escape him by means of a succession of metamorphoses. This is the familiar, sanctioned, enactment of the power of conscience to enforce the norms of the cultural order. The novelty of the scene lies in the problematic edge it introduces at the outset, when Talus arrives. He is not named at first, only referred to as the "yron man." We see him as he appears in his elemental condition, before the imposition from without of definitional limits—or names (the name "Talus" only appears at the moment he is about to trap Malengin). That is, we see the commonality between Talus and Malengin once the names that legitimate their apparent polarity are abstracted. Like Talus, Malengin's element is iron: Talus bears an iron flail, Malengin a staff "whose top was arm'd with many an yron hooke." Briefly, Talus appears vulnerable, subject to interpretation as a figure of but one of the chameleon-like manifestations of the lax conscience—that is, as a figure of one of Malengin's own possible transformations, the guise of permanence and infallibility. The text, in other words, enacts the power of conscience not only to enforce normative assumptions but to problematize them.

So, too, with the pious moral the narrator draws at the conclusion of the scene. Subjected to the kind of treatment convicted traitors might expect from the penal system in Elizabethan England—he is disemboweled and his bones broken—Malengin learns the outcome of defying authority:

> Crying in vaine for helpe, when helpe was past
> So did deceipt the selfe deceiuer fayle.
> There they him left a carrion outcast;
> For beasts and foules to feede vpon for their repast.

(5.9.19)

The master of transformations finds that even his words—his last attempt to break free from Talus—prove as impotent as his strategies of deceit, whose power is now revealed as illusory, a point driven home by the final, ironic transformation into carrion. The official message: deceit, thus decomposed, will have no place in Mercilla's court of equity

Yet the moral passes over one complication in the account of Malengin's entrapment. It is Samient's deceit—her impersonation of a solitary, vulnerable, grief-stricken maid—that lures Malengin out of the rock in the first place. This detail invokes a commonplace casuistical inquiry—when is lying not lying, or when is lying permissible?—but in the context of the episode's concluding moral, the inquiry itself would seem to have been banished from the text along with Malengin. In other words, the concluding moral represents a tacit invitation to ignore the evidence that deceit has not been completely exorcised. Through Samient's action, deceit emanating from quarters attached to Mercilla's power presents itself as a possibility, but also as a possibility destined to be misrecognized. Such narrative details help redefine the space that Malengin occupies in relation to

Mercilla's court not as intrinsically separate and incompatible but as connected, connected through a clandestine textual arrangement that absorbs its potentially subversive insights into the "black hole" of politically endorsed platitudes. There is, then, some question as to what, exactly, the text is reminding us of as Arthur and Artegall meet the guard at the porch, the giant whose duty is to "keepe out guyle . . . / That vnder shew oftimes of fayned semblance / Are wont in princes courts to worke great scath and hindrance" (5.9.22). Even without the occluded detail of Samient's behavior, this passage betrays the instability of its official moral point. Either the court is an anomaly (since courts are generally, the narrator admits, contaminated by "fayned semblance") or, given the chameleon-like character of guile, it is a masterful example of the kind of "fayned semblance" presumed to have been kept out by the guard.[8] The distinction between what belongs intrinsically within and without the court's boundaries has been blurred: another signal that the court in question will participate in the kind of destabilizing action of the court of conscience.

The Knights' Entrance into Mercilla's Court

The spectacle of the punished poet, which appears immediately before the knights reach Mercilla, lends itself to an authoritative, single-textured reading: a cautionary tale of the wages of defying the principle of monarchical omnipotence; a representation, once again, of a ritual purge of "forged guyle"; and an implicit definition of the text itself as the unambiguous opposite of the "lewd poems" responsible for the poet's punishment. Even so, the spectacle is fraught with even more ambiguities than the Malengin episode—ambiguities latent, as Foucault argued, in the very nature of spectacle. To begin with, its spatial position. The spectacle occupies a liminal space, and, as such, represents a site of volatile conversion and change.[9] In two stanzas the spectacle thematizes specifically the problematic status of writing itself, a central locus of the tropic action of language, raising questions about the nature of the authoring and reading presences involved in such action.

For example, the spectacle raises itself to the condition of an anomaly by virtue of the fact that, unlike the surrounding scenes—

the knights' dazzling entry into the hall and the depiction of Mercilla sitting in "rich royall estate"—the spectacle conspicuously excludes any mention of the knights' interpretation of what they see. The throng, we learn, instantly silences itself with amazement and "unwonted terror" at the sight of the knights, and Mercilla's quasi-divine figure is "Admyr'd of many, honoured of all"; but the mutilated poet seems enclosed in a vacuum. Or, more appropriately, he seems to produce the kind of numbing effect associated with Medusa: the knights walk past, their complete unresponsiveness mirroring, in fact, the violent muting of the poet himself. Briefly, two polarized identities—the profane author and his noble readers—converge, as if to point up the politics of interpretation that engages an ethos of necessary silence and suppression, variously produced, both near the margins and near the center of power. In this context, the passage appears at once to define itself as a sustained self-referential episode in the text yet as an episode whose auto-critique will raise the kind of questions that must occupy, figuratively, no place in the text—a medusan episode.

The first stanza seems unproblematic enough in its initial allusion to the efficient cause of the spectacle. Just as the specific punishment merely embodies the terms of an impersonal interpretive organ (the criminal and his punishment are "adiudged so by law"), so the text's definition of the offending behavior seems to echo the terms of the official, and presumably universal, reading: the poet's actions are to be read as "foule" blasphemy of the monarch and the production of "bold speaches" and "lewd poems." What are we, then, to make of the final lines of the first stanza? The initial cause of the punishment—of the official reading of the poet that carries out the terms of the law—is replaced by another: "For the bold title of a poet bad / He on himselfe had ta'en, and rayling rymes had sprad" (5.9.25). To be sure, a legal point of equity is being elaborated here—that the crime must fit the punishment—but there is also the suggestion that the punishment is fulfilling the terms not of an external organ but of an existential reality determined by the poet himself. The condemnation, ultimately, appears to have emanated not merely from without but also from within—a familiar double perspective in the discourse of conscience. As we might expect, the perspective engages further ambiguities in the text.

It is a great convenience, of course, that the moral topography of the book should appear so clearly delineated, with members of the cast of players defining themselves as the contaminated Others. That Adicia, as we have seen, should name herself the "mortall foe / To Iustice" determines the official reading, at least, of her actions in the book while lending a determinate order to the book's allegorical scheme: however interwoven the action and relationships among characters, the narrative can ultimately be reduced to a single, universally held, reading, one in which no dissenting voices contest the distribution of the roles of justice and injustice, good and evil, and so forth. But the spectacle of the poet who, like Adicia, is depicted as having himself determined his status as criminal does not sustain such a seamless vision. The poet, we should note, does not enter the narrative already marked with a revelatory and delimiting name. He is merely "some one" the knights observe. The immediate context of torture and punishment indicates that the name or title he does assume does not necessarily reflect his spontaneous self-definition. It admits interpretation as the product of an external coercive agency: the "bold title of a poet bad" that the poet "on himselfe had ta'en" plausibly refers to the official censure the poet has fallen under by daring to contest the normative truths of the power structure surrounding him. In other words, both the the poet's name and its authoring agency prove unstable and ambiguous categories.

The second stanza amplifies this problem. After the spectacle of the severed tongue, Arthur and Artegall observe another sign—another form of punishment, one that includes a verbal parody both of baptism and of dismemberment. The poet stands beneath a written text that both describes his crime and defines how he is to be known:

> Thus there he stood, whylest high ouer his head
> There written was the purport of his sin,
> In cyphers strange, that few could rightly read,
> *BON FONS*; but *bon*, that once had written bin,
> Was raced out, and *Mal* was now put in:
> So now *Malfont* was plainely to be red,
> Eyther for th'euill, which he did therein,
> Or that he likened was to a welhed
> Of euill words, and wicked sclaunders by him shed.
>
> (5.9.26)

The stanza traces the process of transformation according to which the condemnatory title *Malfont* becomes at once the name of and the fixed judgment against the poet, a process that seems to have little if anything to do with the poet's volition or perspective. The indeterminate "some one" is not so much choosing a self-descriptive name as submitting to the reconstruction of his identity by an external, unknown agency. Note the symbolic excision of what is presumably the poet's figurative "tongue" or language in the substitution of Latin for English in the "cyphers" intended to designate him: an official discourse with hieratic resonances is glossing—in both senses of the word—the discourse of the "lewd poems." Note, too, the recurrent use of the passive voice in the verbs representing the act of writing: it is as though the passage were enacting the legitimizing power of interpretations that define themselves as public, attributable to no particularized agency, therefore impersonal, and, in consequence, incontestable.

What Arthur and Artegall witness, in effect, is the official writing of normative truths, in this case the truths that determine the profile of a socially constituted self. The open-endedness, and the potential subversiveness, of "some one" is circumscribed and disabled under the power of the disembodied gaze of the law or the court of equity. The poet and what the poet writes—interchangeable terms—emerge as functions of their received interpretation under the "law" of equity or conscience, which is, of course, nominally associated with the monarch, whose power is here alluded to in the string of passive verbs I noted above, actions whose agency has assumed an inviolable, godlike character: discernible only through its effects.

It goes without saying that this process of containment has a self-reflexive cast. The spectacle implies that the poet is authored by an external agency—in the largest sense, by a cultural poesis, one that participates, as well, in authoring the "legend of justice" itself, in determining the economy of suppression and selective vision that helps produce canonical readings, for example, of spectacles like the one the text includes. More specifically, the spectacle allegorizes the ontogenesis of the political allegory that dominates book 5. Out of the "raw material" of historicity, of the fluid discourse of the quotidian, comes the Adamic, allegorizing script—the power to name and, by naming, to fix within what looks to be an immovable sphere of controllable meaning. Such imagined fixity betrays itself as illusory, of course: "bon" can turn out to be "Mal." Indeed, that "BON FONS" should be "raced out" and replaced by "Malfont" is both literally and symbolically a destabilizing gesture, as we shall see in a moment; yet it is no less radical a move than the one that precedes it, the move that imposes the controlled allegorical configuration of "bon/Mal font" on the diffuse boundaries of "some one." This is the kind of move book 5 itself repeatedly makes in producing its chain of political allegories, a practice to which the spectacle gives a ritualized and problematized form. Allegory, the spectacle implies, works on discourse like the act of dismemberment on the physical body. Setting up an interpretive telos, it enacts the intention to delimit the range of readings of the text it informs—to cut off or silence the network of discursive operations that will produce "bad" poems, "bad" readings, "bad" poets. And, like the act of dismemberment, allegory employs a rhetoric of authorial invisibility, with invisibility construed as a function of the blurring of readership and authorship, of outside and inside. Just as the severed tongue represents an interchangeable relation between the terms of an external law and the internal condition of the "bad" poet, so the writing over the poet's head defines the imposition of a title from without—the official "reading"—as the externalization and repetition of an internal voice—of authorial intentionality.

What such correspondences add up to is an auto-critique of the text's allegorical mode and yet something more than that: an auto-critique that mimics allegory's self-legitimizing mechanism. The determination of the poet's identity as a function of his passage into an allegorical script; the represented confusion of the authorship of that passage; and the ambiguously framed context of suppression—the ritualized muting of a dissenting voice (or of a misreading)—that stands both as a politic gesture of self-censorship conducted by the dissenting voice itself and as a political, legally enforceable act of retribution against ideological crime—together, these details define allegory itself as a politicized, ideologically charged discourse whose penchant is to obscure and disown such a definition. The spectacle, in other words, anatomizes the legitimizing rhetoric of allegory's tropic structure in terms of a parallel rhetoric located in the Elizabethan discourse of power. The emergence of the ciphers "bon/Mal font"—

abstract terms encoded in a hieratic tongue—invite us to consider allegory's participation in the kind of dehistoricizing impulse that characterizes the judicial and penal actions of the courts of equity and conscience: the impulse to naturalize, to throw out of the arena of historical context and bias, culturally sanctioned norms.

Merely to represent this kind of movement engages the text in a problematic narrative action, problematic because the action can be read both as an assertion of the text's role as promulgator of cultural dogmas and as a disingenuous account of the legitimizing process that yields dogmatic pronouncements. The represented text itself—what Artegall and Arthur read above the poet's head, what they are silent before—is consonant with this ambiguous movement. The canonical, "good," reading, though complex, is straightforward enough: the inscription indicates some essential aspect of the poet and, like a sensitive instrument, it indicates the transformation that the aspect undergoes, the passage from "bon" to "Mal" exemplifying the triumph of reality over illusion and/or the fall from spiritual/ political grace that sin/crime provokes.

Yet the inscription also suggests less accommodating ambiguities, ones that invoke, problematically, the nuances of place and time and person that casuistical inquiry generally raises. Implicitly asking us to imagine a designated place for public adulation doubling as a place for censure, it reinforces the liminal, inherently unstable aspect of public spectacle as a place not of static meaning but of intersecting and often contradictory meanings or readings (a point that, in another context, the spectacle of Anthony Tyrrell's public apostasy at St. Paul's Cross made clear).[10] The temporal references in the stanza further aggravate the effect of instability. The contradictory epithets "bon" and "Mal" seem to exist at once in consecutive and in simultaneous arrangement. The first script we see written over the poet's head, in "cyphers strange," is "BON FONS"; but moments later the script passes into the past perfect tense, registering a more recent act of effacement: "*bon*, that once had written bin, / Was raced out, and *Mal* was now put in." Through this movement, the stanza enacts the passage of time, charging it with significance as a shaping force in the production of would-be authoritative interpretations. Both written interpretations, despite their monolithic appearance, are thus implicated in the vagaries of historicity.

Analogously, they are located in a context governed by the question of their decipherability. Part of their meaning turns on their reception by a readership; and the reception of the scripts proves problematic. We learn that only "few could rightly read" the ciphers spelling out "BON FONS" but that "*Malfont* was plainly to be red." This detail works against the grain of the text's own normative project. To be sure, the insistence on the dichotomous nature of the scripts indicates the impact of an underlying principle of order—the principle of absolute difference—that the text's canonical status rests on. It seems appropriate, as well, that "Malfont" should be easy to read, given that the title passes for the final word on the poet—the truth that every reader, presumably, sees and accepts. But the context established by the other, rival, script tacitly belies the totality of this kind of reading. Readers within Spenser's own literary culture would recognize in the "cyphers strange, that few could rightly read" an allusion to various traditions of secret knowledge (for example, currents of Neoplatonism, hermeticism, and the folklore of magic, not to mention the thematics of secrecy associated with conscience), all of which posit access to gnosis as the privilege of a select readership. In such a hermeneutics of secrecy, what is plain to read—what is easily available to the masses—is hardly likely to be the last word on the subject. And what "few could rightly read" might well be the "right reading"—the higher insight inaccessible to the masses (or, from a politically suspect vantage point, even to the monarch).[11]

Even without this inversion of the text's overt message, the stanza indicates that the reading of the "Malfont" script proves more unstable than we might think, and thus ultimately more open to divergent interpretations than the narrator himself is willing or able to venture. However "plainely" the script might be read, the stanza's closing lines remind us that legibility and transparency of meaning do not coincide. What we follow, as readers of the text, is the narrator's model attempt to behave like a good reader: to delimit the range of significance to be drawn out from the apparent pun he finds in the title. "Malfont" must be appropriate, he observes, for one of two possible reasons: "Eyther for th'euill which he did therein, / Or that he likened was to a welhed / Of euill words, and wicked sclaunders by him shed" (5.9.26). The title seems to indicate either the action of doing evil or the condition of being a source of evil, the root *font* representing a corruption, possibly, of the Latin *facere* in the former case and in the latter the Latin for "fountain" or, as the text records it, "welhed."[12] Whatever the etymological variations, the narrator's reading covers the central exegetical bases: the literal and the figurative stand accounted for, together producing a sign of interpretive plenitude. Yet the very introduction of two alternative readings of "Malfont," however complementary they turn out to be, opens up the possibility that other, more subversive, alternative readings could be projected onto the title. Could be but will not be: the narrative context, in which an alternative title representing a rival value system is mysteriously eradicated, announces the policy of suppression that must be carried out on divergent readings.

The spectacle that Arthur and Artegall pass by without comment contains, as it were, a third, unwritten title, one whose message must, presumably, be lost in the kind of aphasia the heroes represent as they approach the immediate center of power, Mercilla's court. The poet's mutilation, the heroes' silence, and the narrator's narrowly circumscribed reading of the poet's official title enact in concert the text's elusive power to say and unsay the critical truths it possesses about its own place in the legitimizing mechanism that supports Gloriana/Elizabeth's court system. The subtext that the spectacle introduces—showing the politically sensitive bias that informs allegory and allegoresis—is of particular interest in the context of the episode to follow. The political allegory of the trial and judicial murder of Mary Queen of Scots is one of the book's most transparent allegories and at the same time one of the most problematic. The spectacle preceding it foreshadows the kind of critical operation that the trial will conduct—as much on the text's own dialogic counterpoint of historical discourse and allegory, and on the limits of interpretation that each evokes, as on the represented focus of investigation, Duessa.

The Trial of Duessa / Mary Queen of Scots in Mercilla's Court

Then there was brought, as prisoner to the barre,
A Ladie of great countenance and place,
But that she it with foule abuse did marre;

Yet did appeare rare beautie in her face,
But blotted with condition vile and base,
That all her other honour did obscure,
And titles of nobilitie deface;
Yet in that wretched semblant she did sure
The peoples great compassion vnto her allure.

(5.9.38)

Mention of the "rare beautie" with defaced "titles of nobilitie"—together with the allusions in subsequent stanzas to the charge
against Duessa (aspiring "to depryue / Mercilla of her crowne") and
to Duessa's anomalous status (the "vntitled Queene")—clearly opens
a window on the historical record of the Scots case, a matter I want
to return to later. What is worth noting at this titular place in the
episode is the way in which the "tryall of a great and weightie case"
begins on a note—what the casuists would read as a detailed circumstance of person—that points at the same time toward the historical
referent and toward the thematic issue announced in the spectacle.
The initial description of Duessa/Mary Stuart is a rewriting of the
description of the poet. Notice how Duessa appears as a kind of
chiaroscuro of intermingling opposites. The creature of "great countenance and place" and "rare beautie" seems both to fade out and to
remain visible in the context of the creature of "foule abuse" and
"condition vile and base," just as "BON FONS" flickers in and out
of legibility in the context of "Malfont." The principal action that
the prisoner at the bar localizes, again like the poet, is that of suppression: images of dismemberment and effacement recur in the
actions of marring, blotting, obscuring, and defacing that define
Duessa/Mary. Notice, finally, how the construction of the "vntitled
Queene" as a legible text—here described as a misread one—
terminates the stanza, echoing the earlier representation of the narrator's attempt *not* to misread the "vntitled" poet's new title.

The connection between the spectacle of the punished poet and
the initial tableau of the indicted queen at trial is a vital one—even a
scandalous one, though not in the obvious way. I am not arguing
that the poem is attempting to align itself clandestinely with the pro-
Scots faction in the culture's continued reading, in the 1590's, of Mary
Stuart's role in Elizabethan power politics. That is, the poem is not
establishing a critical perspective on the government's and the mon-

arch's engagement in a particular political controversy. Its perspective is metacritical: a perspective that enables us to perceive how the trial of Duessa/Mary elaborates the issues raised in the prefatory spectacle. The initial convergence of the "vntitled" poet and queen invites us to consider the interrelations between the reciprocal actions of writing and reading and the mechanisms of power in Elizabethan culture. Learning the implicit rules of the cultural practice determining the restrictions or taboos at work in the production and reception of texts emerges as an aspect of another imperative: absorbing the implicit rules determining how social and political power is maintained and legitimized. As we enter the Spenserian text of the trial, we are given to suspect that the rules that finally matter are indeed the implicit and self-effacing ones, the ones that sustain, as much in the business of writing and reading as in the exercise of political power, a network of suppression and occlusion, of induced aphasia and misrecognition.

This message is amplified in the episode's probably more transparent conjunction of two kinds of discourse: allegory and historiography (the latter drawing on the historical record to represent specifically the discourse of the state trial of Mary Stuart). The particular interplay of these two discourses in the text reproduces, it turns out, the kind of ambiguous relation we saw in the two parts of conscience (*synteresis/conscientia*): at once normalizing and destabilizing. Independently, both allegory and historiography, like the discourse of conscience, lay claim to a heuristic function, terminating in the disclosure of general or particularized truths. This shared rhetorical equipment, as we shall see, will come into play as the trial episode progresses. Yet, together, the two discourses do not so much reinforce each other's premises as problematize them. Together, the two discourses enter into what we might call a state of ironic synergy.

This state has as much to do with the similarities that the text produces between its allegory and the historical discourse (which includes, notably, the record of the trial) as with the divergences. Let us begin by scanning these two contrasting movements in the text. One of the conspicuous departures of the political allegory from the historical record, which Jonathan Goldberg has commented on, is the translation of Elizabeth's physical absence from Mary's trial into Mercilla's presence at Duessa's. This departure is not the sole one, however.[13] The allegorical representation of Mary's trial itself, ostensibly a summary of the issues and the proceedings constituting the historical event, introduces the implicit question of how to determine at what point the text's tropic, allegorizing operation turns into a distorting lens. Even a cursory glance at the record of the trial indicates that the Spenserian text occludes or "defaces" beyond recognition what are, arguably, the pivotal circumstances of the trial. The strategy of both the defense and the prosecution in the Scots trial, as we have seen in an earlier chapter, was informed by explicit appeals to conscience. In the poem the role of conscience as the presiding spirit of the trial is barely discernible, apparent only in the allusive description of the prosecutor, Zele, as "a person of deepe reach, / And rare in-sight hard matters to reule" (5.9.39). Moreover, Duessa's defense bears little resemblance to Mary's. Mary's resourcefulness in exploiting the discourse of conscience, not to mention her command of the legal issues at stake, turns up in the poem as an admixture of desperate threats (in the figure of Daunger, who threatens "hidden dread / And high alliance vnto forren powre" [5.9.45]) and conventional posturings of the weak female (in the figures of Pittie, Regard of womanhead, and Griefe)—a defense that seems all the more ineffectual in that it is pitted against the culturally validated discourse that the poem assigns exclusively to the prosecution (in the figures of Authority, the Law of Nations, Religion, the Peoples cry and Commons sute, and Iustice).[14] Literally, of course, Duessa has no discourse at all. Her prosecutor, Zele, appears to embody the connection between the hegemonic control of language and the maintenance of a political ascendancy—the image of the eloquent tongue, severed in the spectacle of the criminal poet, returns, restored, in the designated agent of the monarch's conscience or power of equity, who "well could charme his tongue, and time his speach / To all assayes" (5.9.39). In what is arguably more than a mere concession to a convention of allegory, Duessa speaks only through the succession of personified advocates I mentioned above. Unlike her historical referent, Duessa never speaks *in propria persona*; her tongue, like the poet's, has been severed.

I offer this detail as the last departure from the historical record because it is not clear whether it should, in fact, head the list of similarities to the record. The detail of the muted Duessa indicates an ambiguity that runs throughout the political allegories of the book, though nowhere so trenchantly as in this episode. By focusing on two delimited discursive moments, the trial itself and its allegorical representation in the poem, this episode focuses our attention, in turn, on the ambiguous intention of the text: or, more precisely, on the interweaving of its literal and figurative components and on the related problem of where to locate the point at which either component, used as an interpretive measure, will produce a bad or false reading. Literally, the representation of the muted Duessa departs from the historical record; but, figuratively, it accurately conveys a plausible subtext of the trial: that the political context in which Mary spoke annulled the power of her eloquence. Mary's words, falling as they did on deaf ears, were virtually severed from the possibility of generating any viable channel of communication with her interlocutors.

At the literal level, then, the allegory implicates itself, as well as the narrative it contains of judgment against Mary, in a process of distortion—clearly an impolitic, not to say subversive, reading of the text. At the figurative level, the allegory reasserts its integrity as a faithful translation, but at the expense of invoking a reading of the trial that proves ambiguous and, again, suspect. Is Mary to be understood as having been symbolically mute at her trial because, found guilty in advance by a universal judgment (which the trial merely gives a belated and extraneous form to) she possesses no words that can articulate the legitimate truth of her innocence? Or does the symbolic muting indicate the mutilated form of dialog that marginal voices, like those of suspected traitors and usurpers (and "bad" poets), must enter into when they engage in a contest for the right to speak their truth against the truth of an entrenched power structure? All interpretive roads at this point in the text lead not necessarily to a vision of the particular truth of Mary Stuart's innocence and victimization but to the more sweeping insight that more than one truth resides in what the officially sanctioned voice of conscience (Zele) foregrounds as a single, incontrovertible "haynous fact" and that the "fact" that gains legitimacy is the one associated with the constellation of powers in the image of Zele's tongue: the power of conscience, of the monarch, and of speech itself. The textual detail, therefore, does not so much testify to the reciprocal rela-

tion of its figurative and literal interpretations in promulgating what
we might call the poem's encomiastic rubric as it testifies to the collusion of the figurative and the literal in pointing up the metacritical
stance that can be taken on such a rubric: "'true' speech can only be
an act of praise" becomes something like "this poem shows how encomiastic poems observe a rule of occlusion that makes it possible to
claim that 'true' speech can only be an act of praise."

Another way of putting this is to note that the interpretive problems posed by the similarities of the allegory to the historical record
may be at least as great as those posed by the departures. Consider
some of the ways in which the poem, from a canonical viewpoint, is
an embarrassingly faithful mirror of the events of 1586–87. At two
decisive moments—at the climax of Duessa's trial in canto 9 and at
the pronouncement of the death sentence in canto 10—the text contains details that make it possible to perceive a certain tension on the
subject of whose judgment—the monarch's or the people's—finally
counted. (Once Duessa is "guiltie deemed of all," Zele turns his en-
ergy from the "vntitled Queene" to Mercilla herself, urging her to
accept a verdict that in a sense has already been delivered; similarly,
Mercilla pronounces the final "doome" against Duessa under pressure: "Strong constraint did her thereto enforce.") Through such
details the text captures part of Elizabeth's own rhetorical strategy—
her attempt to rewrite her own role in the crisis as that of the "true"
victim—but it also captures, perhaps more daringly, the real political
hazard she entered by engaging in behavior that fueled the constitutionalist impulse of Parliament.

Another detail, this time a formal point: canto 9, departing from
the structural norm both of book 5 and of the trial format on which
the episode patterns itself, ends inconclusively. Mercilla, unable or
unwilling to speak in judgment against Duessa, suspends the narrative action and creates one of the rare moments of suspense in the
poem. In view of the palpable absence of closure, canto 9 may be
said to end, in fact, not with the printed text of stanza 50 but with
the blank space that separates the stanza from the opening lines of
canto 10: a visual gap, a mark of deferral that prompts the reader to
ask, "When will Mercilla speak next? What will her judgment be?"—
to reproduce, in other words, the kinds of questions that were asked
of Elizabeth by her frustrated Parliament and ministers. Finally, let us

consider the final arc of the Duessa section—the passage that moves from Mercilla's suspended judgment at the close of canto 9 to the narrator's digressive tribute to Mercilla's mercy that opens canto 10, followed by the rapidly sketched account of Duessa's end. This passage, filled with labyrinthine turns, as we shall see, defines itself implicitly as a transgressive rewriting of the procrastinating, self-effacing strategy Elizabeth conducted in the winter of 1586–87, a strategy that included the "answer answerlesse" speeches to Parliament, medusan speeches designed to ward off any writing of the Scots case that would bring up the question of Elizabeth's responsibility.

The text would seem, then, least problematic as a canonical writing at the points where it departs from the historical record—at the points, that is, where the text tacitly acknowledges its own status as the record, the end product, of a potentially problematic process of interpretation. The problematic potential, we know, can be arrested or neutralized: the silence of Duessa and the presence of Mercilla can be read, after all, as images that are only apparently false. In them the reader can witness the presumably higher allegorical truth of the represented event that the historical facts alone would not necessarily convey: in Duessa's silence a sign of the ultimate inauthenticity of her position, in Mercilla's presence a sign of the ultimate force of equity in the proceedings. Such an interpretive move would situate the text as an exemplum of one of the commonplaces of Renaissance poetics—the notion, most familiar in Sidney's formulation, that the poet is the "monarch" of "all sciences" because the "speaking picture of poesy" embodies in the "instructing parables" of "pretty allegories" the "abstract and general" wisdom of philosophy and therefore escapes the intrinsic limitations of history, a discourse "tied . . . to the particular truth of things"—that is, to a devalued perspective, one shaped by "old mouse-eaten records" and the "cloudy knowledge of mankind." [15]

The problem with this sort of interpretive move is that it is patently inadequate, especially in view of the way the allegory amplifies the rather different kind of poetics suggested by the narrative context: notably the insight into the politics of allegory and allegoresis suggested by their representation in the spectacle of dismemberment. The vision of the "infallible grounds of wisdom" that the fiction of allegory illumines is a selective vision: thus the allegory of the trial and execution of Duessa speaks, articulating the message not so much through what is conspicuously excluded from the legitimizing, allegorizing text but through what is included.[16] In other words, the very representation of completeness and transparency or neutrality of the allegorical text, which can be adduced from the places where the text seems most thorough in its transmission of the details of the historical case, turns out to be a representation of surfeit—with the allegory itself indicated as the textual evidence of a dismembering process only partially completed. To return to the image invoked in Elizabeth's speeches, the allegory defies the medusan rhetoric associated with the monarch's conscience, memorializing precisely what Elizabeth had designated as off limits, the details destined not to turn up among the "facts" of the case.

Reading the allegory of the trial and execution of Mary Stuart means, then, reading complicitously, for it is allegoresis itself, the text suggests, that must complete the dismembering process of allegory by making sure to misrecognize the impolitic associations of what the text contains. As though conducting a parody of the marquee over the poet's head, the text implies that only its status as "BON FONS" is to be "plainely" read; whatever associations it has with "Malfont" are to remain, like the title "BON FONS" for the poet, neither absolutely legible nor illegible: liminal and therefore elusive. The one clear reference to the spectacle of the poet in the trial—the recovered image of the tongue—indicates how the allegoresis involved in the text takes as its model this kind of parodic relation to the script over the poet's head. Ostensibly, the allegory itself works like the principal discursive structure it incorporates into its fabric, that of the trial. The trial, a self-avowed heuristic enterprise designed to culminate in the discovery and revelation of the truth of a case, helps establish the nominal limits of how the allegory is to be read: as an equally unambiguous and stable pattern of truth.

The image of the tongue introduces an element of strain into this legitimizing operation, for it points up the association between trial, conscience, and spectacle.[17] Consider again Zele's profile: a "person of deepe reach, / And rare in-sight hard matters to reuele" who "well could charme his tongue, and time his speach / To all assayes." No sooner are Zele's credentials established in the allusion to the penetrating gaze of conscience than they are turned into wild cards by the insinuation that Zele's gift is like the orator's or the actor's. The immediate context of this startling line is worth recalling here: the trial episode begins with a charged description of Duessa/Mary—a description that at once establishes the centrality of the circumstance of person in the case and, through the pervasive images of eradication, suggests the difficulty of ascertaining what a complete, stable impression of a person might look like. No help in resolving the difficulty comes from the description of Zele, which reminds us of the public, the staged and the theatrical, dimension of Renaissance conceptions of the person. Instead of the hieratic figure who speaks in Isis Church, in Mercilla's court of equity we meet a figure who drifts from the hieratic pose to the theatrical, someone prepared to carry out the principles of rhetorical decorum Hamlet gives the players at Elsinore: "Suit the action to the word, the word to the action" (3.2.18–19). The "person of deepe reach" doubles as one of surfaces, of chameleon-like adaptability, mirroring the double aspect of conscience itself.

Yet this passage into destabilizing ambiguities furnishes exactly the kind of information that the overt narrative context disowns, so that sustaining the text's normalizing, heuristic aspect emerges as an act contingent on a sustained misreading. The power to "charme," then, works two ways—as a power represented in the text and as a power of the text. As an attribute of Zele, it articulates the unspeakable. It articulates the possibility that the power of conscience derives from "underground," unsanctioned forces that the word "charme" evokes, ones the hieratic agencies of conscience will disclaim: the shamanistic power of rhetoric in word and action and the regions of desire in which rhetoric holds court, where one interlocutor seeks to gain mastery over or submit to another.

This is the kind of "in-sight" the text reveals—what I described above as the allegory's defiance of Elizabeth's medusan rhetoric— only to conceal. That is, the text's own power to "charme" ultimately consists of its mimetic fidelity to the medusan power attributed to the monarch's conscience, in what amounts to a case of mimetic excess. Establishing at the outset an interplay of competing and irreconcilable narrative contexts, the trial episode imitates the interplay of conflicting political and social imperatives that characterizes the dynamics of Elizabethan court culture, a dynamics founded on the culture's naturalized strategies for survival, visibility, and ascendancy. To the degree that the suspect connotation of the charmed tongue associated with Zele and conscience passes as an inconsequential detail—or as one that merely corroborates the normalizing, heuristic context by enlisting the seductive power of rhetoric in the service of Zele's "rare in-sight"—the allegory and the kind of allegoresis it invites appear as a textual imitation of the blind spots that invade the cultural reading of Elizabeth's power and the norms subtending it. This kind of imitation of Elizabeth's medusan conscience is arguably something more than courtly homage or flattery; but that something more cannot be pinpointed in the text. Unlike Zele, the text does not so much reveal its own "rare in-sight" into the mechanism of the power structure it claims to glorify as it enacts the process of virtual dismemberment that impolitic insights must submit to in texts with pretensions to escaping censorship and the cutting off of visibility and of avenues to *fama* in the royal gaze: the kind of dismemberment suffered from the effects of royal disfavor.

We can read in the disingenuously equivocal description of Zele an index of how the representation of the Scots case will situate itself in relation to the medusan power of the discourse of conscience. The text, as though conducting an exposé, locates the power of the petrifying gaze in the cultural practice of sifting out and privileging the circumstantial details that come to constitute the legitimate "history" of an event. The text also locates the petrifying gaze in its own operation: mimesis of the medusan power of conscience is at once a cultural critique and an appropriation or, perhaps, a reclaiming of that power for the text itself, in what the text indicates as the ultimately ungovernable and threatening dynamics of the social practice of writing and reading.

The description of Zele, particularly insofar as it drifts into potentially scandalous language, also announces the interpretive project at stake at the climax of the episode, which begins with the suspense Mercilla brings to the trial by withholding "just vengeance" on Duessa at the close of canto 9. At this point Spenser begins a narrative tour de force in which the allegory appears to be testing the limits of the selective vision it invites, hypothesizing on the extent of its medusan power to eradicate or "deface," like Duessa's "titles of nobilitie," the destabilizing insights that emerge as it moves toward the culminating depiction of Duessa's "wretched corse."

Let us examine more closely, then, the text's treatment of the impolitic insights it points to as, sharpening its mimetic fidelity to the circumstances of time and place, Westminster and Fotheringay in 1586–87, it approaches full disclosure of the *arcana imperii*, the secrets of the monarch's conscience:

> But she, whose Princely brest was touched nere
> With piteous ruth of her so wretched plight,
> Though plaine she saw by all, that she did heare,
> That she of death was guiltie found by right,
> Yet would not let iust vengeance on her light;
> But rather let instead thereof to fall
> Few perling drops from her faire lampes of light;
> The which she covering with her purple pall
> Would haue the passion hid, and vp arose withall.

> Canto 10
> Some Clarkes doe doubt in their deuicefull art
> Whether this heauenly thing, whereof I treat,
> To weeten Mercie, be of Iustice part,
> Or drawne forth from her by diuine extreate:
> This well I wote, that sure she is as great,
> And meriteth to haue as high a place,
> Sith in th'Almighties euerlasting seat
> She first was bred, and borne of heauenly race,
> From thence pour'd down on men by influence of grace.

> For if that Vertue be of so great might
> Which from iust verdict will for nothing start,
> But to preserue inuiolated right
> Oft spilles the principall, to saue the part;
> So much more, then, is that of powre and art
> That seekes to saue the subiect of her skill,
> Yet neuer doth from doome of right depart:
> As it is greater prayse to saue, then spill,
> And better to reforme, then to cut off the ill.

> Who then can thee, Mercilla, throughly prayse,
> That herein doest all earthly Princes pas?
> What heauenly Muse shall thy great honour rayse

Up to the skies, whence first deriv'd it was,
And now on earth it selfe enlarged has,
From th'vtmost brinke of the Armericke shore
Vnto the margent of the Molucas?
Those Nations farre thy iustice doe adore;
But thine owne people do thy mercy prayse much more.

Much more it praysed was of those two knights,
The noble Prince and righteous Artegall,
When they had seene and heard her doome a rights
Against Duessa, damned by them all;
But by her tempred without griefe or gall,
Till strong constraint did her thereto enforce:
And yet euen then ruing her wilfull fall
With more than needfull naturall remorse,
And yeelding the last honour to her wretched corse.

During all which, those knights continu'd there
Both doing and receiuing curtesies
Of that great Ladie, who with goodly chere
Them entertayn'd, fit for their dignities,
Approuing dayly to their noble eyes
Royall examples of her mercies rare
And worthie paterns of her clemencies;
Which till this day mongst many liuing are,
Who them to their posterities doe still declare.

(5.9.50–10.5)

I want to consider, first of all, the general movement of the closing
passage, which involves two kinds of writing: a block of narrative
(5.9.50–10.5.) interrupted by an extended exposition (5.10.1–3). As I
noted above, the narrative that closes canto 9 functions as an aborted
closure. We expect Mercilla's judgment; it is withheld. An anomaly
in the context of the book's structural norm, this moment is also a
fitting conclusion in the context of the episode that begins with the
spectacle of the mutilated poet: the canto ends with the representation of muting extended to Mercilla herself. The muting works, paradoxically, like an echo. It echoes the rhetoric of victimization that
Elizabeth appropriated in her speeches to Parliament. And it echoes
the rhetoric of inviolability that Elizabeth's staged victimization
served. The expected words sealing the unambiguous judgment are
supplanted by the ambiguous gesture of tears, ambiguous because

the text does not clarify whether the tears represent the sorrow of the monarch over the judgment she knows she must make or the sorrow that indicates a commiseration—or a power of equity—so great that the judgment urged by the monarch's advisors will not be uttered.

What, indeed, is Mercilla up to? one may well ask at this point; and the text, in response to the inquiry it elicits, betrays the thematics of secrecy and occlusion that the monarch's conscience exploited in maintaining the illusion of royal inviolability. Consider the concentration of images of shrouding and obfuscation in the last lines of the canto. Echoing the disorienting optical effect of the sign above the poet's head, the text first shows the falling tears as a metaphoric veil blocking out the monarch's words and next shows the tears themselves being veiled as the monarch covers her face with her "purple pall," in a gesture that is more than a model of stately decorum. In this exposed moment, Mercilla responds to the crisis with an explicitly defined strategy of concealment, a pantomime of the desire of those "under the eies of manie," as Elizabeth herself put it, to possess the power represented by the icon of conscience, the chameleon—the power of invisibility.

Mercilla, we learn, "would haue the passion hid." "Passion" is a loaded word, one whose double meaning evokes the politics of ambiguity that informed Elizabeth's behavior as the Scots case drew to a close. The passion to be hidden could be read as Mercilla's indecorous outburst of emotion. Or it could be read as the spectacle of Duessa's final suffering (to some lights her martyrdom), in which Mercilla must perform not as the victim but as the minister of death. In either case, the detail presents itself as a kind of surfeit requiring judicious editing. From one perspective it risks betraying the canonical text as an assemblage of interpretive moves negotiated between author and reader rather than the unmediated vessel of truth: it appears to be a fictional addendum to its historical referent, a textual version of the act it describes, the imposition of a veil over something to be kept secret. (The text makes a secret of the fact that, unlike Mercilla, Elizabeth herself did not hide but made, rather, a spectacle of her grief and, after the execution, of her anger, in an attempt to underscore her own role as victim.) [18] From another perspective the detail risks betraying the canonical text's implicit truth-telling project as a hazardous enterprise, hazardous because such transparency reveals too much. (Read as an allusion to Elizabeth's "passion," the detail transforms the passage into a window giving onto a nominally unreadable message: that Elizabeth made a spectacle of her grief and anger but tried to have Mary killed secretly and in any case indicated in her grief-tinged speeches and in her angry outburst after the execution that her role in the "passion" of Mary's death was to be hidden, in the sense of being misread.) How, indeed, to read this detail, other than to follow the action the text describes: to occlude it?

Two other details provide a narrative context that makes it difficult to ignore how at this climactic moment the text repeatedly cites the act of occlusion as an essential aspect of the politics of misreading employed both in the historical reality and in the text. Consider the "Few perling drops" that Mercilla permits to be seen for a moment before covering her eyes. Why are the tears likened to pearls and not to other adornments of nobility—say, crystals or jewels? Unlike the other possible metaphors, the word "perling" invokes the thematics of concealment. Cataracts, obstructions of the passage of light into the lens, were known as "Pearles of the Eyes."[19] Even in a moment of apparent self-exposure—before Mercilla performs the gesture of covering the tears—the image of the transparent tears turns into one of opacity. The pearling tears thus underscore the evasive strategy represented by the ritual-like use of the purple pall: the royal gaze, symbol of the channels of royal power, is blocked. Through the twice-obscured tears that show Mercilla, like Elizabeth, willing herself absent from the controversy, the text reproduces the paradoxical point of the queen's "answer answerlesse": to read the conscience of the monarch is to misread it—in this case, to transform presence into absence.

A grammatical detail reinforces the point. The metaphor appears not in the substantive but in the participial form: we see not the finished product (tears like pearls) but the process (tears becoming pearls; transparency turning into opacity). The text represents a related transformation with the introduction of Mercilla's purple pall. Here the allegory enacts its dismembering capacity, symbolically cancelling out the nominally higher truth that can be read into Mercilla's presence—the presiding spirit of equity—and replacing it with a truth of a different order—the truth that Mercilla's ritualized absence conveys of Elizabeth's attempt to maintain the illusion of monarchical inviolability by distancing herself, physically and symbolically, from the judicial action against Mary. The image of Mercilla covering herself with a purple pall records Elizabeth's own action of letting the pall-like cloth of state, symbol of the impersonal and abstract authority of the royal crown, substitute for her physical body at Mary's trial.

The sheer range of the allusiveness of this passage contributes to the interpretive problems it poses as substitutes for the expected resolution that the representation of Mercilla's word of judgment would conceivably convey. Not only are there the ambiguities arising from the words I have described; there are also echoes, impolitic ones, of Malengin's regime of duplicity. Mercilla's tearful display, for example, recalls Samient's ruse, and her symbolic vanishing act recalls Malengin's own use of metamorphoses to effect an escape from judgment and punishment. The canto closes, in other words, with the implication that the regimes of Mercilla and Malengin, like the two parts of conscience, *synteresis* and *conscientia*, do not reside in disparate spheres but constitute the alternately concealing and revealing phases of an equivocal text.

Mercilla's final gesture—her representation of the state of her conscience—is, after all, both a revealing and a concealing one: it amplifies the kind of reading cue suggested by the verbal ambiguities in the stanza. We have only to consider the kind of dynamic involved between author and readers of the social text that Mercilla's gesture invokes. An audience sees a woman veil her face. The act produces an image of public mourning and, beyond that, an image that reveals the fact that something is being concealed. The existence of a space of interiority is made visible so that whatever occupies the interior space will be understood to be unintelligible, unyielding to scrutiny. The implicit contract to observe such a message can be read in the gesture's status as ritual, as communal practice (i.e., failure to fulfill the terms of the contract will amount to exclusion from the unifying discourse of the community). In the text, the contract gains a timely frame of reference, given the association of the pall and the cloth of state. The text records, in effect, the "body natural" of the queen being eclipsed by her "body politic." In terms of the reading strategy involved, it records the ascendancy that the body of officially sanctioned, normative readings acquires over private, potentially heterodox ones. What Mercilla's gesture amounts to, then, is a paradoxical act, one that the text mirrors: a representation of the politics of discretionary misreading that, like the purple pall, will occult even as it illumines the interrelated mechanisms of royal power and authoritative discourse.

The narrative resumes four stanzas later (5.10.4–5), again pointing to transgressive insights it shows in the process of being occluded. The account of Duessa's execution (stanza 4) has gained a certain notoriety in readings of book 5 as one of the spectacularly botched moments in the poem, seen either as an example of Spenser's uneven hand or of how, like the moth to the flame, his poem could not help registering signs of the cultural anxiety that the Scots case provoked about the legitimacy of the monarchy and the political and ecclesiastical programs associated with the Tudor crown.[20] Indeed, the allegory at this point appears to go out of control, most conspicuously in the way it fails to localize in the text the two pivotal events that determined the resolution of the case: the decisive judgment of one queen (the signing of the death warrant) and the resulting execution of her rival. To be sure, Duessa turns up at the end of the stanza as a "wretched corse" given the funerary honors owed a dignitary, but how she reached that end is represented through a concatenation of qualifying markers or narrative stammerings ("But," "Till," "And yet euen") that defeat whatever attempt might be made to adduce a direct relationship of cause and effect between Mercilla's actions and Duessa's fate.[21]

Given the text's involvement in the thematics of conscience as I have described it, this sort of representation is predictable. Once again, as it meshes with the details of the historical case that Elizabeth designated as unreadable, the allegory turns into a representation both of mimetic excess and of mimetic excess cancelled out: showing more than a canonical account of the event should, and showing how such a potentially transgressive reading will be eliminated. To perceive the full arc of this narrative action we need to read the stanza describing Duessa's execution not as an isolated unit but as the first of a two-part sequence. The following stanza begins with a segue—"During all which"—that invites us to consider the two

stanzas as simultaneous events. The events: in the first stanza, a potentially destabilizing text; in the second, a representation of how
that text will be quashed. In the second stanza, the knights and their
companions in the court behave as if the problematic events the text
records occupied the same medusan space as the mutilated poet. The
demythologizing circumstances of the case are absorbed into an
economy of mutually advantageous misreading in which both monarch and those under the monarch's gaze are implicated. Not only
the conspicuous failure to produce an ideologically "correct," efful-
gent account of Duessa's end but also the inclusion of signs contra-
dicting Mercilla's inviolability—the reference to the parliamentary
pressure brought to bear on the monarch and the implicit depiction,
in the reference to Mercilla's "more than needfull naturall remorse,"
of Elizabeth's behavior as a contrivance—these circumstances dissolve, like the words "BON FONS," into an illegible text. What re-
places them: a text with no place for a "bad" reading, a text suffused
with the abstractions and shimmering surfaces of courtly etiquette.
The "noble eyes" returning the monarch's gaze see only "Royall examples of her mercies rare / And worthie paterns of her clemencies."
As well they might. Such misreading, the text implies, is part of the
economy of "doing and receiuing curtesies."

In effect, the text enacts the hegemony of the aphasiac regime in
the Elizabethan discourse of power—a medusan power, the political
and social elaboration of the lax conscience, a power that, like the
knights' "continu'd" innocuous reading of Mercilla, remains in force
in return for the continued prospect of survival, of continued visibility, in the court.[22] Even as it makes a show of submitting itself to
the aphasiac regime, producing the kind of unqualified praise promised in the proem, the text problematizes these earmarks of canonicity. In the context of the evident strain involved in coming up with
a "good" account of Duessa's fate, the words of praise that the text
introduces in closing the episode appear not only conventional and
banal but inadequate, inadequate masks over the "conscience," the
interior dimensions, of the crisis.

If the allegory is flawed at this point in the narrative, as some
critics have argued, it is doubly flawed: both in the text of Duessa's
death, which violates the mythology of Elizabeth's inviolability, and
in the represented reading of that text, which shows canonical read-

ings to be inept ones, however politically advisable, indeed necessary, they may be. Flawed, moreover, in its rewriting of the relationship between readers and authors within the discourse of power. Power, it turns out, involves something more than a rhetoric of passive reception of a divinely authored script, the kind of rhetoric that allows the narrator to praise his "Dread Souerayne Goddesse." It involves a rhetoric of indirection and obfuscation, a general cultural project of concealment and aphasia. These so-called flaws are the textual equivalents of the snake bite, "long . . . to be read," that Artegall receives at the end of the book: equivocal marks that chart the progress of their contaminating aspect into unintelligibility.

The narrative's expertise lies in the balancing act it sustains between divergent perspectives—the one approaching political apostasy, like the description of Duessa's execution; the other reclaiming the book's fidelity to the cultural norms it ostensibly retells, like the description of the court's reception of the event. What gives the narrative its unsettling edge, I have been arguing, is that, in the course of the book's progress toward a closure that turns out to be more apparent than real, the anticipatory moments of resolution or normality themselves appear suspect when the narrative context or circumstances are taken into account. How, indeed, is one to distinguish the "worthie paterns" of virtue from their suave dissimulations? How to know whether such a distinction in fact exists? Given the kind of connection that the narrative of the trial insinuates between the articulation of a normative vision and the medusan disablement of critical inquiry, such questions—the unutterable ones—seem all the more to the point. So with the narrative's disarming yet suspect conclusion to the trial episode; so, too, with the most conspicuous assertion of the book's normative project in the episode—the narrator's digression on Mercilla's fabled mercy or equity. Moments like these—where the narrative's reverential and scandalous aspects coincide—attest to the book's recurrent meditation on the involvement of the ungovernable power of writing and reading in the movement of the lax conscience.

In isolation, the narrator's set piece on the virtue of "Mercie" fulfills the book's heuristic function. The narrator takes an opportunity to remind his readers of his own status as a "good" poet and of

Mercilla's universally praised exercise of equity. Yet, in the context of an increasingly problematic narrative, the heuristic adequacy of these two moves is open to question. The previous stanza, which closed canto 9, ended on a note of suspense—a conspicuous withholding of closure—and with the implied presence of at least two unresolved controversial issues, each related to the problem of how authoritative words are constituted and maintained: the rivalry between populist and absolutist conceptions of political sovereignty and the rivalry between competing "facts" in the construction of an allegory of Mary Stuart's last days. In the opening stanza of canto 10 the narrator describes his role in terms that seem, appropriately, to take into account the need for the ambiance of mounting controversy to be dispelled. Echoing the kind of clerical debate recorded by Christopher St. German in the popular legal treatise on conscience and equity called *Doctor and Student*, the narrator observes the controversy among "Some Clarkes" over whether "Mercie," or equity, "be of Iustice part, / Or drawne forth from her by diuine extreate"—whether the unwritten rule of equity takes precedence over the written law; whether Mercilla's as yet unspoken word of equity is more decisive than the "zeale of Iustice" spreading throughout the court; whether the account of Mary Stuart that unequivocally sets "Iustice gainst the thrall" can claim to be the authoritative word on the subject. And the narrator, enacting the power of his word to bring, like the monarch's, an end to controversies, comes up with a judgment that inclines toward mercy: "Sure she [mercy] is as great, / And meriteth to have as high a place" (5.10.1).

To be sure, this looks very much like a verbal figure of *concordia discors*. But the resolution the words announce is merely formal; in practical terms, a judgment that understands each of two potentially competing voices of authority to be "as great" as the other will very likely end up contributing to rather than dispelling a controversy. The narrator's judgment, which literally substitutes itself for Mercilla's judgment in the narrative, represents, in effect, the deferral of the authoritative and unambiguous word that was demanded of Elizabeth in the Scots case: the judgment parodies the queen's equivocal "answer answerlesse." In both cases, a pressing need for clarification of a particularized set of issues is met by a flight into

abstract argument and convoluted verbal play—a flight we will see
invoked again in the economy of courtly "curtesies" immune to all
circumstantial complications.

Thus far I have been reading the narrator's digression as though,
like other parts of the allegory, it were erring on the side of mimetic
excess—carrying its historical similitude too far, into the regions of
the monarch's conscience. There is one sense in which the passage
seems to follow the thematic cue that its digressive status implies, by
departing from what are known to be the historical "facts" of the
case. Let me state the obvious: Mary Stuart was executed. Now let
us turn to the heart of the narrator's theoretical analysis of mercy.
Though strict justice, we learn, enjoys "great might," it also carries a
:ransgressive potential. To "preserue inuiolated right"—to maintain
its integrity—the action of justice "Oft spilles the principall, to
saue the part" and turns into injustice. The paradox was proverbial:
summa ius, summa iniuria; William Perkins discussed the problem
in *EPIEIKEIA, or a Treatise of Christian Equity and Moderation*. His
solution included insights relevant to the problem as it appears in
Spenser's text. Cases of conscience, as Perkins saw them, could not
all be anticipated by the laws: cases were, in effect, variable and
open-ended texts. Reading them required a sensitivity to the norms
which seemed to obtain in them but also a sensitivity to the limits of
the norms, the "ground of mitigation." No lawmakers, "being men,
can foresee, or set downe all cases that may fall out," he argued.
"Therefore when the case altereth, then must the discretion of the
law-maker shew itself, & doe that which the law cannot doe."[23] As
we have seen elsewhere, equity carried a more immediately perceptible transgressive potential than strict justice, in that by definition it
stood for a discursive space that always exceeded the boundaries of
the written text of the law (see Chapter 5). Spenser's text represents
this problematic discursive space in the passage that defines equity
proper. If strict justice has "great might," says the narrator,

> So much more, then, is that of powre and art
> That seekes to saue the subiect of her skill,
> Yet neuer doth from doome of right depart:
> As it is greater prayse to saue, then spill,
> And better to reforme, then to cut off the ill.
>
> (5.10.2)

Even as the subject of an abstract argument, torn from the circumstantial details of its narrative context, equity seems at once to demand and challenge what Perkins would have called the discretionary powers of its readers. The passage turns on a paradox: it looks as though the narrator is describing an action that cannot be undertaken without contradiction. Yet more is going on here than the continuation of the verbal play I described above, especially if we consider that the passage cannot fail to be read with an eye to the narrative context, which in turn asks us to read the narrator's intrusion as a substitute for Mercilla's word of judgment and, therefore, as a text with a clear referential axis.

In this light, the paradox is only the first of the interpretive difficulties the passage raises. Is the narrator suggesting that the paradox merely points to the mysterious, divine-like ways of the monarch's power of equity, according to which Elizabeth's decision to permit Mary's execution was ultimately an act of mercy? Perhaps, but there is nothing in the text that specifically privileges such a reading over the equally plausible one that finds in the contradictory utterance a representation of the kind of ethical and (possibly more important) political checkmate in which Elizabeth in fact found herself. Once again, the destabilizing power of equity and conscience shows its maverick hand, in the words of praise that disclose the virtue most closely associated with the monarch to be impracticable. The implicit, transgressive message: it is not, as Elizabeth would have had it, that the actions of the monarch's conscience cannot be correctly read but that what the monarch claims to do as the inviolable embodiment of equity cannot be done.

Even this message pales before the one that emerges as the narrator closes his theoretical discussion and moves on to what looks like a conventional assertion of universal praise of Mercilla's mercy. "Who then can thee, Mercilla, throughly prayse, / That herein doest all earthly Princes pas?" (5.10.3). The action nearest in the text to this statement, the action that "herein" refers to, is what warrants the "greater prayse"—Mercilla's due: "it is greater prayse to saue, then spill, / And better to reforme, then to cut off the ill" (5.10.2). The action receiving universal praise is one that can have occurred only in the text, for the implication of this passage (several lines before the reference to Duessa's "wretched corse," which finally acknowledges what happened) is that Mercilla did not "spill" or "cut off" Duessa but saved her instead.

Several potentially scandalous insights can be drawn from what amounts to a textual enactment of the action of equity—from the apparent movement of the text out of a position of "strict justice" or fidelity to the known facts to one of interpretive flexibility, one that opens onto an imaginary world that enjoins readers to entertain the possibility of an alternative climax to the case. The passage suggests the power of written texts to rewrite social texts—an act, to be sure, that seems to identify writing as a distorting lens (the work of a "bad" poet) and, more problematically, to identify the rewriting that occurs in canonical texts as an act charged with a legitimizing power so strong that what the canon deems true, for practical purposes, becomes true. The written text, in other words, is exploring the extent to which verisimilitude, the truth measured by the formal arrangement and logic of the written text, can alter or cannibalize details perceived as constituting the truth of the historical record. The regime of verisimilitude shows itself extending beyond the enclosed space of written texts and informing the socially framed idioms like the courtly "curtesies" that will be cited at the close of the episode. Such "curtesies," the text implies, are maintained by a complicitous bond between interlocutors that mirrors the one between written texts and their readers, allowing conventional utterances—like the narrator's hyperbolic appraisal of Mercilla's fame—to assume the place of historical fact. The apparent aberration that the text seems on the verge of articulating—Mercilla's eleventh-hour rescue of Duessa—points up the politics of misreading that the text will later ascribe to the "curtesie" involved in the court's reception of the Byzantine manner of Duessa's dispatching. Whatever the projected closure—whether Duessa is "saued" or "spilled"—the reading will be what courtesy requires: the unabated litany of universal praise.

From one perspective, then, by imagining a context in which an account of Duessa/Mary's salvation enters a canonical reading of the event, the text decenters the received ideological position that defines Duessa/Mary's death as the only possible "good" outcome. From another perspective, one that disabuses us of the limited notion that the text's hidden project is merely to acknowledge a rival ideology, the text indicates a more global and destabilizing insight. It represents what it means to read properly within any ideological system: to observe the taboos surrounding cultural talismans; in the case of the Elizabethan system that the passage encapsulates, to observe the rhetoric of the monarch's medusan conscience, which imagines that whatever the monarch does—however enormous the word or action—will be met by a universally applicable chant of praise—that is, by virtually unseeing eyes.

Another double perspective, one that obtains as well in the vision of the courtly "curtesies" that will close the episode: the text at hand situates itself equivocally in relation to what it represents as the absence of a space for equivocation between texts and readers of royal power. By representing the process itself of eliminating equivocation, along with the prospect of interpretive flexibility that equivocation engenders (a process mirroring the "cutting off" of Duessa and of the poet's tongue), the text blurs the distinction between the act of submitting uncritically to normative interpretive constraints and the act of investigating the mechanism of such constraints metacritically. It blurs the distinction between textual "innocence" or canonicity and the "lewd poems" destined to be placed on the Elizabethan index. It suggests nothing less than the textual equivalent of the regime of the lax conscience, a canonical text that problematizes the scope of canonicity while showing the governing interpretive context to be one that will induce misreadings of the destabilizing insights that have insinuated themselves into the book.

One last consideration. The questions I have been drawing out from the digressive opening of canto 10 are latent in another place— in the blank space or gap in the text that separates cantos 9 and 10 and that serves, in effect, as a parallel text to the one that gives us the scrambled disquisition on equity. The sheer absence of words that follows the final images of Mercilla in canto 9 (the images of veiling and of the frozen arc of a movement) not only underscores the suspense produced by the withholding of Mercilla's decisive judgment. The absence advances, as well, the point that the rest of the episode will indicate in other ways: to the degree that the representation of Mercilla's words mirrors Elizabeth's, it will show the power of the monarch's utterance to depend on the reciprocal relation of two rhetorics, a rhetoric of inviolability and one of unintelligibility. The subtext of absence in this case is, indeed, presence: the representation of what Elizabeth wished her words to amount to—a virtual blank space, a dissolving text received by a state of global misrecognition, deriving from the medusan conscience of the queen. The gap is also a locus that resumes, at a pivotal moment in the narrative, the most searching critical inquiries that punctuate the book, inquiries that, from the canonical perspective, must be "raced out," like the "BON FONS" script. The very fact that the wanted closure appears as a "raced out" part of the text constitutes, for example, an imaginative projection of a legend of justice without any allegorical account of the Scots case. The blank space implicitly poses the questions "Why include this particular allegory at all?" and "Why represent it problematically?" Reading the trial episode in the context of the entire narrative, observing how the episode epitomizes the narrative's involvement in the destabilizing thematics of conscience, indicates the answer to such questions.

The story of the two rival and potentially interchangeable queens (as Elizabeth put it, like "two milke maids") was the culture's most potent symbol of the latently subversive action the twin discourses of conscience and equity brought to their role as the presumed handmaids of the Elizabethan discourse of power. The two queens' rival claims to absolute jurisdiction over the word "conscience," notably over the word's legitimizing function, disclosed the multiple, even contradictory, inflections inherent in the word—as did, in another sphere, the apostate Anthony Tyrrell's scandalous career. This counterpoint of destabilizing circumstances pointed up the disingenuous transparency of the arena of conscience as a legitimizing instrument. And it set up the enabling conditions for all the arena contained—the culture's received normative categories—to be imagined, paradoxically, as they could not, by definition, be imagined: as the self-effacing ciphers—the blank spaces—left by a generalized cultural project of occlusion and misreading, a project indexed by the images of the chameleon, Medusa, and the labyrinth, and oriented toward the action of cutting off the very notion of norms from the corridors leading to the disclosure of that notion as the result of processes informed by ideological imperatives. The blank space in Spenser's text, which represents this paradoxical imagining, encapsulates the narrative project of the entire book and indicates why the trial episode is both appropriate and necessary to the legend of jus-

tice. A fractured narrative that appears seamless only in its function
as a sustained figure of equivocation, the episode enacts even as it
disowns the insolubility of the conflict between the two opposing
ideologies that the discursive confrontation of Elizabeth and Mary
symbolized. More precisely, by charting the passage of a demythologizing insight into a blank space of virtual invisibility, the episode
allegorizes the culture's misreading of the conflict.

In this context, the blank space represents the cloud of misreadings that the equivocal text itself will generate through the confusion
it sustains of textual innocence (as a canonical book of praise) and
textual transgression (as a "lewd poem"). Such textual equivocation,
we have seen, permits the legend of justice to conduct a critical interrogation of the Elizabethan discourse of power—to annul, even
as it makes a show of submitting to, the medusan conscience of the
monarch—and to resist the claims, whether explicit or implicit, of
the readings projected on it to being the authoritative, petrifying
acts of an infallible interpretive power.

It is not enough, however, to speculate as to whether Spenser's
text may be said to cannibalize the rhetoric of the monarch's medusan conscience; for it is in the nature of the text to shift the terms of
such speculation to a higher order, to defamiliarize the cultural hierarchies that make it seem beyond question that acts of cannibaliz-
ing or exploitative mimesis must emanate from the margins and
work on the center of power associated with the monarch. Spenser's
exploration of the conscience of the commonwealth disingenuously
problematizes the hierarchies, so that the Crown and the authoritative discourse it emblematizes may come under speculation as having
originated from a mimesis of the authoring and rewriting practice
that textuality at large exhibits and promotes. From this perspective
the cultural icon of the "Dread Souerayne Goddesse," which nominally governs both commonwealth and the commonwealth's canonical texts, becomes liable to scrutiny as a spectacle of power to the
second degree—a spectacle of the culture's own desire and ability to
produce mirages of stasis as well as the misreadings that will guarantee them.

The rewriting practice of book 5, and particularly of the trial episode, demythologizes not only the relations of power between icon
and text but also the respective iconic uses of allegory and histori-

ography in the Elizabethan discourse of power. Situating itself in the interstices, in a discursive blank space, between the two genres, and problematizing its conjoined effects of distance and proximity with respect to the genres, the episode dislodges both of its generic models from their self-legitimizing credentials, whether historiography's implicit status as the vessel of particularized truths or allegory's as the vessel of a higher, abstracted vision of truth.

As we have seen, the text indicates the politics of interpretation at work in the case of allegory, with the complicitous bond of selective vision between producers and consumers of allegory emblematized in the spectacle of dismemberment. As a canonical narrative, the text of course locates itself within this kind of normative allegorical project and makes itself available to the corresponding, conventional allegoresis. But as a canonical narrative participating in the discourse of conscience, it stands outside this project, representing it, pointing up the metacritical allegory produced from such a vantage point. That is, the text rewrites allegory: in formulaic terms, allegory passes from a sphere in which x equals y to one in which x equals "how y comes into visibility as the obvious or the only reading." The allegory in book 5, in other words, allegorizes its own role in the cultural process of constructing normative visions.

The text's problematic involvement in the historical record of the Scots case engages an analogous rewriting of the premises of historiography. On the one hand, the text seems to emphasize the inadequacy of the conventional allegorical project of screening out or normalizing the vagaries and circumstances of the cases that constitute history, so that the text can be read as the record of an uneasy flight from allegory into the unpalatable and unmanageable facts of history. The text appears to privilege the legitimacy of historical truth; or, to borrow Michael O'Connell's phrase, in book 5 "fiction now waits upon history."[24] On the other hand, the text's ambiguous interweaving of known historical details and fictional accretions or ellipses suggests that the so-called facts of history themselves wait upon ideological bias and upon cultural patterns of fictionalizing—like allegory and allegoresis—that determine the profile and significance of "facts."

Consider the way the text incorporates the essential fact of the Scots case into the final phase of the trial narrative. The corpse turns up almost as an aside in a stanza otherwise focused on the cascade of tempering and temporizing actions of Mercilla, which ends with the image of Mercilla "yeelding the last honour to her [Duessa's] wretched corse." The sheer fact of the death itself is caught up in a net of interpretation. The ambiguous qualifier "wretched"—which signifies both "contemptible" and, with considerably more sympathy, "unhappy"—reminds us that the culture's reception of the fact—the reading of the corpse—was anything but universal. So, too, the evidence of a physical body marked as that of a traitor, and accordingly destroyed, yet marked after death as that of a dignitary indicates both the power of cultural rituals, like executions and state funerals, to impart significance to facts and the complex, not to say tortuous, signification that such rituals in combination can generate.

Consider, too, the welter of ambiguities that characterizes the sole reference to a "fact" in the episode. The prosecution begins with the image of Duessa being appealed "Of many haynous crymes" (5.9.39). The phrase returns in the middle of the prosecution's argument, with one alteration: "Strongly did Zele her haynous fact enforce" (5.9.43). This reference deserves scrutiny, if only because the inclusion of the word "fact" appears a deliberate adjustment of the perfectly adequate and straightforward word "crimes" and because the alteration appears at a point where the narrative's referential axis—the preoccupation of the allegory with the known facts of the Scots case—is becoming most transparent. To be sure, the new word possesses the neutral sense of an empirically verifiable event or action, a connotation, coming into currency in the sixteenth century, that bears on the truth-telling status of the historical discourse invoked in the narrative. But the most current sense of the word in Spenser's time was "an evil deed, or crime."[25] The conflation of the two connotations, one established, one emergent, produces a textual commentary on the involvement of historicism's implicit claims to neutrality in Zele's power to charm—in the rhetorical procedures of fiction. The single ambiguous word indicates, at a pivotal moment in the text, how the corpus of historical facts—like the corpse that emerges at the end of the narrative—is written over, its significance shaped, by interpretive biases that are themselves shaped by the culture's construction of categories like "crime."

The legend of justice thus turns out to be, among other things, a representation of the shared fictionalizing and dismembering actions of historical discourse and allegory and of the political context—subsumed in the image of the state trial—that frames such actions. In this regard, the text weaves into its praise of Gloriana a depiction of the kind of constraints on the vision of their truth-telling project that Elizabethan historiographers found themselves forced to embrace. Sir Fulke Greville struck a note that Spenser's text amplifies when he recalled how, in the course of his futile attempt to probe the conscience of the monarch—to gain permission from Sir Robert Cecil to "peruse all obsolete Records of the Councell-chest"—he had to indicate, as though in response to a casuist's disclosure of the pivotal circumstance of time, how it would be possible for him to present the unmediated transcription he proposed, to "cleerly deliver many things done in that time, which might perchance be construed to the prejudice of this." Greville's response: "I shortly made answer, that I conceived an Historian was bound to tell nothing but the truth, but to tell all truths were both justly to wrong, and offend not only Princes, and States, but to blemish, and stir up against himselfe, the frailty and tendernesse, not only of particular men, but of many Families, with the spirit of an Athenian Timon."[26] A similar parallel of figurative dismemberment and movement into the fact-making regions of fiction marked Camden's revelatory remarks about the process of his writing *The History of the Most Renowned and Victorious Princess Elizabeth*. On the one hand he claimed that the "Love of Truth" had been his only "Incitement . . . to undertake this Work" as well as his "onely Scope and Aim in it"; with the further claim, "Prejudices I have shunned," he insisted that he had had "an Eye to the Truth onely." On the other hand he made the following admission: "Things manifest and evident I have not concealed; Things doubtfull I have interpreted favourably; Things secret and abtruse I have not pried into. The hidden Meanings of Princes (saith that great Master of History) and what they secretly design to search out, it is unlawfull, it is doubtfull and dangerous: pursue not therfore the Search therof.' "[27]

Both Greville and Camden observed and rationalized their submission to the rhetoric of the monarch's medusan conscience and found themselves, in Camden's case, constructing monuments to "Truth" that departed from an equivocation or, in Greville's case, writing no text at all: a blank space in the canon. Theirs was an inchoate insight, directed as it was toward making sense of the paradox they confronted, that to write the truth of Elizabeth's reign was to maintain that the plenitude of truth consisted in its selectivity—in not prying into "Things secret and abtruse" and in massively misreading the "Things manifest and evident." It is Spenser's text that exploits the paradox and enlarges upon the historians' vision. Elizabeth's medusan conscience charted the limits of what could be recognized and articulated in the process of writing her history; her rhetoric allocated the truth of her reign to the nominally idealizing realm of allegory. Demythologizing this process, Spenser's text turns the image of the medusan conscience into an inverted icon: an icon not of the triumph of the monarch's authoritative discourse but of the triumph of the act of writing and of the disturbing yet liberating insight that writing yields. Repeatedly, the legend of justice indicates how all truths—whether historical or allegorical—are written over by a variable text, by the politics of interpretation that have become naturalized in the culture.

Spenser's text, both innocent and transgressive as a canonical text, enacting the instability of the script that attempts to finalize the identity of the punished poet in canto 9, also projects its own generic identity into the blank space. The text constitutes, in effect, a narrative imagining of a genre equipped to represent truth as the site—evoked in the image of the trial in canto 9—where contradictory discourses and ambiguities confront each other, where the image of ideological stability can be read as part of a historical process. Spenser's text, situated in the penumbra of allegory and historiography, introduces a nameless meta-genre without fully inhabiting it, yet indicates the essence of that genre to lie in its power to dissolve generic distinctions. This movement of the text into what we might call a generic wilderness can hardly be accidental. Given the text's entrenchment in the problematic relationship between textuality and power, it is appropriate, as with the insertion of the "flawed" trial episode, that the text should point up the apparent absence of a clearly defined frame of reference against which to determine the text's place on the register of Elizabethan books.

Tropes of Conscience: Gyges' Ring, Spenser's 'Legend of Justice,' and Novelistic Discourse

> Aporia, or the Doubtful. So called . . . because often-
> times we will seem to cast perills, and make doubt of
> things when by a plaine manner of speech wee might
> affirme or deny them.
> —Puttenham, *The Arte of English Poesie* [1]

The indiscernible, disorienting aspect of mental reservation provoked in the semiotics both of social and verbal action a condition
of "self-engendered paradox" that rhetoricians in the Renaissance
called *aporia*.[2] Puttenham's definition rested on the assumption of a
fixed and clear boundary between a "Doubtful" and a "plaine man
ner of speech"—but the practice of mental reservation demonstrated
that such an assumption was, ultimately, untenable. The doctrine
itself did not so much spell out an art of wholesale lying—which
would merely have reinforced the implicit distinction between truth
and its opposite—as it encouraged a metacritical attitude toward the
discursive frame in which the distinction might be raised.

Notably, it described a process of rethinking the relationship between interlocutors in a given dialog. The substance of what passed
between two interlocutors, whether through the language of gesture
or clothing or through spoken or written words, was contingent on
what the casuist Henry Garnet called the "proposition of the mynde"
that either, without knowledge of the other's equivalent action,
might be directing toward a third interlocutor—God. Defenders of
the doctrine posited this silent discourse as the locus of truth—
which was not to say the tangible discourse it shadowed was false.

The difference between the two was not so much qualitative as quantitative—an imperceptible gradient, with the measure determined by the context. Thus by reading casuistically, by scanning the "circumstances of place, tymes, and persons"—for evidence, in effect, of the speakers' mutual displacement of each other as a principal interlocutor in a discourse—one might be able, the explicators of mental reservation argued, to reconstitute what Garnet called the "suppressed particles" of truth within otherwise "ambiguous or imperfect speeches" or behavior.[3] To become accustomed to this practice, however, was to be equipped to perceive, through a leap of the moral imagination, the indiscernible third interlocutor and the silent, "true" discourse it received as relativized constructs: as functions of a play of perspectives within changeable discursive contexts, of which the speakers could have only partial knowledge and over which they could claim only partial control.

The practice of mental reservation enmeshed one in the boundless *aporia* that characterized the hermeneutics of the discourse of conscience, a hermeneutics that informed particularized, contextually responsive performances of language—what Bakhtin called the "dialogic orientation in discourse." This orientation, for Bakhtin the principal feature of novelistic discourse, recognizes the complex and unstable referentiality of the utterance; it recognizes that "between the word [utterance] and its object, between the word and the speaking subject, there exists an elastic environment of other, alien words about the same object, the same theme . . . an environment that it is often difficult to penetrate."[4] Localized in the hermeneutics of conscience, the dialogic orientation showed itself to be both elastic and tension-filled. It showed the inner mechanism or guiding principle—the "conscience"—of discourse to be a socially and politically inflected struggle between competing gambits for semantic hegemony within a given discursive situation.

This hermeneutics, writ small in the practice of mental reservation, was at work more generally in the various manifestations I have described of the confessional act, which informed the Elizabethan discourse of power. Confession, whether considered as a sacramental, juridical, or purely rhetorical performance, provided a model for the dynamic between authorities and subjects, a dynamic of expedience based on the equation of omnipotence and omniscience: revelation as submission. Within this dynamic, the very act of articulating a case of conscience, of exposing an anomaly in the social and theological structures of order, signalled an act of suppression as well. To speak was virtually to silence one's individuated voice, to submit the case to the hegemony of a canonical narrative of the Christian *via*, a narrative that charted the progression from the scrupulous, the guilty, or the doubting to the good conscience—to a state of conformity to an established norm.

But the confessional act also provided a locus for its own undoing as an instrument of submission, insofar as the conscience authoring the conformist narratives was itself the embodiment of an internally dialogized structure, one that called into question, first, the identity of the speaking persona. On the one hand, the word "conscience" implied the coincidence of a private and a public self. *Synteresis* defined one's voice as the echo of an objective, communal voice, a prior, authoritative discourse. On the other hand, "conscience" pointed to a private self that was never completely coterminous with the public self. *Conscientia* articulated an internally persuasive discourse, one representing a subjective appraisal of the circumstances that made one's case unique. That is, *conscientia* defined one's voice as a continually shifting response to the flux of one's social and psychological experience; it represented the intrinsic dialogism—and the intertextuality—of one's discourse, a discourse irreducible to the extrinsic norms implanted in *synteresis*.[5] The persona represented by "conscience" was thus something other than a public self and something other than a private one. It was a representational field in which the self was always becoming; as the doctrine of mental reservation implied, it was always adjusting to its environment and silently criticizing its own status as well as that of its discourse.

The confessional narratives it produced were consequently always something other than what they appeared to be as well, quite apart from what the specific intentions of the author might indicate—as Elizabeth's speeches, Tyrrell's recantations, and the canonical utterances of Spenser's narrator indicate. The closure toward which such narratives moved—conformity to an idealized Christian *via* or to its social and political embodiment in the Elizabethan church-state— was never more than the image of closure, perpetually subject to the narrative disruptions, and to the corresponding contingencies of

meaning, that the further scrutiny of circumstances, posited either
by the observed or the observing conscience, might yield.[6] Similarly,
the truth articulated in such narratives was never more than the image of a truth that, under inspection, would betray its point of origin
not in an eternal logos but at the intersection of the observed and
the observing conscience.

In mythology, the tale of Gyges the Lydian shepherd contained a
similarly probative dimension. The relevant commentaries on the
tale by Protestant controversialists in the sixteenth and seventeenth
centuries imposed limits on its significance, making it a parable for
the political threat of the mental reservations harbored in the lax
consciences of the papists, whose resulting unrestrained power could
lead only to regicide and chaos.[7] A predictable interpretation, given
the kernel of the legend. Within a chasm Gyges discovers a Trojan-
like horse: hollow, containing a giant corpse from whose finger the
shepherd takes a gold ring possessing the power to make its owner
invisible. Wearing the ring, Gyges is able to penetrate into the court,
seduce the king's wife, slay the king, and usurp the throne. So the
doctrine of mental reservation, Thomas Morton observed, was "not
unlike Gyges his ring," for when "our aequivocator . . . shall turne
his aequivocating clause outward to manifest it in speech, he lieth
open and is easily knowen for a disloyal subject; but when he keepeth
it close in his mind, hee is imboldened to practise against his King."[8]

No less predictable, given the dominant ideological stance of non-
resistance to which these lines alluded, was the suppression of the
more penetrating aspect of the tale. It was, indeed, possible to read
the tale as an exposé of the contaminating effect of power in the
hands of those to whom it does not rightfully belong—those who,
as the tale suggested, dwelled beyond the periphery of the recognized centers of power, whether in a pastoral landscape or in the
bowels of the earth. But the absence of a supporting epilogue to the
tale—Lydia does not drift into a reign of terror under a merciless
tyrant—suggests that such a reading did not exhaust the possibilities
of interpretation, that it did not necessarily reflect a privileged perspective. What is striking about the tale is not its depiction of a spiral
of violence and unrest but its circularity: order, or at least the appearance of order, returns. A king has been dislodged but kingship
remains—with a difference. Gyges' progress (a version of the "rags

to riches" story) traces an etiology of royal power in which the unexamined givens at the beginning of the tale are recalled and tacitly questioned at the end. Gyges invests the figure of kingship with a specific history in which the apparently distinct and immutable categories of shepherd and king converge and mirror each other, brought into a dynamic that makes it possible, as it was not at the outset, to think critically about the nature, limits, and origins of royal inviolability and, beyond that, to reflect on the human needs and actions that stratify human society and its languages. At the end, the king no longer simply is; he emerges as a function of a particular context, out of which the royal utterance, should it appear, would sound with the accents of the shepherd. The tale thus invokes an image of a language thinking about itself, about its place as an idiom in connection with others: an image of a language discovering its contingent and polysemous nature and reflecting on the limits of intelligibility, shaped by "circumstances of place, tymes, and persons" that might obstruct the transmission of such a discovery.

This is the image that the Spenserian narrative elaborates in book 5 of *The Faerie Queene*. Spenser's manipulations of the narrative's structure and intertextuality, reconstituting in a literary text the casuistical "circumstances of place, tymes, and persons," sabotage the *mythos* of a fixed horizon of meaning that the "legend of justice" ostensibly projects through the several legitimizing discourses it appropriates. These discourses—of allegory, of historiography, of juridical procedure, of ethical analysis—enter into an interactive and mutually destabilizing relation, in which each discourse's respective claim to embody an authoritative vision or to constitute a securely anchored referential text is qualified by the underlying structure of contingency that the narrative context produces, in which the "circumstances" of narrative disruptions and anomalies point up the informing presence of rival and often incompatible discourses.

One of the most trenchant enactments of this relation occurs at the conclusion of the trial episode—which, as it turns out, bears a resemblance to the multi-textured conclusion of the mythological narrative of Gyges. Spenser's narrative at this point, as at so many others in book 5, turns on a discrepancy between what the narrator reports and what the text—in which the narrator's voice is subsumed—reports by way of constructing a narrative frame in which to situate and evaluate the narrator's language. The movement from the tortuous account of Duessa's execution to the suave representation of the courtly context—a movement we observed in the previous chapter—charts the text's own movement into a metacritical perspective on the discourses that converge in the narrative sequence. The account of the execution represents the limits of the encomiastic conventions of political allegory in the face of the recalcitrant details of a controversial historical event; it represents, too, the failure of historiographical practice to realize its truth-telling intentions or to make them intelligible under the aegis of an ideology of often imperceptible strategies of suppression. The subsequent account, a virtually miraculous—which is to say, suspect—rehabilitation of the encomiastic narrative, subsumes the narrator's reading of the execution into the official but obtuse reading of the "worthie paterns" of the monarch's "clemencies" (5.10.5), a reading that fails to make sense of the narrator's potentially scandalous, if fragmented, insights into the medusan rhetoric of the monarch's conscience. Such a reading, the text suggests, is no less problematic than the one it supplants, because, for one thing, the narrative continuum in which it is situated makes the very act of supplanting part of the profile of the official reading itself. The adequacy of the official reading, then, emerges as a function of the politics of misreading that the text recurrently enacts: in Spenser's narrative, the adequate or "good" reading turns out to be the one that fails to register the processes of occlusion involved in the maintenance of structures of order.

The "legend of justice" thus shows its canonical discourse to be doubly inflected. Whether through the kind of narrative phasing that the trial sequence illustrates or through the scandalous perspectives that the intertextual projection of the Spenserian simile introduces, the "legend" defamiliarizes the abstracted and conventional language of justice and equity it intones by drawing out the subtext that informs such language, the subtext of particularized social negotiations and restrictions. Spenser thus creates a dialogized epic discourse in book 5 that examines the interrelationship of two contradictory conceptions of language: language as a "system of abstract grammatical categories," the unmotivated, unmediated vessel of norms; and language as an "ideologically saturated" heteroglot practice, one that represents, as Bakhtin saw it, "the co-existence of socio-ideological contradictions between the present and the past, between differing epochs of the past, between different socio-ideological groups in the present, between tendencies, schools, circles and so forth."⁹ Through this dialogism, the voice of transparent truth (Puttenham's "plaine manner of speech") yields its formula for transparency: Spenser's "legend of justice" represents the monologic discourse of power—to Bakhtin the "unitary, monologically sealed-off" discourse characteristic of epic poetry—as the mere remains, the emptied sarcophagus, of a heteroglot discourse.¹⁰ In this respect, as a discourse that both represents and exploits the suppressed dialogism of the "simple Truth" the narrator announces in the proem, the Spenserian narrative of book 5 indicates the affinity of the Renaissance epic with the more fully articulated dialogism of the novelistic discourse that Bakhtin found in the novels of the eighteenth century.¹¹

Moreover, the narrative illustrates the common legacy of Spenser's epic and the novel in the internalized dialogism of the casuistry that flourished in the sixteenth century. This casuistry, ultimately aporetic in nature, showed cases of conscience to be something other than momentary lapses in an otherwise ineluctable shepherding of diversity into unity. To borrow an optical metaphor, the anomalies represented by cases of conscience functioned rather like Comenius's "prisms," devices able to "transform the colours of things into a thousand shapes," for which reason, Comenius observed, they were "called fools paradises."¹² So, too, cases of conscience may be thought of as a kind of "fools paradise," despite the strangeness of the association.

Gary Saul Morson has called attention to the connection between Victor Turner's enclosed "rituals of anti-structure," which occupy a central role in Turner's theory of culture, and Bakhtin's study of the ritual of carnival, which occupies an analogous role in Bakhtin's description of novelistic discourse. Both represent liminal events, "securely framed off from the rest of social life," in which the spirit of parody reigns, permitting society to acknowledge the "conventionality of its conventions" and, beyond that, the "historicity of all norms, the unfinished and open quality of all that exists, and a Heraclitian relativity that makes light of all claims of permanence."¹³ Both represent the "fools paradises" of Comenius. One may well wonder how the discourse of conscience, as I have described it in Elizabethan England, can inhabit such a locus. Its parodic elements—which we have observed in social and verbal texts whose integrity is threatened, principally, by the chameleon-like movement, the silent "voice-over," of the lax conscience—contain little, if any, of the jesting quality one associates with the ethos of carnival. The world of Rabelais and Cervantes seems remote. But the distance is only apparent.

The discourse of conscience fosters the same perpetually questioning mode, the same metacritical stance toward the world and toward one's place in it, that carnival's "truths of laughter" invite.[14] Only it raises the stakes. By perpetually questioning its own status and procedures, it demythologizes, from within, the authoritative, sacrosanct discourses it inhabits or refers to, discourses its putative purpose is to valorize. In so doing it implicitly asks whether carnival, or any similar ritual of anti-structure, can mock itself as well as the structures it appropriates. It suggests, then, that laughter or ebullience is not the defining characteristic of the ethos of carnival but rather a function of carnival's distance—its safe, controlled distance—from the norms called into question. And it collapses that distance. It uncovers the scandalous, and subversive, side of carnival's "truths of laughter," only to make visible, and thus subject to scrutiny and criticism, the criteria according to which scandal and subversion are understood as such. It suggests, commensurately, that phenomena like scandal and subversion are in fact a function of the proximity of the carnivalesque mode to the reigning structures of power and order. Its own pervasive aspect—it is hard to avoid traces of the discourse of conscience in the sixteenth century—reminds us, finally, that novelistic discourse itself, essentially anti-generic and anti-canonic, does not so much represent an objectified, framed carnival structure as it does the insinuation of the ethos of carnival itself into hierarchical social structures.

In effect, the discourse of conscience shows how novelistic discourse signals the carnivalization of culture. The myriad anomalies—the cases of conscience—represented in the discourse of conscience may be construed as novelistic events that internalize, and deinstitutionalize, the ethos of carnival. This is not to say, of course, that they endorse an interpretive regime of "unaccountability," of an absolute blindness (a "lax conscience") in reading, that amounts to an *a priori* banalization of all that seems aberrant in a given literary text. Rather, such anomalies present themselves as potential sources of insight, as articulations of the rhetoric of unaccountability, permitting their readers to locate and evaluate evidence of the negotiatory process that occurs between the normative constraints or expectations of an authoritative discourse—a genre—and the particularized, intermingling idioms of the creative artists, their represented subjects, and their companions, the reading audience. Subjected to scrutiny and evaluation as points of rupture in a hierarchically conceived structure of order, the anomalies emerge as points of entry for a transformed, "novelized" perspective, one that deflects the processes of scrutiny and evaluation toward the discursive context that has defined and delimited the anomalies themselves. This is the perspective that insinuated itself into the extra-literary discourse we observed at Richmond and at St. Paul's Cross. So, too, anomalies that figure in the literary discourse of the period, when they refer to conscience or echo the procedures of casuistry, as they do in Spenser's "legend of justice," appear as anomalies with a purpose: as configurations of the metacritical "conscience" of the work itself. They intimate the presence of an emergent novelistic discourse within the canon of Renaissance literature.

Reference Matter

Notes

Introduction

1. King, *A Sermon preached the 5th of November, 1607*, p. 22.
2. Foucault, *The Archaeology of Knowledge*, "Archaeological Description," pp. 135–95.
3. Luther, "Pagan Servitude of the Church," in *Martin Luther*, p. 330.
4. Cited in Tentler, *Sin and Confession*, p. 159.
5. E. Amann, "Laxisme," in *Dictionnaire de théologie catholique*, vol. 9, pt. 1, p. 41.
6. A relevant discussion of the taboo phenomenon is in Douglas, *Purity and Danger*, pp. 7–40.
7. For a detailed discussion of the various medieval constructions of conscience, see Potts, *Conscience in Medieval Philosophy*.
8. Perkins, *A Discourse of Conscience*, in *William Perkins, 1558–1602*, p. 9.
9. Moore, "Uncertainties in Situations," in *Law as Process*, pp. 39–40.
10. "Conviction and Attainder of Robert Lalor," in Petti, *Recusant Documents*, p. 190.
11. Persons's observation is in a letter to Alfonso Agazzari, November 17, 1580, in Hicks, *Letters and Memorials*, p. 59. A good general discussion of the English Protestant casuists' relationship to the precedent of Catholic casuistry is in Thomas F. Merrill's introduction to his edition of two of Perkins's treatises (*A Discourse of Conscience* and *The Whole Treatise of Cases of Conscience*), in *William Perkins, 1558–1602*, pp. ix–x.
12. Hall, "Cases of Piety and Religion," *Resolutions and Decisions*, in *The Works*, vol. 7, p. 363.
13. For the attack on the "Maeandrian turnings and windings" of Jesuit casuistry, see King, *A Sermon preached the 5th of November, 1607*, pp. 26–27. The "sleeveless aunsweres" of the recusants under interrogation were detailed in Munday's pamphlet *A Discoverie of Edmund Campion*, sig. Ciiiiv.
14. Strype, *Annals*, vol. 2, pt. 2, p. 285.
15. Perkins, *The Whole Treatise of Cases of Conscience*, p. 145.
16. White, "Bakhtin, Sociolinguistics and Deconstruction," p. 137.
17. Ibid., p. 138.

18. Ibid., p. 140.

19. "All theories of *langue, deep structure, basic systemic sentences*, and *différance* are metaphysical in that they are attempts to isolate a pure and unmotivated language anterior to the use of actual speech by social groups" (White, "Bakhtin, Sociolinguistics and Deconstruction," in *The Theory of Reading*, p. 140). The text of casuistry, I am arguing, shows us how and why the "actual speech by social groups" produces and maintains such a rarefied image of language.

20. Bakhtin, "Epic and Novel," in *The Dialogic Imagination*, p. 31.

21. Bakhtin, "Discourse in the Novel," in *The Dialogic Imagination*, pp. 366–71.

22. Ibid., p. 371. What I try to show in the following chapters is how casuistry promoted what Bakhtin called the "Galilean perception of language" typical of novelistic discourse: "one that denies the absolutism of a single and unitary language—that is, that refuses to acknowledge its own language as the sole verbal and semantic center of the ideological world. It is a perception that has been made conscious of the vast plenitude of national and, more to the point, social languages—all of which are equally capable of being 'languages of truth,' but, since such is the case, all of which are equally relative, reified and limited, as they are merely the languages of social groups, professions and other cross-sections of everyday life" (pp. 366–67). Bakhtin briefly mentioned the role of conscience in the development of the dialogism that characterizes novelistic discourse. (He noted the "representation of the struggle waged by the voice of conscience with other voices that sound in a man" [p. 350].) Because he understood conscience as a unitary voice only (the internalized presence of an authoritative word), the few remarks he made on the subject of conscience suggest that he did not appreciate the intrinsic dialogism of conscience.

23. "Le caractère peu cohérent, et à la limite irrationel, de la description bakhtinienne du genre romanesque marque déjà le fait que cette catégorie n'occupe pas dans le système la place qui lui convient" (Todorov, *Mikhail Bakhtine*, p. 139).

24. Holquist, "Introduction," in Bakhtin, *The Dialogic Imagination*, p. xxxi.

25. Accordingly, I have chosen not to introduce the term "novelistic" into the body of the argument. While Bakhtin's particular understanding of the iconoclastic and *sui generis* narrative practice of novelistic discourse would make the use of the term appropriate throughout the study, to my mind it would be hard to keep at bay the resulting implication that the texts at hand are caught up principally in an etiological script pitched toward the "finished product" of what are conventionally known as novels. This study, then, ex-

amines the role of casuistry in the production of narrative from an angle that neither demands a Bakhtinian conception of novelistic discourse nor risks the reductionism that can follow from importing a literary term, however flexible its perimeters, into a study in which literary texts constitute only one part of a larger cultural problematic.

One

1. *Holinshed's Chronicles*, p. 133.
2. *John Stubbs's Gaping Gulf*, p. 79.
3. Sir John Puckering, Speaker of the House of Commons, speech to Elizabeth I, in *Cobbett's*, p. 1196.
4. "Sir Philip Sidney's letter to queen Elizabeth, concerning her marriage," in Strype, *Annals*, vol. 2, pt. 2, p. 642.
5. The counterpoint of perceived threats to political and social stability by the two factions is conveyed in Strype's discussion of the problems to the Elizabethan government posed by puritans and papists in 1580; see Strype, *Annals*, vol. 2, pt. 2, pp. 331–51. It was not uncommon for the religious and political dissidence of puritans and papists to be described as twin aspects of a common abuse of conscience. The seventeenth-century preacher Robert South thus criticized both groups' exploitation of the presumed inviolability of conscience: "He who looks well into this argument, looks into the great *Arcanum*, and the *Sanctum Sanctorum* of Puritanism; which indeed is only reformed *Jesuitism*, as Jesuitism is nothing else but *Popish Puritanism*: And I could draw out such an exact parallel between them, both as to principles and practices, that it would quickly appear, that they are as truly brothers, as ever were *Romulus* and *Remus*; and that they sucked their principles from the same *wolf*" (South, "Obedience for Conscience-sake, the Duty of Good Subjects," p. 130).
6. Cited in Neville Williams, *Elizabeth I*, p. 66.
7. Elton, *England Under the Tudors*, p. 289.
8. The text I am using of Elizabeth's two speeches to Parliament in November 1586 is the one printed in *Holinshed's Chronicles*, pp. 933–35, 938–40. For a detailed account of the tensions between queen and Parliament that formed the context of these speeches, see Neale, *Elizabeth I*, vol. 2, pp. 122–44.
9. Naunton, *Fragmenta Regalia*, pp. 5–6.
10. Ibid., p. 5.
11. C., *A Declaration of the ends of traytors*, sig. Aiii–Bii.
12. For an account of the textual history of the speeches, see Neale, *Elizabeth I*, vol. 2, pp. 130–33, and Read, *Lord Burghley and Queen Elizabeth*, p. 363.

13. See Douglas's account of constructions of power in the passive voice in "Passive Voice Theories in Religious Sociology," in *In the Active Voice*, pp. 1–15. Elizabeth's conspicuous absence from the opening of Parliament could also be construed as an extension of the performative power of the royal utterance or gesture: absence indicating, in this case, the queen's desire that her power should include the power to make things *not* happen. The most useful discussion of the performative aspect of language is in Austin, *How to Do Things with Words*.

14. Nicolas, *Life of William Davison*, pp. 117–19.

15. Rait and Cameron, *King James's Secret*, p. 194.

16. *Cobbett's*, p. 1241.

17. Ibid., pp. 1242–43.

18. Letter to Davison, cited in Read, *Lord Burghley and Queen Elizabeth*, p. 364.

19. "Sentences written by the lord treasurer Burghley; occasioned upon the death of Mary queen of Scots; and upon queen Elizabeth's displeasure towards him on that account," in Strype, *Annals*, vol. 3, pt. 2, p. 405.

20. Cited in Greaves, *Elizabeth I, Queen of England*, p. xiii. A contemporary, though no more sympathetic, appraisal of Elizabeth sought to attribute the queen's elusiveness to the instruction of men likely to be associated with casuistry and the direction of conscience. Shortly after Elizabeth's coronation, the Spanish ambassador de Quadra wrote these words: "I have lost all hope in the affairs of this woman. She is convinced of the soundness of her unstable power . . . besides this, her language (learned from Italian friars who brought her up) is so shifty that it is the most difficult thing in the world to negotiate with her. With her, all is falsehood and vanity!" (cited in Luke, *Gloriana*, p. 94).

21. Strype, *Annals*, vol. 3, pt. 1, p. 529.

22. *Cobbett's*, p. 1172.

23. Ibid., p. 1169.

24. For a discussion of the relevance of Paul's view of secular authority to sixteenth-century political theory, see Holmes, *Resistance and Compromise*, pp. 39–46; see also Skinner, *Foundations*, vol. 2, pp. 15–19.

25. For a discussion of Parliament's efforts to coerce Elizabeth into taking action against Mary in 1572, see Neale, *Elizabeth I*, vol. 1, pp. 262–90.

26. *Cobbett's*, p. 1173.

27. Ibid., p. 1170.

28. Perkins, *A Discourse of Conscience*, in *William Perkins, 1558–1602*, p. 9.

29. Rait and Cameron, *King James's Secret*, p. 109.

30. Strype, *Annals*, vol. 3, pt. 1, p. 530.

31. *Cobbett's*, vol. 1, p. 1172.
32. Ibid., p. 1173.
33. Ibid., p. 1162.
34. Ibid., p. 1163.
35. For a general discussion of the relationship between Crown and Parliament in Elizabethan England, see Elton, *England Under the Tudors*, pp. 395–420.
36. *Cobbett's*, p. 1161.
37. Ibid., p. 1171.
38. Ibid., p. 1165.
39. Strype, *Annals*, vol. 3, pt. 1, p. 531.
40. *Cobbett's*, p. 1197.
41. Ibid., pp. 1197–98.
42. The text of Elizabeth's first speech appears in *Holinshed's Chronicles*, pp. 933–35.
43. Bernard of Clairvaux, cited in "The Steps of Humility and Pride," in *The Works of Bernard of Clairvaux*, p. 73, n338.
44. An illuminating discussion of the implications of the *arcana imperii* theme is in Goldberg, "The Theater of Conscience," in *James I and the Politics of Literature*, pp. 113–63. The historical context of the term is discussed in Kantorowicz, "Mysteries of State."
45. *Scottish Calendar* (ix.154) cited in Neale, *Elizabeth I*, vol. 2, p. 121.
46. Lea, *A History of Auricular Confession*, pp. 289–90.
47. The Babington Plot was, of course, the most conspicuous of the plots associated with the papists, and it constituted part of the case against Mary. See the supplication by the "estates of the realm," which prompted Elizabeth's first speech to Parliament on the subject of Mary, in *Cobbett's*, pp. 1190–92.
48. See Kantorowicz, *The King's Two Bodies*, and Girard, *Violence and the Sacred*.
49. For a good discussion of the Thomist evaluation of moral action, see Potts, *Conscience in Medieval Philosophy*, pp. 122–36.
50. Tutiorism, together with its development, successively, into probabiliorism and probabilism, is discussed in Thomas Deman, "Probabilisme," *Dictionnaire de théologie catholique*, vol. 13, pt. 1, pp. 418–619. See also Lea, *A History of Auricular Confession*, pp. 285–411. For a more recent, excellent general discussion of the historical development of casuistical schools of thought, see Jonsen and Toulmin, *The Abuse of Casuistry*.
51. I discuss the relationship between equity and conscience in Chapter 5.
52. Sanderson, "Sermon ad clerum I," in *Twelve Sermons*, p. 22.

53. *Holinshed's Chronicles*, p. 935.
54. The text of Elizabeth's second speech appears in *Holinshed's Chronicles*, pp. 938–400.
55. *Spenser: Poetical Works*, pp. 469–70.
56. For a discussion of the structure of the homily and the rhetorical tradition informing it, see Murphy, "Ars praedicandi: The Art of Preaching," in *Rhetoric in the Middle Ages*, pp. 269–355.
57. Tilley, *A Dictionary of the Proverbs*, p. 117.
58. *The Compact Edition of the Oxford English Dictionary*, vol. 1, p. 623.
59. A concise history of the association of Solomon and Ecclesiastes is in "Koheleth (Ecclesiastes) or the Philosophy of an Acquisitive Society," in Bickerman, *Four Strange Books of the Bible*, pp. 139–67.
60. This was not the first time Elizabeth had used Ecclesiastes to signal the impenetrability of the royal conscience; in the formal address that prorogued the Parliament of 1585, the queen warned Parliament against its attempt to probe too deeply into the purposes behind her actions. Defending her concern to protect the "true Christian religion," she made this observation: "And so you see that you wrong me too much, if any such there be, as doubt my coldness in that behalf, for if I were not persuaded that mine were the truth of God's will, God forbid that I should live to prescribe it to you. Take heed lest Ecclesiastes say not too true, 'They that fear the hoary frost, the snow shall fall upon them.' I see many over-bold with God Almighty, making too many subtle scannings of His blessed will as lawyers do with human testaments" (Rice, *The Public Speaking of Queen Elizabeth*, p. 85).
Scriptural citations pertaining to Elizabeth's speeches are from the 1560 edition of the Geneva Bible (Madison: University of Wisconsin Press, 1969); other Scriptural citations are from the 1611 edition of the King James Version (Oxford: Oxford University Press, 1896).
61. Homilies and commentaries in the sixteenth century seized the point, citing Ecclesiastes in admonitions to resist judgments based on the deceptive appearances of outward things. Consider the reference Sandys made to Ecclesiastes 9 in his sermon "made in Paul's, on the day of Christ's nativity": "For touching outward things, we cannot certainly judge the hatred or love of God by them. In these external events, 'The same condition is to the just and to the wicked, to the good and pure, and to them that are polluted, to him that sacrificeth, and to him that sacrificeth not. As is the good, so is the sinner; he that sweareth as he that feareth an oath'" (Sandys, *Sermons*, p. 31). Consider, too, Calvin's discussion of God's foreknowledge: "As all future events are uncertain to us, so we hold them in suspense, as if they might incline to one side or the other. Yet in our hearts it nonetheless remains fixed that nothing will take place that the Lord has not previously foreseen. . . .

In this sense the term 'fate' is often repeated in Ecclesiastes . . . because at first glance men do not penetrate to the first cause, which is deeply hidden. And yet what is set forth in Scripture concerning God's secret providence was never so extinguished from men's hearts without some sparks always glowing in the darkness . . . we ought undoubtedly to hold that whatever changes are discerned in the world are produced from the secret stirring of God's hand . . . if anyone would judge by the present state of things, which men God pursues with hatred and which ones he embraces in love, he labors in vain and troubles himself to no profit, 'since all things happen alike to righteous and impious . . . to those who sacrifice victims and to those who do not sacrifice' (Eccl. 9:2). From this it follows that God does not everlastingly witness his love to those for whom he causes all things to prosper, nor does he always manifest his hate to those whom he afflicts. And he does this to prove the innate folly of humanity, since among things so necessary to know it is grasped with such great stupidity. As Solomon had written a little before, one cannot discern how the soul of a man differs from the soul of a beast because both seem to die in the same way (Eccl. 3:19)" (*Calvin: Institutes of the Christian Religion*, vol. 20, pp. 209–210, 585). Against such a context, Elizabeth's use of the Scriptural commonplace demonstrated the interrelation of her political position and an epistemological and theological issue, producing, as it were, a Christian frame for the rhetoric of the *arcana imperii*.

62. The maintenance of royal power, then, depended on what René Girard has called the "single principle" we can perceive in other cultural spaces, "in primitive religion and classical tragedy alike, a principle implicit but fundamental. Order, peace, and fecundity depend on cultural distinctions; it is not these distinctions but the loss of them that gives birth to fierce rivalries and sets members of the same family or social group at one another's throats" (Girard, *Violence and the Sacred*, p. 49).

63. Alcibiades's drunken entrance at the close of the *Symposium*, for example, carried a certain unmistakable bacchic resonance. Standing "with a mass of ribbons and an enormous wreath of ivy and violets sprouting on his head," he appeared as an avatar of the god who embodied a disturbing duality: Dionysius, the minister both of order and of chaos. See *The Collected Dialogues of Plato*, p. 564. On the double aspect of Dionysius, see Girard, *Violence and the Sacred*, p. 28. Note also Plutarch's understanding of the difference between Apollo and Dionysius, which considers implicitly the chameleon-like aspect of Dionysius: "Dionysius they depict in many guises and forms . . . [to him they attribute] a certain variability" ("The E at Delphi" 389b, quoted in Slater, *The Glory of Hera*, p. 212). For Thucydides the hero was the minister mostly of chaos. Alcibiades' "wild courses went

far to ruin the Athenian state," he observed. The Athenians "feared the extremes to which he carried the lawlessness of his personal habits, and the far-reaching purposes which invariably animated him in all his actions." Even if the Athenian people were finally to blame for having "speedily shipwrecked the state," in Thucydides' view their action was a predictable response to a leader who had become a figure of ambiguity, of dangerous double meanings. They removed him because beneath the glittering military commander they perceived, rightly or wrongly, one who was "aiming at tyranny." See *Thucydides* [*The Peloponnesian War*], p. 190.

Through Renaissance editions and translations of these sources, the figure of Alcibiades reached the sixteenth century as an unresolved enigma. Works that drew on them might either extoll Alcibiades's virtues or associate his behavior with moral and political corruption. Thus when Ludovico da Canossa, in *The Book of the Courtier*, sought a model for his perfect courtier—an ideal shaped by the Ciceronian model for the good orator—he chose Alcibiades: "And even as we read that Alcibiades surpassed all those peoples among whom he lived, and each in the respect wherein it claimed greatest excellence, so would I have this Courtier of ours excel all others in what is the special profession of each" (Castiglione, *The Book of the Courtier*, p. 38). Castiglione's Count had read Nepos, who had lavished praise on the Athenian: "With whomsoever he was, he was reckoned a leading man, and mightily beloved" (Nepos, *The Lives of Illustrious Men*, p. 59). Readers of Plutarch would have found it difficult to reconcile such unqualified esteem with the *imago* that Plutarch had chosen for the hero: "For among other qualities and properties he had (whereof he was full) this as they say was one, whereby he most robbed men's hearts: that he could frame altogether with their manners and fashions of life, transforming himself more easily to all manner of shapes, than the chameleon. For it is reported, that the chameleon cannot take white colour: but Alcibiades could put upon him any manners, customs or fashions, of what nations soever, and could follow, exercise, and counterfeit them when he would, as well the good as the bad" (Plutarch, *The Lives of the Noble Grecians and Romanes*, p. 223). Nepos's phrase was perhaps more apt than he might have wished: "In this man, nature seems to have tried to do all that it was capable of accomplishing" (Nepos, *The Lives of Illustrious Men*, pp. 52–53).

64. One of the central documents in the Judeo-Christian tradition that helped cement the chameleon's association with moral depravity is Leviticus, in which the chameleon is listed among the unclean animals. See Douglas's discussion of the phenomenon of the Leviticus proscriptions in *Purity and Danger*, pp. 41–57. William Baldwin's *Treatise of Moral Philosophy* (1547) gives a representative example of how the image of the chameleon was used in dis-

cussions of moral problems in the sixteenth century: "Lyke as a Chamell hath all colours saue whyte: so hath a flatterer al poyntes saue honestie" (Tilley, *A Dictionary of the Proverbs*, p. 91). Note especially, among other examples in Tilley, the association of chameleons and the problem of religious dissidence: "Chameleons take all colours but the white, And Schismaticks all fancies but the right" (Howard, *New Sayings*, p. 2, cited in Tilley, *A Dictionary of the Proverbs*, p. 91).

65. Alciati, "In adulatores, emblemata LIII," in *Emblemata cum commentariis*, p. 255.

66. Lodge, *Wit's Miserie and the World's Madnesse*, p. 4.

67. Thomas Browne discussed this proverbial characteristic of the chameleon in chapter 21 ("Of the Chameleon") of *Pseudodoxia Epidemica*, in *The Works of Sir Thomas Browne*, pp. 257–67. Among writers in Elizabeth's time, Shakespeare used this piece of lore, notably in *Hamlet*. In response to Claudius's ingratiating question "How fares our cousin Hamlet?" Hamlet replies, "Excellent, i'faith; of the chameleon's dish; I eat the air, promise-crammed" (3.2.93).

68. For a discussion of Renaissance views of feeding imagery and its relation to the assimilation of texts, see Cave, *The Cornucopian Text*. See also Starobinski, "The Inside and the Outside."

69. Perkins, *A Discourse of Conscience*, in *William Perkins, 1558–1602*, p. 68.

70. Elizabeth's own translation of the *Consolatio* is printed in Pemberton, *Queen Elizabeth's Englishings of Boethius, Plutarch and Horace*.

71. Lydgate's account of Alcibiades is in book 3 of *Fall of Princes*; my citations are from *Lydgate's Fall of Princes*, pp. 420–21. In the *Consolatio* of Boethius, Lady Philosophy's words about Alcibiades are as follows. "Fix your gaze on the extent, the stability, the swift motion of the heavens, and stop admiring base things. The heavens are not more remarkable in these qualities than in the reason by which they are governed. The beauty of your person passes swiftly away; it is more fleeting than spring flowers. And if, as Aristotle says, men had the eyes of Lynceus and could see through stone walls, would they not find the superficially beautiful body of Alcibiades to be most vile upon seeing his entrails?" (Boethius, *The Consolation of Philosophy*, p. 55).

72. Plutarch, *The Lives of the Noble Grecians and Romanes*, p. 223.

73. For a general history of the rhetoric of monarchical inviolability and the implicit association with invisibility, see Kantorowicz, "Mysteries of State," pp. 74–91, especially the maxim of Boniface VIII: "Sancta Sedes omnes iudicat, sed a nemine iudicatur." The analogous power of conscience appears in a remark made by Edward Aglionby in the House of Commons, April 11, 1571, arguing that there was "no human positive law to enforce

conscience, which is not discernible in this world" (cited in Caraman, *The Other Face*, pp. 35–36).

74. Warner, *Albions England*, p. 247.

75. Accounts of the complicity of Elizabeth's ministers in not arresting the progress of the death warrant despite signs that Elizabeth was still in doubt can be found in Camden, *The History of the Most Renowned and Victorious Princess Elizabeth*, pp. 290–300; Nicolas, *Life of William Davison*, pp. 108–29; Neale, *Elizabeth I*, vol. 2, pp. 136–44.

76. The two men's protestations of innocence included, inevitably, references to conscience (Burghley associating the privilege of enjoying the monarch's gaze with the support derived from the "pillar of [his] conscience" [Strype, *Annals*, vol. 3, pt. 1, p. 540]). However such language may have empowered the two outcasts in moral or psychological terms, it could do nothing for them politically, particularly insofar as Elizabeth had made it clear that in the political arena the power of conscience was to be understood to belong to the monarch alone. The business of disabling her position could not come from a direct assault but only from an indirect one, as the Spenserian narrative of book 5 of *The Faerie Queene* shows (see Chapters 4–7).

77. Kantorowicz, *The King's Two Bodies*, p. 11.

78. Cited in ibid., p. 13.

79. Strype, *Annals*, vol. 3, pt. 1, p. 540.

80. The report of the Spanish ambassador is cited in Zeeveld, *The Temper of Shakespeare's Thought*, p. 147; the commentary is Zeeveld's, p. 147.

81. A concise analysis of the semantic complexities involved in the word "conscience" is in C. S. Lewis, "Conscience and Conscious," pp. 181–213.

82. Kantorowicz, *The King's Two Bodies*, pp. 7–9.

83. Ibid, pp. 16–20.

84. Pierce, *Conscience in the New Testament*, pp. 40–53.

85. For a discussion of the connection between conscience and the Greek *ate*, see Dodds, "From Shame-Culture to Guilt-Culture," in *The Greeks and the Irrational*, pp. 38–42.

86. Kreihing, *Emblemata Ethico-Politica, carmine explicata*, p. 38.

Two

1. South, "Obedience for Conscience-sake, the Duty of Good Subjects," p. 140.

2. Puttenham, *The Arte of English Poesie*, pp. 196–97. An absorbing reading of the Tiberian rhetoric of royal power in Jacobean England is in Goldberg, *James I and the Politics of Literature*, pp. 55–112.

3. Brosnan, "Mental Restriction and Equivocation," p. 461.

4. For a general discussion of the classical, patristic, and medieval anteced-

ents of sixteenth-century discussions of equivocation and mental reservation, see Lea, *A History of Auricular Confession*, pp. 401–11. For an illuminating account of the subversive potential of equivocation in Jacobean England, see Mullaney, "Lying Like Truth."

5. Garnet, *A Treatise of Equivocation*, p. 9. Further references to this treatise are from this edition, pp. 12–13, 104.

6. The chief work of Azpilcueta, a doctor of canon law and casuist who taught at the Universities of Toulouse, Salamance, and Coimbra, was the *Manuale sive Enchiridion confessariorum et paenitentium*; Garnet's discussion of mental reservation derives in part from another of Azpilcueta's works, the *Commentarius in cap. Humanae aurea*, 22, q. 5: "de veritate responsi partim verbo, partim mente concepti; et de arte bona at mala simulandi." For a discussion of the connections between Garnet's treatise and the major casuistical documents of the sixteenth century on the subject of mental reservation, see Malloch, "Father Henry Garnet's Treatise of Equivocation."

7. Cicero, *De officiis*, III, 52. The practice of mental reservation in Elizabethan England was seen by one commentator to be a symptom of "modern times" rather than a sign of a particular religious affiliation. Sir John Davies, making a report of the proceedings against recusants held in the Castle Chamber, Dublin, in April 1613 recalled Cicero's phrase when he observed that "when those of the religion in Queen Marie's daies were examined by Bishopp Bonner uppon articles which did drawe them into an apparant perill of theire lives, none of them were ever found to aequivocate or to use anie mentall reservacion; but they aunsered truly and directly, though they paid the price of theire lives for it. And so do all Protestantes at this day which happen to fall into the Inquisicion. Howbeit, for a man to hold his peace when hee neede not to speake, it is oftentimes good Christian policy, but 'aliud est tacere, aliud caelare,' saith Cicero" ("Case of Concealment or Mental Reservation," in Petti, *Recusant Documents*, p. 255).

8. Citations in this paragraph and the next are from Persons, *A treatise tending to mitigation*, p. 402.

9. "Popish teachers affirme, that in some cases, they may sweare in a doubtfull meaning. And this they practise in time of daunger, when beeing convented before the Magistrate, and examined, they answer Yea in word, and conceive negation, or No in their minds. A practise most impious, and flat against this excellent Rule of the Prophet, that a man should sweare in truth, judgement, & justice" (Perkins, *The Whole Treatise of Cases of Conscience*, in *William Perkins, 1558–1602*, p. 142). Perkins's view on the subject was in fact much more complex than the above statement suggests. Consider, for example, his appropriation of the scholastic distinction between lying and concealing: "For it is one thing to speake against our knowledge,

and another to speake that which we knowe. And concealements, if there be a reasonable cause, and if it be not necessarie for us to reveale the thing concealed, are not unlawfull. Thus Abram speakes the truth in part, calling Sara his sister, and conceales it in part, not confessing her to be his wife" (*An exposition*, p. 211). Perkins also makes a distinction between "dissembling" and "sembling" or "fayning," the latter obtaining "when something is spoken not contrayr, but beside, or divers to that which we thinke" (*An exposition*, p. 211).

10. "Leake's Relation of the Martyrdom of Father Southwell," in Pollen, *Unpublished Documents*, p. 334.

11. Southwell, *An Humble Supplication*, p. 44.

12. Perkins, *The Whole Treatise of Cases of Conscience*, in *William Perkins, 1558–1602*, p. 142.

13. Persons, *A treatise tending to mitigation*, p. 429.

14. Ibid., pp. 414, 416.

15. "The Case of Concealment or Mental Reservation," in Pollen, *Unpublished Documents*, p. 249.

16. Morton, *A Full Satisfaction*, p. 99.

17. Persons, *A treatise tending to mitigation*, pp. 442–43.

18. "An Act for the better discovering and repressing of Popish Recusants," Prothero, *Select Statutes*, p. 256.

19. A good general discussion of the benefit of clergy is in Elton, *Reform and Reformation*, pp. 53–56.

20. Holmes, *Elizabethan Casuistry*, pp. 64–65, 52–53.

21. Munday, *A Discoverie of Edmund Campion*, sig. Ciii–iv.

22. Bilson, *The true difference betweene Christian subiection and unchristian rebellion*, pp. 35–36.

23. "And be it further enacted . . . that every person or persons being subject of this realm which after the said forty days shall know and understand that any such Jesuit, seminary priest, or other priest abovesaid shall abide, stay, tarry, or be within this realm or other the Queen's dominions and countries, contrary to the true meaning of this Act, and shall not discover the same unto some Justice of Peace or other higher officer within twelve days next after his said knowledge, but willingly conceal his knowledge therein; that every such offender shall make fine and be imprisoned at the Queen's pleasure" ("Act against Jesuits and Seminary Priests" [1585], in Hughes and Fries, *Crown and Parliament in Tudor and Stuart England*, p. 127).

24. Letter to Aquaviva, in Pollen, *Unpublished Documents*, p. 325.

25. Wark, *Elizabethan Recusancy in Cheshire*, p. 89. The relevant parts of

Regnans in excelsis are printed in Morey, *The Catholic Subjects of Elizabeth I*, p. 56.

26. See Kingdon, *The Execution of Justice*, p. 128.

27. Morey, *The Catholic Subjects of Elizabeth I*, p. 86.

28. "In our commoun, I dare not defyne that it is a mortall synne not to confesse or to denye, so long as he useth no fraude or periurye, or any such plea as may pervert the judgement. For in the civill law the whole judgement dependeth on the partyes confession; in the commoun law it consisteth in the tryall of the countrey, which if the defendant accept, it seemeth no more is required of hym. And so we see that in all ages it was the custom of never so notorious thieves to pleade not guyltye, neyther have I ever heard of any doctour which hath reprehended it" (Garnet, *A Treatise of Equivocation*, pp. 70–71).

29. Holmes, *Elizabethan Casuistry*, pp. 52–54, 63–66.

30. Accounts of the Ingram and the Freeman cases are printed in Pollen, *Unpublished Documents*, pp. 284, 350.

31. Sandys, "A Sermon preached in York, at the celebration of the day of the Queen's entrance into her reign," in *Sermons*, p. 64; Topcliffe's remark is printed in Pollen, *Unpublished Documents*, pp. 105–6.

32. Wark, *Elizabethan Recusancy in Cheshire*, pp. 91–92, 102–105.

33. Persons, *A treatise tending to mitigation*, pp. 549–50. The text Persons refers to is Athanasius, "Apology of our Holy Father Athanasius, Archbishop of Alexandria, in vindication of his flight, when he was persecuted by Duke Syrianus."

34. For a good introductory account of the Priscillianist heresy, see the essay by Harold B. Jaffee that prefaces Augustine's treatise "Against Lying," in *Saint Augustine*, pp. 113–20. References cited in my discussion are from King, *A Sermon preached the 5th of November, 1607*, pp. 26–27.

35. Cited in Caraman, *The Other Face*, p. 41.

36. For a survey of the recent discussions among historians regarding the degree of the papist community's quiescence in the early years of Elizabeth's reign, see Holmes, *Resistance and Compromise*, pp. 11–22.

37. The Act of Uniformity is printed in Prothero, *Select Statutes*, p. 17. Bacon's observations on the government's duty to find the appropriate method of shaping the consciences of the queen's subjects are in "Certain Observations upon a Libel," in *The Works of Francis Bacon*, p. 254. In the same treatise Bacon takes pains to neutralize the subversive potential of conscience by allocating its political function to the sovereign alone: "Causes of conscience, when they exceed their bounds, and prove to be a matter of faction, lose their nature; and . . . sovereign princes ought distinctly to

punish the practice or contempt, though coloured with the pretence of conscience and religion" (p. 254).

38. See Read, *Lord Burghley and Queen Elizabeth*, pp. 235–55.

39. See Neale, *Elizabeth I*, vol. 2, pp. 241–90.

40. A good discussion of the general ineffectiveness of *Regnans in excelsis* is in Elton, *England Under the Tudors*, p. 303.

41. Morey, *The Catholic Subjects of Elizabeth I*, pp. 59–65.

42. The proclamation is printed in Hughes and Larkin, *Tudor Royal Proclamations*, p. 469.

43. See Kingdon, *The Execution of Justice*, p. 13. Burghley describes Sanders's death in a way that suggests Burghley was attempting to make Sanders's fate illustrate the ravaging action of a guilty conscience; he notes "the strange manner of the death of Dr. Sanders, the Pope's Irish legate, who . . . wandering in the mountains in Ireland without succor, died raving in a frenzy" (p. 31). See also Morey's discussion of Sanders, in *The Catholic Subjects of Elizabeth I*, pp. 64–65.

44. On the subject of the role of the printing presses in the English mission see, especially, Southern, *Elizabethan Recusant Prose*, pp. 353–56; and Rostenberg, *The Minority Press and the English Crown*.

45. Persons's career as controversialist and as author of devotional literature is covered in Southern, *Elizabeth Recusant Prose*, pp. 184–85, and in Basset, "The Mystery of Robert Persons," in *The English Jesuits*, pp. 55–96.

46. In a letter to Agazzari, November 17, 1580, Persons related the events that led up to the scandal of Campion's document: "When they first came into this island, the Jesuits heard that the cunning of their adversaries was such that, if they captured any men who were distinguished for learning or had a considerable reputation with the people, they were wont to keep them shut up in dark prisons and, spreading meanwhile false rumours either of their recantation or of their obstinate refusal to see the light, never allowed them to tell their case in public. And so by way of providing a cure for this inconvenience by a salutary piece of foresight, they prepared in advance written answers and deposited them with a loyal friend of theirs, with the intention and purpose that, if they should be taken prisoners at any time, they would ask for them back and, with their signatures attached, take them to the Royal Council. In the meantime it came to pass that the person, to whose charge the matter had been entrusted for some reason or other handed a copy of these documents to another man, and he to a second; so that in a few days time the thing reached the hands of a countless number of men, including the Queen's Councillors themselves." The effect: "by the reading of which the spirits of the Catholics seemed to be raised, whilst the heretics were dumbfounded, the enemy were inflamed with anger—so much

so that many proclamations were made against us, and the public treasurer, Cecil by name, when administering the oath lately in the Queen's name to the new Mayor of London, publicly complained in very grave terms of the Pope and the Jesuits, who, he said, had conspired against the English state" (Hicks, *Letters and Memorials*, pp. 57–58).

47. The remark about the seditious nature of papists is Burghley's, in Kingdon, *The Execution of Justice*, p. 6; Bacon's remark is in "Certain Observations upon a Libel," in *The Works of Francis Bacon*, p. 249.

48. By the time Campion's "Challenge" appeared, in 1580, the Tudor government had already shown its disposition to act on its legislation against the missionaries in England: one seminary priest had been put to death in 1577, sentenced under the 1571 Act against the Bull from Rome. For details see Morey, *The Catholic Subjects of Elizabeth I*, pp. 60–61.

49. The "Challenge" is printed in Basset, *The English Jesuits*, pp. 454–56.

50. The mission also had a clearly pragmatic aspect, seeking sustenance and financial support from the upper echelons of society, the peerage and the gentry. Consider Persons's remark to Agazzari: "All last summer we spent very usefully preaching in the country, being escorted in each county by a number of young men of gentle birth, of whom there are quite a lot here who volunteer to be our servants (as they themselves term it). Very generously they pay our expenses as well as their own" (Hicks, *Letters and Memorials*, p. 59).

51. Letter of Christopher Buxton to the rector of the English College, Rome, September 12, 1587, in Pollen, *Unpublished Documents*, p. 149.

52. Bacon, "Certain Observations upon a Libel," in *The Works of Francis Bacon*, pp. 254–55.

53. The remark was made by the judge presiding at the conviction of Robert Lalor early in 1607 ("Conviction and Attainder of Robert Lalor," in Petti, *Recusant Documents*, p. 190).

54. The politicization of conscience implied by Paul's use of the term in Romans as a mechanism for inducing obedience to secular authority was made explicit and topical in the "Homily against Disobedience and Wilful Rebellion" as well as in the oath required of public officials according to the 1559 Act of Supremacy. See *Certain Sermons*, pp. 211–17; and Prothero, *Select Statutes*, pp. 1–13.

55. See Kingdon, *The Execution of Justice*, pp. 6–7. Burghley's impression of the dangers of the papists is echoed in the 1591 Proclamation castigating the Jesuits, who were described as attempting "by falsehood, by hypocrisie, and by underminings of our good subjects under a false colour and face of holines, to make breaches in mens and womens consciences, and so to traine them to their Treasons . . . a secret infection of treasons in the bowels of our

Realm" (cited in Southwell, *An Humble Supplication*, p. 63). The attitude penetrated into private discourse as well. The notorious Topcliffe, interrogator of recusants and priests, noted that in their responses to the Bloody Questions administered to induce treasonous statements from papists, the priests "albeit theie speak faier, yet they seeme to carrie fowle and traiterous harts, and if they hurt not, it is not for want of will to attempt it, but for lacke of force to accomplish it" ("Letter to the Lords concerning the Seminary Priests," in Pollen, *Unpublished Documents*, p. 106).

56. Persons to Agazzari, November 17, 1580, in Hicks, *Letters and Memorials*, p. 59. While it is not clear whether the missionary priests had substantial training in public disputation, it is nonetheless likely that most of them had a modicum of training in casuistry, as suggested by William Allen's description of the priorities of the mission: "Since all the labourers we send are employed in administering the sacraments and above all things in hearing confessions (for the people have hardly any pastors now but them) we take care that they are most carefully instructed in the whole catechism and in pastoral matters, and are not ignorant of ecclesiastical penalties and censures, or of the way to deal with their people in such cases" (cited in Knox, *The First and Second Diaries of the English College, Douay*, pp. xxxviii–xlii).

57. The official ban that the ecclesiastical hierarchy of the Catholic Church in the seventeenth century placed on the practice of mental reservation and the doctrine of probabilism, which allowed the practice of mental reservation its fullest extension, can be understood as an attempt within the Church itself to arrest the dismantling process generated from within its own pastoral discourse. On the history of mental reservation and probabilism after the sixteenth century, see Thomas Deman, "Probabilisme," in *Dictionnaire de théologie catholique*, vol. 13, pt. 1, pp. 418–619; see also E. Amann, "Laxisme," in *Dictionnaire de théologie catholique*, vol. 9, pt. 1, pp. 37–86. Blaise Pascal's role in fueling the controversy over probabilism is discussed in Jonsen and Toulmin, *The Abuse of Casuistry*, pp. 231–49.

58. Holmes, *Resistance and Compromise*, pp. 6–9. See also Holmes, *Elizabethan Casuistry*, pp. 1–9.

59. For a discussion of the *communicatio in sacris* tradition, see Rose, *Cases of Conscience*, p. 73. Holmes discusses the Scriptural loci used in the tradition, especially 2 John 10–11: "If there come any unto you, and bring not this doctrine, receive him not into your house, neither bid him Godspeed: For he that biddeth him Godspeed is partner of his evil deeds." Holmes notes that the Rheims New Testament gloss orients this passage explicitly toward the topical issue of church attendance in England; see Holmes, *Resistance and Compromise*, p. 85. The rule was not rigid, however;

marriages with schismatics were tolerated, as, occasionally, were marriages with heretics. See Holmes, *Resistance and Compromise*, pp. 113–14.

60. Holmes discusses the impact of the Council of Trent on the English mission in *Resistance and Compromise*, pp. 84–89; a useful analysis of the political implications in England of the papal bull *Regnans in excelsis*, which excommunicated Elizabeth, appears in Elton, *England under the Tudors*, pp. 303–10.

61. Cited in Holmes, *Resistance and Compromise*, p. 87.

62. The most useful discussion of conciliarism and Marsiglian theory in sixteenth-century political thought is in Skinner, *Foundations*, vol. 1, pp. 61–65; vol. 2, pp. 114–23. Persons's involvement in resistance theory is analyzed in Clancy, *Papist Pamphleteers*. According to Holmes, Persons's central argument seems to have been that Catholics in England did not "'repugn' or 'resist' any of the realm's temporal laws, but simply refused to obey the 'pretended laws of religion' because they believed in conscience and could prove that they were 'against the laws of God and not consonant to any just and truly called laws of our country'" (*Resistance and Compromise*, p. 37). Note that the Protestant tradition was equally able to support resistance theory; Calvin held that civil law was not binding in conscience. See *Institutes of the Christian Religion*, vol. 21, pp. 1183–84.

63. Holmes, *Resistance and Compromise*, p. 102.

64. References in this discussion to the case-books are from Holmes, *Elizabethan Casuistry*, pp. 38–40, 63–66, 74–77.

65. Rose discusses the concept of *metus iustus* in *Cases of Conscience*, pp. 85–87.

66. Discussions of the recusancy laws, their terms, and the limits of their application are in Morey, *The Catholic Subjects of Elizabeth I*, pp. 67–69, and Rose, *Cases of Conscience*, pp. 15–17.

67. Langdale, "A treatise to prove that attendance at the Protestant church was in itself no sin . . . ," cited in Southern, *Elizabethan Recusant Prose*, p. 143. As Holmes notes, Persons observed that the Langdale pamphlet "was widely spread among Catholics in the provinces" (Holmes, *Resistance and Compromise*, p. 93). Persons's remark is printed in "The Memoirs of Father Robert Persons," in Pollen, *Miscellanea II*, pp. 179–81.

68. Persons's remarks in this discussion of the subject of church attendance are from *Reasons of Refusal*, cited in Southern, *Elizabethan Recusant Prose*, pp. 141–42.

69. Waldern was one of a number of recusants imprisoned in and around London after the passage of the 1593 penal law against popish recusants (35 Eliz., c. 2); see "Examination of Imprisoned Recusants," in Petti, *Recusant Documents*, p. 80.

70. "The goinge and not goinge is not made a signe distinctiue betwene C. & P. for puritans refuse to go to the churches of P. againe & P. do not account yt a speciall marke" (Langdale, cited in Southern, *Elizabethan Recusant Prose*, p. 143).

71. Prothero, *Select Statutes*, p. 92.

72. The language of the homily describes treason in a way that evokes the Calvinist sense of the numberless sins of the soul: "For he that nameth rebellion nameth not a singular or one only sin, as is theft, robbery, murder, and such like; but he nameth the whole puddle and sink of all sins against God and man; against his prince, his country, his countrymen, his parents, his children, his kinsfolks, his friends, and against all men universally" ("Homily against Disobedience and Wilful Rebellion," in *Certain Sermons*, p. 225).

73. Haigh, *Reformation and Resistance in Tudor Lancashire*, p. 277. In Lancashire, described by the Privy Council as "the very sink of popery," a pattern appears to have emerged: "the recusant household with an 'occasional-conformist' head seems to have been common among the gentry" (p. 275). Morey notes that by the end of the century "there was a large number of conformists" in Yorkshire; see Morey, *The Catholic Subjects of Elizabeth I*, p. 213.

74. Haigh, *Reformation and Resistance in Tudor Lancashire*, p. 94.

75. The 1571 Act of Treason, for example, proscribed several external signs of papistry: the "vain and superstitious things" included the *agnus dei*, holy pictures, beads, and so forth—proscriptions that did not directly address the more complex problem of the church-papists, or even of the recusants. Haigh's observation is apposite: "In large, especially northern, parishes with dispersed settlements and many chapels, recusants were extremely difficult to detect" (Haigh, *Reformation and Resistance in Tudor Lancashire*, p. 267). Moreover, as Haigh suggests, variations in the statistics concerning recusants are difficult to interpret because the "number of of recusants detected reflects the intensity of the search," a point that James I's remark to Parliament reflected: "I think there are more recusants discovered, but not that there are more indeed than heretofore" (p. 260). Economic factors seem to have played a role in the hermeneutics of the dissident culture as well: "As proof of absence from church on four successive Sundays was required, the well-to-do recusant could avoid the £20 fine by moving house before the month expired, an easy matter for those owning houses in more than one county or with an abundance of relatives" (Morey, *The Catholic Subjects of Elizabeth I*, p. 141). Elliot Rose points out that the laxity of the church wardens and the practice of "private arrangements" between wardens and recusants were instrumental in producing a protective shield around the dissident population . See Rose, *Cases of Conscience*, pp. 61–62. For a discussion

of the relation between repetitive, ritualized activity and conversion, see MacMullen, *Christianizing the Roman Empire*, pp. 52–58, 74–85. More generally, see Geertz, "Religion as a Cultural System," in *The Interpretation of Cultures*, pp. 87–125.

76. For a discussion of the political problems raised by the *rebus sic stantibus* clause, see Mattingly, "William Allen and Catholic Propaganda in England." See also Holmes, *Resistance and Compromise*, pp. 41–43. One sixteenth-century document gives an idea of the scandalous impact of the clause on the Protestant power structure in Elizabethan England: "The pope that now is, to animate his workmen, and free them from danger, hath agreed, like a fox, to wink at the bull of Pius V. A qualification is made thereof in that which might touch his brokers. The bull shal not so bind them; but if they be taken seducing her majesties subjects, and examined for their allegiance, by dispensation they may profess it frankly. But will you know how long? *Donec publice eusdem bullae executio fieri potest* [i.e., Until the execution of the said bull may be done publicly]. Will you know how long? Until the catholics by competent forces shall be able to resist" (*That such papists as of late times have been executed were by a statute of Edward III, lawfully executed as traitors; A treatice*, in Strype, *Annals*, vol. 3, pt. 2, p. 341).

77. Earle, "A Church-papist," in *Microcosmographie*, pp. 27–28.

78. Cited in Basset, *The English Jesuits*, p. 42.

79. Ibid., p. 43.

80. Details of the disguise Thomas Holford wore at the time of his arrest are included in "The Arrest of Thomas Holford, 18 and 23 May, 1585," in Pollen, *Unpublished Documents*, pp. 109–11.

81. An exemplary martyrology from the period, focusing on the Christ-like victimization of the missionary priests, is William Allen's *A Briefe Historie of the Glorious Martyrdom of Twelve Reverend Priests*.

82. The case-book citations on the subject of fasting are taken from Holmes, *Elizabethan Casuistry*, pp. 37–40, 69–74, 105–6. The central role of intention in the determination of a resolution of a case of conscience derives prominently, of course, from Aristotle's *Nichomachean Ethics*, which informs Henry Garnet's treatise on equivocation, as we have seen. In the seventeenth century, Pascal's *Lettres provinciales* satirized what had become the scandalous practice of "directing the intention," associated with Jesuit casuistry. See Pascal, *The Provincial Letters*.

83. Perkins, *A Discourse of Conscience*, in *William Perkins, 1558–1602*, p. 32.

84. "Whether it is lawfull to eate eggs on fridayes in England?" in Holmes, *Elizabethan Casuistry*, pp. 40–41.

85. See N. Iung, "Scandale," *Dictionnaire de théologie catholique*, vol. 14, pt. 1, pp. 1248–49.

Three

1. "Father Richard Holtby on Persecution in the North," in Morris, *Troubles*, vol. 3, p. 121.

2. Cited in Neville Williams, *Elizabeth I*, p. 261.

3. Southwell's remark appears in a letter to Aquaviva, July 25, 1586: "Some [priests] for whom a ransom was paid have been set at liberty unconditionally. But the poursuivants whose business it is to arrest them, prowl about the city lynx-eyed" (Pollen, *Unpublished Documents*, p. 308). Whether or not the pursuivants should be numbered among the effective agents of the government's intelligence network is a point in dispute; Read argues that it would be "inaccurate to number these men as parts of Walsingham's secret service, although doubtless he obtained from them occasionally very useful information in regard to the movements and plans of the Catholics" (*Mr. Secretary Walsingham*, p. 336). Contemporary references such as Southwell's suggest that the pursuivants were nonetheless perceived as extensions of the government's invasive machinery of scrutiny. On the subject of the Elizabethan intelligence network in general, see, in addition to Read, Plowden, *Danger to Elizabeth*.

4. "A Yorkshire Recusant's Relation," in Morris, *Troubles*, vol. 3, p. 69.

5. Plowden, *Danger to Elizabeth*, p. 226.

6. The point I am trying to underscore is not that the social relations between divergent religious groups were, in practice, unrelievedly tense and polarized. Historians of the period have, as a rule, downplayed the cloak-and-dagger atmosphere that one might find tempting to imagine to have prevailed. See, for example, Aveling's reading of Catholic-Protestant relations in *The Handle and the Axe*. What I want to emphasize is the kind of interpretive practice implied in the sporadic nature of the Tudor intelligence network and articulated in the casuistical manuals used in the English mission, a practice that assumed a social text in which no detail could be overlooked or taken as innocuous and that assumed an interpretive context that was characterized, as recusant documents suggest, by the widespread sense among dissidents that the "conscience" of the government could be anywhere, notably in the imperceptible penetration of pursuivants and spies into apparently secure communities.

7. An economic motive may well have encouraged the ideological division between the two religious groups. For a discussion of this phenomenon in the early Tudor period, see Elton, "Informing for Profit." See also Read, *Mr. Secretary Walsingham*, p. 318. Government proclamations during Elizabeth's reign recurrently attested to the perceived need for informers as well as for the promise of financial reward. One proclamation, possibly prompted by the bull of Sixtus V in 1588 urging rebellion against the mon-

arch, denounced seditious publications of Catholics and urged everyone in the realm to "inquire and search" for such publications; in reward for such a service, informers were to receive "the moity of all the goods and chattels of the said offender, which should be so apprehended or detected by them" (Strype, *Annals*, vol. 3, pt. 2, p. 91). Morey's observation on the subject of the social tension—and the implicit interpretive challenges—associated with the congruence of recusants and informers is illuminating: "After the passing of the 1581 Act [the Act against Reconciliation with Rome] recusants were at risk from the common informer, who could obtain a third of the fine in the event of a conviction, one-third going to the Queen and the remainder to the poor of the parish, a least in theory. In the Hilary Term of 1581–82, Hugh Cuffe sued twenty-four recusants living in twelve different counties, but his occupation had its risks, and in 1599 Catholics living in the Whitby district attacked and drove out a common informer and his companions" (cited in Aveling, *Northern Catholics*, p. 125).

8. Read, *Mr. Secretary Walsingham*, p. 320.

9. Witness the wording of the Act against Popish Recusants (1593), which includes an indictment of "sundry and seditious persons, who terming themselves Catholics and being indeed spies and intelligencers not only for her Majesty's foreign enemies but also for rebellious and traiterous subjects born within her Highness' dominions . . ." (Hughes and Fries, *Crown and Parliament*, p. 130).

10. The text of Parry's letter to Burghley is cited in Strype, *Annals*, vol. 2, pt. 2, p. 366.

11. Citations from the Parry case are taken from *Cobbett's*, pp. 1095–1111.

12. Strype, *Annals*, vol. 3, pt. 1, pp. 378–79.

13. "Life of William Weston," in Morris, *Troubles*, vol. 2, p. 206. In "The Fall of Anthony Tyrrell," which I discuss later in the chapter, Robert Persons names five apostate priests, but it seems probable, to judge from his remark, that there were more: he gives the names "of Anthony Tyrrell, and that of John Nichols, of Laurence Caddy, of Richard Bayne, Edward Osborne, and some others" (*Troubles*, vol. 3, p. 316). The popular association of pastoral care and secret knowledge associated with the confessional dialog was not exclusive to the papists. Secrecy was recognized as a necessary attribute as well of those Protestant ministers who were sought out as spiritual counsellors. William Perkins, the Puritan casuist, noted that "the person to whom confession [understood loosely outside the sacramental context that the papists endorsed] is made, must be a man of trust and fidelity, able and willing to keepe secret things that are reveiled, yea to burie them (as it were) in the grave of oblivion, for 'Love covereth a multitude of sinnes'" (*The Whole Treatise of Cases of Conscience*, in *William Perkins, 1558–1602*, pp. 89–90).

14. Unless otherwise indicated, my citations in this discussion are from Persons's "The Fall of Anthony Tyrrell," in Morris, *Troubles*, vol. 2, pp. 392–410.

15. Strype, *Annals*, vol. 3, pt. 2, p. 433.

16. Morris, *Troubles*, vol. 2, pp. 402–24.

17. Foucault, *Discipline and Punish*, p. 233.

18. Perkins, *A Discourse of Conscience*, in *William Perkins, 1558–1602*, p. 74.

19. A list of the available instruments of torture can be found in Tootell, *Dodd's Church History of England*, pp. 150–51. A description of the torture known as the "wall," which was used in the much-publicized case of Robert Southwell, is printed in Pollen, *Unpublished Documents*, pp. 333–34. See also Pollen's discussion of the "wall" in "Warrants to Torture Christopher Bale," in *Unpublished Documents*, pp. 178–79. Of all the torture devices used against recusants and priests, the "wall" is perhaps the most provocative, because of the way in which it evokes what we can call the "unaccountability" topos that marked the queen's rhetorical stance in relation to the pursuit of religious dissidents. The "wall" takes us beyond Foucault's impression of the significance of the physical body of the condemned in the public spectacle of punishment; in the case of the "wall" the prisoner's own body becomes the instrument of torture, with no direct external intervention—it is as though the agents of the governmental authorities were merely witnesses to the criminal's self-destruction, a role Elizabeth herself attempted to ascribe to herself in her speeches on Mary. As Pollen puts it, "Hung up by the hands, the mere weight of the body [did] the work of the rackmaster, and even more efficiently, because it worked slowly and noiselessly" (*Unpublished Documents*, p. 178).

20. The watchfulness of Tyrrell's companions was not merely a symbolic act, however: through it, the companions pieced together evidence of Tyrrell's treachery, which they used to extract a confession from Tyrrell. See Morris, *Troubles*, vol. 2, pp. 205–7.

21. The citations regarding the activities of Tyrrell and his prison companions are from "The Life of Father William Weston, S.J.," in Morris, *Troubles*, vol. 2, pp. 203–8.

22. Morris, *Troubles*, vol. 2, p. 204. Weston's remark also suggests that the dynamic involved in the acquisition of "tokens and signs" involved the suppression on the part of Tyrrell's companions of signs of their own suspicion of the priest—i.e., Tyrrell's companions must have found it expedient to adopt the chameleon-like behavior of church-papists, spies, and others involved in elaborating the labyrinthine social text of the discourse of conscience.

23. The citations from Persons's discussion of Tyrrell's scandalous enact-

ment of the confessional utterance in the sermon at St. Paul's Cross are from "The Fall of Anthony Tyrrell," in Morris, *Troubles*, vol. 2, pp. 487–97.

24. An analogous appeal involved a royal audience: Bishop Sandys praised the virtue of the "upright conscience" as the locus of unambiguous truth in the sermon he delivered before Elizabeth I in 1558; see Sandys, *Sermons*, p. 58.

25. Hall, "Cases of Piety and Religion," *Resolutions and Decisions*, in *Works*, p. 359.

26. The phrase comes from Robert Sanderson's definition of the doubting conscience: "Doubting properly is motus indifferens in utramque partem contradictionis when the mind is held in suspense between two ways, uncertain whether or both to take to; when the scales hang even . . . and in aequilibrio, without any notable propension or inclination to the one side more than to the other" (cited in Kelly, *Conscience*, p. 61).

27. Citations regarding the Tyrrell case are from Morris, vol. 2, *Troubles*, pp. 497–501.

28. Tyrrell also claimed that it was precisely because of his association with hyprocrisy that his words could be believed. In a letter to Elizabeth, written before the first St. Paul's Cross episode (that is, after he had abandoned his role as spy and returned to the Catholic faith), he argued that his case was a means "whereby you may the better be warned of the nature of a true loyal subject, from him that playeth the counterfeit and hypocrite" (Strype, *Annals*, vol. 3, pt. 2, p. 426). This remark, though no doubt intended by Tyrrell to justify his past career and to deny the problematic aspect of his renewed status as English Catholic and as self-proclaimed loyal subject of the queen, also indicates the kind of destabilizing action typical of the discourse of conscience. Under the pressure to resolve the contradiction between his personal sense of innocence and his appraisal of his public identity as criminal, Tyrrell makes a statement that dismantles the polarized relation of the "true subject" and the "hypocrite," so that the act of correctly reading the true subject depends on the surrounding context or frame that the true subject's own association with hypocrisy provides.

Tyrrell emerged once from relative obscurity in 1602 to give testimony before the Ecclesiastical Commissioners, who under the direction of Bishop Richard Bancroft were investigating the practice of exorcism in the realm; Bancroft's chaplain, Samuel Harsnet, later included Tyrrell's testimony in "A declaration of egregious Popish Impostures," in *Dictionary of National Biography*, vol. 57, p. 439.

29. Persons's attempt to salvage Tyrrell as a model for the Christian community finds an analog in the mechanism of the *Spiritual Exercises* of Ignatius Loyola as understood by Roland Barthes; in both cases, the outcome, as

Barthes observes of the *Exercises*, is "to make the withholding of the Mark itself into an ultimate sign" (*Sade, Fourier, Loyola*, p. 75).

30. Morris, *Troubles*, vol. 2, p. 316. The "scruple of conscience" is not necessarily the driving force behind the confession, however; Persons locates the phrase at the head of a catalog of motives: "scruple of conscience, fear of God's judgments, hope of salvation, terror of eternal condemnation, love of justice, zeal of truth, and for defence of innocency, which in their passion they had slandered" (p. 316).

31. "The kind of deflection I have in mind [in discussing terministic screens] concerns simply the fact that any nomenclature necessarily directs the attention into some channels rather than others" (Burke, "Terministic Screens," in *Language as Symbolic Action*, p. 45). It is worth noting that Burke's discussion of the selectivity of perception at issue in what he calls "terministic screens" draws on Pascal's satire in *The Provincial Letters* of the Jesuit casuists' procedure of "directing the intention"—a procedure that effectively promoted laxity in cases of conscience.

32. Casuists themselves recognized that the confessional utterance might well function as a screen for duplicity. See, for example, Bernard's discussion of "hypocritical confession" in "The Steps of Humility and Pride," in *The Works of Bernard of Clairvaux*, pp. 73–74.

33. Perkins, *A Discourse of Conscience*, in *William Perkins, 1558–1602*, pp. 72, 75.

34. Ibid., pp. 66–69.

35. Bernard, "The Steps of Humility and Pride," in *The Works of Bernard of Clairvaux*, p. 78.

36. Bourdaloue, "Sermon . . . sur la fausse conscience," in *Oeuvres de Bourdaloue*, vol. 3, p. 44.

37. Perkins, *A Discourse of Conscience*, in *William Perkins, 1558–1602*, p. 68; Bourdaloue, "Sermon . . . sur la fausse conscience," in *Oeuvres de Bourdaloue*, p. 49; Augustine's *dictum* is cited in Bourdaloue, p. 44.

38. Potts, *Conscience in Medieval Philosophy*, pp. 135–36. The "double bind" problem appears in Protestant casuistry as well; see Perkins, *The Whole Treatise of Cases of Conscience*, in *William Perkins, 1558–1602*, pp. 100–101.

39. Bourdaloue, *Oeuvres de Bourdaloue*, p. 46. On the question of the accountability of conscience and the development of invincible ignorance in the lax conscience, see E. Amann, "Laxisme," in *Dictionnaire de théologie catholique*, vol. 9, pt. 1, pp. 38–39. For a discussion of the Aristotelian background to the casuistical descriptions of the lax conscience, see Fülöp-Millar, *The Power and Secret of the Jesuits*, pp. 156–62.

40. "Les Juifs sortant de la synagogue dirent donc à Jean-Baptiste: Qui

êtes-vous? afin que nous puissions rendre rèponse à ceux qui nous ont en-
voyés? Que dîtes-vous de vous-même? Je suis, répondit-il, la voix de celui
qui crie dans le désert: préparez la voie du Seigenur, et la rendez droite"
(Bourdaloue, *Oeuvres de Bourdaloue*, p. 41).

41. Bernard's descriptions of the lax conscience as an abyss and as a reptile are cited in Bourdaloue, *Oeuvres de Bourdaloue*, p. 48.

42. Douglas's discussion of the Leviticus passage and the cultural significance of the category of the unclean in general is in *Purity and Danger*,
pp. 41–57.

43. Burghley, in Kingdon, *The Execution of Justice in England*, pp. 6–7.
The 1593 Act against Popish Recusants is printed in Prothero, *Select Statutes*,
p. 92.

44. La Rochefoucauld, *Maximes et reflexions diverses*, p. 42.

45. Kingdon, *The Execution of Justice*, p. 6.

46. The relationship of conscience and scandal is discussed in N. Iung,
"Scandale," in *Dictionnaire de théologie catholique*, vol. 14, pt. 1, pp. 1246–54.

47. Scandal, in other words, represents the rupture in the organization
and containment in cultural systems of taboo and of the unclean, as described by Douglas in *Purity and Danger*; the words of Bourdaloue on the
subject of the potentially uncontainable contamination of scandal are apposite: "Le scandale n'est pas un péché purement personnel, mais comme une
espèce de péché originel qui, se communiquant et se répandant, infecte
l'âme, non-seulement de son propre venin et de sa propre malice, mais de la
malice encore de ceux sur qui il s'étend et sur qui il se répand" ("Sermon sur
le scandale," in Bourdaloue, *Oeuvres de Bourdaloue*, p. 35). The phenomenon
of "passive scandal," which takes into account the informing perspective of
the observing conscience in the construction of scandal, is discussed in
N. Iung, "Scandale," in *Dictionnaire de théologie catholique*, vol. 14, pt. 1,
p. 1248.

48. For a discussion of the role of the *adiaphora* in the English reformation, see Verkamp, *The Indifferent Mean*.

49. More's discussion of the scrupulous conscience is in *A Dialogue of
Comfort against Tribulation*, in *The Complete Works*, vol. 12, p. 112. More's
praise of Jean Gerson is in *De Tristitia Christi*, in *The Complete Works*, vol.
14, pt. 1, p. 315.

50. Though the scrupulous and the lax conscience exist in technically
polarized states, Taylor's discussion of the dangers of the scrupulous conscience implies that the passage from one state to the other may occur imperceptibly: "If the scruple prevails upon his weakness so far as to rifle the
better reasons, the conscience loses its rule and its security, and the scruple
passes into a doubt, and the law into a consultation, and the judgment into

opinion, and the conscience into an undiscerning, undetermined faculty" (*Ductor Dubitantium*, vol. 9, p. 267).

51. "An Act to retain the Queen's subjects in obedience (1593)," in Prothero, *Select Statutes*, pp. 90–91.

52. Prothero, *Select Statutes*, p. 91.

Four

1. Bourdieu, *Outline of a Theory of Practice*, pp. 168–70.

2. Raymond Williams, *Marxism and Literature*, pp. 128–35, esp. pp. 133–34. See also Bryson's discussion of semiotic "practical activity" in *Vision and Painting*, p. 51.

3. Raymond Williams, "Structures of Feeling," in *Marxism and Literature*, pp. 128–35.

4. Unless otherwise indicated, the edition I am using is *Edmund Spenser: The Faerie Queene*.

5. Sidney, *A Defence of Poetry*, p. 27.

6. Interpretations that have provided a useful context for my reading, though with different emphases, are in Strong, *Gloriana*, pp. 95–107; Hotson, *Shakespeare by Hilliard*, pp. 29–32; and Goldberg, *Endlesse Worke*, pp. 153–57.

7. For basic discussions of iconography of the sieve, see Hotson, *Shakespeare by Hilliard*, p. 29, and Strong, *Gloriana*, p. 95.

8. For a sense of the various significances of the motto, see Strong, *Gloriana*, pp. 95–97, and Hotson, *Shakespeare by Hilliard*, p. 30.

9. See Chapter 1 for a discussion of the official connection in Elizabeth's discourse of power between the monarch and conscience.

10. I am grateful to Stephen Orgel for pointing out the political relevance of the mythologizing of Elizabeth's chastity at this point in her reign and for pointing out the connection between Elizabeth and the chaste Dido in Elizabeth's personal iconography. For an alternative reading of the Dido reference in the portrait, see Orgel, "Shakespeare and the Cannibals," pp. 58–62.

11. On the function of the ordeal, see Hexter, *Equivocal Oaths and Ordeals in Medieval Literature*.

12. See Strong, *Gloriana*, pp. 105–6, for a discussion of the iconography of imperialism and the central paradigm of Charles V in the iconography.

13. Camden, *Remaines*, p. 101.

14. The portrait thus appears to participate unambiguously in the ethos of similitude that Foucault sees as the fundamental conceptual orientation in the sixteenth century. See, especially, "The Prose of the World," in *The Order of Things*, pp. 17–45.

15. The appearance of "obviousness" relates to Bryson's discussion of the denotative, easily assimilable codes that reign in painterly discourse before Alberti; see *Vision and Painting*, pp. 60–68.

16. Strong, *The Cult of Elizabeth*, p. 43.

17. Bryson, *Vision and Painting*, p. 106.

18. The account is cited in Hotson, *Shakespeare by Hilliard*, p. 31.

19. Merritt Hughes gives a summary of the history of the Virgilian Dido in "Virgil and Spenser," p. 336.

20. *The Aeneid of Virgil*, pp. 760–67.

21. Neville Williams, *Elizabeth I*, p. 168.

22. Stubbs, *Gaping Gulf*, cited in Neville Williams, *Elizabeth I*, p. 201.

23. Petrarch, in *Lord Morley's Tryumphes of Fraunces Petrarke*, pp. 109, 115.

24. Sandys, "Upon the fourteenth book of Ovids Metamorphosis," in Ovid, *Ovids Metamorphosis English'd*, p. 262.

25. Ovid, *Heroides and Amores*, pp. 97–99.

26. Strong, *Gloriana*, p. 68.

Five

1. Unless otherwise indicated, the edition I am using is *Edmund Spenser: The Faerie Queene*.

2. The structure of conscience was double, insofar as *synteresis* existed in conjunction with *conscientia*, that part of conscience responsible for determining the practical application of general precepts according to the shifting weight of particularized contexts—the *circumstantiae* of a case.

3. Sidney, *A Defence of Poetry*, p. 47.

4. I use the word "narrator" rather than "poet" throughout my reading of the poem. The word "poet" implies the identity of the first-person speaker and the historical author; as I hope my analysis in Chapters 5–7 demonstrates, the poet represented as the "I" in the narrative is more precisely understood to be the narrator—to be a persona constituted in the text that the author uses to embody a particular perspective on the represented action. Chatman's discussion of Booth's distinction between the "implied author" and the narrator indicates how I see the relationship between Spenser and the narrator in the poem: "[The author] is 'implied,' that is, reconstructed by the reader from the narrative. He is not the narrator, but rather the principle that invented the narrator, along with everything else in the narrative, that stacked the cards in this particular way, had these things happen to these characters, in these words or images. Unlike the narrator, the implied author can *tell* us nothing. He, or better, *it* has no voice, no direct means of communicating. It instructs us silently, through the design

of the whole, with all the voices, by all the means it has chosen to let us learn" (Chatman, *Story and Discourse*, p. 148).

5. Perkins, *EPIEIKEIA*, p. 482.

6. For an account of Spenser's professional association with the courts of equity, see Graziani, "Elizabeth at Isis Church."

7. West, *Symboleography*, p. 174; McCutcheon, "Justice and Equity," p. 410. For background on the Tudor courts of equity, see C. Allen, *Law in the Making*, pp. 383–425, and Pollock, *Essays in the Law*, pp. 180–98.

8. McCutcheon, "Justice and Equity," p. 409; West, *Symboleography*, p. 173.

9. West, *Symboleography*, p. 174v.

10. "Equity is a Roguish thing, for Law wee have a measure know what to trust too. Equity is according to the conscience of him that is Chancellor, and as it is larger or narrower soe is equity. Tis all one as if they should make the Standard for the measure wee call A foot, to be the Chancellors foot; what an uncertain measure would this be; One Chancellor has a long foot another A short foot a third an indifferent foot; tis the same thing in the Chancellors Conscience" (Selden, *Table Talk*, p. 49).

11. West, *Symboleography*, p. 174v.

12. For useful background on the significance and history of *Doctor and Student* in Tudor England, see T. F. T. Plucknett's introduction in *St. German's Doctor and Student*, pp. xi–lxvii.

13. *St. German's Doctor and Student*, p. 97. For a discussion of the relation between divine and natural law in contemporary legal theory, see Pollock, "The History of the Law of Nature," in *Essays in the Law*, pp. 31–79.

14. See Vinogradoff, "Reason and Conscience in Sixteenth-century Jurisprudence."

15. Aristotle's discussion of equity in the *Nicomachean Ethics* is in book 5, chapter 10. Citations are from *Nicomachean Ethics*, pp. 141–42.

16. See the introduction to the Selden Society edition of *Doctor and Student* for an account of St. German's role in the development of equity in the discourse of common law. See also C. Allen, *Law in the Making*, pp. 406–15.

17. For an account of the theory of dereification see Berger and Luckmann, *The Social Construction of Reality*.

18. Eedes's sermon was published in *Six Learned and godly Sermons*, pp. 84–102.

19. Eedes, *Six Learned and godly Sermons*, p. 99.

20. Ibid., pp. 91–92.

21. The conceptual problem associated with equity—what Selden called its "Roguish," uncontainable, aspect—had for Eedes a specific political dimension: the absorption of common law jurisdiction by chancery lawyers,

who were technically responsible for administering equity. See McCutcheon, "Justice and Equity," pp. 405–10.

22. West, *Symboleography*, p. 175.

23. For a discussion of the relationship of the *ius gentium* to divine and positive law, see Pollock, *Essays in the Law*, pp. 31–79.

24. West, *Symboleography*, pp. 175–76.

25. The *pharmakon* of writing, in Derrida's argument, is the "best of all medicines," the action of pure and inviolable *logos*—"the *eidos*, truth, law, the *epistēmē*, dialectics, philosophy"—manifesting itself in opposition to the qualitatively different, both inferior and exterior, action of writing, which functions merely as a mnemonic device, a simulacrum of the *logos*. Writing, too, lays claim to the medicinal power of the *pharmakon*, by setting itself up as a compensatory supplement to the *logos*: as the mechanism enabling the *logos* to repeat itself, to extend, as it were, its life. (The point appears most clearly in the *Laws*, where, to borrow Derrida's phrase, "the immutable, petrified identity of writing . . . assures the law's permanence and identity with the vigilance of a guardian"—indeed, with the vigilance of conscience itself. For a view of the Greek sense of conscience as a nursemaid, see Pierce, *Conscience in the New Testament*, pp. 51–52.) Yet it is precisely in its capacity as a medicinal supplement that the *pharmakon* of writing appears to be a poison, a penetrating, contaminating agent. This action reveals itself in what is perhaps the most powerful charge against writing: the charge that writing is a displacement and an adulteration of the living memory (*mnēmē*) of the *logos* by its surrogate, the inert, rote repetition (*hypomnēsis*) of the *logos*. That the possibility of displacement, surrogation, and adulteration exists, however, suggests that the *logos* is not as inviolable as it would appear to be. Writing, the figure of repetition, exposes the breach that exists in the *logos*, which, if it is to subsist, must manifest itself through the figure of repetition—must engage in the action of writing itself, must attempt to fill up a space already possessed by writing, the space where the possibility of re-presenting (and misrepresenting) the *logos* exists. What writing contaminates, then, is the ethos of plenitude, "infinite self-presence," and the absolute otherness of the *logos*, by implicating itself in the structure of the *logos*. Thus we find Socrates in the *Phaedrus* referring to the *logos* as "another sort of writing: not merely as a knowing, living animate discourse, but as an inscription of truth in the soul." In other words, the action of the *pharmakon* dissolves the convenient network of absolute oppositions—inside/outside, speech/writing, good/evil—on which the fiction of the ontologically prior, hermetic structure of the *logos* depends. Indeed, the *pharmakon* itself has no fixed composition: "Having no stable essence, no 'proper' characteristics, it is not, in any sense of the word . . . a *substance*." It is rather "the prior

medium in which differentiation is produced." See Derrida, "The Pharmakon" and "Plato's Pharmacy," in *Dissemination*, pp. 95–117, 120–28.

26. See C. Allen, *Law in the Making*, pp. 406–10, for a discussion of the
alternative myths of the relation of equity to the law. Though it is not my
purpose to explore in greater detail the implication of either myth, it is
worth noting that the myth that places equity before the law has imperialist
connotations that would have been flattering to Elizabeth and certainly harmonious with the official discourse of power that honored the conscience
of the monarch as the supreme locus of truth and justice in the realm. On
the alternative (constitutionalist vs. imperialist) views of equity see also
Kermode's discussion of book 5 of *The Faerie Queene* in "'The Faerie
Queene' I and V," in *Shakespeare, Spenser, Donne*, pp. 33–59.

27. There are minor variations on this pattern of closure at the end of the
cantos. For example, at the end of canto 4, the Radigund/Artegall conflict
is only temporarily suspended after the first day of battle; but the canto does
have a sense of closure in that an agreement is made to join in single combat
and the terms are agreed upon: the "jurisdiction" of victor is to be absolute.
Canto 5 ends on a note of irresolution with Artegall's imprisonment and
Clarinda's double-speak machinations, prolonging his "thraldome"—but
note how the narrator's prolepsis seals this open-ended moment: the canto
ends by projecting the moment of closure to come: "Vntill his owne true
loue his freedome gayned, / Which in another Canto will be best contayned"
(5.5.57). In other words, a sense of "resolution" is maintained, even explicitly
insisted upon, precisely at a moment that could have been left unresolved.
The point of insisting on such images of closure, formal or otherwise, is to
do justice to Spenser's radical departure from the narrative norm his narrator
has set up when the political allegory turns to the scandal of the trial of
Mary Queen of Scots. Canto 9 ends with a double suspension, both formal
and thematic, in the representation of the muted Mercilla, who does not
speak the words of judgment the court is anticipating—and the suspension
is all the more powerful for appearing in a context of patterned narrative
resolutions. For a detailed discussion of this episode, see Chapter 7.

28. Foucault argued that the sixteenth century was predominantly an age
that focused on similitudes and resemblances, that its preoccupation was to
emphasize the overall unity, and the intelligible pattern, of the world under
God. See "The Prose of the World," in *The Order of Things*, pp. 17–45. The
argument turns essentially on epistemological and cosmological considerations; in the moral and ethical sphere, however, the notions of difference
and discreteness occupied an important place in the conceptual order of the
period. It was the project of casuistry to articulate the force of such notions
by promoting a method of examining the particularized formation and pur-

poses of a moral act; by privileging the circumstantial, contextual substance of a case; and by defining the epitome of cultural breakdown in terms of the triumph of the system of analogy, represented by the lax conscience.

29. See Fletcher's useful and persuasive analysis of the temple, in a different context from the one on which I focus, in *The Prophetic Moment*, pp. 259–304.

30. For a discussion of euhemerism see Seznec, "The Historical Tradition," in *The Survival of the Pagan Gods*, pp. 11–36.

31. Seznec, *The Survival of the Pagan Gods*, p. 22.

32. Sidney, *A Defence of Poetry*, p. 59.

33. Isis, we should note, was known as the creator of the alphabet and of writing; see Seznec, *The Survival of the Pagan Gods*, p. 16.

34. The sixteenth century had both senses of the word "invent"—whether "to come upon, find" or "to devise . . . fabricate" (*The Compact Edition of the Oxford English Dictionary*, vol. 1, p. 1476).

35. "Letter to Raleigh," in *Edmund Spenser: The Faerie Queene*, p. 16.

36. It should be noted that the concluding stanzas drift entirely into a "present" temporal reference, with the narrator entering the conventionally paired discourses of self-abasement and praise of the monarch; at this point, the discourse of euhemerism, with the perspective it offers of observing the process according to which official discourses come into being, is conveniently—perhaps necessarily—abandoned. By the time the reader has reached the end of book 5, it will be possible to see the very act of abandoning such a discourse, with its potentially scandalous insight, as part of a continually developing message in the poem about the politics of suppression that subtend canonical texts like *The Faerie Queene*.

Six

1. The contextual emphasis that casuistry promotes can be understood in terms of the Marxist philosophy of language that Bakhtin endorsed, which focused on the shaping roles of historical context and praxis in language. See Voloshinov, *Marxism and the Philosophy of Language*. Casuistry invokes as well the kind of attention to context that Smith discusses more generally in *On the Margins of Discourse*.

2. The interpretive project of casuistry amounts to a problematizing action, one that shows the conventional nature of its own methodology; to take the perspectival metaphor I use literally, casuistical analysis produces a narrative equivalent of the kind of destabilizing action that occurs in visual narrative when the Albertian laws of perspective become themselves a part of the subject matter rather than the "invisible" frame for the painted sub-

ject. See Chapter 4 for a discussion of this phenomenon in the "Siena Sieve" portrait of Elizabeth.

3. One of the assumptions governing my argument is that the Horatian understanding of decorum obstructs rather than helps one's understanding of how Spenser's narrative works. However "epic" in its general emphases and tone, Spenser's poem does not, it seems to me, rely on the broadly drawn ("skiagraphic") effects or global perspectives that Horace, among others, saw as characteristic features of the epic. Horace would have argued, as Trimpi puts it, that the "stylistic excellences appropriate to epic should not be made to fear a critic looking with a sharp eye for inaccuracies in the refined detail characteristic of paintings made for close inspection and of poems written for leisurely perusal" (*Muses of One Mind*, p. 101). As though leading the reader into a transgressive act of reading, Spenser's verse form and the conceptual frame of conscience both invite the kind of "close inspection" that the prescriptions of literary decorum would seem to exclude. For a further discussion of the Horatian notion of decorum in ancient literary theory, see Trimpi, pp. 130–63.

4. Unless otherwise indicated, the edition I am using is *Edmund Spenser: The Faerie Queene*.

5. Discussions of the political relevance of the Radigund episode as an allegory of the rivalry between Mary Queen of Scots and Elizabeth I are in Graziani, "Elizabeth at Isis Church"; and O'Connell, *Mirror and Veil*, pp. 140–47.

6. Lewis has a concise treatment of Knox's work in *English Literature in the Sixteenth Century*, pp. 199–200. For an illuminating discussion of the context of Elizabethan courtly and sexual politics that framed the work, see Montrose, "The Elizabethan Subject," pp. 303–40.

7. Spenser's use of the word "hungry" turns on the ambiguity of the word; the context Spenser indicates suggests he is thinking of "hungry" in the sense of "eaten with hunger or keen appetite" (*The Compact Edition of the Oxford English Dictionary*, vol. 2, p. 1394).

8. For a discussion of the disturbing effect of sites that blur distinctions between inside and outside, see Starobinski, "The Inside and the Outside."

9. The fundamental treatment of the distinction between showing and telling remains Booth's, in *The Rhetoric of Fiction*, pp. 3–20.

10. For a sense of the referential value of what the narrator's behavior indicates, see Montrose's analysis of the connection between political frustrations and sexual politics in Elizabeth's court, in "The Elizabethan Subject," pp. 307–18.

11. Elizabeth's peroration turned on the antithesis between the admission of conventional "sexly weakness" and the "delight" at knowing "that God

hath made me this instrument to maintain His truth and glory, and to defend this kingdom, as I said, from peril, dishonor, tyranny, and oppression" (from "The 'Golden Speech' of 1601," in Rice, *The Public Speaking of Queen Elizabeth*, p. 109).

12. How appropriate that the narrator should connect Britomart's newly acquired titles to the common preposition "as," which in this context takes on an ambiguous character: to read of Britomart's reign "as Princess" and of her subsequent adoration "as a Goddesse" is to perceive that the titles do not so much identify what Britomart is or has become, perhaps, as point up what she is understood by common consent to resemble. She becomes a princess provisionally, a goddess metaphorically, in both cases at one remove, at least, from the authentic embodiments of the designated powers.

13. The appropriate image at this point in the narrative, one that would convey a successful absorption of the tensions in the discourse of accomodation I have been discussing, would be the image of the hermaphrodite; but such an image is withheld at this point.

14. The text can be read, in other words, as illustrating a point of law and equity, with equity, suppressing its deregulatory aspect, yielding to the law and, in a parallel construction, with the individual conscience (including the monarch's) yielding to the public conscience as defined by the *doxa* of traditional (i.e., phallocentric) cultural norms.

15. That the "proper," the true, order of things in the narrative should be established by a woman—by a person outside the structure of power, just as equity is technically outside the structure of the law—illustrates how the *logos* of male dominance and authority depends on the self-cancellation of a female presence. Thus Britomart enacts the role of equity in its condition of existing after the law: she submits to a law that denies her own access to power. Yet Britomart also enacts the alternative conception of equity as existing prior to the law: it is by Britomart's action that the law of male domination can reassert itself and its "true," authorless status.

16. Another way of seeing how Spenser's narrative equivocates at this point is to see how it represents the very category of the poem's readership as sensitive to the winds of political necessity in shaping norms for interpretation. The designated community of "readers" of the Britomart/Artegall relationship is the Amazon community, who accept as natural (as "True Iustice") the kind of social and political organization that Artegall and Britomart import into their land. It is not necessary to argue that Spenser himself was self-consciously critical of the "True Iustice" brought to the land of the Amazons in order to see how the text draws an analogy between the conversion trope (whereby the Amazons "see the light") and the establishment of a

cultural context in which dissent is systematically silenced, whether for good or for ill.

17. The paradoxical character of the narrative—representing the process of making certain representations unintelligible—can be understood in terms of Raymond Williams's discussion of "structures of feeling." Spenser's text in book 5 works rather like the example Williams gives (*Marxism and Literature*, p. 34) of the "semantic figures" in works by Charles Dickens and Emily Brontë, which represent poverty not as a particularized symptom of "social failure or deviation" (i.e., the dominant structure of feeling in early Victorian ideology) but as a connecting instance of a "general condition" of isolation and exposure in society (an emergent structure of feeling). Spenser's narrative, at once traditional and iconoclastic, explores the ambiguity of the inexpressibility topos that Elizabeth herself used in her speeches to Parliament: the narrative makes its own apparent insufficiency the vehicle of its most nuanced and startling perspectives. The narrative constructs a logic of discrepancies and anomalies that opens up the possibility of reformulating traditional questions about the nature of the epic, of monarchical sovereignty, and so forth, by representing various existing social, political, and literary structures as caught up in an economy of power that depends on the force of scandal, of the suppression of demythologizing inquiries, to survive.

18. Useful background on the role of Artegall as the exemplar of equity can be found in Fletcher, *The Prophetic Moment*, pp. 228–87. See also Nelson, "The Legend of Justice: The Idol and the Crocodile," in *The Poetry of Edmund Spenser*, pp. 256–75.

19. In addition to the cited heuristic methods, Spenser's narrative also exploits the convention of the tournament, in canto 3, which celebrates the "spousals of faire Florimell" and enriches the narrative with a description of the stylized resolution to conflicts that the jousts represent. Given the narrative's recurrent treatment of the cultural crisis embodied in the Scots case, it is not surprising that the tournament should be capped by an encounter between two rival ladies, Florimell and her false semblant, who, brought together, create a dilemma that is both interpretive and political. Faced with the "true saint beside the image set," Florimell's spouse, Marinell, is virtually immobilized:

> Ne wist he what to thinke, or to deuise;
> But, like as one, whom feends had made affrayd,
> He long astonisht stood, ne ought he sayd,
> Ne ought he did, but with fast fixed eies
> He gazed stil vpon that snowy mayd;

Whom euer as he did the more auize,
The more to be true Florimell he did surmize.

(5.3.18)

Spenser expands the arena in which the monarch's medusan rhetoric of petrification operates. It is not merely the presence of Gloriana that controls
the responses of her subjects or viewers but Gloriana's representation as
well; more problematically, the petrified response is reconsidered in the narrative as a response not to divine-like authority but to a crisis of authority—in effect, a case of conscience brought about by rival claims to truth.
The particular resolution that Spenser brings to the crisis is both fully conventional and politically astute. The narrator brings a sudden and dramatic
end to the confusion by describing how the false Florimell melts away like
snow in the presence of the sun: a projection of the ardent wish (attributable
to more than Elizabeth alone) that Mary, like the false Florimell, "vanish
into nought" through no observable agency of destruction. It is worth noting, in this context, that the narrator allows himself the luxury of describing
in some detail the horrified response of the onlookers to the disappearance
of the threatening rival. It is not relief they feel but "senselesse horrour" at
the mystery of the sudden disappearance. The onlookers want to understand
the process that has brought about the resolution to the crisis, and they
remain frustrated in that desire. Spenser's own text will provide a cipher for
the kind of process that is instrumental in the maintenance of royal authority
and that the depicted onlookers themselves are not given access to in the
represented tournament.

20. For a discussion of the coercive rhetoric of conscience, see Chapter 1.

21. The omniscient character of conscience is perhaps nowhere more
clearly described than in William Perkins's phrase "Nay it is (as it were) a
little God sitting in the middle of men['s] hearts" (*A Discourse of Conscience*,
in *William Perkins, 1558–1602*, p. 9).

22. In his edition of *The Faerie Queene*, Gough notes: "In the watchfulness of Britomart and Talus, by which her life is saved, Spenser refers to the
activity of Elizabeth's spies, who repeatedly frustrated the designs of the
plotters" (cited in *The Works of Edmund Spenser*, p. 211). The connection
between Talus, the figure of conscience, and the allusion to the spy network
that Gough perceives is apposite in the context of my general argument
about the thematics of conscience in Elizabethan England.

23. Artegall's position in fact illustrates the force of equity as a sensitive
register of context in the determination of right and wrong. The reliable
means of discerning the difference between the two categories is not the
crude instrument of the scale but the "mind" and "eare" of the judge, Arte-

gall argues: "In the mind the doome of right must bee: / And so likewise words, the which be spoken, / The eare must be the ballance, to decree / And iudge, whether with truth or falshood they agree" (5.2.47). To amplify Artegall's own words, we might say he is acknowledging the importance of taking into account the acoustics of the uttered word in its specific context as a central guide in making sense of its meaning. The argument approaches that made by the casuists in analyzing the practice of mental reservation; see Chapter 2.

24. The Adicia narrative may be said to play on the ambiguous status of the entropic vision that the narrator articulates in the proem, referring obliquely as it does to the transformation of the wilderness from a lost yet yearned for idyllic space, the pre-lapsarian site of a past "golden age," to a degenerate space associated with a primitive ("saluage") culture temporally antecedent to the "civilized" world of Gloriana's court, which now embodies the idea of the recovered "golden age."

25. Thus constituted, icons function, of course, as central instruments in the sociology of religion; see Geertz, "Ethos, World View, and the Analysis of Sacred Symbols," in *The Interpretation of Cultures*, pp. 126–41.

26. The selectivity of perception I refer to works as a narrative embodiment of what Burke referred to as "terministic screens," with the qualification that Burke's language-oriented description needs to include the broader semiotic map I have sketched in showing the identifying marks of the discourse of conscience in political, social, and religious words and behavior. "Not only does the nature of our terms affect the nature of our observations, in the sense that the terms direct the attention to one field rather than to another. Also, many of the 'observations' are but implications of the particular terminology in terms of which the observations are made" (*Language as Symbolic Action*, p. 46).

27. For a discussion of Bourdaloue's analysis of the lax conscience, see Chapter 3.

28. Gough gives a convenient summary of the political allegory of Burbon as Henry of Navarre; see *The Works of Edmund Spenser*, pp. 259–60.

29. Perkins borrows Thomas Aquinas's distinction between concealment and lying: "It is one thing to speak against our knowledge, and another to speake that which we knowe. And concealements, if there be a reasonable cause, and if it be not necessarie for us to reveale the thing concealed, are not unlawfull. Thus Abram speakes the truth in part, calling Sara his sister, and conceales it in part, not confessing her to be his wife. Gen. 12. 10. Thus Samuel by Gods appointment reveales that he came to Gilgall to offer sacrifice, and conceales the annointment of David, that he might save his life. 1 Sam. 16.5" (*An Exposition*, p. 211). Perkins's understanding of "fayning" in

the same document is apposite here: "Some call [it] simulation: not dissembling, but rather sembling (if I may so terme it). And that is, when something is spoken not contrary, but beside, or divers to that which we thinke. And this kind of fayning, if it be not to the prejudice of truyth, against the glorie of God, and the good of our neighbor, and have some convenient and reasonable cause, is not unlawfull. . . . Josua having besieged Ai, meant not to fliew, yet doth he faine a flight, that he might draw his enemies out of the citie and destroy them. Jos. 8.5. There is a kind of deceit called 'dolus bonus,' that is, 'a good deceit,' and of this kind was the act of Josua. Thus Physitians for their good, use to deceive the senses of their impotent patients. Thus parents insinuate unto their children, terrible things, of the beare, and the bull-begger, that they may keepe them from places of hurt and danger. And this may be done without fault, for it is one thing to contrary the truth, and another to speake or doe something diverse unto it without contrarietie" (p. 211).

30. An illuminating discussion of the rhetoric of the absolute monarch's control over temporality and reading is in Marin, *Le portrait du roi.*

31. "Now this extremity of the law, is in this case (when there is good cause, why in a Christian consideration of some circumstances, this justice should be mitigated) so farre from justice, as indeed it is flate injustice. And herein is the proverbe true: *summa ius, summa injuria*: that is, the extremitie of the law is extreme injury. And of this doth the Holy Ghost meane, Eccles. 7.7, Bee not over just, that is, presse not justice too far, nor urge it too extremely in all cases, lest sometimes you make the name of justice, a cover for cruelty" (Perkins, *EPIEIKEIA*, p. 61).

32. We can see here the narrative relevance of the metaphor for equity of the Lesbian rule: the narrative enacts equity's power to perform as a flexible interpretive measure, one attuned to the shifting dynamic of power relations behind the concept of "True Iustice."

33. *The Compact Edition of the Oxford English Dictionary*, vol. 1, p. 1970.

34. For a discussion of the political allegory of the Grantorto episode, see Bennett, *The Evolution of The Faerie Queene*, pp. 194–95.

35. Natalis Comes's commentary is cited in *The Works of Edmund Spenser*, p. 229.

36. For an alternative view of Hippolytus, see Devereux's reading of Euripides' play, in which he sees the youth as a "sex phobic," in *The Character of the Euripidean Hippolytus.* Spenser himself gives his readers a model for interpreting Hippolytus in book 1, in which the youth appears as the innocent victim of his "wanton stepdame's" false accusations of treason (1.5.36–39).

Seven

1. Unless otherwise indicated, the edition I am using is *Edmund Spenser: The Faerie Queene*.

2. Cain, *Praise in The Faerie Queene*, pp. 136–41.

3. For a discussion of the *pharmakon*-like property of equity, see Chapter 5.

4. The allegory, in other words, plays on the force of the word "person" in Renaissance culture as a theatrical role or performance. Mercilla's presence is not only an allegorical embodiment of equity and of Elizabeth but a narrative substitute for the absent Gloriana and, subsuming these associations, a representation of the role-playing of absolute power involved in the machinery of royal spectacle. For a discussion of the connotations of "private" and "public" spheres in the word "person," see Goldberg, *James I and the Politics of Literature*, pp. 148–55.

5. Lewis, *English Literature in the Sixteenth Century*, p. 393.

6. Though the prefix "anti" is from the Greek for "opposite" and "ante" from the Latin for "in front of," "anti" also functions as a variant of "ante"; see *The Compact Edition of the Oxford English Dictionary*, vol. 1, p. 92.

7. For a discussion of the association of mental reservation and the lax conscience, see Chapter 2.

8. The ambiguity of the image of the court opens up the larger question of the narrative's resistance to a stable generic identity: the shifting perspective of the court mirrors the interplay of encomium and satire in the text.

9. The concept of liminality is treated in Turner, *The Ritual Process*, pp. 94–130.

10. See Foucault's discussion of the ambiguous status of the spectacle of public punishment in *Discipline and Punish*, pp. 45–47.

11. For a discussion of various traditions of secret knowledge in the Renaissance, see Haydn, *The Counter-Renaissance*. See also D. C. Allen, "The Symbolic Wisdom of the Ancient Egyptians," in *Mysteriously Meant*, pp. 107–33.

12. The Latin *fons* also alludes to the baptismal font, the site of the healing action of the divine word through baptism. Thus conceived, the poet's words appear as a parodic version of the divine word and thus as scandalous, as the text indicates.

13. "In one crucial detail, the trial of Duessa does not replicate Mary's. It presents Mercilla in the seat of judgment, and thereby implicates her. Elizabeth, on the other hand, had absented herself from Mary's trial just as she had avoided meeting Mary during all the years of her English imprisonment" (Goldberg, *James I and the Politics of Literature*, p. 12).

14. In the trial Mary did, in fact, use the argument about the hazard of

alienating foreign powers that her death might provoke, but the poem transforms the context in which she made the argument: no longer is the point part of a sustained legal argument, as it was in the actual trial; instead it figures as part of the tactics of female wiles. In other words, the resonance of a legitimizing discourse is located in the position of the prosecution alone. What the poem shows is how the interpretation of the context in which an utterance is made radically alters the significance of the utterance itself. See "Language, Speech, and Utterance" and "Verbal Interaction" in Voloshinov, *Marxism and the Philosophy of Language*, pp. 65–98.

15. Sidney, *A Defence of Poetry*, p. 30.

16. Ibid., p. 32.

17. Examples of the social practice illustrating the association of trial and spectacle are in Bellamy, *The Tudor Law of Treason*, pp. 132–38.

18. See Chapter 1.

19. *The Compact Edition of the Oxford English Dictionary*, vol. 2, p. 2107. The citation is from Gabelhouer's *Book of Physike* (1599). There is one sense in which the word "perling" could be read as corroborating the book's canonical message: "to render clear and pellucid" (*The Compact Edition of the Oxford English Dictionary*, vol. 2, p. 2107). Yet the narrative's earlier association of the word *clarus* with hidden deception, in the figure of Clarinda, would undercut the impact of this alternative sense of the word. See Chapter 5.

20. A case in point is O'Connell's judgment about the damaging effects on the poem's "mythic fiction" of Spenser's decision to construct an "increasingly close allegorization of the trial of the Queen of Scots," in *Mirror and Veil*, pp. 151–56.

21. See Cain's illuminating discussion of this stanza, in which he sees worked out in miniature the poem's ironic juxtaposition of its idealized encomiastic program and a recalcitrant political reality, in *Praise in The Faerie Queene*, p. 142. One way to measure the degree to which the poem problematizes the relationship of cause and effect between supposed criminal action and the public spectacle of punishment is to read Duessa's end against the example of Munera in canto 2. The details of Munera's fate are boldly drawn: her hands and feet are "Chopt off, and nayld on high that all might them behold" (5.2.26). Later she is thrown over the castle wall, into the "flood . . . / And there her drowned in the durty mud" (5.2.27).

22. The description of Mercilla's response to Duessa's "fall" gives us an indication of the implicit directive to misread that the court in stanza 50 is depicted as having understood. In "ruing her wilfull fall" the verb is polysemous: it means not only to repent of a personal transgression or "to regard or think of (an event, fact, etc.) with sorrow or regret" but also "to wish that (something) had never taken place or existed" (*The Compact Edi-*

tion of the Oxford English Dictionary, vol. 2, p. 2596). The court's response in stanza 50 suggests the fulfillment of the wish—to behave as if the sentence of death had never been acted on.

23. Perkins, *EPIEIKEIA*, p. 62.

24. O'Connell, *Mirror and Veil*, p. 149.

25. The word "fact" could mean "an action, deed, course of conduct (L. *factum*)" and, among other meanings, "an evil deed, a crime. In the 16th and 17th century the commonest sense" (*The Compact Edition of the Oxford English Dictionary*, vol. 1, p. 947). We should note that Spenser's use of the phrase "haynous fact" after "haynous cryme" is itself ambiguous. The second phrase could be merely an instance of Spenser's intensifying descriptive habit of doubling. But we cannot reasonably exclude the more challenging alternative: that Spenser was writing at a time when the ambiguity of the word "fact" was turning it into a word endowed with a specific semantic range of flexibility and that what Spenser's alteration of "cryme" to "fact" indicates is a growing awareness that "fact" could be read, by itself, in its neutral sense—in other words, that Spenser wanted both to reorient the reader toward the still-current sense of "fact" as "crime" and to problematize that sense.

26. *Sir Fulke Greville's The Life of Sir Philip Sidney*, pp. 218–19.

27. Camden, *The History of the Most Renowned and Victorious Princess Elizabeth*, pp. 5–6.

Envoy

1. Puttenham, *The Arte of English Poesie*, p. 234.

2. Norris, *Deconstruction*, p. 49.

3. Garnet, *A Treatise of Equivocation*, p. 17.

4. Bakhtin, *The Dialogic Imagination*, p. 276.

5. To be sure, the casuists themselves, committed to the heuristic potential of casuistry, argued that the discourse of *conscientia* must be reducible to the norms posited in *synteresis*. They prescribed a normative operation to the relationship between the two parts—the two voices—of conscience by invoking, as a model, the relationship between the major and minor premises of the syllogism. Yet this very operation, while intended to insure the primacy of *synteresis* in defining the self, also made it impossible to consider *synteresis* in isolation from *conscientia*. That is, the operation tacitly recognized the contextual underpinning of *synteresis*—its suppressed dialogic relation to *conscientia*.

6. Thus, at the end of a vexing case concerning the "liklihood" of committing sin by breaking a "solemne oath," taken "by feare and compulsion"

at the hands of thieves, to aid the criminals and "withall never disclose the parties," William Perkins wrote: "For my part, I leave it in suspense" (*The Whole Treatise of Cases of Conscience*, in *William Perkins, 1558–1602*, p. 109).

7. The principal account of Gyges is in Plato's *Republic* (2:359), in Hamilton and Cairns, *The Collected Dialogues of Plato*, pp. 606–8.

8. Morton, *A Full Satisfaction*, p. 84.

9. Bakhtin, *The Dialogic Imagination*, p. 291.

10. Ibid., p. 296.

11. The connection I make between Spenser's epic and the novel was not one Bakhtin would likely have made because of the way he polarized the discourse of the epic and of the novel, as he did the media of poetry and prose: "In the epic there is one unitary and singular belief system. In the novel there are many such belief systems, with the hero generally acting within his own system. For this reason there are no speaking persons in the epic who function as representatives of different languages—in the epic, the speaker is, in essence, solely the author alone, and discourse is a single, unitary authorial discourse" ("Discourse in the Novel," in *The Dialogic Imagination*, p. 334). What I have tried to show in my reading of book 5 is how Spenser's orchestration of the narrative structure permits us to see the agency of the author as distinct from that of the represented narrator; it is the gap between narrator and author that initiates the fragmenting of the "single, unitary authorial discourse" of the epic in Spenser's narrative.

12. *The Compact Edition of the Oxford English Dictionary*, vol. 2, p. 2305.

13. Morson, "The Heresiarch of *Meta*," p. 422.

14. The phrase "truths of laughter" is cited in ibid.

Works Cited

Alciati, Andrea. *Emblemata cum commentariis.* Ed. Claude Mignault. Padua: Pauli Frambotti Bibliopolae, 1661.

Allen, C. *Law in the Making.* 1927. Rev. ed. Oxford: Clarendon Press, 1964.

Allen, D. C. *Mysteriously Meant: The Rediscovery of Pagan Symbolism and Allegorical Interpretation in the Renaissance.* Baltimore: Johns Hopkins University Press, 1970.

Allen, William. *A Briefe Historie of the Glorious Martyrdom of Twelve Reverend Priests, Father Edmund Campion and His Companions, with Contemporary Verses by the Venerable Henry Walpole, & the Earliest Engravings of the Martyrdom.* Ed. J. H. Pollen, S.J. London: Burns & Oates, 1908.

Aristotle. *Nicomachean Ethics.* Trans. Martin Ostwald. Indianapolis: Bobbs-Merrill, 1962.

Athanasius. "Apology of our Holy Father Athanasius, Archbishop of Alexandria, in vindication of his flight, when he was persecuted by Duke Syrianus." In *Historical Tracts of S. Athanasius, Archbishop of Alexandria.* A Library of Fathers of the Holy Catholic Church, Anterior to the Division of the East and West. Oxford: John Henry Parker, 1843. 188–209.

Augustine. *Saint Augustine: Treatises on Various Subjects.* Ed. Roy J. Deferrari. The Fathers of the Church Series, vol. 16. New York: Fathers of the Church, 1952.

Austin, John. *How to Do Things with Words.* Ed. J. O. Urmson and Marina Sbrisà. 2nd ed. Cambridge: Harvard University Press, 1975.

Aveling, Hugh. *The Handle and the Axe: The Catholic Recusants in England from Reformation to Emancipation.* London: Blond & Briggs, 1976.

———. *Northern Catholics: the Catholic Recusants of the North Riding of Yorkshire, 1558–1790.* London: Chapman, 1966.

Bacon, Francis. *The Works of Francis Bacon.* Ed. Basil Montague. Vol. 2. Philadelphia: Parry & McMillan, 1859. 3 vols.

Bakhtin, M. M. *The Dialogic Imagination.* Trans. Caryl Emerson and Michael Holquist. Ed. Michael Holquist. Austin: University of Texas Press, 1981.

Barthes, Roland. *Sade, Fourier, Loyola.* Trans. Richard Miller. New York: Hill and Wang, 1976.

Basset, Bernard, S.J. *The English Jesuits: From Campion to Martindale.* New York: Herder and Herder, 1968.

Bellamy, John. *The Tudor Law of Treason.* London: Routledge & Kegan Paul, 1979.

Bennett, Josephine W. *The Evolution of The Faerie Queene.* 1942. Reprint. New York: Burt Franklin, 1962.

Berger, P. L., and T. Luckmann. *The Social Construction of Reality: A Treatise in the Sociology of Knowledge.* Garden City, N.Y.: Doubleday, 1966.

Bernard of Clairvaux. *The Works of Bernard of Clairvaux, Treatises II.* Trans. M. Ambrose Conway, OCSO. Cistercian Fathers Series, no. 13. Washington, D.C.: Cistercian Publications, 1977.

Bickerman, E. J. *Four Strange Books of the Bible.* New York: Schocken, 1984.

Bilson, Thomas. *The true difference betweene Christian subiection and unchristian rebellion.* Oxford: J. Barnes, 1585.

Boethius. *The Consolation of Philosophy.* Trans. Richard Green. The Library of Liberal Arts. Indianapolis: Bobbs-Merrill, 1962.

Booth, Wayne. *The Rhetoric of Fiction.* 2nd ed. Chicago: University of Chicago Press, 1983.

Bourdaloue, Louis. *Oeuvres de Bourdaloue.* Vol. 3. Paris: Firmin Didot Frères, 1840. 3 vols.

Bourdieu, Pierre. *Outline of a Theory of Practice.* Cambridge: Cambridge University Press, 1977.

Brosnan, J. Brodie. "Mental Restriction and Equivocation." *Irish Ecclesiastical Record* 16:2 (1920): 461–70.

Browne, Sir Thomas. *The Works of Sir Thomas Browne.* Ed. Geoffrey Keynes. Vol. 2. London: Faber & Gwyer, Ltd., 1928. 6 vols.

Bryson, Norman. *Vision and Painting: The Logic of the Gaze.* New Haven: Yale University Press, 1983.

Burke, Kenneth. *Language as Symbolic Action: Essays on Life, Literature and Method.* Berkeley: University of California Press, 1966.

C., R. *A Declaration of the ends of traytors and false conspirators against the state.* London: J. Charlewood for T. Gubbins at T. Newman, 1587.

Cain, Thomas. *Praise in The Faerie Queene.* Lincoln: University of Nebraska Press, 1978.

Calvin, John. *Calvin: Institutes of the Christian Religion.* Trans. Ford Lewis Battles. Ed. John T. McNeill. Library of Christian Classics, vols. 20 and 21. Philadelphia: Westminster Press, 1960.

Camden, William. *The History of the Most Renowned and Victorious Princess*

Elizabeth, Late Queen of England. Ed. and intro. Wallace T. MacCaffrey. Chicago: University of Chicago Press, 1970.

———. *Remaines concerning Britain.* London: J. R. Smith, 1870.

Caraman, Philip. *The Other Face: Catholic Life Under Elizabeth I.* London: Longmans, 1960.

Castiglione, Baldesar. *The Book of the Courtier.* Trans. Charles S. Singleton. Garden City, N.J.: Anchor Books, 1959.

Cave, Terence. *The Cornucopian Text: Problems of Writing in the French Renaissance.* Oxford: Clarendon Press, 1974.

Certain Sermons or Homilies (1547) and A Homily against Disobedience and Wilful Rebellion (1570). Ed. Ronald B. Bond. Toronto: University of Toronto Press, 1987.

Chatman, Seymour. *Story and Discourse: Narrative Structure in Fiction and Film.* Ithaca: Cornell University Press, 1978.

Clancy, Thomas H. *Papist Pamphleteers: The Allen-Parsons Party and the Political Thought of the Counter-Reformation in England, 1572–1615.* Chicago: Loyola University Press, 1964.

Cobbett's Complete Collection of State Trials. Vol. 1 London: R. Bagshaw, 1809. 10 vols.

Derrida, Jacques. *Dissemination.* Trans. Barbara Johnson. Chicago: University of Chicago Press, 1981.

Devereux, George. *The Character of the Euripidean Hippolytus.* Chico, Calif.: Scholars Press, 1985

Dodds, E. R. *The Greeks and the Irrational.* Berkeley: University of California Press, 1951.

Douglas, Mary. *In the Active Voice.* London: Routledge & Kegan Paul, 1982.

———. *Purity and Danger: An Analysis of Concepts of Pollution and Taboo.* Harmondsworth: Penguin, 1970.

Earle, John. *Microcosmographie; or, A Piece of the World Discovered; in Essays and Characters.* Bristol: W. Crofton Hemmons, n.d.

Eedes, Richard. *Six Learned and godly Sermons.* London: A. Islip for E. Bishop, 1604.

Elton, G. R. *England Under the Tudors.* 2nd ed. London: Methuen, 1974.

———. "Informing for Profit: A Sidelight on Tudor Methods of Law-Enforcement." *Cambridge Historical Journal* 11 (1953): 149–67.

———. *Reform and Reformation: England, 1509–1558.* Cambridge: Harvard University Press, 1977.

Fletcher, Angus. *The Prophetic Moment: An Essay on Spenser.* Chicago: University of Chicago Press, 1971.

Foucault, Michel. *The Archaeology of Knowledge.* Trans. A. M. Sheridan Smith. New York: Pantheon Books, 1972.

320

Works Cited

———. *Discipline and Punish: The Birth of the Prison.* Trans. Alan Sheridan. New York: Vintage Books, 1979.

———. *The Order of Things: An Archaeology of the Human Sciences.* New York: Vintage Books, 1973.

Fülöp-Millar, René. *The Power and Secret of the Jesuits.* Trans. F. S. Flint and D. F. Tait. New York: Viking Press, 1930.

Garnet, Henry. *A Treatise of Equivocation.* Ed. David Jardine. London: Longman, Brown, Green, and Longmans, 1851.

Geertz, Clifford. *The Interpretation of Cultures.* New York: Basic Books, 1973.

Girard, René. *Violence and the Sacred.* Trans. Patrick Gregory. Baltimore: Johns Hopkins University Press, 1977.

Goldberg, Jonathan. *Endlesse Worke.* Baltimore: Johns Hopkins University Press, 1981.

———. *James I and the Politics of Literature.* Stanford, Calif.: Stanford University Press, 1989.

Graziani, René. "Elizabeth at Isis Church." *PMLA* 79 (1964): 378–83.

Greaves, Richard L., ed. *Elizabeth I, Queen of England.* Problems in European Civilization. Lexington, Mass.: D. C. Heath, 1974.

Greville, Sir Fulke. *Sir Fulke Greville's The Life of Sir Philip Sidney.* Ed. Nowell Smith. 1907. Reprint. Folcroft, Pa.: Folcroft Library, 1971.

Haigh, Christopher. *Reformation and Resistance in Tudor Lancashire.* London: Cambridge University Press, 1975.

Hall, Joseph. *The Works of the Right Reverend Joseph Hall, D.D.* Ed. Philip Wynter, D.D. Vol. 7. Oxford: Oxford University Press, 1863. 10 vols.

Haydn, Hiram. *The Counter-Renaissance.* New York: Scribner, 1950.

Hexter, Ralph. *Equivocal Oaths and Ordeals in Medieval Literature.* Cambridge: Harvard University Press, 1975.

Hicks, L., S.J., ed. *Letters and Memorials of Father Robert Persons, S.J.* London: Catholic Record Society, 1942.

Holinshed's Chronicles of England, Scotland, and Ireland. Vol. 4. London: J. Johnson et al., 1808. 4 vols.

Holmes, P. J. *Resistance and Compromise: The Political Thought of the Elizabethan Catholics.* Cambridge: Cambridge University Press, 1982.

———, ed. *Elizabethan Casuistry.* London: Catholic Record Society, 1981.

Hotson, Leslie. *Shakespeare by Hilliard.* Berkeley: University of California Press, 1977.

Hughes, Merritt. "Virgil and Spenser." *University of California Publications in English* 2 (1928): 263–418.

Hughes, Paul L., and Robert F. Fries, eds. *Crown and Parliament in Tudor and Stuart England: A Documentary Constitutional History, 1485–1714.* New York: G. P. Putnam's Sons, 1959.

Hughes, Paul L., and James F. Larkin, eds. *Tudor Royal Proclamations.* Vol. 2. New Haven: Yale University Press, 1964. 3 vols.

Jonsen, Albert R., and Stephen Toulmin. *The Abuse of Casuistry: A History of Moral Reasoning.* Berkeley: University of California Press, 1988.

Kantorowicz, Ernst H. *The King's Two Bodies: A Study in Medieval Political Theology.* Princeton: Princeton University Press, 1957.

————. "Mysteries of State: An Absolutist Concept and Its Late Medieval Origins." *Harvard Theological Review* 48 (1955): 65–91.

Kelly, Kevin T. *Conscience: Dictator or Guide? A Study in Seventeenth-Century English Protestant Moral Theology.* Studies in Theology and Church History. London: Geoffrey Chapman, 1967.

Kermode, Frank. *Shakespeare, Spenser, Donne.* London: Routledge & Kegan Paul, 1971.

King, John. *A Sermon preached the 5th of November, 1607.* Oxford: J. Barnes, 1607.

Kingdon, Robert M., ed. *The Execution of Justice in England by William Cecil and A True, Sincere, and Modest Defense of English Catholics by William Allen.* Folger Shakespeare Library. Ithaca, N.Y.: Cornell University Press, 1971.

Knox, Thomas Francis, ed. *The First and Second Diaries of the English College, Douay, and an Appendix of Unpublished Documents.* London: D. Nutt, 1878.

Kreihing, Johannes, S.J. *Emblemata Ethico-Politica, carmine explicata.* Antwerp: I. Meursium, 1661.

La Rochefoucauld. *Maximes et reflexions diverses.* Ed. Jean-Pol Caput. Nouvelles Classiques Larousse. Paris: Librairie Larousse, 1975.

Lea, H. C. *A History of Auricular Confession and Indulgences in the Latin Church.* Vol. 2. Philadelphia: Lea Brothers & Co., 1896. 3 vols.

Lewis, C. S. "Conscience and Conscious." In *Studies in Words.* 2nd ed. London: Cambridge University Press, 1964. 181–213.

————. *English Literature in the Sixteenth Century, Excluding Drama.* Oxford: Oxford University Press, 1954.

Lodge, Thomas. *Wit's Miserie and the World's Madnesse.* London: A. Islip, sold by C. Burby, 1596.

Luke, Mary M. *Gloriana: The Years of Elizabeth I.* New York: Coward, McCann & Geoghegan, 1973.

Luther, Martin. *Martin Luther: Selections from His Writings.* Ed. John Dillenberger. Garden City, N.Y.: Anchor Books, 1961.

Lydgate, John. *Lydgate's Fall of Princes.* Ed. Dr. Henry Bergen. Early English Text Society. Extra Series, no. 222. London: Oxford University Press, 1924.

MacMullen, Ramsey. *Christianizing the Roman Empire*. New Haven: Yale University Press, 1984.

McCutcheon, J. Wilson. "Justice and Equity in the English Morality Play." *Journal of the History of Ideas* 19 (1956): 405–10.

Malloch, A. C. "Father Henry Garnet's Treatise of Equivocation." *Recusant History* 15 (Oct. 1981): 387–95.

Marin, Louis. *Le portrait du roi*. Paris: Editions de Minuit, 1981.

Mattingly, Garrick. "William Allen and Catholic Propaganda in England." *Travaux d'Humanisme et Renaissance* 28 (1957): 325–39.

Montrose, Louis. "The Elizabethan Subject and the Spenserian Text." In *Literary Theory / Renaissance Texts*. Ed. Patricia Parker and David Quint. Baltimore: Johns Hopkins University Press, 1986. 303–40.

Moore, Sally Falk. *Law as Process: An Anthropological Approach*. London: Routledge & Kegan Paul, 1978.

More, St. Thomas. *The Complete Works of St. Thomas More*. Ed. Louis L. Martz and Frank Manley. Vols. 12 and 14. New Haven: Yale University Press, 1976. 14 vols.

Morey, Adrian. *The Catholic Subjects of Elizabeth I*. Totowa, N.J.: Rowman and Littlefield, 1978.

Morris, John, ed. *The Troubles of Our Catholic Forefathers*. Vols. 2 and 3. London: Burns & Oates, 1877. 3 vols.

Morson, Gary Saul. "The Heresiarch of *Meta*." *PTL: A Journal for Descriptive Poetics and Theory of Literature* 3 (1978): 407–27.

Morton, Thomas. *A Full Satisfaction concerning a Double Romish Iniquitie; hainous Rebellion, and more then heathenish Aequivocation*. London: Richard Field for Edmond Weaver, 1606.

Mullaney, Steven. "Lying Like Truth: Riddle, Representation and Treason in Renaissance England." *ELH* 47 (1980): 32–47.

Munday, Anthony. *A Discoverie of Edmund Campion, and his Confederates, their most horrible and traiterous practises, against her Maiesties most royall person, and the Realme*. London: Edward White, 1582.

Murphy, James. *Rhetoric in the Middle Ages*. Berkeley: University of California Press, 1974.

Naunton, Sir Robert. *Fragmenta Regalia: Memoirs of Elizabeth, Her Court and Favourites*. London: Charles Baldwin, 1824.

Neale, J. E. *Elizabeth I and Her Parliaments*. 2 vols. London: Jonathan Cape, 1953, 1957.

Nelson, William. *The Poetry of Edmund Spenser*. New York: Columbia University Press, 1963.

Nepos, Cornelius. *The Lives of Illustrious Men, Written in Latin by Corne-*

lius Nepos and Done into English by Several Hands. Oxford: H. Crutten-don, 1684.

Nicolas, Nicholas Harris. *Life of William Davison.* London: J. Nicholas & Son, 1823.

Norris, Christopher. *Deconstruction: Theory and Practice.* New York: Methuen, 1982.

O'Connell, Michael. *Mirror and Veil: The Historical Dimension of Spenser's Faerie Queene.* Chapel Hill: University of North Carolina Press, 1977.

Orgel, Stephen. "Shakespeare and the Cannibals." In *Cannibals, Witches, and Divorce: Estranging the Renaissance.* Ed. Marjorie Garber. Selected Papers from the English Institute, 1985. New Series, no. 11. Baltimore: Johns Hopkins University Press, 1987. 40–66.

Ovid. *Heroides and Amores.* Trans. Grant Showerman. The Loeb Classical Library. 1914. 2nd ed. Cambridge: Harvard University Press, 1977.

———. *Ovids Metamorphosis English'd, mythologized, and represented in figures.* . . . Trans. George Sandys. London: J. L. for Andrew Hebb, 1640.

Pascal, Blaise. *The Provincial Letters.* Trans. A. J. Krailsheimer. Harmondsworth: Penguin, 1967.

Pemberton, Caroline, ed. *Queen Elizabeth's Englishings of Boethius, Plutarch and Horace.* Early English Text Society. Original Series, no. 113. Millwood, N.Y.: Kraus Reprint, 1981.

Perkins, William. *An exposition upon the five first chapters of the Epistle to the Galatians.* Cambridge: J. Legat, 1604.

———. *EPIEIKEIA, or a Treatise of Christian Equity and Moderation.* In *The Work of William Perkins.* Ed. Ian Breward. Abingdon, Berkshire: Sutton Courtenay Press, 1970. 477–510.

———. *William Perkins, 1558–1602.* Ed. Thomas F. Merrill. Nieuwkoop: B. De Graaf, 1966.

Persons, Robert. *A treatise tending to mitigation.* 1607. Ilkley: Scolar Press, 1977.

Petrarch. *Lord Morley's Tryumphes of Fraunces Petrarke: The First English Translation of the Trionfi.* Ed. D. D. Carnicelli. Cambridge: Harvard University Press, 1971.

Petti, Anthony G., ed. *Recusant Documents from the Ellesmere Manuscripts.* London: Catholic Record Society, 1968.

Pierce, C. A. *Conscience in the New Testament.* Studies in Theology. London: SCM Press, Ltd., 1958.

Plato. *The Collected Dialogues of Plato.* Ed. Edith Hamilton and Huntingdon Cairns. Princeton: Princeton University Press, 1961.

Plowden, Alison. *Danger to Elizabeth: The Catholics Under Elizabeth I.* New York: Stein & Day, 1973.

Plutarch. *The Lives of the Noble Grecians and Romanes.* Trans. Thomas North. London: Richard Field for Thomas Wight, 1595.

Pollen, J. H., S.J., ed. *Miscellanea II.* London: Catholic Record Society, 1906.

———. *Unpublished Documents Relating to the English Martyrs.* London: Catholic Record Society, 1908.

Pollock, Sir Frederick. *Essays in the Law.* London: MacMillan, Ltd., 1922.

Potts, Timothy C. *Conscience in Medieval Philosophy.* Cambridge: Cambridge University Press, 1980.

Prothero, G. W., ed. *Select Statutes and Other Constitutional Documents Illustrative of the Reigns of Elizabeth and James I.* Oxford: Clarendon Press, 1894.

Puttenham, George. *The Arte of English Poesie.* Kent English Reprints: The Renaissance. Kent: Kent State University Press, 1970.

Rait, Robert S., and Anne I. Cameron, eds. *King James's Secret: Negotiations Between Elizabeth I and James VI Relating to the Execution of Mary Queen of Scots, from the Warrender Papers.* London: Nisbet, 1927.

Read, Conyers. *Lord Burghley and Queen Elizabeth.* London: Jonathan Cape, 1960.

———. *Mr. Secretary Walsingham and Queen Elizabeth.* Vol. 2. Oxford: Clarendon Press, 1925. 3 vols.

Rice, George P., Jr., ed. *The Public Speaking of Queen Elizabeth: Selections from Her Official Addresses.* New York: Columbia University Press, 1951.

Rose, Elliot. *Cases of Conscience: Alternatives Open to Recusants and Puritans Under Elizabeth I.* London: Cambridge University Press, 1975.

Rostenberg, Leona. *The Minority Press and the English Crown: A Study in Repression, 1558–1625.* Niewkoop: B. De Graaf, 1971.

St. German, Christopher. *St. German's Doctor and Student.* Ed. T. F. T. Plucknett and J. L. Barton. London: Selden Society, 1974.

Sanderson, Robert. *Twelve Sermons.* London: R. B. for R. Dawlman, 1637.

Sandys, Edwin. *The Sermons of Edwin Sandys.* Ed. John Ayre. The Parker Society Publications, vol. 41. Cambridge: Cambridge University Press, 1841.

Selden, John. *Table Talk.* London: Reeves and Turner, 1890.

Seznec, Jean. *The Survival of the Pagan Gods: The Mythological Tradition and Its Place in Renaissance Humanism and Art.* Trans. Barbara F. Sessions. Bollingen Series, no. 38. 1952. Reprint. Princeton: Princeton University Press, 1972.

Sidney, Sir Philip. *A Defence of Poetry.* Ed. J. A. Van Dorsten. Oxford: Oxford University Press, 1966.

Skinner, Quentin. *The Foundations of Modern Political Thought.* 2 vols. Cambridge: Cambridge University Press, 1978.

Slater, Philip E. *The Glory of Hera*. Boston: Beacon Press, 1968.

Smith, Barbara Herrnstein. *On the Margins of Discourse*. Chicago: University of Chicago Press, 1978.

South, Robert. "Obedience for Conscience-sake, the Duty of Good Subjects." In *The English Sermon*. Ed. C. H. Sisson. Vol. 2, pp. 126–43. Cheshire: Carcanet Press, 1976. 3 vols.

Southern, A. *Elizabethan Recusant Prose, 1559–1582*. London: Sands, 1950.

Southwell, Robert. *An Humble Supplication to Her Majestie*. Ed. R. C. Bald. Cambridge: Cambridge University Press, 1953.

Spenser, Edmund. *Edmund Spenser: The Faerie Queene*. Ed. Thomas P. Roche, Jr., and C. Patrick O'Donnell, Jr. New Haven: Yale University Press, 1978.

———. *Spenser: Poetical Works*. Ed. J. C. Smith and E. de Selincourt. 1912. Reprint. Oxford: Oxford University Press, 1977.

———. *The Works of Edmund Spenser*. Variorum edition. Ed. Edwin Greenlaw et al. Vol. 5. Baltimore: Johns Hopkins University Press, 1936.

Starobinski, Jean. "The Inside and the Outside." *The Hudson Review* 28 (1975): 333–51.

Starr, George. *Defoe and Casuistry*. Princeton: Princeton University Press, 1971.

Strong, Roy. *The Cult of Elizabeth*. London: Thames and Hudson, 1977.

———. *Gloriana: The Portraits of Queen Elizabeth I*. London: Thames and Hudson, 1987.

Strype, John. *Annals of the Reformation*. 4 vols. Oxford. Clarendon Press, 1824.

Stubbs, John. *John Stubbs's Gaping Gulf, with Letters and Other Relevant Documents*. Ed. Lloyd E. Beery. Folger Shakespeare Library. Charlottesville: University Press of Virginia, 1968.

Taylor, Jeremy. *Ductor Dubitantium, or, The Rule of Conscience in All Her General Measures; Serving as a Great Instrument for the Determination of Cases of Conscience*. In *The Whole Works of the Right Rev. Jeremy Taylor, D.D.* Ed. The Reverend Alexander Taylor. Vols. 9 and 10. London: Longman, 1855. 10 vols.

Tentler, Thomas N. *Sin and Confession on the Eve of the Reformation*. Princeton: Princeton University Press, 1977.

Thucydides. *Thucydides [The Pelopponesian War]*. Trans. Benjamin Jowett. Vol 2. Oxford: Clarendon Press, 1900. 3 vols.

Tilley, Morris P. *A Dictionary of the Proverbs in England in the Sixteenth and Seventeenth Centuries*. Ann Arbor: University of Michigan Press, 1966.

Todorov, T. *Mikhail Bakhtine: Le principe dialogique*. Paris: Editions du Seuil, 1981.

Tootell, Hugh, ed. *Dodd's Church History of England*. Vol. 3. London: C. Dolman, 1839. 5 vols.

Trimpi, Wesley. *Muses of One Mind*. Princeton: Princeton University Press, 1983.

Turner, Victor. *The Ritual Process: Structure and Anti-structure*. Chicago: Aldine, 1969.

Verkamp, Bernard J. *The Indifferent Mean: Adiaphorism in the English Reformation to 1554*. Athens: Ohio University Press, 1977.

Vinogradoff, Sir Paul. "Reason and Conscience in Sixteenth-century Jurisprudence." In *Collected Papers*. Vol. 2, pp. 190–204. Oxford: Clarendon Press, 1928. 2 vols.

Virgil. *The Aeneid of Virgil*. Trans. Allen Mandelbaum. New York: Bantam, 1961.

Voloshinov, V. N. *Marxism and the Philosophy of Language*. Trans. Ladislav Matejka and I. R. Titunik. Cambridge: Harvard University Press, 1986.

Wark, K. R. *Elizabethan Recusancy in Cheshire*. Manchester: Chetham Society, 1971.

Warner, William. *Albions England*. 1612. Reprint. New York: G. Olms, 1971.

West, William. *Symboleography. The art, description or image of instruments*. London: R. Tothill, 1590.

White, Allon. "Bakhtin, Sociolinguistics and Deconstruction." In *The Theory of Reading*. Ed. Frank Gloversmith. Totowa, N.J.: Barnes & Noble, 1984. 123–46.

Williams, Neville. *Elizabeth I, Queen of England*. London: Sphere Books, Ltd., 1971.

Williams, Raymond. *Marxism and Literature*. Oxford: Oxford University Press, 1977.

Zeeveld, W. Gordon. *The Temper of Shakespeare's Thought*. New Haven: Yale University Press, 1974.

Index

In this index an "f" after a number indicates a separate reference on the next page, and an "ff" indicates separate references on the next two pages. A continuous discussion over two or more pages is indicated by a span of page numbers, e.g., "57–59." *Passim* is used for a cluster of references in close but not consecutive sequence.

Library of Congress Cataloging-in-Publication Data

Gallagher, Lowell, 1953–
    Medusa's gaze : casuistry and conscience in the Renaissance /
Lowell Gallagher.
        p. cm.
    Includes bibliographical references and index.
    ISBN 0-8047-1859-8 (acid-free paper)
    1. English literature—Early modern, 1500–1700—History and
criticism. 2. Casuistry in literature. I. Title.
PR428.C28G35 1991
820.9´353´09031—dc20   90-39914
                                                            CIP

∞   This book is printed on acid-free paper